Imaginative Mapping

HARVARD EAST ASIAN MONOGRAPHS 422

Imaginative Mapping

Landscape and Japanese Identity in the
Tokugawa and Meiji Eras

Nobuko Toyosawa

Published by the Harvard University Asia Center
Distributed by Harvard University Press
Cambridge (Massachusetts) and London 2019

The Harvard University Asia Center publishes a monograph series and, in coordination with the Fairbank Center for Chinese Studies, the Korea Institute, the Reischauer Institute of Japanese Studies, and other facilities and institutes, administers research projects designed to further scholarly understanding of China, Japan, Vietnam, Korea, and other Asian countries. The Center also sponsors projects addressing multidisciplinary and regional issues in Asia.

The Harvard University Asia Center gratefully acknowledges the support of the Association for Asian Studies First Book Subvention Fund.

Library of Congress Cataloging-in-Publication Data

Names: Toyosawa, Nobuko, author.
Title: Imaginative mapping : landscape and Japanese identity in the Tokugawa
    and Meiji eras / Nobuko Toyosawa.
Other titles: Harvard East Asian monographs ; 422.
Description: Cambridge, Massachusetts : Published by the Harvard University
    Asia Center, 2019. | Series: Harvard East Asian monographs ; 422 |
    Includes bibliographical references and index.
Identifiers: LCCN 2018057659 | ISBN 9780674241121 (hardcover : alk. paper)
Subjects: LCSH: National characteristics, Japanese—History. | Cultural
    Landscapes—Japan. | Geographical perception—Japan. | Japan—Historical
    geography. | Japan—History—Meiji period, 1868-1912. | Japan—History—Tokugawa
    period, 1600–1868.
Classification: LCC DS830 .T68 2019 | DDC 952/.025—dc23 LC record available at
    https://lccn.loc.gov/2018057659

Index by the author and Michael Goldstein

♾ Printed on acid-free paper

Last figure below indicates year of this printing
28 27 26 25 24 23 22 21 20 19

For my family

Contents

Tables and Figures

Tables

Figures

Acknowledgments

I have received generous support from many people and have incurred numerous debts in researching and writing this project. Any shortcomings in the arguments presented here are solely my responsibility. I am pleased to finally thank those who helped me complete this book.

This project evolved out of my doctoral research. My thesis adviser at the University of Illinois, Urbana-Champaign, Ronald P. Toby, and thesis committee members, Elizabeth Oyler, Robert Tierney, Brian Ruppert, and numerous others, most notably Atsuko Ueda, Kevin M. Doak, Theodore Hughes, Sho Konishi, Emanuel Pastreich, the late David Goodman, and the late JaHyun Kim Haboush, offered intellectual support and insights that shaped my ideas about narrative, identity, and Japan. Setsuko Noguchi at the Japanese Studies Collection at the library offered much help every time I needed to find articles and other materials. Many of these colleagues have since left Champaign, but I am very grateful to them for their patience and tireless encouragement, as well as their willingness to show me what is entailed in embarking on a scholarly pursuit.

I am indebted to Narita Ryūichi at Japan Women's University. He allowed me to attend his graduate seminar and oversaw my studies on Shiga Shigetaka. His encouragement for me to meet the late Kamei Hideo at Hokkaidō University proved very important, not only because of the actual visit but because it allowed me to experience the sense of place and feel the significance of Sapporo. This enabled me to expand my spatial and historical imagination regarding the time when Shiga studied there in the 1880s. For my study of early modern Japanese history, I am thankful to Yokota Fuyuhiko, professor emeritus at Kyoto University. We met in Chicago in 2016, but his studies on the social structure of reading publics and reader cultures first caught my eye and helped me understand the making of early modernity long before we met.

Several scholars generously provided feedback that tremendously helped me reconceptualize my dissertation into a book. At the University of Southern California, I received guidance from Gordon Berger, David Bialock, Philip J. Ethington, Janet Goodwin, and Joan Piggott. Tomoko Bialock has been of invaluable help since then to obtain access for me to rare and special collection materials. Special thanks are due to the amazing scholars from the program in Digital Humanities at UCLA, most notably Yoh Kawano for his enduring support, faith in my work, and friendship. He never failed to suggest answers to my questions relating to the digitization and visualization of maps, itineraries, and other textual materials with which I was in danger of being swamped. On every occasion, he came up with solutions almost instantly, always exceeding my expectations. I will be forever grateful to him for producing the maps and the direction charts for this book.

My breakthrough moments came during my postdoctoral fellowship at the University of Chicago. I offer many thanks to all the excellent undergraduate and graduate students who challenged me in my early modern Japanese history courses. Their questions were instrumental in encouraging me to rethink the notion of authority, the idea of public and private, and the process of state formation and community formation, and they forced me to reimagine the space of early modernity without the bias of presentist perceptions. I was very fortunate to experience the company of enthusiastic, kind, and critical colleagues. I am grateful to all of them, especially Michael Bourdaghs, Kyeong-Hee Choi, Jacob Eyferth, Chelsea Foxwell, Paola Iovene, Reggie Jackson, Ashton Lazarus, Hoyt Long, and James E. Ketelaar. I am truly indebted to Susan L. Burns, who critically read my manuscript at different stages and helped me clarify my thoughts and arguments in an encouraging manner. This study would have been completely different had I not taken the time to revise it again in Chicago, deciding to incorporate the outstanding resources the late Okuizumi Eizaburō had assiduously built up as part of the collection of Japanese studies. I also thank Kiku Hibino and Ayako Yoshimura for their assistance during and after my fellowship.

Most recently, I received generous support from the Oriental Institute of the Czech Academy of Sciences, where I now work. I am deeply thankful to the director, Ondřej Beránek, and my boss, Jakub Hrubý, for providing me with just about everything I needed to complete this book. I extend my gratitude to my copyeditor, Steven Patten, for carefully reading the entire manuscript in a very timely manner. The anonymous readers for the Harvard University Asia Center deserve special thanks for their valuable suggestions, many of which I followed with appreciation. I am sincerely grateful to Robert Graham and his team for producing this book with much enthusiasm.

I was blessed with the support of wonderful friends, who all had a profound influence on me in relation to my thoughts on the production of knowledge, different forms of activism, and being a historian. Robert I. Hellyer, Emer O'Dwyer, Yi Wang, Valerie Barske, Hilary Snow, Robert Goree, Kazumi Koga, Isomae Jun'ichi, Aratake Ken'ichirō, Chris Gerteis, Matt Perry, and James Babb have given fantastic support and continue to be my inspiration. David L. Howell and Mariko Tamanoi have been exemplary scholars in every sense of the word ever since I met them at the Social Science Research Council Dissertation Workshop. I am profoundly indebted to them for their support and faith in my project from a very early stage, which was at times the only positive light I saw.

Last but not least, I am forever thankful to my family—my parents, my sisters, and their terrific families. During my long years of study, they all remained hopeful and optimistic about me and my work. This book would not have been possible without their understanding and support and so, with utmost gratitude, I dedicate this book to them.

A Note to the Reader

First, all Japanese names appear in the traditional Japanese order, that is, surname followed by given name. I refer to individuals using the name by which they are most commonly known, for example, Ieyasu for Tokugawa Ieyasu, and Shiga for Shiga Shigetaka. I also make reference to conventional period names, which correspond with a sequence of imperial reigns, and employ provincial names of Tokugawa Japan and systems of measurement of that time. I provide the equivalent of the dates, prefectures, distances, directions, and the like in the text.

Second, chapter 3 provides the reader with provincial maps of the Genroku era (1688–1704), namely, the maps of Yamashiro and Ōmi. The Genroku maps are marked with labels and images that have multiple orientations, and they are different from today's maps that align a set of geographic data with a known coordinate system. I created the English labels as truthfully as possible, reflecting the multidirectionality of the original maps. The early modern spatial philosophy determined certain directions, times, and orientations to be inauspicious, which greatly affected the construction of city and village. Mapmakers likely strove to preserve these details of the direction and orientation of buildings, natural features, village, and other structures of the time.

Third, in chapter 6, characters on illustrations, including the map, are to be read from right to left.

Unless otherwise noted, all translations are my own.

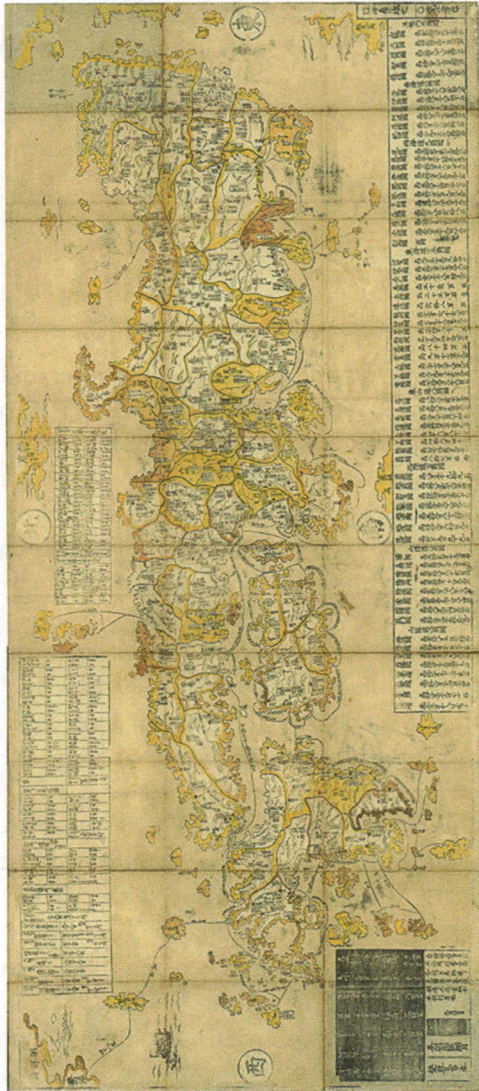

FIGURE 1.1. "New Edition: Map of All Provinces of Japan" (*Shinhan Nihonkoku ōezu*) made by Ishikawa Ryūsen (dates unknown). This map is better known as "Outline Map of Our Country" (*Honchō zukan kōmoku*). This is one of the six editions of popularly circulated *Nihonkoku ōezu*, whose first edition appeared in 1687, with the last being dated to 1713. The map includes tables that show the travel distances to various post stations via different highways, as well as distances to foreign countries. The table in the lower right section indicates the annual rice yields of all sixty-six provinces of Japan. This kind of map had emerged by the late seventeenth century, providing useful information for travelers and sightseers. For more information regarding this map, see Yonemoto, *Mapping Early Modern Japan*. Courtesy of the Geospatial Information Authority of Japan.

INTRODUCTION

> If geography is invisible . . . this may be due to the deliberately his-
> torical or archaeological approach which privileges the factor of
> time . . . As you write, "Each periodization is the demarcation in
> history of a certain level of events, and conversely each level of
> events demands its own specific periodization, because according
> to the choice of level different periodizations have to be marked
> out and, depending on the periodization one adopts, different
> levels of event become accessible . . ." It is possible, essential even,
> to conceive [of] such a methodology of discontinuity for space
> and the scales of spatial magnitude.
>
> —Michel Foucault, "Questions on Geography"

Prime Minister Abe Shinzō attempted to revive the ideologically
charged "beautiful Japan" concept by placing his national goals directly onto the Japanese landscape in his 2006 publication *Toward a Beautiful Japan* (*Utsukushii kuni e*). On one hand, he wished to transform
Japan into a more independent, equal, defense-capable nation and break
away from the country's postwar system, based on pacifism. On the other
hand, he was hopeful that his idealization of a powerful Japan would
make Japanese youth more confident and proud of their country (*jishin
to hokori no moteru kuni*), which would result in the proliferation of popular nationalist sentiment in Japan.[1] Setting aside the potential of Abe's
anachronistic mode of inspiration as the nation's leader, his beautiful
Japan was the manifestation of the conservative agenda of the nation's
leadership, echoing the militarism and imperialism of wartime Japan that
should never be repeated. What interested me was that Abe mobilized
the landscape as a political ideology, whose power has often given rise to
the gradual formation of social and subjective identities in the past.[2] His

1. Abe S., *Utsukushii kuni e*, 231–32.
2. Mitchell, *Landscape and Power*, 1.

attempt to reinvent Japan by reawakening wartime values that led the nation into committing unspeakable crimes deserves focused attention.

Geographer Denis Cosgrove has also pointed out that landscape is a "way of seeing" that allows social groups to create a sense of belonging by bonding themselves with the land and other human groups that inhabit the land.[3] These studies discuss the fascinating power of landscape that is capable of naturalizing cultural constructs while setting up certain "natural" ways of observing the view and its affective relationship with people. Considering that the "natural" ways of viewing the land are never natural but are produced by people who impose certain ideas onto the landscape and narrativize them as part of the natural view, the landscape metaphor requires rigorous analysis. Of course, the imposition could result in the projection of positive ideas, but the ideological nature attached to the landscape metaphor remains. In this regard, Julia Thomas has explored the "power behind the seemingly mild stereotype of Japan's permanent love of nature" in her *Reconfiguring Modernity: Concepts of Nature in Japanese Political Ideology*. Through a semiotic and hermeneutic approach that treats nature as a metaphor for ideological themes, she has concluded that in the case of Japan, "whoever can define nature for a nation defines that nation's polity on a fundamental level."[4]

This book is interested in this intriguing power of the landscape, which seemingly presents us with special qualities of geographic beauty while masking the ideological claims of law, prohibition, control, or violence, as manifested in the view. W. J. T. Mitchell has perceived landscape as "a body of determinate signs" and has demonstrated the possibilities of reading landscape through the interpretive approach, in the same way we would treat any other textual system.[5] He cautions us that because of the multiple meanings existing in the landscape, which often function as a tool to create a certain sense of intimacy and affective feelings, the discourse of social or cultural identity needs to be analyzed meticulously in the distinct historical context by considering what political forces have been mobilized in the "natural" landscape. Following his lead, this study examines landscape as a textual space and reveals how during

3.   Cosgrove, *Social Formation and Symbolic Landscape*, xiv.
4.   Thomas, *Reconfiguring Modernity*, 2–10.
5.   Mitchell, *Landscape and Power*, 2.

the Tokugawa (1603–1868) and Meiji (1868–1912) eras the landscape played a major role in producing a narrative of Japan, engendering a unifying sense of community.

The landscapes I introduce in this book mostly emerge in the essays and treatises written by scholars and intellectuals after the seventeenth century. For instance, in the mid-seventeenth century, scholars such as Hayashi Razan (1583–1657), Kaibara Ekiken (1630–1714), and Yamazaki Ansai (1618–82) created an overarching narrative of the past by developing the idea that Japan was a country created and ruled by the deities (*shinkoku*). They wished to present Japan as equal to a civilized China, so they adopted the conceptual framework of the Chinese knowledge system, namely, the system of thought and metaphysics known as Neo-Confucianism. Based on the topographic reports that the country had thus far produced, they projected a mirror image of *shinkoku* Japan against the sagely country (*seijinkoku*) of China. By drawing on the divine traces found in local topography, Ekiken, for instance, produced a narrative of *shinkoku* Japan into the traditional discourse of the spirit of dead people and the divine spirit of the deities (*kishin*) in East Asia.

Starting with my analysis of the production of this seventeenth-century *shinkoku* Japan in the medium of *kishin* discourse as a meta-narrative, the first four chapters trace the changing discourse of *kishin* and *shinkoku* Japan up to the early nineteenth century. In response to the mounting level of crisis and anxiety, as symbolized in poor harvests, natural disasters, and the frequent sight of foreigners crossing the waters near the Japanese archipelago, the *shinkoku* narrative became strongly reflective of the need to establish spiritual guidance for the community. My analysis identifies the reciprocal interaction between the changing narrative of *shinkoku* Japan and popular anxieties that conceived the signs of disquiet as indicating the failures of the Tokugawa shogunate and the subsequent shift away from the ideal state of harmony under heaven. Paralleling the rise of Nativism (Kokugaku) in the late eighteenth century, when a group of scholars questioned the source of legitimacy enjoyed by the shogunate and founded a school of thought that stood in opposition to Confucianism, the *shinkoku* Japan discourse became a narrative of spiritual salvation in the nineteenth century.

The collapse of the shogunate in 1868 meant the breakdown of the Neo-Confucian cosmology as the dominant worldview of Japan. The change certainly did not happen overnight, but as the reference point for civilization quickly shifted to the West rather than China, the principal knowledge system that structured and represented the universe also moved from Neo-Confucian metaphysics to Western knowledge. With the waves of Western imperialism infringing the national and cultural borders of Japan in the last decades of the nineteenth century, however, the young intellectuals became increasingly apprehensive about the overt Westernization programs of the Meiji state. Fully aware of the invasive power of the Western knowledge that was threatening the autonomous realm of knowledge in Japan, the "new generation" vehemently condemned the government's Westernizing policies in the fields of diplomacy, national industry, education, and other areas.[6] Instead, they advocated the preservation of Japan's national essence (*kokusui*) as the vital means by which Japan might survive in the competitive world because they were fearful of losing their distinct identity and cultural roots. Trying to strike a balance between progress and tradition—necessary if their nation were to maintain its status as a civilized member of the modern world—the elite formed intellectual societies and spread the idea of a civil society, constitutional government, and other modern notions of the nation-state throughout the 1880s.

One of the active antigovernment groups, the Society for Political Education (Seikyōsha, 1888), is at the heart of my analysis in the final two chapters, with a special emphasis on two major writers, Miyake Setsurei (1860–1945) and Shiga Shigetaka (1863–1927). The group identified culture as central to what constitutes the national identity and emphasized the preservation of Japanese culture as the critical task and the pillar around which to build the nation. Like the Tokugawa scholars who strove to present Japan as a civilized equal to China, Seikyōsha writers vigorously engaged in mapping Japan by using newly available sources of knowledge. Seeking to develop a narrative thread, Setsurei and Shiga appropriated certain theories, rhetoric, and language on beauty from Western knowledge and reformulated the *shinkoku* Japan idea by shifting the focus from the unverifiable *kishin* to the remarkable milieu of the Japanese archipelago. The modern science of geography enabled Shiga to theorize on the marked geographic beauty of the archipelago as a

6. Pyle, *New Generation in Meiji Japan.*

proven source for nourishing Japanese artistic sensibility in his *On the Landscape of Japan* (*Nippon fūkeiron*, 1894).[7] Finding new ground on which to build Japan's strength as a modern nation, Setsurei wrote *Truth, Goodness, and Beauty: The Japanese* (*Shin zen bi: Nipponjin*, 1891), among other publications, in which he defined the inner aspects of the Japanese through these philosophical notions. As Japanese art had created a colossal craze for Japonism in Europe, reaching its peak in the 1860s and 1870s, the designation of Japanese art as the embodiment of the Japanese spirit gained currency at the end of the nineteenth century. In this intellectual climate, Setsurei and Shiga invented a narrative of Japan as a strong and beautiful country, whose features were woven into scientific validity drawn from modern geography and philosophy. The message of a sublime Japan displaced the prior semiotic configuration of landscape as *kishin*, allowing its geographic beauty to be the symbol of Japan's national essence.

Seikyōsha writers incorporated Western knowledge as a means of providing a scientific rationale for the potential of modern Japan. When the geopolitical balance in East Asia was shifting rapidly in the last decade of the nineteenth century, exploding in the form of the Sino-Japanese War in 1894, Shiga's *Nippon fūkeiron* appeared as a timely manifestation of Japanese supremacy to sway popular support in the direction of defending the national homeland. In this sense, Shiga and other Seikyōsha writers successfully guided their readers to support not only Japan's aggression in the war against China but also its ensuing imperial visions in East Asia, this being regarded as a way of protecting their beautiful affective homeland. One of the goals of this study is to consider the relationship between the recurring discourse of Japanese landscape and Japan's cultural identity and the relationship between aesthetics and nationalism and to do so by examining the time and context that triggered the discursive mobilization of the landscape. I direct the reader's attention to the power of landscape that tames our thinking process, allowing us to accept the

---

7. Western literature represents the periodicals of the Seikyōsha activists as *Nihon* (Japan) or *Nihonjin* (The Japanese), but Urs Matthias Zachmann offers the correct Romanization as *Nippon* or *Nipponjin*. Zachmann, *China and Japan in the Late Meiji Period*, 165.

ideological claims placed on the landscape as natural, beautiful, sublime, or otherwise.

By teasing out the continuities and discontinuities in the mode of envisioning a community, *Imaginative Mapping* reveals how scholars since the mid-seventeenth century have shaped and visualized Japan vis-à-vis the dominant cultural Other. One of the implications is that Japan has had an inseparable affinity with Asia since ancient times, and these ties were not trifling but offered a vital means by which to delineate the space of Japan as an independent entity. The writing of local history and topography that embraced the idea that Japan was *shinkoku* followed the most authentic scholarship model of East Asia, Chinese historiography, while reviving *fudoki* (the record of the "wind" and "earth") that originated in Japan's official history writing in the eighth century.[8] As already mentioned, to attribute a civilized status to the representation of Japan, scholars used the Chinese knowledge system and created a discursive sphere of Japan as a Chinese equivalent.

In other words, the efforts to produce Japan's spatial unity as *shinkoku* rested on the complex negotiations involved in ordering Japan's indigenous space in accordance with the supreme knowledge structure and conceptual framework of China. The representation of Japan as a separate entity was therefore made possible through the civilized Chinese knowledge system and, in turn, the efforts of Razan, Ekiken, and others to spatialize Japan were followed by the need to eliminate those traces of China from the discourse of *shinkoku* Japan. When I use the word *spatialize*, I mean the act of representing the given space by verbalizing it in the form of textual or visual narrative, and I do so with full awareness that this involves an unequal power relationship. The power struggle may be between the civilized center and the periphery to create a mirroring self-image and self-knowledge of Japan versus China, or the land in some local regions in its struggle with the shogun's capital of Edo, or later in the Meiji era in creating an image of Japan versus the West. For our purposes, it is important to remember that the spatialization of Japan was prompted

8. For an insightful analysis on understanding Japan's experience with modernity based on *kanbun* écriture, see Saitō Mareshi, *Kanbunmyaku no kindai*, *Kanbunmyaku to kindai Nihon*, and *Kanji sekai no chihei*; Komori, *Buntai toshite no monogatari* and "Kaisetsu: shisō toshite no buntai."

and mediated by the Other, even though the representations of Japan imply its exclusively *Japanese* space. The insistence on Japanese purity or the irreducible quality of Japanese culture stems from the fact that the articulation of Japan goes back to the adaptation of Chinese or Western knowledge systems. Precisely because of the presence of the foreign in the very conceptual structure Japan had adopted, the process would never be complete without eradicating traces of the Other from the framework.

Another notable implication of the early modern production of the *shinkoku* narrative is that the *shinkoku* idea did not appear in a vacuum in the late eighteenth century with the founding of Kokugaku that centered on Motoori Norinaga (1730–1801) or Hirata Atsutane (1776–1843). In fact, the idea had been extant all along as many warriors of the prior "country at war" (Sengoku) period (1467–1568) adopted the idea of heaven's way or the heavenly way (*tendō*) and positioned themselves as righteous rulers with the mandate of heaven. Even during the peaceful era under the regime of the Tokugawa shogunate, the idea of Japan as *shinkoku* continued to circulate, as we can see in the case of *Japan's Treasury for the Ages* (*Nippon eitaigura*), written by Ihara Saikaku (1642–93), for example. Saikaku mentioned the importance of worshiping the deities and Buddha (*shinbutsu*) in accordance with the virtues of the world (*yo no jingi*) because the culture of worship was the basis of Japan's culture (*wakoku no fūzoku*) and the characteristic that made it the country of the deities (*wagakuni wa shinkoku nari*).[9] What was new in the seventeenth century was, I argue, that the idea signaled the Japanese difference from China, Korea, and India, where Confucianism and Buddhism still shaped the dominant intellectual outlook.[10] The examination of the *shinkoku* narrative allows us to see, on one hand, the ongoing presence of the deities and supernatural beings in popular spirituality, while allowing us to understand how the discourse of *shinkoku* in the seventeenth century related to the writings of the Kokugaku scholars of the eighteenth and nineteenth centuries. Especially with regard to the perception and interpretation of the Divine Age narrative reproduced by Norinaga in *The Commentaries of the Kojiki* (*Kojikiden*), the analysis of the changing narrative of *shinkoku*

9.   Ihara, *Nippon eitaigura*, 2.
10.   On the conceptualization of Japan among *shintō* scholars before Motoori Norinaga's Kokugaku discourse, see, for example, Maeda T., "Shin, ju, butsu no sankyō."

explains why this idea resurfaced and how it became a point of contention in the scholarly debates in the early modern period.

Today, Japan's "national seclusion" (*sakoku*) thesis is no longer as
prominent as in earlier historiography, with a number of studies revising
the assumption by clarifying the nature of shogunate diplomacy and foreign policies.[11] These works have turned our attention to more subjective
analyses of Japan's historical experience, such as the maturing power of
the shogunate and other examples of local growth that resulted from the
daimyo's participation in countrywide commerce, trade, politics, and arts
and culture.[12] Within this context of ripening social processes leading
toward the great peace, domainal authorities achieved a stabilization of
the regions under their rule.[13] For example, record keeping was a vital
means of tracing the line of authority for the domain, and those who
had a knowledge of Neo-Confucianism dedicated themselves to sorting
out their local records of history and topography, including *shintō* and
Buddhist temple properties. The information from the past amounted
to numerous compilations of local topography for the domain.[14] As
opposed to the chaos consuming the center of civilization due to the

11.   Arano, Ishii, and Murai, eds, *Kinseiteki sekai no seijuku*; Asao, *Shōgun kenryoku
no sōshutsu*; Hellyer, *Defining Engagement*; Mitani, *Escape from Impasse*; Toby, *State and
Diplomacy*; Toby, *'Sakoku' to iu gaikō*.

12.   Scholars have investigated different sets of practice in local governance. Most
radically, Timon Screech perceives these 280 domains as multiple states, based on the
fact that each had its own local conditions. While I disagree with his use of the term
state, the diversity in the community does force historians to be attentive to the differences among the domains and analyze them within their specific historical contexts.
Screech, *Shogun's Painted Culture*, 11–18. See also Kozakai, *Kinsei Nihon no dogō to chiiki
shakai*; Ooms, *Tokugawa Village Practice*; Takano, *Kinsei seiji shakai eno shiza*.

13.   In this regard, Yokota Fuyuhiko has written extensively about the strong popular desires and prayers for peace, stability, and prosperity of the region and the country
in the early Tokugawa period. According to him and others, the three unifiers were well
aware of the popular longing for peace and actively informed the populace about its
arrival. Yokota, *Tenka taihei*, 11–15. See also Takahashi S., *Edo no heiwaryoku*; Takano,
Kinsei daimyōke kashindan to ryōshusei; Watanabe T., *Kinsei hyakushō no sokojikara*.

14.   I use *shintō*, not Shinto, to distinguish the practice of the indigenous worship
of deities during the early modern era. Before the Meiji state established state Shinto by
subordinating local deities under the Sun Goddess of Ise Shrine, there were a variety of
local practices related to the worship of local deities. See Breen and Teeuwen, *New History of Shinto*; Hardacre, *Shintō and the State*; Koyasu, *Kokka to saishi*.

crushing setback of the Manchu takeover of the Ming dynasty in 1644, local scholars in Japan recognized that they were living in a new epoch of great peace under the Tokugawa shogunate. Reflecting the shogunate's refusal to acknowledge the Qing dynasty as the legitimate successor to Ming China, scholars vigorously produced local historiography, and their ability to produce refined scholarship enabled them to conceive of Japan's new place in East Asia. Concurrently, many scholarly activities altered the nature of the domain as a communal space, which was at first given to the daimyo as territory for them to rule militarily. The strong militaristic tendencies and values that existed in the formative years of Tokugawa were replaced with a new set of more civic values as political and commercial changes redefined the nature of the rule that prompted the domain to construct new social relations.

In this manner, analyzing the mode of imagining Japan in Tokugawa and Meiji Japan allows me to make a case for envisioning the emergent notion of cultural community and the dissemination of the idea of Japan, which were already taking place during the Tokugawa period. This means that the practice of imagining cultural community existed in the early modern era, even before the modern sense of self appeared in the late nineteenth century.[15] By shedding light on the formation of the early modern speaking subject, this study explores Japan's experience with modernity in a different way. I emphasize the significance of the early modern subject because even though recent scholarship has revealed the refined system of local governance and their community-making efforts in the Tokugawa era, these cases have not been part of the mainstream narrative of Japanese history. More precisely, scholars see modernity as emerging exclusively from contacts with the Western nations and characterize the interaction with the West as the beginning of the modern era in Japanese history. By casting Western knowledge as the universal sign of modernity, they often dismiss the stabilization of the political, economic, and social orders in Tokugawa society as being extraneous. Can we continue to see the universality of Western knowledge as the sole force behind the quest for modernity in Japan? The present study challenges this view by offering a novel interpretation of subject formation and argues that

15. See Wakao, "Kinsei ni okeru 'Nihon' no ishiki no keisei," 14–45.

after the seventeenth century scholars gradually but firmly established a speaking subject for the collective unity of Japan.

As the following pages demonstrate, whether they claimed to be Neo-Confucian or *shintō* scholars, local scholars attempted to embark on the invention of the subjective position of Japan and established a unified cultural community in the face of the cultural authority of China. I resist the urge to categorize local scholars as Confucian or *shintō* because even when they themselves claimed to be Neo-Confucian scholars, one can find more than one school of thought in their conceptualization of the universe, and it is difficult to delineate the intellectual borders between them.[16] Without clearly identifying them as *shintō* or Neo-Confucian, I maintain a focus on the general desire to ascertain the domainal authority that belonged to the broader country, and try to capture the motivation of these scholars in the Tokugawa and later in the Meiji eras, who strove to posit the "national" speaking subject against the cultural reference of the time. Many scholars broadly shared the intellectual world of the time—Confucianism, *shintō*, Buddhism, and Daoism, or Western knowledge. By interpreting the cosmology and attributing distinct features to Japan, they posed an independent entity of Japan to disseminate the awareness of Japan.

To be clear, I emphasize that the feelings of community I present in the first four chapters clearly do not signify the birth of the nation in the modern sense, and my intention is not to argue in favor of placing the Tokugawa period as the beginning of the modern era in Japanese history. The sense of collective unity I describe is not the same as the modern sense of nationalism that functions as a political or cultural ideology to configure the populace into national subjects. The absence of any apparatus of the modern nation-state in the Tokugawa period makes it clear that the shogunate did not have a level of power similar to the Meiji state, which was founded as a modern state in 1868. Nonetheless, the cultivation and spatial dissemination of the idea of Japan clearly existed before the arrival of Commodore Matthew Perry (1794–1858) in 1853 or the sub-

---

16.   I agree with the approach taken by Wakao Masaki and others rejecting the identification of early modern Japan as "the age of Confucianism" or Buddhism. Early modern Japan had its own cosmology that was irreducible to any specific teaching or thought. Wakao, "Shin, ju, butsu no jidai."

sequent rapid incorporation of Western knowledge. Therefore, I propose to use intellectual maturity as the measurement tool for tracking Japan's path toward modernity, arguing that the Chinese knowledge system provided the means for establishing the historical agency needed to pose an imaginary Japan. Through reference to the case of the early modern subject in Japan, I wish to amplify the debates on modernity and nationalism for non-Western countries before the West came to disseminate modern concepts of nationhood. By comparatively analyzing the two modes of imagining Japan, we can discern the sophisticated growth of knowledge structures, as well as the expansion of the intellectual capacity of scholars.

This study represents a reappraisal of Japan's engagement with the rest of the world, a process through which Japanese scholars identified the major characteristics of their people and culture. It is not absolute but arbitrary to gauge how the collective identity of Japan materialized as modern or premodern because it depends on the work of later historians, who have been instrumental in identifying the defining features of modernity. The periodization of national history is often determined by close correspondence with the model or standards of other national histories. More specifically, one national history can be divided into certain periods in accordance with the periodization of other national history models; for Japan, the standard adopted was based on the Western periodization model, which itself built on the West's experience with modernity. By continuing to follow this chronology model, we deem the Western experience with modernity to be universal. As mentioned, I would contest the idea that the universality of modernity should be drawn only from the West's experience. The efforts to represent people in a collective manner began in seventeenth-century Japan, even when geographic borders were ambiguous.[17] The desire to posit a community resulted in these cases of imaginative mapping, and this awareness of the putative unity of Japan testifies to a path toward modernity, which is a different road but allows us to investigate modernity as a universal phenomenon also arising in non-Western countries.

17. Batten, *To the Ends of Japan*; Howell, *Geographies of Identity*; Murai et al., *Kyōkai no Nihonshi*; Nenzi, *Excursions in Identity*.

In fact, some recent studies have already defended the existence of an indigenous mode of community before the nation-building project of the Meiji state. For example, Eiko Ikegami in *Bonds of Civility: Aesthetic Networks and the Political Origins of Japanese Culture* has visualized the lively emergence of various aesthetic spaces in early modern Japan and argued that Tokugawa Japan witnessed a number of civic and artistic trends that unified the people. Ikegami has convincingly shown that people of different social status were connected by a sense of civility and beauty and formed the aesthetic spaces where active exchange, networking, and communication took place. The premise of her study is the need to understand the historical development of the cultural identity of Japan through the activities that existed in "the domain of private citizens under a feudal regime."[18] By identifying the space and time of early modern Japan as proto-modernity, however, *Bonds of Civility* illustrates how spaces in Tokugawa Japan became closer to and similar to an established set of ideas of the state of being modern by expanding the social, cultural, political, and economic networks available to people. This developmental model is reflective of Ikegami's sociological approach, which assumes that society is inherently heading toward modernity. In this regard, I hold a different position, that is, that the maturing processes arise from their specific political, social, or economic conditions, and the later scholars look at the historical experience of regions and characterize them as feudal or proto-national in the chronology of the development and progress of national history. When historical forces move a country dynamically toward social formation, the specific conditions of the time pave the way for the formation of a community, but whether the community becomes modern or remains primitive in nature depends on their respective contexts.

In this sense, Susan Burns's *Before the Nation: Kokugaku and the Imagining of Community in Early Modern Japan* has crucially influenced my conceptualization of this project. By showing the disconcerting nature of Kokugaku discourse and practice in the time of Motoori Norinaga, Burns's analysis of the four Kokugaku scholars demonstrates the contentious nature of the establishment of the *Kojiki* and the *Nihon shoki* as valid accounts of Japan's early history. Laying out Norinaga's concerns regard-

18. Ikegami, *Bonds of Civility*, 381.

ing the danger of disorder in society and his commitment to reviving the message of the founding deities and "the way" of the country, Burns's book reveals that Norinaga primarily cared about the need to recover the way of the deities to show his students how they could lead a stable spiritual life and regain the heart of Japanese-ness. In a similar vein, recent studies by Federico Marcon (*The Knowledge of Nature and the Nature of Knowledge in Early Modern Japan*) and Maki Fukuoka (*The Premise of Fidelity: Science, Visuality and Representing the Real in Nineteenth-Century Japan*) present well-studied cases of the indigenous epistemological "progress" in Tokugawa Japan. Arguing that what enabled Tokugawa scholars and artists to pursue their inquiries were the shared concerns for knowledge of the natural world and the development of classification systems, these studies amply demonstrate that the means by which Japanese scholars were able to achieve the state of being modern was substantially different from that of the Western scholars, but they, too, were able to reach that state through their reference to their own findings and analyses.[19] Without being directly influenced by Western discoveries in the field of natural sciences, artists and scholars nurtured their taxonomy of the natural world, which was considerably similar to Western discoveries in the natural sciences. *Imaginative Mapping* takes its rightful place among these existing and innovative studies by offering a subjective reading of the historical experience of Japan in the early modern and modern eras, and highlights how the discourse of modern Japan came into being in response to these specific historical and social conditions.

Chapter Summaries

Chapter 1 begins with an exploration of the shogunate's topographic projects in the form of the land surveys (*kenchi*) and provincial mapmaking (*kuniezu*) that followed the establishment of the Tokugawa shogunate. The aim of the shogunate's topographic projects was to control local lords to achieve the unification of the entire country, but local scholars emerged

19. Burns, *Before the Nation*; Fukuoka, *Premise of Fidelity*; Marcon, *The Knowledge of Nature and the Nature of Knowledge*.

as valuable players in implementing the shogunate's projects, often for their own purposes. Chapter 1 argues that they shared the desire for the peace of the region and initiated the compilation of topography in a style of writing reminiscent of the ancient *fudoki*, which dates back to the eighth century. By exploring how the *fudoki* compilation emerged and was revived through the work of Kaibara Ekiken from Chikuzen province (today's Fukuoka), this chapter demonstrates that *fudoki* were a valuable means for consolidating the region under the rule of the daimyo, while also showing how *fudoki* contributed to the stabilization of the political center in Edo, the Tokugawa shogunate.

Chapter 2 shifts the focus to the cosmology of the seventeenth century, with a special emphasis on Kaibara Ekiken's interpretation of Zhu Xi Neo-Confucian metaphysics. Originally inspired by the *kishin* discourse of ancient China, he uses a number of traditional East Asian theories of space and cosmology to define the place of Japan in the broader world. In the process, he identifies the direction of the East as the place of abundant *yang ki* and with this metaphysical explanation is able to validate the claim that Japan was *shinkoku*. With the results of his investigation of local topography revealing layers of history, particularly traces of the deities in the ancient past, Ekiken was able to equate them with the *yang ki* of the metaphysical world and produced a narrative of Japan where various spirits of the dead were floating around. This chapter argues that this revival of the ancient *fudoki* as Japanese history writing represented his effort to delineate Japanese differences from an external cultural authority while also analyzing his theorization of the way of the deities (*shintō*).

Chapter 3 explores how Ekiken tried to disseminate the message of *shinkoku* Japan through the publication of commercial guidebooks. I examine one of the published guidebooks from his lifetime, *The Excellent Views of the Capital* (*Keijō shōran*, 1706) and introduce how Ekiken narrativized Japan as *shinkoku* by interpreting the topography of the capital of Japan. Based on the idea that the capital of "peace and harmony" (Heiankyō) was topographically ideal by showing the correspondence with the four deities (*shijin sōō*) that surround the space, Ekiken's guide selected certain places that laid claim to hosting the divine footsteps of deities from the ancient past. By the end of the seventeen-day tour, the reader would be fully aware of the remarkable qualities of the capital (*miyako no fūdo*) that naturalized the idea of *shinkoku* Japan. The numerous markers of divine connections existing throughout the capital, such as temples, shrines, and other sites, as well as the religious devotees who zealously came to visit sacred places, completely effaced the initial *kishin* idea in Ekiken's narrativization of Japan's capital.

Chapter 4 explores the rise of Nativism and how the Kokugaku discourse intersected with the idea of *shinkoku* Japan. Building on the existing scholarship setting out the political and social conditions that contributed to the conceptualization of the cultural community of Japan around the Kokugaku scholars, this chapter analyzes how the discourses produced by Motoori Norinaga and Hirata Atsutane intensified the reconceptualization of the deities of Heaven and Earth and consequently advanced the idea of *shinkoku* Japan. It underscores how the participation of Norinaga and Atsutane furthered the *shinkoku* Japan narrative, enabling the imagining of Japan and the visualization of community at a critical moment in Japanese history, ultimately making it the foundational narrative of Japan's cultural identity.

Chapter 5 moves on to the modern era and examines the production of the narrative of Japan after Japan's cultural authority shifted from China to the West. I analyze one of the cofounders of Seikyōsha, Miyake Setsurei, who theorized about the interiority of the Japanese nation by carefully weaving the universal principles of progress and the Hegelian notion of absolute spirit in his vision of modern Japan. Setsurei's 1891 publication of *Truth, Goodness, Beauty* reflected his attempt to position Japan in the modern world by identifying Japan's mission to do so by means of the humanitarian discourse of achieving world peace. Fluent in the history of Western philosophy, he re-presented the character and quality of the Japanese people in philosophical terms, aiming to revise the dominant understanding of the centrality of the West when Japan under the Meiji state belonged to the backward East, thus embodying premodernity. In so doing, Setsurei elevated Japanese art, which had fueled the growth of Japonism in late nineteenth-century Europe, to the activities and expressions of the Japanese spirit, while identifying the archipelago as the space that nourished Japan's artistic sensibilities.

Chapter 6 examines Shiga Shigetaka, another cofounder of Seikyōsha, who had extensive knowledge of geography, especially human geography, which explored humanity's bond with nature. Drawing on his knowledge of geography, climatology, and economics, Shiga created a distinct vision

of a beautiful Japan that was firmly grounded in its agricultural and economic strength. Being a prolific writer and an excellent poet of classical
Chinese poetry, he employed his literary talents in his writing and combined it with his specialization in geography. As a result, Shiga's visualization of an ideal Japan significantly contributed to the creation of sublime
Japan, doing so by establishing the Japanese landscape as the symbol of
Japan's national spirit, one that was filled with vitality and movement.

The final two chapters capture the transformative process of knowledge structures from Neo-Confucian metaphysics to the more articula-
ble language of empirical science. However, the transfer from one mode
of knowledge to the next was complex, involving the revival or realign-
ment of the old epistemology. As we know from various cases in which
the zealous efforts of the Meiji state to import Western knowledge to
Japan were met with violence and protests, the shift from the old mode of
imagining community to the new was difficult. What proved useful was
the *fūdo*-based thinking, which testifies to the importance of *fūdo* as being central to the history and identity of Japan by creating a deeply rooted
affinity with the landscape and people. Indeed, Seikyōsha's nationalist aestheticism derived from the familiar *fūdo*-based awareness of imagined
Japan. This study stresses the power of the unifying narrative to create
an imagined community, but the power came from the recurring affective notion of *fūdo*, which had the capacity to nurture the mental landscape in the reader's mind.

CHAPTER I

Local Topography in Seventeenth-Century Japan

> Discursive formation of a much higher complexity than a geographic proper name is required in order that the unity of a group thus named be a social reality, that is, that the members of the populace identify themselves with that unity through the medium of the name. The geographic proper name "America," for instance, exists, but this does not imply that there is a community called "America."
>
> —Sakai, *Translation and Subjectivity*

In the second half of the seventeenth century in Japan, an upsurge in books about local topography emerged, including *The Record of the Counties in Aki and Bingo Provinces* (*Geibi-koku gunshi*), *The Unified Record of Higo Province* (*Higo kokugun ittōshi*), and *The Fudoki of Hitachi Province* (*Hitachi no kuni fudoki*).[1] With the word *fudoki* (a record of the "wind" and "earth"; often translated simply as regional gazetteer) or a phrase such as "record of" a particular region attached to the end of the title, these books contain lists of county and village names, temples and shrines, local specialties, and information about the region's natural features and historical background. They usually begin with an author's

---

1. *Geibi-koku gunshi* covers the topography and history of eight counties in the province of Aki and six counties in Bingo province, and this compilation was finished in 1663. There is a preface written by Hayashi Gahō (1618–88), one of the sons of Hayashi Razan (1583–1657). The record shows that Lord Hosokawa Tsunatoshi (1643–1714) of Kumamoto ordered Kitajima Setsuzan (1636–97) to compile *Higo kokugun ittōshi* in 1667. The date of completion remains unclear, and there is no record of this text in the *Union Catalogue of Early Japanese Books*. Shirai, *Nihon kinsei chishi hensanshi kenkyū*, 50–55.

note about how they tried to record the beauty and richness of their home region while maintaining the ancient *fudoki* style, the traditional genre of topographic writings that originated in the Nara period (710–94).[2]

Comprising sixty-five volumes in total, the ancient *fudoki* (*ko-fudoki*) is known as "the first compilation of topography and ethnography (*chishi minzokushi*) of our country."[3] The imperial court ordered the compilation of the topographic reports of local regions, province by province, which was finally finished in the sixth year of Enchō (928). The revival in the seventeenth century was slightly different from the ancient *fudoki* of *Fudoki of Izumo Province* (*Izumo no kuni fudoki*) and *Fudoki of Harima Province* (*Harima no kuni fudoki*). The variety of titles indicates that the seventeenth-century *fudoki* were not categorized by province, and the compilation did not originate with an order of the court or the Tokugawa shogunate. As the following pages demonstrate, the people in local regions made *fudoki*-like texts on their own.

The central concern of this chapter is to understand why they mobilized this particular tradition of writing at this specific time. Historians often regard the official topographic programs of mapmaking (*kuniezu*), land surveys (*kenchi*), and related topographic projects from the formative years of the Tokugawa as the shogunate's orders to institute the political structure referred to as the *baku-han* (*bakufu* and domain) system. They claim that the *baku-han* system, which was built on land-based mediation, sustained the basis of shogunate rule for over 260 years. This chapter complicates this view by arguing that the "great peace under Heaven" (*tenka taihei*) of the Tokugawa was not solely because of the firm grip of the shogunate over the regional lords. The identity of the domain (*han*) in the early seventeenth century was colored by a sense of loyalty and military allegiance to the shogun. Nonetheless, military lords had to establish their authority in the domains and govern the rural communities, and to this end, many officials shaped their local politics by adopt-

2. Scholars often call the original compilation of *fudoki* in the early history of Japan ancient *fudoki* (*ko-fudoki*) and distinguish it from the later compilation of local topography in the Tokugawa period. *Ko-fudoki* includes compilations that began with the edict of 713 and continued to 925. Hashimoto Masayuki, *Ko-fudoki no kenkyū*, 1–4.

3. Yoshino, "Hanrei," *Fudoki*, 1.

ing traditional political philosophy from China.[4] By drawing on the political structure of the Zhou dynasty (1022–256 BCE) in China, for example, where the emperor tasked regional lords of various ranks, such as *hankoku*, *hanchin*, *hanshin*, and *hanpo*, with managing the vast feudal empire as benevolent leaders, some domainal officials of hereditary vassals of the Tokugawa focused more on the idea of *hanpo*, that is, to assist the shogunate.[5] Others in the large holdings privileged the meaning of *hankoku* and concentrated on creating a semi-autonomous country of their own.[6] Because the villages were divided into different yet connected groups that together sustained rural life, although in a complicated manner, I argue that the topographic projects were an effective means of installing domainal authority on the provinces.[7] By highlighting the efforts of domain leaders in the seventeenth century, this chapter shows how they shaped the basis of their rule, which led to various centers emerging on the periphery that stabilized the entire realm.[8]

The Unification of Japan and Land Distribution

The victory of Tokugawa Ieyasu (1542–1616, r. 1603–5) at the Battle of Sekigahara in 1600 marked him as the *tenkabito* (a person who reaches Heaven by winning battles).[9] He followed the establishment of the domains

4. Itō, *Kinseishi no kenkyū*, 464–45.

5. Takano, *Hankoku to hanpo no kōzu*, 10. See also Kanai, *Hansei*; Yamaguchi, *Bakuhansei seiritsushi no kenkyū*.

6. Takano, *Hankoku to hanpo no kōzu*, 10; Roberts, *Mercantilism in a Japanese Domain*.

7. For a detailed analysis of what the peasants did in their villages in the early modern era, see Ooms, *Tokugawa Village Practice*.

8. Yokoyama, "Jo: Antei shakai," 13; Abe Y., *Nihon shushigaku to Chōsen*, 158–60; Abe A., "Juka shintō to kokugaku," 504–6. In English, see, for example, Roberts, *Performing the Great Peace*.

9. The term *tenkabito* is usually used to describe the three unifiers of Oda Nobunaga (1534–82), Toyotomi Hideyoshi, and Tokugawa Ieyasu, who came to unify and rule the realm through their military tactics and wisdom and ended the Sengoku era. During the transitional period from the medieval to the early modern era, becoming the *tenkabito* meant taking on the actual role of ruler of the realm without the need for imperial appointment as shogun. Asao, "Tenkabito to Kyoto," 19–20.

by rewarding local lords with a piece of land to rule over as territory (*ryōchi*) and subsequently launched several topographic land surveys and mapmaking projects, placing them under his own control.[10] The territories obtained from the opposing side became available to Ieyasu, the Tokugawas, and those who had helped secure Ieyasu's victory. Reducing the land holdings of families and vassals of the former *tenkabito* Toyotomi Hideyoshi (1537–98) from 2,000,000 *koku* to 650,000 *koku*, Ieyasu took away a total of 6,400,000 *koku* from the pro-Toyotomi warriors after the battle.[11] *Koku* or *kokudaka* was the annual rice yield, which measured the wealth and power of the domain through reference to its level of agricultural productivity, an estimation of how many people the domain could feed.[12]

The regional lords with powerful holdings of 10,000 *koku* or more were called daimyo, and they were subject to the official process of registering their land possession with the shogunate, which became known as "granting the territory" (*ryōchi ategai* or *ryōchi ando*).[13] Through this

10. Fujii, *Edo jidai no kanryōsei*, 11–15; Roberts, *Mercantilism in a Japanese Domain*, 15.

11. The shogunate held 4.2 million *koku* of territories (*tenryō*) scattered throughout the country at a time when the total daimyo territories amounted to 18 million *koku* and the total territories of all banner men (*hatamoto*) were 2.6 million *koku*. Motoyama, *Kinsei jusha no shisō chōsen*, 3–4. According to the *Rules for the Responsibility of the Senior Council* (*rōjū shokumu teisoku*), dating from 1634, those who held *kokudaka* amounting to less than 10,000 were called banner men (*hatamoto*). They formed the shogunate's armed forces. Hereditary (*fudai*) daimyo, independent of the Tokugawa vassalage but loyal to the shogunate, were clearly distinguished from the outside (*tozama*) daimyo, the latter becoming loyal to Ieyasu only after the Battle of Sekigahara. Yamaguchi, "Han taisei no seiritsu," 159–66.

12. One *kokudaka* was approximately the amount of grain a male adult would consume in a year, about 150 kilograms. *Kokudaka* did not automatically mean that the domain produced exactly the same amount of grain, as evidenced in the case of the Matsumae domain in Ezo, where they did not produce any rice. In such cases, *kokudaka* was used to demonstrate levels of prestige. David Howell explains that the shogunate originally used the *kokudaka* system "to calculate both the military forces a lord could reasonably expect to support and, concomitantly, the scale of public-works projects he could be called on to supervise." Eventually it became "above all a measure of its lord's standing within the community of daimyo." Howell, *Geographies of Identity*, 23.

13. In June 1635, the *Various Points of Laws for Warrior Houses* (*Buke shohatto*) was revised, and the shogunate clearly defined the status of daimyo as being those who had 10,000 *koku* or more. Yokota, *Nihon no rekishi*, vol. 16, *Tenka taihei*, 87–89.

mediation, Ieyasu established control over other powerful daimyo, particularly the ones in the western parts of Japan who were slow to recognize him as *tenkabito*. Later, the "issuance of the territory documents in Kanbun 4" (*Kanbun inchi*, 1664) during the rule of the fourth shogun, Tokugawa Ietsuna (1641–80, r. 1651–80), marked the completion of the first phase of land distribution, and the procedures linked to land allocation were standardized.[14] For the remainder of the Tokugawa era, the renewal of documents (*ryōchi aratame*) took place through the process of ceremonially confirming the daimyo's rule of the domain by issuing the documents (*ryōchi hanmotsu*), accompanied with the shogun's letter with a red seal (*shuinjō*).[15] Daimyo permanently lost their ownership and the right to rule only in April 1868 when the Meiji state ordered them to return papers of *hanmotsu* and *shuinjō* shortly after the Meiji Restoration.[16]

To be sure, even after the 1660s, the domains continued to shift because daimyo were never guaranteed the right to rule the same territory and were subject to punishment by confiscation (*kaieki*), reduction (*genpō*), or transfer (*tenpō*) of the territory.[17] Furthermore, as historian Philip Brown has claimed, the standardization of the types of shogunate land surveys, especially in the early seventeenth century, was "only for

14.   Asao, *Shōgun kenryoku no sōshutsu*; Kitajima, *Edo bakufu no kenryoku kōzō*, 321–23; Ōno M., "'Ryōchi hanmotsu/ shuinjō' sairon"; Takagi S., "Edo bakufu no seiritsu," 117–53; Tokugawa, *Shinshū Tokugawa Ieyasu monjo no kenkyū*.

15.   Land surveys and mapmaking grew out of the practice adopted by many Sengoku daimyo, some of which may be traced back to their lords Oda Nobunaga and Toyotomi Hideyoshi. Berry, *Hideyoshi*. For example, the format of *shuinjō* issued by Ieyasu remained the same as Hideyoshi's, and Ieyasu used the same size and quality of *shuinjō* as Hideyoshi. Fujii, *Tokugawa shōgunke ryōchi ategaisei*, 326–43. For the rule of the northernmost island of Ezo, see the detailed analysis by Kaiho, "Wajin seiken no seiritsu" and "Tōitsu seiken, Matsumae han."

16.   Aoyama Tadamasa notes that the way the daimyo returned these documents to the Meiji state varied, and the *Record of Restoration* (*Fukkoki*) does not preserve all documents of *ryōchi ategaijō* from all 260 daimyo houses because some were lost in a fire. But he states that 166 out of 260 daimyo houses returned these documents to the Meiji state. Aoyama T., "Joshō: kinsei ni 'han' wa atta ka," 4–5.

17.   By drawing on Fujino Tamotsu's study, Philip Brown shows 235 cases of confiscation of daimyo territory in peacetime from 1601 to 1760. Brown explains that the daimyo ended up receiving a larger slice of territory in most of these cases, but this number shows how unstable the territory was for the daimyo in the first half of the Tokugawa period. Brown, *Central Authority and Local Autonomy*, 20–24.

policy, not of methods," implying the premature nature of these topographic projects.[18] The inconsistency involved in these projects reflected the varying ways the first three shoguns dealt with powerful daimyo. For example, Ieyasu had begun distributing land before he was appointed shogun in 1603, and the distribution procedures were revised repeatedly until 1615, when the Toyotomi were destroyed during the siege of Osaka because up to this point, the shogunate had consisted of the officials of both Ieyasu and Toyotomi Hideyori (1593–1615). They shared the administrative duties of the new government, working jointly to conduct the land surveys that determined which lands should be received by their chief vassals. Asao Naohiro points out that the siege of Osaka was an important opportunity for Shogun Hidetada (1579–1632, r. 1605–23) to obtain the support of the "outside" (*tozama*) daimyo, who swore military allegiance to Ieyasu only after the Battle of Sekigahara.[19] With little influence over the *tozama* daimyo, who were spread across the western parts of the archipelago, land mediation functioned as a tool for establishing Hidetada's shogunal power, while providing the daimyo with the opportunity to participate in the shogunate centered political system for decades to come.

Another major topographic project was making provincial maps. When land was assigned to a daimyo as territory, a procedure was adopted that allowed the shogunate to keep track of daimyo landholdings and

18. Brown, *Central Authority and Local Autonomy*, 71. In this regard, Luke Roberts mentions the inaccuracies found in the official assessment of agricultural production, which resulted from the inconsistent land surveys and the subsequent assessment of taxes. Roberts, *Performing the Great Peace*, 53–56.

19. Asao, *Shōgun kenryoku no sōshutsu*, 234. Fujii also explains that Ieyasu, not Hidetada, held the military command for the western regions beyond Suruga (today's Shizuoka prefecture) prior to 1617, and Hidetada's issuance of the *shuinjō* in 1617 to the various daimyos in the western provinces of the realm was a symbolic gesture that indicated he had finally come to place them under his control. Fujii, *Tokugawa shōgunke ryōchi ategaisei*, 126. See also Kasaya's studies that examine a series of the shogun's tactical attempts, especially in the first thirty years, to dismantle the basis of legitimacy of the Toyotomi house centering on and beyond Osaka Castle. After the Battle of Sekigahara, there were no territories of the Tokugawa daimyo in western Japan beyond Kyoto, and the ensuing presence of daimyo with a large province-holding capacity (*kunimochi daimyo*) in western Japan remained a crucial challenge to the shogunate. Kasaya, "Joron," 3–25; Kasaya, *Sekigahara kassen*; Kasaya, *Sekigahara kassen to Ōsaka no jin*.

collect taxes from them. The shogunate initiated land surveys to obtain information about the daimyo's territory, such as the size of every village and its level of productivity, and the results were recorded in the book of the surveyed land (*kenchichō*) and the book of villages (*gōchō*) (figures 1.1 and 1.2). Based on the results of the land surveys, the shogunate calculated the taxes to be levied on the daimyo, and these numbers were recorded in *gōchō*. *Gōchō* listed all the villages that existed in the territory with their annual rice yields, and *gōchō* formed an important resource by containing information about the economic power of each daimyo.[20] Based on the data in *gōchō*, the shogunate made provincial maps, which also marked all the villages with their names and their annual rice yields in a color-coded manner (figures 1.3 and 1.4). The symbolic meaning associated with knowing everything about the domains that the daimyo ruled—village names, their annual rice yields, local histories, and natural features—was an important message that the shogunate was above the regional lords.[21] To make this point absolutely clear, the shogunate preserved these vital documents of local domains in the shogun's library, Momijiyama bunko.

In the early years of the shogunate, the land surveys were difficult to perform because of poor survey technology and a lack of resources.[22] It was also difficult simply because some territories included undeveloped land, and in some cases more lands were made available for rice cultivation after the surveys ended so the domains could meet the allocated taxes. Although the full picture of the land surveys is hard to obtain, due to the limited extant proof of *gōchō*, the process was long and complex

20. For a complete record of *gōchō* during the Genroku (1688–1703) and Tenpō (1830–43) periods, see *Naikaku bunko shozō shiseki sōkan*, vols. 55–56. They are also available at the Digital Archive of National Archives of Japan, https://www.digital.archives .go.jp/DAS/pickup/view/category/categoryArchives/0300000000/0302000000/00.

21. The local administration differed significantly from province to province, and in this sense, the Tokugawa village exhibited ever-changing practice. Ooms states that data on the land and people were essential to the shogunate and domain's offices, which in his view facilitated domination over local governance. Ooms, *Tokugawa Village Practice*, 110.

22. See also Murakami, *Edo bakufu Hachiōji sennin dōshin*; Narumi, "Kinsei ezu ni miru sokuryō"; Ōishi, *Jikata hanreiroku*.

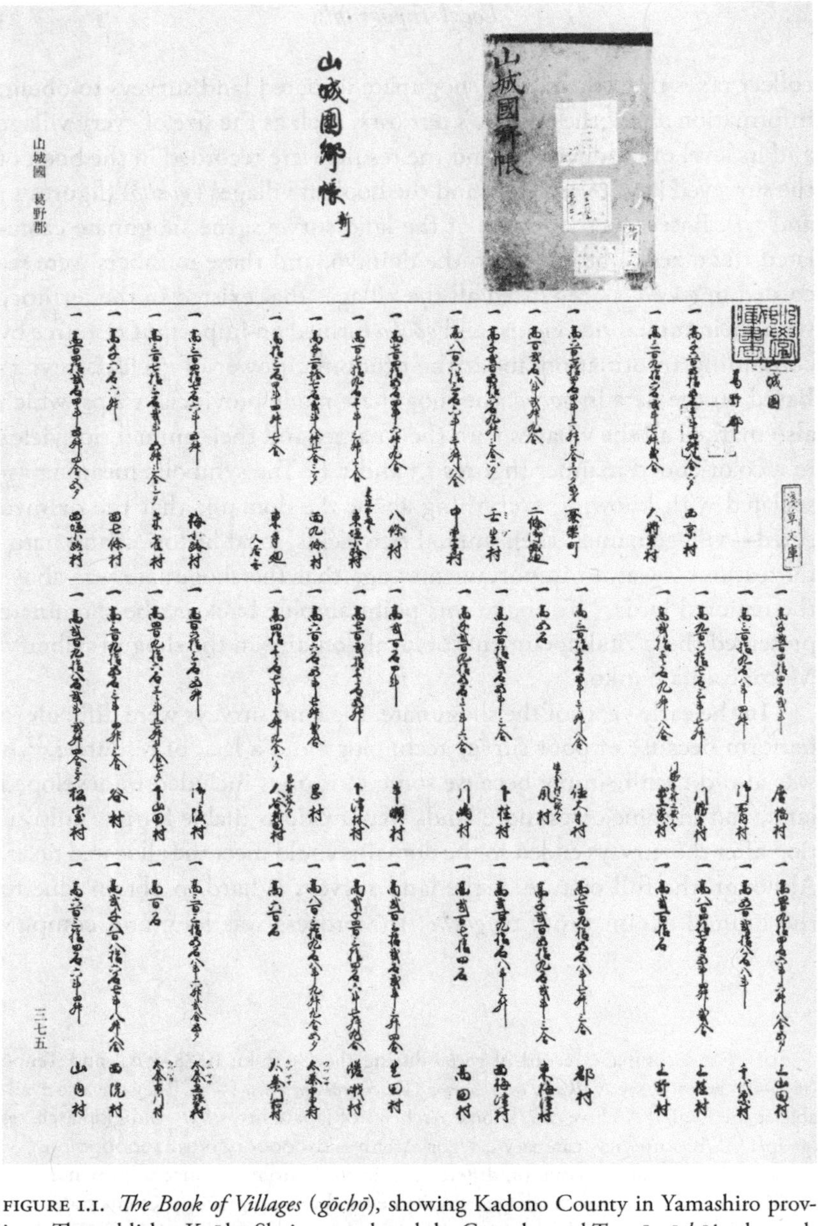

FIGURE 1.1. *The Book of Villages* (*gōchō*), showing Kadono County in Yamashiro province. The publisher Kyūko Shoin reproduced the Genroku and Tenpō *gōchō* in the multivolume set of government historical documents ("Yamashiro no kuni gōchō," in *Naikaku bunko shozō shiseki kankōkan*, 55:375). Today the originals are available at the Digital Archive of National Archives of Japan. Courtesy of Kyūko Shoin. https://www.digital.archives.go.jp/DAS/pickup/view/category/categoryArchivesEn/0300000000/0302000000/00.

FIGURE I.2. *The Book of Villages* (*gōchō*), showing Soekami County in Yamato province ("Yamato no kuni gōchō," in *Naikaku bunko shozō shiseki kankōkan*, 55:383). Courtesy of Kyūko Shoin.

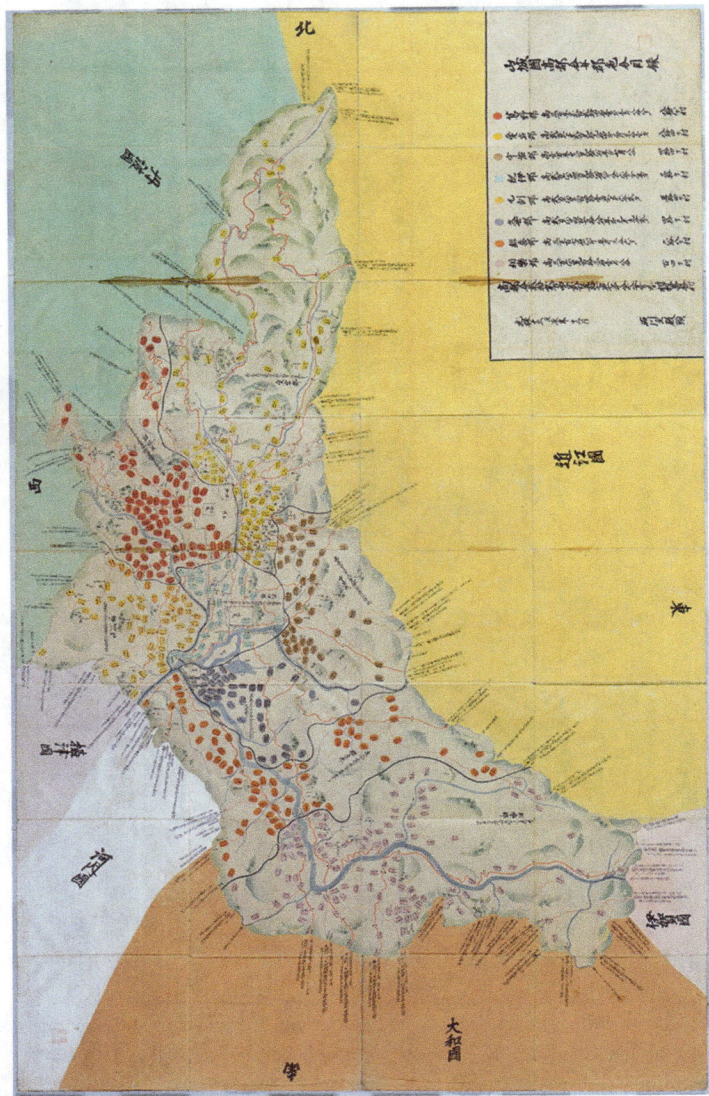

FIGURE 1.3. Provincial map of the Genroku-era (1688–1703) Yamashiro province. The production of provincial maps began in 1696 and was completed by 1702. The shogunate standardized the process, with each oval shape marking a village, along with its name and annual productivity level (see close-up in figure 1.4). National Archives of Japan houses the Genroku *kuniezu*, as well as *kuniezu* made in the Tenpō era (1830–43). Courtesy of the Digital Archive of National Archives of Japan. https://www.digital.archives.go.jp/DAS/pickup/view/category/categoryArchivesEn/0300000000/default/00.

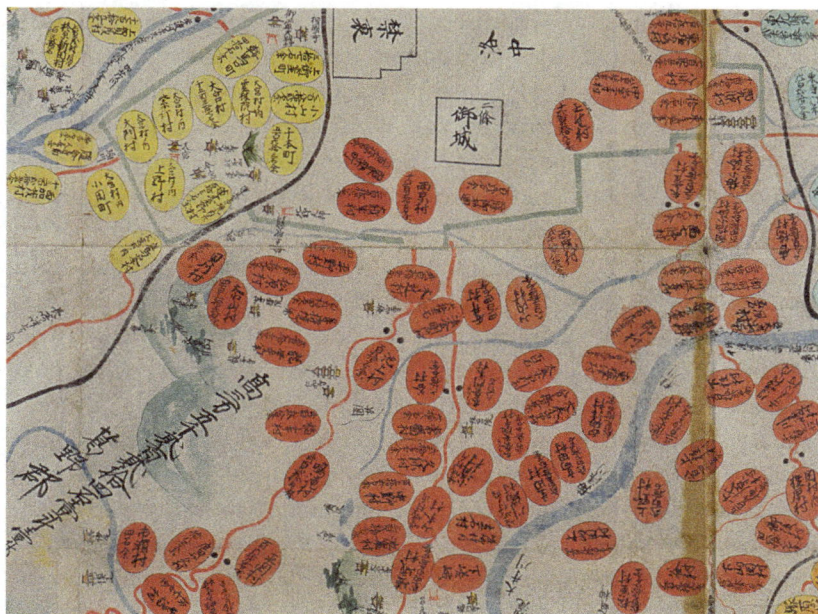

FIGURE 1.4. Close-up of figure 1.3. The black and red lines represent the major roads, with blue indicating rivers, lakes, and ponds. The two small black circles superimposed on the highways represent milestones.

because of the conflicting interests of the shogunate and the domain.[23] The autobiography of Tokugawa samurai Katsu Kokichi (1802–50), for example, offers a clue about how the land survey and the calculation of taxes took place.[24] Kokichi's brother, who was the shogunate official, sent Kokichi to the village in Shinano province (present-day Nagano prefecture) to determine the rice tax for the coming year because the brother was in poor health and unable to perform the duty. Kokichi declared an exceptionally small amount of tax to be paid on all the paddy fields in the village, which made the villagers extremely happy. Of course, this was a rare case, and unless the representatives included a lenient official like Kokichi, the estimation of taxes might be more than the village could

23.   See, for example, Izumi, *Kinsei zenki gōsondaka*; Katō, "Nanbuhan ni okeru chihō chigyōsei;" Watanabe T., *Kinsei hyakushō no sokojikara*.

24.   Katsu, *Musui's Story*, 52.

actually produce. One study shows how the shogunate provided the domain lords with detailed instructions, pressuring them to report the productivity of the land by calculating the amount of "unhulled rice harvested per square *shaku* (ca. 30 cm)" with "allowances being made for variables such as soil type" to compile in the *gōchō*.[25] The shogunate's imposition often resulted in an overestimation of annual rice yields, which caused long-term problems in the domain governance, thus forcing the domain to exploit farmers. In a similar light, Kawamura Hirotada notes that the *kuniezu* compilation during the Shōhō period (1644–47) under the rule of Tokugawa Iemitsu (1604–51, r. 1623–51) was particularly demanding because of numerous rules on the domains about how to make the map. The shogunate's instructions included the submission of a "map of the castle and castle-town" (*jōezu*) and the "book of the roads" (*michi no chō*) together with *kuniezu* and *gōchō*.[26] Considering that Iemitsu launched other policies to enhance the shogunate's authority, such as the deification of Ieyasu at the enlarged Nikkō Tōshōgū shrine, these instructions indicate Iemitsu's attempt to ensure the daimyo's allegiance to the shogunate.

25.   Unno, "Cartography in Japan," 396. Unno notes that the "final register defined the value of the cultivated land according to its yield in *koku*." As Sugimoto further explains, reporting only the agricultural yields to the shogunate became a problem because the domain might have other sources of revenue from sea and mountains, which were not calculated as the yield. The land survey was limited to arable land, but the daimyo might hope to increase productivity by developing the mountainous areas. Areas such as mountains, fields, forests, and seas were, however, not part of their possession but belonged to the shogunate, and this also led to disputes and discontent, necessitating another mapmaking project aimed at redrawing the borders. See Sugimoto, *Ryōiki shihai no tenkai*, 21–76.

26.   Kawamura, *Edo bakufusen kuniezu no kenkyū*, 385–97. In this regard, Berry poses an intriguing question in relation to why the Tokugawa regime was able to impose cartographic logic when mapmaking was still a new skill in the early modern states. When reading Ooms's *Tokugawa Village Practice* concurrently, we note his argument that the domain lords became the "imperial conquerors," installed into their domains through land mediation and emerging as an effective tool of the shogunate, who used them to actively reshape the landscapes under their control. Although my interest is in the narrativizing process of creating the defining identity of Japan, I agree with Berry and Ooms that the process of provincial mapmaking played a seminal role in the social engineering. Berry, *Japan in Print*, 54–103; Ooms, *Tokugawa Village Practice*, 71–191.

The shogunate's oppressive demands with regard to mapmaking and land surveys indicate that these projects were exhaustive and the domains had to conduct extensive research to comply with the shogunate's instructions. One of the requirements the shogunate insisted on was the collection of all the village names and for these to be written in the correct *kanji* compounds. Having the names recorded using the correct characters was vital because there were villages with the same name, which caused confusion when collecting taxes. Likewise, because the names of the counties and villages appeared on *gōchō*, provincial maps, and the *hanmotsu* documents that guaranteed the daimyo's ownership and right to rule, it was necessary to stipulate the names correctly and register them and their annual yields for official use. The shogunate instructed the domain to present proof that validated the histories of the village names and how the characters were selected. Being "correct" meant that each name had to be verified through reference to *Japanese Names for Things: Annotated and Classified* (*Wamyōshō*, also known as *Wamyō ruijushō*) and the household encyclopedia known as *setsuyōshū*.[27] Moreover, the shogunate made it clear that in cases where the domain's explanations disagreed with shogunate sources, the domain explanations would be deemed inadequate and the shogunate would provide its own information and resources with official privileged status.

The domains struggled to meet these instructions, and sometimes they were unable to fully respond to orders. Besides the pressure from above, many local domains faced a number of difficulties from village communities that were struggling with the transition to the new era. There was a need to intervene in the native structures and networks that had controlled the life of the village up to this point, which presented considerable challenges to the lord because he and his retainers were

27. *Wamyōshō* is a dictionary edited by Miyamoto no Shitagō (911–83) during the Heian period (794–1185). This text is also known as *Wamyō* or *Shitagō ga wamyō*, and it lists 2,600 Chinese terms that are organized in the traditional classification order, starting with the "On Heaven" (*ten no bu*), "On Earth" (*chi no bu*), "On Grass and Trees" (*sōmoku no bu*), and so on. Yokota Fuyuhiko makes a note that during the Tokugawa period, more supplementary information was added to the original *setsuyōshū* and it evolved into an encyclopedia, while different types (more than 300 versions) of *setsuyōshū* emerged for the convenience of users. Yokota, "Kinsei no shuppan bunka to 'Nihon'," 109–14.

newcomers in a land where most village residents had lived all their lives.[28] In other words, managing the villages involved dismantling the existing structures and instituting a new line of authority under the daimyo, which was obviously important for the stability and prosperity of the domain. Here the compilation of *fudoki* proved useful.

Governing the Domain

Let us now turn to *Aizu fudoki*, which sheds light on why and how the lord of Aizu, Hoshina Masayuki (1611–73, r. 1643–69), decided to revive the tradition of *fudoki*. *Aizu fudoki* is often viewed as a reflection of the shogunate's will to revitalize its central authority by compiling national history, but as I will demonstrate, it was also Lord Masayuki's deeply personal commitment to improving the position of his domain within the Tokugawa political order. Masayuki was a son of the second shogun, Hidetada; he was also a stepbrother of the third shogun, Iemitsu, and of the lord of Mito, Tokugawa Mitsukuni (1628–1701). With these blood connections, he was an influential force in the shogunate and remained powerful as a regent to the fourth shogun, Ietsuna.[29] Masayuki is known to have made decisions for the shogunate in close consultation with Zhu Xi Neo-Confucian teachings and launched a number of moralizing policies, such as establishing "family precepts" (*kakun*), securing the relationship between the daimyo house and retainers, and cultivating ethical

28. Fujii, *Tokugawa shōgunke ryōchi ategaisei*; Kitajima, *Edo bakufu no kenryoku kōzō*, 321–23; Ōno M., "'Ryōchi hanmotsu/ shuinjō' sairon"; Takagi S., "Edo bakufu no seiritsu"; Tokugawa, *Shinshū Tokugawa Ieyasu monjo no kenkyū*.

29. Takano Nobuharu points out that daimyo who were related to the Tokugawa family rarely engaged in shogunal politics directly, except for Hoshina Masayuki, the eighth shogun Tokugawa Yoshimune (1684–1751, r. 1716–45) who came from one of the three branch families of Tokugawa (*gosanke*), Kii Tokugawa, and later Matsudaira Yoshinaga (1828–90, r. 1838–58). However, they normally occupied positions that were critical to shogunal politics to support the Tokugawa house. Takano, *Daimyō no sōbō*, 62–63.

relationships within the domain.[30] Many of his efforts to tone down the militaristic tendencies of the warriors coincided with the shogunate's early undertakings to establish cooperative relationships with other daimyo.[31] Masayuki surrounded himself with scholars and invited Yamazaki Ansai (1619–82) to be a Confucian lecturer for Aizu in 1665. His close relationship with Ansai, who formed a school of thought known as *Suika shintō*, is well known. He also studied *shintō* with Yoshikawa Koretari (1616–94), the disciple of the Yoshida *shintō*, and received the *shintō* spiritual title of Hanitsu reijin (God of Hanitsu Spirit) from Koretari. Apart from lecturing Masayuki on *shintō*, Koretari conferred the four esoteric transmissions of Yoshida *shintō* on Masayuki in the year before his death.[32]

Having become the new lord of Aizu in 1643, after being transferred from Dewa province (present-day Yamagata prefecture), Masayuki encountered the old local forces from previous eras, embodied in the form of the "head of the village" (*gōgashira*), a figure who virtually controlled the village life of Aizu during the Sengoku era. He needed to work with these former leaders of the land and ultimately to weaken their power to restructure the village community. Religious institutions in Aizu also had to come under the authority of the domain.[33] In the process, Masayuki used the wisdom of the ancient sages of China, including the moral teachings of Zhu Xi Neo-Confucianism, to allocate different domain groups to their appropriate place in society.[34] The compilation of *fudoki* also

30. For example, Masayuki forbade the practice of *junshi* (follow the master to the grave) to strengthen the loyalty of the vassals to the daimyo house and stabilize the rule of the domain. However, the practice continued. Taniguchi, "Junshi, adauchi, shinjū," 80. Masayuki is also remembered for severely punishing Yamaga Sokō (1622–85) in 1666, following his criticism of the discussion on human nature presented by Zhu Xi in his *Seikyō yōroku* (Essential Lexicography of Sagely Confucius Teachings). Both Masayuki and Sokō valued moral teachings as a way of stabilizing the domain, but they disagreed about whose teaching was the best. Maeda K., *Aizuhan ni okeru Yamazaki Ansai*, 1–7. See also Taira, *Kinsei Nihon shisōshi kenkyū*, 5–12.

31. Takano, *Hankoku to hanpo no kōzu*, 483; Yokota, *Tenka taihei*, 24–30.

32. Maeda K., *Aizu-han ni okeru Yamazaki Ansai*, 125–27.

33. Masayuki worked to dissolve the power of the former lords of Aizu but did not exclude them. He commemorated their historic achievements by building monuments and maintaining their presence in the historical memory. Takano, *Daimyō no sōbō*, 195.

34. Taira, *Kinsei Nihon shisōshi kenkyū*, 9.

proved effective in various ways for the new lord. First, he needed to acquaint himself with the local topography and history, and second, his understanding of local topography and specialty items allowed him to strategize the development of local industries. The first *Aizu fudoki* was compiled under Masayuki's supervision during the fifth and sixth years of the Kanbun era (1665–66). This *fudoki* is often called *Kanbun fudoki* (*Fudoki* of the Kanbun Era, 1661–72) and is distinguished from later compilations. The Aizu domain continued to compile *fudoki* in the subsequent eras to keep updating the topographic information, which materialized as *Jōkyō fūzokuchō*, completed in the Jōkyō era (1684–88), and *Bunka fudoki*, compiled in the Bunka era (1804–18).[35] The domain actively produced other *fudoki*-like texts throughout the Tokugawa period to supplement and revise the topographic information of Aizu. All of these texts were closely modeled on the original *fudoki* of the eighth century.

Japanese historian Shirai Tetsuya places *Aizu fudoki* in close dialogue with the shogunate's efforts in the 1664 *ryōchi aratame* process, when the shogunate issued instructions to all the domains regarding the renewal process for their land holdings.[36] The shogunate appointed special officials (*ryōchi shuin aratame bugyō*) to renew the documents concerning the territory, and they collected all previously issued documents to reissue a new set.[37] The shogunate required a report on some of the county names from the Aizu domain in March 1664, and the shogunate requested the domain turn in the report with the prior *hanmotsu* documents. However, as Shirai shows, Aizu domain could not verify all the names the sho-

35. Shōji, "Josetsu," 4–12.

36. By this time, the previous land surveys and assessments of taxes had accumulated enough results for the daimyo territories, so there was no longer a need to conduct new land surveys. Instead, the focus shifted to refining the processes of mapmaking and issuing documents concerning the daimyo territories. From Ietsuna's time, therefore, the new shogun symbolically called for *ryōchi aratame* (domain renewal) or *tsugime ando* (land allocation process in transition), collected the *ryōchi hanmotsu* and *shuinjō* that were issued by the former shogun, and reissued the set of documents under his authority.

37. In addition to the existing practice of issuing *ryōchi hanmotsu*, the shogunate decided to issue a new *ryōchi mokuroku* (catalog of the counties and villages in the territory), which listed all villages in the province under the district's names, along with their annual production of *kokudaka*. Fujii, *Tokugawa shogunke ryōchi ategaisei*, 303–6.

gunate had ordered, apart from the ones in Ōnuma and Asaka counties. As a result, some place names in the counties of Aizu were different from the official reference sources when the domain submitted the requested documents.[38] The shogunate officials demanded that a senior retainer of the House Elder (*karō*) of Aizu, Tanaka Masaharu (1613–72), explain the divergent information concerning these names. The shogunate specifically instructed him to make inquiries with those older people in Aizu who were knowledgeable about these names and the local topography and present a report with written proof explaining the origins and histories of the place names.[39]

Because the Aizu officials could not produce adequate explanations in response to the shogunate's inquiries, the renewal documents from Ietsuna were written using incorrect characters for the counties that Aizu failed to verify. When the *hanmotsu* documents arrived from the shogunate in June 1664, Masayuki realized that not only were the characters wrong but the annual rice yields for these places had also been estimated incorrectly. Therefore, in August 1664 Masayuki ordered the domain to conduct a thorough topographic survey of Aizu, ordering another House Elder, Tomomatsu Kanjūrō (1622–87), to tour the domain to collect necessary information.[40] Kimura Tadanari in the county magistrate (*koori bugyō*) office, and another official, Mukai Yoshishige, who was also a scholar of Kōshōgaku (evidential study, philology in modern knowledge) and specialized in researching place names, traveled with Tomomatsu.[41] Masayuki was determined to correct the incorrect names and replace the annual yields of these places with more reasonable numbers. Instead of presenting the correct names of the counties to the shogunate, he produced *Aizu fudoki* by drawing on the recovered historical documents recording the details of the region to explicate the rise and fall of almost all counties and districts in Aizu.

Aizu fudoki embodied the painstaking efforts adopted by the domain to collect varying pieces of information about Aizu. The text is densely written in the classical Chinese style (*kanbun*), and many details are

38.   Shirai, *Nihon kinsei chishi hensanshi kenkyū*, 35.
39.   Shirai, *Nihon kinsei chishi hensanshi kenkyū*, 36–43.
40.   Shirai, *Nihon kinsei chishi hensanshi kenkyū*, 35.
41.   Maeda K., *Aizuhan ni okeru Yamazaki Ansai*, 51; Shōji, "Kaidai," 25.

quoted texts from various historical records, which was the way used to validate the claim in the study of Kōshōgaku. For instance, the first two sentences read, "the region of Aizu is the southwestern part of the province of Ōshū [another name for Mutsu province]. The counties of Aizu, Yama, Ōnuma, and Kawanuma are together known as the four counties of Aizu (*Aizu shigun*)."[42] Before the third sentence appears, there is a section written in a smaller font that consists of various references (*katchū*), amounting to a total of nine sentences. This *katchū* section provides an explanation for the *Aizu shigun*, which the second sentence has just mentioned. The beginning of *katchū* reads as follows:

> In regard to the four counties of Aizu (*Aizu shigun*), originally Aizu formed one county but soon became divided and called itself Yama. Yama was, then, split into Ōnuma and Kawanuma, and Aizu County disappeared and instead Inagawa appeared [and replaced the original Aizu]. This explanation is, in fact, wrong. *Wamyōshō* states that the two counties of Ōnuma and Kawanuma exist today below Shirakawa, and there are nine sections in a village below Aizu. *Waka* poems or old documents mention the mountains and rivers of Yama, Ōnuma, and Kawanuma by calling them altogether Aizu's mountains and rivers.[43]

In this fashion, the section attempts to clarify the confusion over the four counties of Aizu by citing *Wamyōshō*, *Later Collection* (*Gosenshū*, also known as the *Gosen wakashū*, compiled in 951), and *Collection of Ten Thousand Leaves* (*Man'yōshū*), which mention one or more of the four counties of Aizu. By refuting the explanation that Aizu County had disappeared and become Inagawa County, the excerpt supports the ongoing existence of Aizu, which continued to be mentioned in the popular medium of poetry. Poets and writers continued to call the mountains and rivers of Yama, Ōnuma, and Kawanuma counties Aizu mountains and the rivers of Aizu because Aizu never disappeared from the mental map or memory of the people there. By citing other sources and offering other explanations about the four counties, the attempt here was to deestablish the privilege attached to the official sources, thus showing that the on-

42. Shōji, *Aizu fudoki fūzokuchō: Kanbun fudoki*, 38.
43. Shōji, *Aizu fudoki fūzokuchō: Kanbun fudoki*, 38.

going local trends were not necessarily captured in the official reference texts.

Aizu fudoki demonstrated the complex history of the Aizu region, where the boundaries had shifted many times in the past and the names had changed accordingly. The various native sources used in *Aizu fudoki* recorded and explained the region's conflicting history, which was not necessarily reflected in the official records of the shogunate because court authority had waned in the late Heian era, and the record was not kept up to date. Suggesting that some of the information used by the shogunate was outdated because their sources were from the medieval era, *Aizu fudoki* placed greater emphasis on the sources they had employed. It showed the value of local records, such as the information in the *Renewed Record of All Things* (*yorozu aratamechō*), and local poems and songs as a vital resource when identifying the places in Aizu and more accurately reflecting the changing histories of Aizu. At the same time, following the style of *The Record of the Great Ming* (*Da Ming Yitong zhi*, 1461), the authoritative text of China's traditional historiography, *Aizu fudoki* was written in the official scholarly language of *kanbun*, with the use of *katchū* and many references to the official history texts following the Kōshōgaku style of scholarship.[44] The prefaces to *Aizu fudoki* were written by the two most prominent scholars of the time, Hayashi Shinobu (better known as Gahō, 1618–88), a son of Hayashi Razan (1583–1657), and Yamazaki Ansai. *Aizu fudoki* exemplified a sense of authenticity by preserving the traditional format, writing style, and prefaces of noteworthy scholars and tried to claim the status of being a genuine successor to the antiquarian *fudoki*.

In particular, Yamazaki Ansai's preface highlights the historical significance of Masayuki's compilation as a revival of the ancient *fudoki* that occurred under Empress Genmei (661–721, r. 707–15). Written in *kanbun*, the preface begins:

44. *Aizu fudoki* begins its narrative by designating the territorial borders and describing the topography, while quickly referencing the official historical texts to illustrate the rise of the Aizu region. It lists the most updated historical information on the status of shrines and temples in the domain, local specialty produce, the natural features of local topography, and the names and histories of various places in the domain. See, Shōji, *Aizu fudoki fūzokuchō: Kanbun fudoki*.

From the beginning of heaven and earth, there was our Japan, the country
of the deities (*shinkoku*). Succeeding the deities, Izanagi and Izanami built
the pillars of the country and asked their children to rule Japan (*Ōyashima*).
They each had a space to rule. This is what is known as the *Urayasu no
kuni* (peaceful country) of Japan. . . . Empress Genmei renewed the names
of the provinces, counties, districts, and villages, and . . . initiated unpre-
cedented reforms. . . . Our *fudoki* were kept by Dajōkan (Council of State),
but the royal throne declined, and the offices were abolished. *Fudoki* became scattered around throughout the country, and the missing volumes
were never supplemented. . . . Hoshina Masayuki of Aizu asked [me] about
the origin of Japan (*Ōyashima*) and regretted the loss of *fudoki* very much.
[To revive the lost tradition], he personally made *fudoki* of Aizu. How auspicious this book is! . . . let us wait for the completion of the countrywide
fudoki.[45]

Ansai identified the ancient *fudoki* as the local record of ancient Japan
under the imperial government of Empress Genmei. Even though these
were precious records, many of them went missing due to the decline of
the imperial court. Emphasizing the historic importance of the ancient
fudoki, Ansai elevated Masayuki's personal dedication to the domain
and his achievement in raising *Aizu fudoki* to the level of official history,
while expressing his wish to see other provinces following Masayuki's
lead. Ansai ended his preface by remarking on the potential for *fudoki*
to contribute to the compilation of a "national" history (*kokka shūsei no
kuwadate*).

Aizu fudoki included a number of smaller compilations, such as the
twenty-four-volume *Origins of Temples and Shrines* (*Jisha engi*), which
validated the historical origins (*engi*) of the temples and shrines in
Aizu, their historical origins and development (*raireki*), and treasures
(*hōmotsurui*) housed within. By declaring information about the wealth,
treasures, and possessions of the temples and shrines, the religious institutions became obligated to pay taxes to the domain. In return, they
received the domain's protection for restoration projects and other repairs,
if necessary. By publicizing the origins of the temples and shrines in the
distant past, these institutions risked being negatively evaluated about

45. Yamazaki, "Aizu fudoki jo," 36–37.

their identity if Kōshōgaku scholars disproved their claims. In other words, obtaining the temple and shrine details and including them in *Aizu fudoki* was a means of signifying that the domain's authority reached as far as the religious institutions, thus placing them under the domain's control. Besides the sources from temples and shrines, *Aizu fudoki* drew largely on sources such as *yorozu aratamechō* and *Record of the Land* (*tochichō*), which had been preserved at some *gōgashira* households up to this point.[46] The inclusion of these sources similarly meant that the domain was able to successfully shift the power dynamics of the local communities in their favor and obtain access and the right to house these documents under their authority. Masayuki achieved his objective of placing both religious institutions and the former structures of the village communities under the control of Aizu domain by compiling *Aizu fudoki*.

In this way, Masayuki's *Aizu fudoki* challenged the authenticity of the shogunate's reference sources while observing the ancient *fudoki* of the official history project of the past. By adhering to this traditional format and authoritative writing style, such as the 1461 *Da Ming Yitong zhi*, *Aizu fudoki* legitimized itself as a valid scholarly production of local topography. The shogunate officials were considerably impressed with Masayuki's *Aizu fudoki* and *Five Confucian Works in Aizu* (*Aizu gobusho*), which also included prefaces written by three eminent scholars. After viewing *Aizu fudoki*, the shogunate officials allowed the Aizu domain to submit a petition to the grand inspectors (*Ōmetsuke*) to update the incorrect names of the four counties in their *hanmotsu* documents, with the possibility of presenting evidence to Shogun Ietsuna. Unfortunately, the figures for the annual rice yields and the place names in the registered documents were not altered right away, and the domain had to wait until the renewal process during the fifth shogun, Tsunayoshi (1646–1709, r. 1680–1709) in 1684.[47]

46. Yamazaki, "Aizu fudoki jo," 36–37; Shōji, "Hanrei," 18–19.

47. In 1684 and 1685 Tsunayoshi issued the *ryōchi* documents, not only to the daimyo but also the small temples and shrines excluded in Ietsuna's time. The results of the Tsunayoshi's *shuin aratame* can be found in *Jōkyō gohanmotsu goshuin aratameki* (Record of Renewed Documents and Red Seal Papers issued during the Jōkyō era, 1684–88), housed in the National Archives of Japan.

Although Masayuki did not achieve his immediate goal of correcting the place names and their annual rice yields, the domain's painstaking efforts resulted in a number of successes, and the production of *Aizu fudoki* became well known among other domains. *Aizu fudoki* became the model record documenting the complex histories of Aizu, and the changing names were straightened out and recorded accurately in the registered documents. The scale and depth of the *Aizu fudoki* compilation, made possible by sending his senior officials to all corners of the domain, made Masayuki the leading authority. His influence consequently became preeminent, creating proper hierarchical order and places for all people in the region, including the native leaders of *gōgashira* and the village communities. He was undeniably motivated by the desire to reduce the domain's tax burden, but as his reverence for the moral teachings of Zhu Xi Neo-Confucianism reveals, Masayuki was also driven by his wish to govern the domain in line with the virtues of Neo-Confucianism.

. My analysis of the *Aizu fudoki* compilation reveals what the land-based mediation between the shogunate and respective daimyo entailed in the long run. Masayuki's accomplishment was deeply rooted in his political ideals, including his desire to rule his territory as a benevolent leader (*meikun*), and this message was appealing to those daimyo in different regions who faced similar hardships.[48] Not all the lords followed Masayuki's lead, but because they were equally confronted with the challenges of thoroughly acquainting themselves with the local topography to establish their domainal authority, Masayuki's *Aizu fudoki* sent a message that domainal authorities should be responsible for recording the complex history of their own lands, thus prompting a resumption of the *fudoki* compilation.[49] Those who were motivated to achieve stability in the domain extended the Neo-Confucian teachings beyond the household

48.   Kasaya, "Joron: Tokugawa jidai tsūshi yōkō," 28–29; Taira, *Kinsei Nihon shisōshi kenkyū*, 437–38.

49.   In addition, the daimyo read and studied war tales (*gunki mono* or *gunki monogatari*), such as *Nobunaga ki* (Chronicle of Oda Nobunaga, 1622) by Oze Hoan (1564–1640) and the fourteenth-century *Taiheiki* (Chronicle of Great Peace), in the seventeenth century. These tales were written in such a way as to justify the rise of the military figure and set the right path for the future, so they were widely used to educate the members of the daimyo house, the retainers, and other members in the domain. Fujii, "Kinsei zenki no daimyō to jikō," 140–41; Wakao, *'Taiheiki yomi' no jidai*; Yokota, *Tenka taihei*, 11.

(*ie*) of the military houses, and the domains, led by their leading scholars, adopted the idea of history writing as an effective use of the past, using it "to convey the moral messages and judgments vouchsafed by Heaven" as moral teachings within domain life.[50] Hayashi Gahō presided over the office of the shogunate at the time of renewing the domain documents with *Wamyōshō* and *setsuyōshū* in hand, and he worked closely with local domains by offering advice on the style and structure of *fudoki*.[51] Following the completion of *Aizu fudoki*, the latter half of the seventeenth century witnessed an upsurge in books about local topography as those who were close to the center actively encouraged other daimyo to undertake their own *fudoki* projects.

The conditions surrounding the production of *Aizu fudoki* reveals that the shogunate's official land survey and mapmaking programs required a significant amount of cooperation from local domains and provinces. The impressive finished products of the provincial maps and the books of villages, as well as the individually distributed *hanmotsu* documents, might seem to reflect the authority of the shogunate. Contrary to this view, the shogunate officials alone could not have achieved the level of perfection that characterizes these artifacts. The shogunate officials were unfamiliar with the local topography unless they were from the region, a fact that required local people to be in charge and carry out the project. The official topographic projects were made possible by the efforts of local scholars and officials, creating an opportunity for local scholars, officials, and farmers to participate in the intellectual labor for the domain and the shogunate. In this regard, Sugimoto Fumiko and others have already shown that local officials mostly conducted the land surveys and made the maps by following the instructions given by the shogunate.[52] Moreover, the ongoing project of mapmaking—which is referred to by the imperial reign as *Keichō kuniezu* (1604), *Kan'ei kuniezu* (1633), *Shōhō kuniezu* (1644), *Genroku kuniezu* (1697), and *Tenpō kuniezu* (1835)— was not conducted in a regular cycle, precisely because the situation

---

50. Ng, *Mirroring the Past*, x–xi.

51. Gahō assisted Kurokawa's *Geibi-koku gunshi*, *Higo kokugun ittōshi*, and the *Hitachi no kuni fudoki*. He worked with Mito Mitsukuni, who was well aware of Hoshina Masayuki's *Aizu fudoki*. Shirai, *Nihon kinsei chishi hensanshi kenkyū*, 50–55.

52. See Sugimoto et al., *Ezugaku nyūmon*; Sugimoto, *Ryōiki shahai no tenkai*; Kawamura, *Edo bakufu no Nihon chizu*; Kawamura, *Edo bakufusen kuniezu no kenkyū*; Unno, "Cartography in Japan."

sometimes forced the shogunate to redraw the provincial borders in *kuniezu* and other official documents.[53] Because there was often more than one domain in a province, border disputes between residents were frequent. More precisely, the domains were in charge of governing the local population, but if the policies of one domain differed from others in the province, it generated local disputes of various kinds.[54] Official topographic investigations were called for when the authorities had to resolve local disputes over the provincial borders or renew the number of annual rice yields to adjust taxes.

Considering the cases that led to the renewal of the official documents, the provincial maps and books of villages are artifacts of the efforts of local communities and their solidarity. Indeed, various local scholars were involved in the process of verifying place names for the making of *gōchō* and eventually *fudoki* by referencing the historical texts.[55] Historian Haga Shōji, for example, writes that the Owari domain in today's Aichi prefecture began compiling *fudoki* of the province in 1698 after deciding that the details of local shrines and temples had to be recorded.[56] Yokoi Tokimochi (dates unknown), a magistrate of the office of temples and shrines (*jisha bugyō*), compiled *The Record of Owari Province* (*Bishū shi*) with two Confucian scholar assistants, Fukada Masamuro (d. 1663) and Koide Kaitetsu (also known as Tōsai, 1666–1738). They received additional aid from a handful of officials and *shintō* priests, who helped them sort out and validate the historical details through reference to the documents housed in the religious institutions. The death of Lord Tokugawa Tsunanari (1652–99) delayed the project, but it was eventually

---

53. Out of these five times, the shogunate called for the making of *Nihon-zu*, a map of Japan, in 1638, 1644, and 1696 based on the provincial maps that had just been submitted to the shogunate.

54. Unoda, "Kinsei juka no keiseiron," 35–36.

55. Ōno M., "'Ryōchi hanmotsu/ shuinjō' sairon," 27.

56. In 1607, Ieyasu's son, Tokugawa Yoshinao (1601–50), became the first lord of Owari domain. The domain consists of the entire province of Owari and a chunk of land in Mino province. Domain and province names did not always overlap, but in the case of Owari, the domain ruled the entire province and pieces of land in other provinces. Owari Tokugawa was one of the three *gosanke* houses, along with Mito and Kishū Tokugawas. For a detailed history of Owari, see, for example, Nagoya City Museum website, http://www.museum.cicty.natoya.jp.

completed in 1752 as *The Record of Owari Province* (*Bishū fushi*).[57] The work of local scholars, with the knowledge of Kōshōgaku, who verified the correct characters and histories, was valuable evidence for the domain charged with governing the local province.

As Federico Marcon and others have argued, with the exception of monks associated with the Gozan monasteries, there were no socially recognized "scholars" before the Tokugawa period.[58] The new networks of scholars gave impetus to the *fudoki*-like compilations, such as the production of temple and shrine origin stories (*jisha engi*), local specialties (*dosankō*), and names of places (*nayose*) by cataloging the fame attached to various places in the region. These projects provided local scholars with opportunities to cultivate, practice, and improve their Kōshōgaku skills by collecting, validating, and systematizing the topographic and historical information of their region. At the same time, the compilations of local topography and history generated the compilations of the history of spiritual sites, such as *jisha engi*, and accounts of the origins of pilgrimage (*junrei engi*). These texts became profoundly important as information sources for commercial publications, which were used in more informal guidebooks and handbooks for ordinary tourists, as well as in other self-study books.[59] In the eighteenth century, before setting out on their journeys, tourists were able to study the history of the shrines and temples in the pilgrimage destinations and leisure travel sites. The popularity of pilgrimage and travel increased the number of designated "sites of amulets" (*fudasho*) where travelers received religious tokens. Many sites with religious or spiritual significance became known widely through the production of "stories of the origins" (*engi mono*) that offered narrative overviews of various religious institutions. The compilations of *fudoki* and *fudoki*-like texts had a great effect on popular tourism and travel culture in the mid-Tokugawa period.

---

57. Haga S., *Shisekiron*, 39.

58. Marcon, *The Knowledge of Nature and the Nature of Knowledge*, 52–54; Motoyama, *Kinsei jusha no shisō chōsen*, 23–24.

59. New books under the category of *jisha engi* and *junrei engi* were vigorously produced from the eighteenth century onward. See, for example, Tsutsumi, *Kinsei bukkyō setsuwa*; Tokuda, *Chūsei no jisha engi to sankei*; Tsutsumi and Tokuda, *Jisha engi no bunkagaku*.

Kaibara Ekiken, "Fudoki," and History Writing

Kaibara Ekiken was one of the enthusiastic scholars of local topography who played an instrumental role in spreading *fudoki*-like productions throughout the country. Even though Ekiken lived away from the political and cultural centers of Edo and Kyoto in Chikuzen province (present-day Fukuoka) and was a masterless samurai (*rōnin*) from 1650 to late 1656, he earnestly studied during this time in Nagasaki, Edo, and Kyoto, receiving financial support from his family. When the third lord of Kuroda domain in Chikuzen, Kuroda Mitsuyuki (1628–1707, r. 1654–88), replaced Lord Tadayuki (1602–54) in 1654, Ekiken was called back to Kuroda and became heavily involved in transforming domain politics into a civil and cultural administration (*bunchi seiji*).[60] Unlike the time under Tadayuki, who had a strong inclination toward military rule (*budan seiji*), during Mitsuyuki's time the Kuroda domain flourished.[61] These policies were mainly selected and adopted by Tachibana Kanzaemon (dates unknown) and his son Tachibana Gorōzaemon (dates unknown), who recruited Ekiken to domainal service and remained his strong supporters thereafter. The Kuroda domain sent Ekiken to Kyoto to study *materia medica* (Honzōgaku) for about four years; during this time Ekiken became an ardent student of court music in Kyoto, an interest that brought him into contact with the most prominent scholars of the time. Ekiken's close relationship with leading scholars suggests that he was well informed about the developing trends of local *fudoki* compilation. He traveled widely in his lifetime, visiting Edo twelve times, Kyoto twenty-four times, and Nagasaki five times, extending these trips to enjoy the tourism-worthy places along the way.[62]

Ekiken is said to have repeatedly requested the Kuroda domain to allow him to write a sequel *fudoki* to the original *Chikuzen fudoki*, and he finally received approval in 1688.[63] Besides *fudoki*, he produced a number of other important works for the Kuroda domain, such as the *Gene-*

---

60. Inoue T., *Kaibara Ekiken*, 20–23.
61. Inoue T., *Kaibara Ekiken*, 24–28.
62. Inoue T., *Kaibara Ekiken*, 106–7.
63. Kaibara E., "Chikuzen no kuni zoku fudoki," 1.

alogy of the Kuroda Family (*Kuroda kafu*), *The Vassals of the Kuroda* (*Kuroda kashinden*), *The Abbreviated Account of the Kuroda* (*Kurodaki ryaku*), and *Biography of Loyal and Righteous Men of the Kuroda* (*Kuroda senkō chūgiden*). Ekiken and his assistants made trips to various locations to complete these history projects. After reaching a local place, Ekiken conducted field research by asking local temple and shrine residents, as well as other inhabitants, about local histories and topography, following this up with a careful investigation of his findings by referencing official history sources and following the Kōshōgaku evidential method.[64] As is often the case with these domain documents, many of the accounts that Ekiken produced for the Kuroda remained unpublished because they contained strategic information concerning the domain. However, Ekiken's scholarship quickly earned him a reputation, and scholars from other domains obtained hand-copied and draft versions of his writings and circulated them as highly prized scholarship.

Ekiken endorsed virtues derived from Neo-Confucian teaching and used them to enhance the prestige of the Kuroda domain. He was not just involved in producing family lineage books and *fudoki* for the domain but also in restoring the valuable historical accounts of the country. Sharing Hoshina Masayuki's regrets about the lost records of the country, Ekiken wrote similarly in his unpublished essay "The Record of Scenic Japan" (*Fusō kishō*) about the importance of *fudoki*. Defining topographic writings (literally, the writings on the earth, *chishi*) as "important documents of our realm," Ekiken treated them as documents that had recorded the "wind and earth of our land" (*honchō no fūdo no koto*) since antiquity.[65] He lamented that *fudoki* did not survive the civil wars of the medieval era, especially the violent destructions associated with the Meitoku Rebellion in 1391 and the Ōnin Rebellion (1467–77). The century-long civil strife destroyed the cultural capital of Kyoto, and Ekiken observed the regrettable state of *fudoki* in the early modern period as follows:

64. Itasaka, "Kaibara Ekiken *Azumaji no ki*," 418. See also a catalog of Ekiken's personal library, "Ganko mokuroku," that shows a list of reference texts he used in writing the historical texts. Kyūshū Shiryō Kankōkai, "Ganko mokuroku," 4–39.

65. Kaibara E., "Fusō kishō," 311.

Fudoki of Yamashiro Province (*Yamashiro fudoki*) only has records about Kuze District, and many parts of *Fudoki of Iga Province* (*Iga fudoki*) are also missing. *Fudoki of Owari Province* (*Owari fudoki*) has four volumes, and they are written in a more detailed manner than other provinces, which is rare. There are a few citations from *fudoki* in [an annotation of *Man'yōshū* called] *Man'yōshūshō* written by the scholar Sengaku (b. 1203) and in [an annotation on poetry called] *Shirin Saiyōshō* by scholar Yua (b. 1291). They can be used as proof of *fudoki*.[66]

The excerpt confirms the fragmented state of the extant *fudoki* and indicates Ekiken's attempt to locate textual evidence in contemporary texts. Indeed, he owned copies of some of the ancient *fudoki*, including *Fudoki of Ise Province* (*Ise fudoki*) and *Yamashiro fudoki*, plus a hand-copied version of *Fudoki of Izumo Province* (*Izumo fudoki*) and *Fudoki of Bungo Province* (*Bungo fudoki*), indicating that he had studied the original *fudoki* carefully.[67] Because of the considerable difficulty he experienced in locating the originals, Ekiken sought to confirm the existence of *fudoki* by finding historical texts that referenced *fudoki*, such as *Man'yōshūshō*.[68] He was informed about contemporaneous scholars who had reproduced similar works of the ancient *fudoki*, such as the ten-volume set of *Record of the Yamashiro Province* (*Yōshū fushi*, 1684) by Kurokawa Dōyū (d. 1691) and *Record of the Province of Yamashiro* (*Yamashiro kokushi*) by Ōshima Kyūma (dates unknown).[69] The essay "Fusō kishō" makes clear that Ekiken thought it possible to revive or reconstruct the original *fudoki*.

66. Kaibara E., "Fusō kishō," 311.
67. Ekiken held a copy of numerous topographic texts that were produced by his contemporary scholars, such as *Aizu fudoki* and *Record of Izumi Province* (*Senshūshi*). He held a copy of the first volume of *Fudoki* of Cambodia (*Shinrō fudoki*), published during the Yuan dynasty. Kyūshū Shiryō Kankōkai, "Ganko mokuroku," 10, 19, 29, 33, and 37; Kyūshū Shiryō Kankōkai, "Kazōsho mokuroku," 52.
68. Scholars today explain that the lack of creative or artistic qualities in the ancient *fudoki* provided the authorities little incentive to preserve these records. Akimoto, *Fudoki no kenkyū*, 1041–45.
69. Kaibara E., "Fusō kishō," 333. There are few records about *Yamashiro kokushi*, which consists of nine volumes. The author and publication date are not listed in the *Nihon kotenseki sōgō mokuroku*, although Ekiken identifies the author as Ōshima Kyūma in the text.

It is intriguing that Ekiken, along with Hoshina Masayuki, Hayashi Gahō, Yamazaki Ansai, and others, was interested in *fudoki* and thought they were more important than other more canonical historical texts, such as the *Man'yōshū*, *The Record of Ancient Matters* (*Kojiki*), and *The Chronicles of Japan* (*Nihon shoki*). Many historians in the past, including Ekiken, have identified the 713 edict by Empress Genmei as the first imperial order instigating *fudoki* compilation. Ekiken wrote in "Fusō kishō" that Empress Genmei ordered five home provinces and seven circuits (*kinai shichidō*) to compile *fudoki*, and each province made its historical record of *fudoki* in the fifth month of year six of Wadō (713).[70] Recognizing the significance of the 713 edict, Ekiken quoted the entirety of the edict in "Fusō kishō" as follows:

Good characters shall be given to the names of the villages and districts in the "home provinces and seven circuits" (*kinai shichidō*). Identify and record what the province produces and what grows in the province, such as silver and copper, plants and trees, birds and animals, and fish and insects, and so on; also comment on the fertility of the earth. The origins of the names of mountains, rivers, plains, and fields, and also unusual tales that are orally transmitted from generation to generation by the elders shall be investigated; include all these details in this historical report and present it to the court.[71]

The instruction to revise the local place names with "good characters" meant they should record the name using *kanji* characters, reflecting the supremacy of the Chinese culture at the time. The instruction to identify the special products of the province and discuss the fertility of the land in the region indicates the empress's desire to learn about the richness of

---

70. Kaibara E., "Fusō kishō," 311.

71. Kaibara E., "Fusō kishō," 311. This edict was originally compiled in *Shoku Nihongi*, on the second day of the fifth month in the sixth year of Wadō. Naoki, *Shoku Nihongi*, 147–48. Mark Funke translates the "good character" as "good Chinese characters" and reiterates this point in his interpretation of the edict as "all place names should have two Chinese characters." "Good characters" might have implied Chinese characters rather than Japanese *kana* at this time, but the character *ji* does not necessarily mean Chinese characters. For example, the *Morohashi Dai kanwa jiten* offers the meaning of *ji* as *fumi* (letter) or *moji* (character), among others. Funke, "Hitachi no kuni fudoki," 2–3; Morohashi, *Dai kanwa jiten*, 318; Shirai, *Nihon kinsei chishi hensanshi kenkyū*, 27.

the land she ruled. At the same time, the emphasis on the place origin stories implies that although the names were written in different characters in different times, it was considered valuable to remember all names that represented the place.

Even though Ekiken designated the edict documented in *The Chronicles of Japan Continued* (*Shoku Nihongi*) as evidence of the imperial order of *fudoki* compilation, scholars have disputed the validity of the edict at length, largely because nowhere in it does the term *fudoki* appear, and scholars today have concluded that the term *fudoki* was never used in any official documents until the Heian period.[72] More precisely, the earliest evidence of the use of the term was found in the eleventh-century poetry anthology *Literary Essence of Our Country* (*Honchō monzui*), in an exchange between senior councilor Miyoshi no Kiyoyuki (847–919) and Emperor Daigo (r. 897–930) in 914.[73] Some scholars of the Nativist (Kokugaku) school of thought in the nineteenth century, such as Hirata Atsutane (1776–1843), or Japanese ethnologist Orikuchi Shinobu (1887–1953), paid a lot of attention to *fudoki* because they saw signs of Japan's original community in the numerous poems and descriptions included. Kokugaku scholars positioned *fudoki* in a close relationship with *Man'yōshū*, for instance, as a guide to annotate and interpret the poems in *Man'yōshū*. In the end, they concluded that the *fudoki* project was extensive and had taken place over a long period of time; it is difficult to determine when the project started but it is likely that this was well before the 713 edict was issued.[74]

72. Aoki M., *Izumo Fudoki*, 25. For instance, Tanaka Takashi argues that the compilation order very likely followed the completion of *Kojiki* in 712, but his supporting evidence for this claim is an imperial rescript titled "An order to edit national history (*kokushi*)," which includes the term *kokushi* for national history, but not *fudoki*. Tanaka T., "Kaidai," 7–8.

73. This document, comprising twelve points from Kiyoyuki's opinions (*iken fūji jūnikajō*) advised him to employ the *fudoki* from the prior time to better control the administration of the local estate administration. Here the term *fudoki* was used as a reference for verifying estate policies, with the specific example of a district called Nima no gō that "was mentioned in the *fudoki* of Bitchū (Western part of Okayama prefecture)" being provided. Kamio, *Kodai ritsuryō bungaku kō*, 62. For *Honchō monzui*, an anthology of Chinese prose and poetry by Japanese writers, edited by scholar Fujiwara no Akihira (989–1066), see, for example, Shirane, *Traditional Japanese Literature*, 248.

74. Kamio, *Kodai ritsuryō bungaku kō*, 56–63.

The cultural authenticity of the *fudoki* has also been debated. Ethnologists and Kokugaku scholars have suggested that *fudoki* contained signs of Japan's original cultural identity, but there are other scholars who have argued compellingly that *fudoki* were an example of Japan's adaptation of China's political culture as recorded in the *Book of Jin* (265–420) (*Shinjo* in Japanese, *Jin shu* in Chinese).[75] This is a contentious debate about the adaptation of culture during the classical period, when Japan was vigorously adopting the Chinese practice of compiling national history, among other things. Especially during the Tang dynasty (618–906) in China, there were various kinds of topography compilation in the visual form and the textual narrative format, and the compilations expanded even more once the Northern Song dynasty (960–1126) had united the country.[76] Many of the topographic compilations in classical Japan followed these continental practices and produced similar maps and topographic reports. Intriguingly, the Yamato court maintained the Japanese name, *fudoki*, in their compilation of history.[77] Although Japan's first governing body, the Yamato court, exuberantly adapted structures of the Tang dynasty in China and established what is known as the *ritsuryō* (a combination of a criminal code *ritsu* and an administrative code of *ryō*) system in the early eighth century, Joan Piggott, a historian of early Japan, has argued that *fudoki* compilation was in fact an indigenous tradition that developed at the time of "the emergence of Japanese kingship" when the kings generated a "unified culture integrating most of the archipelago" as Nihon (Japan).[78] In other words, although there was an overwhelming presence of Chinese culture in the administrative systems and political structures of the court, the court still sought to balance local and native traditions and foreign Chinese culture and affirmed provincial

75. Kurano, "Kaisetsu," 290.

76. For a detailed analysis of the compilation of local topography in the Tang and Song dynasties of China, see Aoyama S., *Tō Sō jidai no kōtsū to chishi chizu no kenkyū*, 447–522.

77. Aoki M., *Izumo Fudoki*, 24–26.

78. Joan Piggott identifies the eighth century as the beginning of "Japan" and distinguishes this from its prior realms. Emperor Shōmu ruled as *tennō* (heavenly sovereign) and was "supported by a bureaucracy more than 7,000 strong in a realm configured by Chinese-style laws, the *ritsuryō*." Piggott, *Emergence of Japanese Kingship*, 1–5.

cultures by compiling *fudoki*.[79] Therefore, the court implemented *fudoki* to obtain the topographic and historical information of the villages and districts, but more important, the real purpose was to demonstrate the rich and abundant local topography and histories the court then claimed to control.

In this regard, Mark Funke offers a fascinating analysis that captures the conflicting concerns of the imperial court at this time. He emphasizes that the compilation of *fudoki* under Empress Genmei aimed to supplement the two chronicles of *Kojiki* and *Nihon shoki*, which left out other accounts of the deities' activities.[80] In a similar light, a scholar of religion, Isomae Jun'ichi, has observed that the compilation of *Nihon shoki* was "an epoch-making event" because the compilers sorted out various legendary and historical accounts into one, although these accounts "had been preserved in fragmented form" until then.[81] Isomae further points out the exclusive nature of *Nihon shoki* that narrativized only appropriate events relevant to the expansion of the rulers and their imperial lineage during the age of the gods (*jindai* or *kamiyo*). In short, other accounts of the deities had existed prior to the production of *Nihon shoki*, but *Nihon shoki* suppressed and obliterated them from memory and the official history of Japan because those accounts did not adhere to the story of the imperial lineage adopted in *Nihon shoki*. By contrast, *fudoki* recorded the time before the establishment of the grand narrative of the creation story and documented in detail the age of the deities and their activities all over the Japanese archipelago. The nature of *fudoki* was a survey of the "geographical extent of the imperial line's involvement in the development of the land."[82]

In this fashion, the discussion of modern scholarship informs us regarding the historical significance of *fudoki*. Of course, we do not know how much Tokugawa scholars knew about these debates over the historical validity of such chronicles. Regardless of the contentious points in

79. Funke, "Hitachi no kuni fudoki," 1–3; Aoki M., *Izumo Fudoki*, 3.

80. Funke, "Hitachi no kuni fudoki," 1. See also Higo, "Kiki seiritsu no rekishi shinri teki kiban," 368–80.

81. Isomae, "Myth in Metamorphosis," 361. See also Isomae and Thal, "Reappropriating the Japanese Myths," 34; Isomae, *Japanese Mythology*, 10.

82. Higo, "Kiki seiritsu no rekishi," 366.

historiography, it is important to acknowledge that *fudoki* again became important among scholars in the seventeenth century, including Ekiken. They prioritized *fudoki* as the valid and vital historical source for Japan's past by establishing the validity of the 713 edict and the court's attempt to compile the history of Japan. Ekiken particularly played a noteworthy role in solidifying the special significance of *fudoki* by providing, for the first time, the sequel to the original *fudoki*, titled *Chikuzen Fudoki Continued* (*Chikuzen no kuni zoku fudoki*, hereafter cited as *Zoku fudoki*), completed in 1709. Moreover, almost 100 years after Ekiken's death in the early nineteenth century, the shogunate rediscovered his *Zoku fudoki* and designated it as the model text for the *fudoki* compilation of other domains. With the aim of compiling *fudoki* for all provinces to generate a sense of togetherness under shogunate authority, Hayashi Jussai (1768–1841), the head of the Neo-Confucian Academy in Edo (Shōheikō), issued an edict in 1803 concerning the mandate for *fudoki* compilation in every domain. Jussai sent an order concerning "the Compilation of Topographic Reports of Various Provinces" (*shokoku chiri no sho* or *shokoku chishi*) in the form of an "internal order" (*naimei*) and instructed daimyo to observe the following three points when producing their *fudoki*: write in Japanese-style writing (*kanabun*), investigate fully and objectively the facts of the historic sites (*koseki jijitsu*), and model their works on *Zoku fudoki*, not the Chinese historiography or the Japanese texts modeled on the Chinese texts.[83]

When domestic and international problems were challenging the moral and political authority of the shogunate in the early nineteenth century, the shogunate's decision to mandate the *fudoki* compilation was a means of reasserting its legitimacy over the domains and identifying

---

83.   Shirai, *Nihon kinsei chishi hensanshi kenkyū*, 157–61. Evidence suggests that Tokugawa Ieyasu was interested in the practice of recording history, such as the dynastic history of China, but he did not call for the countrywide compilation of *fudoki*. Ieyasu possessed various topographic texts in his private libraries in his residences in Edo, Kyoto, and Sunpu, including copies of the *Da Ming Yitong zhi* and *Fangyu Shenlan* (Excellent Views of the World), a famous guidebook of scenic places in China under the Southern Song dynasty, comprising about seventy volumes. Shirai, *Nihon kinsei chishi hensanshi kenkyū*, 29; Akimoto, *Fudoki no kenkyū*, 1044.

itself as the symbolic center.[84] The chief senior councilor and regent to the eleventh shogun Tokugawa Ienari (1773–1841, r. 1787–1837), Matsudaira Sadanobu (1759–1829) was in charge of instituting a number of reforms at this time, which became known as the Kansei Reforms that were in line with Neo-Confucian virtues and morality.[85] Sadanobu also supported the publications of the *Veritable History of the Tokugawa* (*Tokugawa jikki*) and *Revised Version of the Genealogies of the Houses in the Kansei Period, 1789–1801* (*Kansei chōshū shokafu*), which were useful in validating the genealogy and other relationships of the retainers in compiling *fudoki*.[86] These compilation projects were the means for understanding the family lineages of vassals and retainers and placing the provinces under the shogunate's control to enhance authority when the crisis that eventually led to the overthrow of the shogunate in the mid-nineteenth century occurred.

The designation of Ekiken's *Zoku fudoki* as the model texts for the *fudoki* compilation in the nineteenth century was based on the fact that it was written in Japanese *kanabun*. At a time of mounting crisis, gathering local history and topographic reports compiled in Japanese was seen as

84.　Haga S., *Shisekiron*, 298–99; Takagi H., "'Kyōdo ai' to 'aikokushin' o tsunagu mono."

85.　The reforms imposed the enforcement of Neo-Confucianism as the orthodox field of study in schools sponsored by the shogunate (Kansei Prohibition of Heterodox Studies) in 1790. The prohibition encouraged Neo-Confucian-inspired studies, such as the compilation of historical texts, family and domain lineages, and other works following Chinese historiography. Fujita, *Kinsei no sandai kaikaku*, 110; Shirai, *Nihon kinsei chishi hensanshi kenkyū*, 105–6; Takahashi A., "Kinsei kōki no rekishigaku to Hayashi Jussai." For more information on Sadanobu's reform, see, for example, Ooms, *Charismatic Bureaucrat*, and Screech, *Shogun's Painted Culture*. Screech identifies Sadanobu as the ultimate author of Japanese culture. It was he who constructed unifying notions of Japanese culture when there existed over 200 domains or "states" according to his use of the term. Screech's overt emphasis on the role of Sadanobu in creating cultural unity, however, overlooks valuable studies that have highlighted the emergence of a "national" culture before Sadanobu. In addition to the role of the print culture that gave rise to the culture of movement, see, for example, Vaporis, *Tour of Duty* for a study on the transformation of regional cultures brought about as a result of the alternate attendance system.

86.　*Kansei chōshū shokafu* was a sequel to *Kan'ei shoka keizuden* (A Collection of the Genealogies of Some Houses in the Kan'ei Period, 1624–44), which was produced under the third shogun, Iemitsu. This genealogical work offered a history of 1,400 *hatamoto* (banner men) and daimyo houses, which amounted to a massive 1,530 volumes. National Institute of Japanese Literature, *Union Catalogue of Early Japanese Books*, http://base1.nijl.ac.jp/infolib/meta_pub/KTGSearch.cgi.

an effective way of producing a sense of community. The shogunate recognized the symbolic value of *kanabun* in Ekiken's text and embraced Japanese-style writing. However, what motivated Ekiken to choose this form of inscription in the early eighteenth century when classical Chinese was the most respected language of official scholarship? As mentioned earlier, many local scholars, including Hoshina Masayuki and Yamazaki Ansai, were interested in reviving the *fudoki* tradition, and they wrote their *fudoki* and the prefaces in the Chinese style of writing, *kanbun* and followed the authentic Chinese historiographies of the past. This was because Tokugawa scholars routinely employed the *kanbun*-style of writing, and they did not necessarily perceive *kanbun* as a foreign language, regarding it more as the language of authentic scholarship in East Asia. In fact, intellectual historian Koyasu Nobukuni identifies Ogyū Sorai (1666–1728) as the first scholar to recognize *kanbun* as a foreign language (*igengo*) and explain the linguistic difference between Chinese and Japanese.[87] Of course, Ekiken was capable of reading *kanbun* and he used *kanbun* in his scholarship, which means his use of *kanabun* in his *fudoki* was deliberate. This was a very innovative attempt, a clear indication of his awareness of the self and other.

This point—that is, the employment of the Japanese *kanabun* style in the traditional writing of *fudoki*—is vital to our understanding of the significance of Ekiken's scholarship and deserves a fuller examination in the next chapter. There I reveal the broader significance of the decision to write the *fudoki* in Japanese-style writing by asking what Ekiken's idea of Japan was and from where he adopted the rationale to validate the Japanese difference by producing a narrative of Japan. As we move on to the next chapter, we need to remember that local scholars were central to *fudoki* production as the land-based mediation matured in different regions. As they restored the local history records and embarked on the full-scale topographic projects for their domains, they came to see numerous signs of divine traces inscribed in the local landscape, especially in the place names of their regions. As a result of the topographic research conducted in the method of Kōshōgaku, the divine traces in various regions were made visible, and Ekiken established a link between the remnants of the age of the gods and *fudoki* as a record of the history of Japan.

87. Koyasu, *Soraigaku kōgi*, 14–15.

CHAPTER 2

The "Country of the Deities"

Narrative is a meta-code, a human universal on the basis of which transcultural messages about the nature of a shared reality can be transmitted. Arising, as Barthes says, between our experience of the world and our efforts to describe that experience in language, narrative "ceaselessly substitutes meaning for the straightforward copy of the events recounted."

—Hayden White, *The Content of the Form*

The presence of local scholars rose in the early eighteenth century because many of them advanced in their professional lives to become domain lecturers (*hanju* or *jushin*). Kaibara Ekiken, a lecturer from Chikuzen province, lived in a time when lively intellectual debate flourished in the cities, as recorded in the "Chronology of Teacher Ekiken" (*Ekiken sensei nenpu*). In this document, compiled some time after Ekiken's death by his nephews, Kaibara Yoshifuru (1664–1700) and Kajikawa Kakyū (dates unknown), we find a list of scholars who had direct or indirect influence on the formation of Ekiken's thought. For instance, the year 1630, when he was born, reads:

Hayashi Dōshun [better known as Razan (1583–1657)] was forty-eight years old; Ishikawa Jōzan [(1583–1672)] was forty-eight years old; Matsunaga Sekigo [(1592–1657)] was thirty-nine. . . . [By this year] Lord Kuroda had ruled Chikuzen for thirty years; Ōsaka Castle's fall, sixteen years ago, marked the demise of the Toyotomi; Eight years had passed since Tokugawa Iemitsu [(1604–51, r. 1623–51)] became the [third] shogun. . . . Foreign ships in Nagasaki were forbidden to bring Western books into Japan.[1]

1. Ekikenkai, "Ekiken sensei nenpu," 1.

This combination of notable scholars of the time and the remarks that indicate political stability—such as the thirty years of Kuroda's rule, the passing of enemies to the shogunate, and the ban on foreign books—implies that 1630 marked the dawn of an era of political solidity and subsequent economic prosperity. The inclusion of more scholars, such as Nakae Tōju (1608–48), Yamazaki Ansai (1619–82), Andō Seian (1622–1701), Kinoshita Jun'an (1621–98), Yamaga Sokō (1622–85), Itō Jinsai (1627–1705), and Matsushita Kenrin (1637–1704), hints at the lively discussions on good government, the economy, and human nature that were taking place in the private schools of these scholars in the cultural capitals.[2] The wide variety of schools of thought in place—Buddhism, *shintō*, Confucianism, Neo-Confucianism, Daoism, what is known as the Wang Yangming school of Confucianism today, and others—allowed Ekiken to develop his own intellectual orientation and contributed to the formation of his narrative of Japan.[3]

This chapter continues to examine Ekiken's works to demonstrate how he invented a narrative of Japan as the country of the deities by creatively reviving the ancient records of *fudoki* and reinterpreting the traditional discourse of the "spirits of the dead" (*kishin*) in ancient China.[4] The idea of *shinkoku* had long existed in Japan, appearing in the fourteenth-century *Chronicle of Gods and Sovereigns* (*Jinnō shōtōki*) by Kitabatake Chikafusa (1293–1354) and being witnessed in the ban of Jesuit missionaries (*Kirishitan bateren tsuihō no rei*, 1587), in which Toyotomi Hideyoshi

2.   Ekiken's diary shows that he visited Matsunaga Sekigo, Yamazaki Ansai, Kinoshita Jun'an, Matsushita Kenrin, Mukai Genshō (1609–77), and Inō Jakusui (1655–1715) in Kyoto. For the major scholars of the Tokugawa period, see, for example, Koyasu, *Edo shisōshi kōgi*; Tsuda, *Banzan Ekiken: dai kyōikuka bunko*, 21–22.

3.   Koyasu Nobukuni states that the Wang Yangming school of thought did not exist in early modern Japan, and only a few scholars had an intellectual orientation toward such learning. Meiji intellectuals, such as Inoue Tetsujirō, Miyake Setsurei, and others, wrote about the Wang Yangming school of Confucianism, and it then emerged as a school of thought opposed to Zhu Xi Neo-Confucianism and other Confucian schools. Koyasu, *Hōhō toshite no Edo*, 96.

4.   I have translated the notion of *kishin* as the spirits of the dead, but the Chinese theories of *kishin* are numerous because the idea had existed since the ancient times and changed over time. For a concise history of the *kishin* debates in Chinese philosophy, see Miura K., *Shushi to ki to shintai*, 67–129.

referred to Japan as the country of the deities, standing up against the Christian God. However, I argue that Ekiken's narrativization of Japan as *shinkoku* at this time was innovative.[5] He drew on the discourse of *kishin*, according to which the bodies of the dead return to Earth while the spirits evaporate into space like phantoms. By equating the spirits of *kishin* with the divine spirits of the deities in Japan, Ekiken produced a vision of *shinkoku* Japan that contrasted with the sagely country of China (*seijinkoku*) while actively adopting the conceptual frameworks of Zhu Xi Neo-Confucianism.

His attempts were timely as seventeenth-century East Asia had just witnessed a significant shake-up of the existing order: the Manchu take-over of the Central Kingdom and the demise of the Ming dynasty (1368–1644). As Tajiri Yūichirō has observed, the end of the Ming encouraged not only Japan but also Korea, which established itself as "small China" (*shō Chūka*) and claimed the authenticity of a society based on Confucian rituals.[6] Unlike in Korea, Confucianism had not yet taken deep root in the culture, political structure, or ethics of Japan by that time, and Tajiri explains that scholars instead drew on the idea of *shinkoku* as the central idea to solidify Japanese identity.[7] Emerging within the context of the changing geopolitical conditions in East Asia, as if to compete with the Manchu, who were historically viewed as the northern barbarians (*hokuteki*) in the Sino-centric civilization hierarchy, Ekiken and other leading scholars in Japan arose from a situation characterized by the prevailing peace and stability created under the Tokugawa shogunate. His goal was to develop a clear identity for Japanese people to mark the country's new position in East Asia and to do so by building a new intellectual relationship with China.

5. For different versions of Hideyoshi's letter, see Kanda, "'Tendō' shisō to 'shinkoku' kan."

6. Tajiri, "Kinsei Nihon no 'shinkoku'ron," 110–13. For a detailed account of the limited social integration of Confucianism in early modern Japan, see, Paramore, *Japanese Confucianism*, 16–117.

7. Tajiri, "Kinsei Nihon no 'shinkoku'ron," 110–13.

Neo-Confucianism and Japanese Scholars
in the Early Seventeenth Century

Since the seventeenth century, Japanese scholars had studied Zhu Xi Neo-Confucianism by reading the dialogues between Zhu Xi (1130–1200) and his students through such texts as *A Collection of Discussions between Zhu Xi and His Disciples* (*Zhuzi yulei* in Chinese, *Shushi gorui* in Japanese), Zhu Xi's commentaries on the Confucian classics, commentaries on Zhu Xi's writings by Chinese and Korean scholars, and other texts by Song scholars.[8] The abstract metaphysics of Zhu Xi generated many questions for his students, including Ekiken, and the interpretation of Zhu Xi Neo-Confucianism became a major bone of contention among them.[9] Let us first understand the discourse of Neo-Confucianism, a system of thought and knowledge that Zhu Xi perfected.

Zhu Xi presented an elaborate metaphysics that explicated the inner workings of the cosmos through the basic concepts of "principle" (*ri* in Japanese, or *li* in Chinese), "energy flow" (*ki* in Japanese, *qi* in Chinese), and five elements.[10] In this philosophical tradition, *ki* was further divided into two energies, *yin* (darkness) and *yang* (light), and the interaction between *yin* and *yang* was believed to have created the five elements of fire, water, wood, metal, and earth. The various combinations of these elements produced the constituent parts of all beings and phenomena in

8.   Seventy years after Zhu Xi's death, his students produced 140 volumes of *Shushi gorui*. This is a collection of dialogues between Zhu Xi and his students, and it is filled with the spirited discussions on notable topics and themes that students recurrently raised. Zhu Xi's responses often capture his sincere attempts to offer his best advice and words of warning. The first six volumes are about the basic conceptions of Zhu Xi's Neo-Confucian metaphysics, such as *ri*, *ki*, *kishin*, and human nature. Yoshikawa and Miura, *Shushishū*.

9.   Kaibara E., "Taigiroku," 166–69, 173–75. See also Abe Y., *Nihon shushigaku to Chōsen*; Abe A., "Shushi no kyūri no nisokumen," 2–3; Inoue A., "Kindai Nihon ni okeru Li Taikei kenkyū no keifugaku."

10.   Shimada Kenji divides Zhu Xi Neo-Confucianism into six major groups: metaphysics, *ri-ki* theory, ethics and human nature, methodology for learning, annotations for the Confucian classics, and his critiques on the theories of official history and political philosophy. Shimada K., "Kaisetsu," 13.

the universe.[11] Yoshikawa Kōjirō offers a summary of Zhu Xi's metaphysics as follows:

> Every being in the universe is moving toward a certain direction. What directs the movement of all things is called *ri*. . . . Every existence in the universe is made of *ki*, and *ki* always moves in a certain direction. The union of different *ki* constitutes all things that exist and all phenomena that take place in this universe. The ways *ki* is combined with other *ki* create different things, and the different combinations make shapes and features of all things different. And yet, the movement of each *ki* is consistent because all *ki* are made of [the same] *ki* that moves toward a certain direction in accordance to *ri*. . . . Everywhere *ri* is found, therefore, there is *ki* . . . and there is no *ri* where no *ki* is found.[12]

Zhu Xi's major idea was that everything in the universe was made of *ki*, and all *ki* moved in a certain direction because what is called *ri* was found in *ki* and guided the movement of *ki*. *Ki* itself was a material substance and the fundamental matter that gave shape to all things in the cosmos in accordance to *ri*. For example, for humans, *ki* took the shape of the human body, and an individual's body, language, and everything that formed the person was the result of the movement of *ki*. *Ri* was the human mind or its original nature (*sei*), and *sei* could be nourished through learning, so a proper education involving the study of the ethics of the ancient sages was imperative to the cultivation of the mind.

Confucius (552–479 BCE) valued the Five Classics: the *Book of Odes*, *Book of Documents*, *Book of Changes*, *Book of Rites*, and the *Spring and Autumn Annals*. Zhu Xi selected the Four Books of *Great Learning*, *Doctrine of the Mean*, *Analects*, and *Mencius* on the grounds that they explained the notion of *ri* better.[13] Zhu Xi's notion of principle, encompassing the all-knowing, almighty power of *ri*, appeared to be a human construct (not a cosmic principle) to many scholars in Japan. Most notably, Itō Jinsai called for a return to the original words of Confucius by valuing his original texts, such as *Analects* and *Mencius*, as the source of the true

---

11. Furth, *Flourishing Yin*, 23.
12. Yoshikawa, "Kaisetsu," 2.
13. Yoshikawa, "Kaisetsu," 4–5.

words of Confucius.[14] Ekiken also disagreed with Zhu Xi's notion of *ri* and instead prioritized *ki* by insisting that *ri* was not innate but discoverable by observing the movement of *ki*. Ekiken argued that *ri* did not exist prior to the existence of *ki*, and *ri* was only identifiable by studying the movement and patterns of *ki* (*ki no ri*).[15] Yet Ekiken did not reject Zhu Xi's cosmology in its entirety or deny the existence of *ri*. In Ekiken's view, *ri* did not exist independently from *ki* because *ri* and *ki* were once one and the same in the state of chaos (*konton*), and thus one must first understand how the whole universe operates to understand how *ri* works. In fact, by distinguishing himself from Zhu Xi and claiming that *ri* and *ki* were in a different state even though they were once the same, Ekiken stood firm with the scholars who interpreted *ri* and *ki* as being inseparable (*riki ittai ron*). It was necessary to understand the relationship between various *ki* that embody *ri* within it to understand what the principle was all about.

Zhu Xi's privileging of *ri* over *ki* was reflective of the historical time when supernatural beings strongly shaped people's understanding of the universe and their view of how the supernatural would affect the natural and human worlds.[16] The "spirits of the dead" (*kishin*) were believed to harm the world of the living if they were not pacified through proper ritual performances. For example, Confucius valued the spirits of the dead in Heaven and Earth, including the spirits of the ancestors, stating

14.   Jinsai began a school of thought, antiquarian learning (Kogigaku or Kogaku), at his private academy, the Hall of Ancient Learning (Kogidō), in Kyoto. Koyasu, *Shisōshika ga yomu rongo*, 5–11.

15.   Ekiken did not privilege the human mind/heart as being innately good, but he believed in the possibility of improving it through learning. Ekiken differed from the thought and philosophy of the Wang Yangming School that privileged the mind as the supreme decision maker and claimed its autonomy rather uncritically. Tsujimoto, "'Gakujutsu' no seiritsu," 168–70.

16.   Zhu Xi's dialogue with his disciples recorded various stories of mystical beings they claimed to have witnessed or experienced, some reminiscent of the notion of Buddhist reincarnation. For instance, a student asked Zhu Xi if it was possible for a human to be reborn as a beast because he had seen a boy with hairy pigs' ears in the county of Yongchun (in today's Fujian Province). Yoshikawa and Miura, *Shushishū*, 288–89. See also Lewis, *Construction of Space in Early China*, 13–76, for the development of the idea that the union of Heaven and Earth produced all life, including the body and the cosmos, in early Chinese philosophy.

that they should be respected and worshiped to secure their descendants' prosperity. Therefore, the spirits of the dead occupied an important topic in Confucianism, and the discussion about *kishin* was the theme of volume three of *Zhuzi yulei*, as well as significant parts of the *Commentaries on the Four Books* (*Shishu jizhu* in Chinese, *Shisho shitchū* in Japanese) and *Queries on the Four Books* (*Shishu huowen* in Chinese, *Shisho wakumon* in Japanese).[17] The dialogues between Zhu Xi and his students help us understand the anxiety many felt about the unknown power of the spirits of the dead, as well as the desire to control them. By making references to the Song scholars of Confucianism, Zhu Xi identified *kishin* in his annotations on the *Doctrine of the Mean* as follows:

> The Cheng brothers of the Song dynasty said, "*Kishin* (鬼神) are fine workings of Heaven and Earth, and they are the traces of all changing phenomena in the universe." Zhang Zai said, "*Kishin* are the effects of two *ki* [*yin* and *yang*]." I think, if we conceive two *ki* [in this universe], the first group of the spirits of the dead (鬼) is the spirits of *yin*, and the second group of the spirits of the dead (神) is the spirits of *yang*. If we conceive one *ki* [in this universe], the second [group of the] spirits of the dead (神) are the energies that extend to come here, while the first [group of the] spirits of the dead (鬼) are the energies that withdraw and go back there. In fact, they are actually one and the same [because *yin* and *yang* are originally the same *ki*].[18]

The references to the scholars of the Song dynasty (Northern Song 960–1126, Southern Song 1127–1279) of China, the Cheng brothers of Cheng Yi (1033–1107) and Cheng Hao (1032–85), as well as Zhang Zai (1020–77), show that their philosophical discourses constituted the foundations of Zhu Xi's thought.[19] They articulated two kinds of *ki*, which were *yin* and *yang*, and *yin* and *yang* were attributed to the two kinds of the spirits of the dead. Nonetheless, since *ki* before being divided into *yin* and *yang*

---

17.   Koyasu, *Shisōshika ga yomu rongo*, 189.
18.   Koyasu, *Kishinron*, 32.
19.   The Cheng brothers and Zhang Zai, along with Zhou Dunyi (1017–73) and Shao Yong (1011–77), were essential philosophers whose philosophical discourses became the basis of what Zhu Xi completed as Neo-Confucianism. Tsuda, *Banzan Ekiken*, 45.

were the same in nature, these two spirits of the dead could also be traced back to one and the same *ki*.

Zhu Xi defined the first group of the spirits of the dead as *yin* and the second group as *yang*. By referring to *yin* and *yang* as the intricate workings of *ki*, he reduced these spirits to the movement of *ki* and designated a place for the spirits of the dead within his cosmology. As a result, his discourse on the universe successfully contained the spirits, which had been viewed as a hazard in the time of Confucius, as part of *ki*.[20] He theorized the role of rituals in the reverence and celebration of the spirits and ultimately contained human fears and anxieties. Reflecting this reciprocal place of *kishin* in the human community of worship and rituals, the Kogigaku scholar Itō Jinsai defined *kishin* as follows:

> *Kishin* are Heaven and Earth, mountains and rivers, ancestors' shrines (*sōbyō*), the gods of five rituals (*goshi*), and all supernatural beings that cause happiness and misfortune (*kafuku*) [to human beings]. These are all works of *kishin*. Zhu Xi said, "the first spirits of the dead are the spirits of *yin* when the second spirits of the dead are the spirits of *yang*." I think what Zhu Xi meant was that, although there is a term *kishin*, *kishin* could not exist between Heaven and Earth without [the mediation of] *yin* and *yang*. Thus, Zhu Xi defined it as he did [that the first group of the spirits of the dead is *yin* when the second group is *yang*]. Indeed, this is a definition of a true scholar of Confucianism. However, it is wrong for scholars of our time to say that wind, rain, frost, and dew, sun, moon, day and night, and things that come and go are all works of *kishin*.[21]

The last sentence contradicts Zhu Xi's view; he had stated that all phenomena, including wind, rain, and frost, were the workings of *yin* and *yang*, and thus those of *kishin*. Jinsai might have rejected the mythoreligious elements in popular beliefs that explained some climatic phenomena as being acts of the supernatural, as Koyasu Nobukuni has argued.[22] For our purposes, it suffices to show that Jinsai, too, accepted the definition of *kishin* as the workings of *yin* and *yang* as explained by Zhu Xi.

20.   Miura K., "Shushi kishinron no rinkaku," 741–84.
21.   Koyasu, *Kishinron*, 13.
22.   Koyasu, *Norinaga to Atsutane no sekai*, 158.

Later scholars, such as Ogyū Sorai (1666–1728), said that in fact the sages of the past (*sen'ō*) had invented the realm of the supernatural to confine these spirits, which were believed to be harmful, so that rulers could establish themselves as legitimate sovereigns in the role of administering proper rituals.[23] By positioning the objects for worship, Sorai argued, the rulers legitimized their place in society, and their acts and teachings aimed to control the popular minds. As I discuss further in chapter 4, the discourse of *kishin* continued to flourish in late Tokugawa Japan. Now we direct our attention toward the idea of *kishin* in Ekiken's scholarship.

Kishin and Ekiken's Shinkoku Japan

Although there is no entry for the term *kishin* in the *Dictionary of Things in Japanese* (*Nihon shakumyō*), which was created by Ekiken, he defined it by separating the term into two parts. Under the first spirits of the dead (*oni*) and the second spirits of the dead (*kami*), we find the following definitions for these two characters. He wrote about *oni* and *kami* in the following quotations:

> A person who dies and still has his/her spirit (*rei*) becomes the first spirit of the dead, called *oni*. It is, so to speak, a ghost (*yūrei*). The character *yin* is the Japanese reading for this spirit of the dead (*oni*). A person who is alive is *yang*, and the dead person is *yin*. Also, the soul (*tamashii*) of *yin* and *yang* is called *onigami* as we see in the preface to the *Collection from Ancient and Modern Times* (*Kokinshū*, also known as *Kokin wakashū*, 905). The preface talks about the invisible *onigami* . . . . In India, horrifying creatures with horns and tusks (*kiba*) are called "evil beings" (*yasha*), which in Japan are commonly known as *ki* (*oni*). In one theory, *ki* is hidden because *onigami* is invisible.[24]
>
> *Kami* or *shin* is above, as we see in the *Annotations on Jikji* [a Korean Buddhist document, *Anthology of Great Buddhist Priests' Zen Teachings*, *Jikishishō*, also known as *Jindai jikishishō* in Japanese]. *Kami* live above and

---

23. Koyasu, *Soraigaku kōgi*, 162–63, and *Jiken toshite no Soraigaku*, 16–19.
24. Kaibara E., "Nihon shakumyō," 34–35.

are to be revered. Also, the Japanese reading of *yin* and *yang* is "gimi," so *kami* also means *yin* and *yang*. This is because *kami* is the spirit (*rei*) of *yin* and *yang*. There is another theory that *kami* is the abbreviation of the middle character of the word "mirror" (*kagami*) according to the *Jikji* . . . . Without the character "above" (*ue*), however, any attempt to read *kami* for *kagami* is wrong (*higagoto*).[25]

The fact that there is no term *kishin* as a compound in his dictionary suggests that Ekiken consciously or unconsciously excluded this word from his dictionary of things in Japanese names. Nonetheless, as someone who earnestly studied Neo-Confucian discourses, Ekiken was undoubtedly familiar with the notion of *kishin* and continued to debate the idea because it was *ki*, which was fundamental to all things in the universe. Indeed, the perception of *kishin* had a profound significance for Ekiken. Some readers might already have noticed, but Ekiken's idea of Japan as *shinkoku*, the country of the "divine" spirits, shares the same character as the second character of *kishin*. The character "divine" is the character "gods" (*kami*), and in the following I explicate how the foundation of Ekiken's *shinkoku* narrative was inspired by the discourse of *kishin* that focused on the second group of spirits.

Ekiken's *shinkoku* idea is found in his unpublished essay, "Precepts for the Deities in Heaven and Earth" (*Jingikun*), which he wrote toward the end of his life. Nowhere in the essay do we find the term *kishin*, but the excerpt is embedded with *kishin* discourse. By embracing the idea of worshipping the gods for the well-being of the country, Ekiken wrote as follows:

> Celebrating the deities in Heaven and the deities on Earth (*amatsu kami kunitsu kami*) has been the rule of our country. People are the masters of the deities. The deities increase their awe by obtaining reverence from people. People will live without trouble when they receive blessings from the deities. Thus, in the past, the kings of the world of the dead (*meiō*) first aided and nurtured their people and then revered the deities. It would not be the ancient way if the kings, without caring for people, worshiped and

25. Kaibara E., "Nihon shakumyō," 7.

celebrated the deities, spent money on them, and made people suffer. That would be against the way.

Japan is the country where the deities have emerged and ruled since the ancient past (*jōko*), and that is why Japan is named the "country of the deities" (*shinkoku*) just as China (*morokoshi*) is called the "country of the sages" (*seijinkoku*). People who were born and live in Japan, thus, all know the way of the deities (*shintō*).[26]

This passage valorizes the importance of performing rites and celebrating the deities to keep the spirits content and maintain the stability and peace of the country. By placing the people above the deities—as the masters of the deities—Ekiken made it clear that worship and proper rituals were the responsibility of the people. These acts made it possible for them to receive the gods' blessings; this, in turn, brought about stability for the community. By accepting the *shinkoku* narrative that the gods emerged in the ancient age and were succeeded by human emperors in the ensuing reigns, he claimed that Japan had been *shinkoku* ever since. According to Ekiken, Japan had been *shinkoku* just as China was the country of the Confucian sages.

However, as we have already observed in the previous chapter, Ekiken and other scholars did not take account of the divine age described in the chronicles of *Kojiki* and *Nihon shoki* at face value but tirelessly sought to validate the idea of *shinkoku* through topographic investigations of *fudoki*. This means that *kishin* discourse inspired him to perceive the spirits as floating around the universe, including the space of the Japanese archipelago, and he tried to show the divine traces by studying the topography of various locales rather than accepting the chronicles where someone had recorded a particular group of gods as being involved in the formation of the imperial lineage. If we follow the discourse of *kishin* that perceived various movements of the spirits in terms of *yin* and *yang*, *fudoki* would appear to be more authentic texts that captured the experience of the age of the gods. Thus, not just Ekiken alone but other contemporary scholars were also enthusiastic about validating the topographic inscriptions through the evidential method of Kōshōgaku. In short, the land

26.   Kaibara E., "Jingikun," 641.

had inscriptions of various divine traces, and the landscape articulated the history behind each place.

By perceiving historical events that took place in the archipelago as fundamental flows of energy, Ekiken investigated the actual place as a sight of authentic historical inscriptions. His unfinished essay "A Record of Scenic Japan" (*Fusō kishō*) illustrates his understanding of space and Japan's place within it as follows:

> Japan (*Nihon*) is located in the middle of the Eastern Seas (*tōkai*). The vitality (*shōge* or *seiki*) [literally, "pure *ki*"] in Heaven and Earth originates in the East, and the East is where harmonious *ki* (*waki*) vigorously exists. Therefore, Japan is the country of the deities (*shinkoku*), and the honesty of the people and their customs and manners (*fūzoku*) are superior to those of other countries (*shoshū*), both now and then.[27]

In the traditional understanding of space in East Asia, the East was not necessarily the preeminent direction in terms of cartography or cosmology.[28] In China, the imperial palace was often situated in the northern part of the capital, while the rulers consistently occupied the central position and mapped all other elements of society in relation to their proximity to the ruler. By contrast, grounding Japan in the East allowed Ekiken to position the Japanese archipelago in the saturated space of vital *ki*, which was in the direction of the East. This gesture of privileging the East was shared by a number of Japanese writers, such as Hayashi Razan and Gahō, who valorized and established the East as the superior position in relation to China. Historically we find confirmation of this understanding, for example, in a letter from Prince Shōtoku (574–622), addressed to a Chinese emperor, in which he describes himself as a prince of Japan, a place where the sun rises. It was believed that *ki* had first emerged in the East, which made *ki* in the

27. Kaibara E., "Fusō kishō," 314.
28. For example, Lewis analyzes the case of the Bright Hall (*mingtang*) of the ancient royal and imperial palace in China as a microcosm of the ideal spatial construction. Historically, the Bright Hall was made the Grand Academy, the ancestral temple, or the world model. Its significance was not about the particular direction but its proximity to the center. Lewis, *Construction of Space in Early China*, 248–84.

East pure and original.[29] *Shōge* was rightly abundant in the East because that was where the divine *kishin* gathered. Following this traditional understanding of space, Japan occupied a privileged space filled with abundant untainted *ki* and was thus determined to be the country of the deities.

The activity of the vibrant *ki* is the essential element in the designation of Japan's place and identity. To support this claim, Ekiken also referenced numerous historical texts as evidence to establish that Japan had been mentioned in various official records.[30] Citing the section of the fifth year of the reign of Emperor Seimu (83–190, r. 131–90) in *Nihongi* (another name for *Nihon shoki*), Ekiken quoted the section in which Seimu instituted the system of counties and provinces for the first time. Then he validated this piece of information by further quoting from volume eleven of the *Chronicle of Old Events in the Previous Ages* (*Kujiki* also known as *Sendai kuji hongi*), citing a passage that describes the appointment of provincial governors (*kuni no miyatsuko*) to 144 provinces throughout the archipelago. The existence of these positions was confirmed by the poems contained in the *Collection of Ten Thousand Leaves* (*Man'yōshū*), which mentions the provinces of Yoshino, Nanba, Hatsuse, and Hase.[31] After citing a number of texts to provide textual references for the chronology of the development of Japan, Ekiken combined textual evidence with the spatial meanings of the East to demonstrate that Japan was *shinkoku*.

Ekiken went on to state that the Japanese people had some qualities in common with the gods, such as simplicity, honesty, and trustworthiness. These qualities of the people were "superior to those of other countries," and he ended the introduction with another remark on the direction of the East. It reads:

29. Mizuno, *Eki, fūsui, reki, yōjō, shosei*, 56–68.
30. These texts constitute the majority of the canonical works of *Kokushi taikei* (History of Japan, 1897–1904), a collection of primary and historical writings from the premodern period. Economist and historian Taguchi Ukichi (1855–1905) compiled this collection, which consists of a seventeen-volume main portion and a fifteen-volume sequel. The work was completed between 1897 and 1904.
31. Kaibara E., "Fusō kishō," 310.

Japan is located in the East of four oceans under heaven. The East is the beginning of *yang ki* (*yōki*) where the sun rises. It is also the direction that belongs to the spring when many new lives are born. Additionally, since it [Japan] is the country of the deities (*shinkoku*), the land (*kokudo*) and people's manners and customs (*fūzoku*) are superior to other barbarians (*shoi*). China is located in the middle, and it is the country of the sages (*seijin no kuni*). Thus, China is unquestionably a superior country (*jōkoku*), and Japan is indeed inferior to China. And, how could the outer barbarians (*gaii*) come close to China? [Even so,] Japan is a country that fits more with the name of men of virtue (*kunshi*) than China, and it was perfect [for Emperor Jinmu] to call Japan the Country of Rich Autumn Harvests (*Toyo akitsu su*). . . . People say that the East is the first direction. Thus, Japan should be the first country of all.[32]

Once again, with such characteristics as the place of *yang ki*, the place where the sun rises first, the place that "belongs to the spring," and the place where new lives are born, the East is privileged. It nurtures the people and the *fūdo* (literally, the "wind" and "earth") and environment of Japan. This is why Emperor Jinmu appropriately named the country *Toyo akitsu su* in praise of the rich harvests in the autumn.[33] The excerpt highlights Japan's privileged location as the source of the country's divine nature. If we recall how Zhu Xi and the Song scholars identified *kishin* as the "fine interactions of *yin* and *yang*," Ekiken clearly interpreted the "effects of *ki* that exist between Heaven and Earth" in the same way as the movement of incessant energy within the Japanese archipelago. Although nowhere do we see the term *kishin*, this concept made Japan the country of the divine spirits, *shinrei*, in Ekiken's representation.

Ekiken also showed that historically, the auspicious place of Japan had been known to other countries in East Asia. By quoting ancient historical texts to claim that Japan was mentioned in the historical records in China, he championed certain aspects of the Japanese people in his essay "Fusō kishō." However, he also acknowledged the purpose of writing

32. Kaibara E., "Fusō kishō," 331.
33. Kaibara E., "Wajiga," 558.

history and the production of scholarship, which Japan urgently needed to improve. He stated,

> *Tōiden* (or *Tōi retsuden*, The Biography of Eastern Barbarians) of *Gokanjo* (Book of the Later Han, *Hou Han Shu* in Chinese) [which is volume eighty-five] is the first text that made reference to Japan (*wakoku*). Since then, other historical records and various books have mentioned Japan many times. . . . Recently Matsushita Kenrin [1637–1703], who is passionate about Japan studies (*wagaku*), wrote a book called *Ishō Nihonden* (Commentary on Japan in Foreign Texts, 1688). In it, Kenrin wrote in detail about how various Chinese texts (*kara no sho*) made reference to Japan.
>
> Japan is located in the Eastern Sea (*tōkai*) where the vitality of pure *ki* (*shōge* or *seiki*) in Heaven and Earth begins . . . . The Japanese people embrace the way, and many aspects of Japan are indeed superior to those of China (*Chūka*), and of course, other countries outside of civilization (*gaikoku*). According to the *Gokanjo waden* (on Japan), "there are many Japanese people who are over a hundred years old" [quoted from the original text]. Even now, many people live to between eighty and ninety years old. The life of people in China (*Morokoshi*) or other countries (*shokoku*) is shorter. Ancient people considered Japan as a country of the men of virtue (*kunshikoku*), and they also called it the land of immortality (*fuji no kuni*). That is indeed true. . . . However, Japan's crudity in writing (*bunpitsu*) is what places Japan behind China. This is the weakness of Japan. . . . Without knowing the letters, the country is powerless. Even the successes, virtuous deeds, the bravery of warriors or their names will not be remembered without the letters to preserve those accounts in writing. Thus, the Japanese must enrich scholarship.[34]

Admitting that China was far more civilized than Japan because they had superior scholarship and literature, Ekiken acknowledged that the Japanese were not good at writing and had not produced adequate scholarship. He was critical of how scholars before him had produced scholarship that made Japan "powerless" in the past. He pointed out the lack of historical accounts of brave warriors, the virtuous acts of historical figures, and the names that should have been remembered, and he acknowledged that Japan lagged behind China.

---

34.   Kaibara E., "Fusō kishō," 314.

At the same time, Ekiken's positioning of Matsushita Kenrin's *Ishō Nihonden* simply as a book "about how various Chinese texts (*kara no sho*) made reference to Japan" seems to be filled with meaning. As Ronald Toby has revealed, the various references that old Korean and Chinese texts made about Japan were often "wrong" because they were the observations of foreigners and recorded somewhat exotic aspects of Japan. Ancient Korean and Chinese scholars only made notes about strange differences in the way of doing things. In this light, Toby argues that Kenrin's book aimed to "correct" some of the observations by employing the Kōshōgaku method, thus interfering in the Chinese and Korean historiography of Japan and for the first time providing the correct and validated account of Japan.[35] Considering his close relationship with Kenrin, Ekiken was aware of his views and could well have commented on the problems associated with foreign historiographies that misrepresented Japan, thus evaluating Kenrin's work more highly. However, Ekiken refrained from making any remarks on the foreign historiography but only used it to show that Japan had been mentioned in foreign historiography since the time of *Gokanjo*.

In this regard, historian Kate Nakai has discussed the dilemma of Japanese scholars that endorsed the Confucian virtues of benevolence and righteousness and the authority of the sages. They sought to "de-Sinify Confucianism" while affirming the "Sinitic essence of the way of the sages" in their intellectual activities that permeated Tokugawa Japan.[36] In light of Ekiken's high regard for Chinese scholarship, Japan's potential to surpass China was very ambiguous. What Ekiken attributed to Japan in the excerpt above were remarks such as long life expectancy, being a country of immortality (*fuji no kuni*), and the existence of good manners. These points are rather subtle and could hardly be seen as aspects that might distinguish it from China. We can only conclude that Ekiken's will to improve the status of Japanese scholarship was fraught with tension. At the same time, we know from other sources that his scholarly activities not only enriched scholarship in Japan but also contributed to the expansion of popular education to include women and

---

35. Toby, "Foreign Texts/Native Readings," 144.
36. Nakai, "Naturalization of Confucianism in Tokugawa Japan," 165.

children.[37] Recalling Ekiken's enthusiasm for reviving the ancient *fudoki*, we might read this excerpt in a similar light and locate his desire and attempts to improve the status of Japanese scholarship. Ekiken introduced Kenrin's work as a notable example of Japanese scholarship, and there were scholars like Kenrin in the early modern era that took a valuable step forward by producing outstanding work. Together with scholars like him, Ekiken was engaged in the production of advanced historiography in Japan, namely, the revival of *fudoki* in *kanabun* as a means of challenging Chinese historiography.

When observed along with Ekiken's publication of didactic texts and popular educational texts using *wabun*, it becomes clear that his passion for improving the scholarship of Japan was not just his attempt to compete with China for the quality or quantity of historiography. Ekiken was interested in educating people with the fine and distinct quality of Japan, as he often remarked in the prefaces to his essays. Indeed, he was convinced that if perceived as the fine workings of *yin* and *yang*, everything could be explained as evidence of the working of *ki*, even the *fūdo* of Japan. He actually stated in the preface to *Zoku fudoki* that "everything between Heaven and Earth concerns us all, and we should seek to investigate the principles that are yet to be identified."[38] As Tetsuo Najita has argued, Ekiken's interest in articulating nature empirically was rooted in his belief that the direct observation of nature would reveal the interworking of Heaven and Earth, thus identifying various patterns and logics that exist in the cosmos.[39] Ekiken was highly motivated in his desire to understand Japan's place in the universe by studying the working of various *ki*. The next section offers my analysis of his visualization of Chikuzen, and I delve into how the traditional discourse of *kishin* guided his investigation of what Japan was, as well as his conceptualization of the space of Japan as representing the fine interactions of *ki* and *kishin*.

37.   Tsujimoto, *Shisō to kyōiku no mediashi*; Tsujimoto, "Moji shakai no seiritsu," 138–46; Tsujimoto, *Manabi no fukken*, 126–56; Wakao, "Shin, ju, butsu no kōsaku."

38.   Kaibara E., "Chikuzen no kuni zoku fudoki: jijo," 1.

39.   Najita, *Visions of Virtue*, 45–56. See also Matsumura, "Kunshi no chi," 179–98; Miura S., "Taigiroku ni itaru michi"; Tsujimoto, "Kinsei ni okeru 'ki' no shisōshi oboegaki," 39–76.

Kishin as the Meta-Narrative for the "Chikuzen no kuni zoku fudoki"

In 1688, at the age of fifty-nine, Ekiken embarked on compiling *fudoki* of his province with the help of his nephew, Kaibara Yoshifuru. By the mid-seventeenth century, the Kuroda domain in Chikuzen province had a good grasp of their local topography (figure 2.1). Ekiken's two prefaces stress the historical importance of knowing one's own topography, which confirms the significance of the compilation to the domain and avows the virtue of the lord of the domain (figures 2.2 and 2.3). As the title *Chikuzen no kuni zoku fudoki* suggests, *Zoku fudoki* maintains a close resemblance to the original *fudoki* in terms of its scope and content, as well as the detailed information it provides about place names, their natural features, and local special products. Considering that Ekiken wrote *Zoku fudoki* with a strong desire to revive the practice of the original *fudoki*, it is no surprise that its contents resemble the original *fudoki* (figure 2.4).[40] The entire *Zoku fudoki* consists of thirty volumes and is divided into four sections—(1) two volumes of "summary" (*teiyō*), (2) twenty-one volumes of the "counties of Fukuoka, Hakata, and fifteen counties" (*Fukuoka Hakata oyobi jūgo gun no ki*), (3) five volumes of "old castles and battlefields" (*kojō kosenjō no ki*), and (4) two volumes of the "native products of Chikuzen" (*dosankō*). The contents in the second and third sections overlap, with the counties, old castles, and battlefields recurrently mentioned. *Zoku fudoki* contains extensive and comprehensive information about Chikuzen province, including many stories Ekiken heard from local people. Concerning this point, Ekiken made a note that he had tried very hard to substantiate the validity of the popular claims and stories by thoroughly scrutinizing local documents.[41] This suggests that he recognized that although empiricism in scholarship was absolutely important, a sense of place might not be fully recorded in the written texts. Thus, he appreciated popular sentiments and the memory attached to these local places

---

40. Matsumura, "Kunshi no chi," 208–9; Inoue T., *Kaibara Ekiken*, 136–48.

41. Kaibara E., "Chikuzen no kuni zoku fudoki," 1. The number of volumes in *Zoku fudoki* has variations. The 1911 *zenshū* edition has 30 volumes in total whereas the Takeda collection version has 31 volumes.

and tried to preserve the broader cultural *fūdo* of the locality, which included many popular feelings. In this sense, Ekiken's *Zoku fudoki* was an attempt to preserve the affective affinity that people had with their local places.

From the outset, the sheer number of places included in *Zoku fudoki* makes it hard to determine whether Ekiken had a set of criteria for selecting these places rather than others. *Zoku fudoki* communicates to the reader, first and foremost, that this compilation is a completely exhaustive work, and it does so by detailing the names, types of Buddhist sect and the lineage of the shrine, depth of the rivers and height of mountains, species of trees and weeds, and more. Yet Ekiken sometimes had to make choices about what to include and what to omit. With regard to his choices, he wrote as follows in the preface:

> In the section on the counties, I have exhaustedly recorded the way all the remarkable mountains stand (*ichijirushiki yama no tatazumai*), the flow of the rivers, the vast fields, the deep hearts of ponds (*ike no kokoro fukaki*), the drifting islands (*kuga o hanaretaru shimajima*), the famous old sites and places as read about in poems and stories, and the places where shrines and temples of today and earlier times stand. Some of these places may, after all, turn out to be not as good as we have been told. Equally, there are places that surprise us greatly by presenting amazing beauty [even if one has never heard of them before]. Thus, I have even included places that have never acquired the status of *utamakura* (conventionalized places in *waka* poetry) yet still present rare beauty because they deserve our attention. In the section on the old castles and battlefields, "*kojō kosenjō*," I have offered historical accounts, such as information about who owned the castle, as well as stories about the battles that were fought there, and I have combined them with what people say about them today. . . . (An annotation section of *katchū* is inserted, noting that in total, there are one hundred and sixty old castles, and twenty-five battlefields.) There are, in total, nine hundred and thirty-four districts that I mention in this book.[42]

Including such a large number of battlefields and old castles indicates Ekiken's empathetic feelings toward his home domain, which existed because of the sacrifices made by many brave soldiers who had defended

---

42.   Kaibara E., "Chikuzen no kuni zoku fudoki," 3.

FIGURE 2.1. Map of Chikuzen province (1779). The inscription reads, "Hand-copied in late February of the eighth year of An'ei (1772–80) by Akashi Yukinobu (dates unknown)." While this map is about 100 years older than Ekiken's *Zoku fudoki* production, the Fukuoka Prefectural Library estimates that it is an actual reproduction based on the map made in the first half of the Kan'ei era (1624–43). Such a judgment is made through reference to the roads and townscape of Nōgata and Akizuki domains. Courtesy of Fukuoka Prefectural Library, Local Materials Division.

castles and fought for their lives. It also indicates the sense of relief signified by the end of the Sengoku era. The way Ekiken describes the landscape of Chikuzen is similarly reflective of the peaceful era in which he lived, sounding almost as if he was observing a person to capture the grace and remarkable beauty of the landscape. These descriptions confirm that while providing a comprehensive list of almost all the castles and battlefields, Ekiken's goal was also to highlight the local sentiments engraved in places.

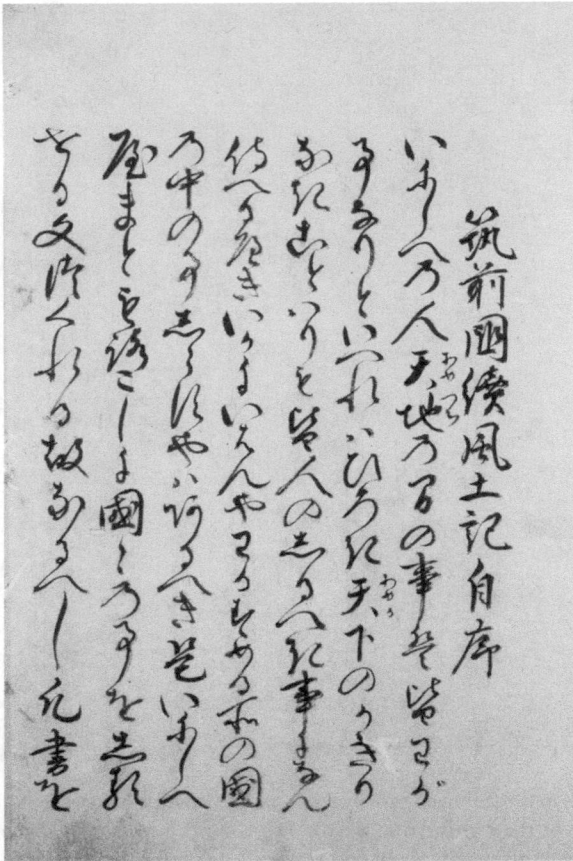

FIGURE 2.2. "Preface" (*Jijo*) to the *Chikuzen no kuni zoku fudoki* by Kaibara Ekiken. Ekiken included two prefaces in the thirty-one volumes of *Zoku fudoki*. Courtesy of Fukuoka Prefectural Library, Local Materials Division, Takeda Collection.

The sense of place that appears in *Zoku fudoki* enhances the reading experience. The reader discovers how Ekiken's narration reinvigorates certain historical moments, thus allowing the reader to imagine what the actual events were like in any given historical time. By presenting vivid descriptions of the battles, enemy attacks, and the like, Ekiken encourages readers to visualize the historic, victorious moments, thus creating a stimulating reading experience. The combination of statistical details, such as the "summary" section introducing each of the seventeen towns, and

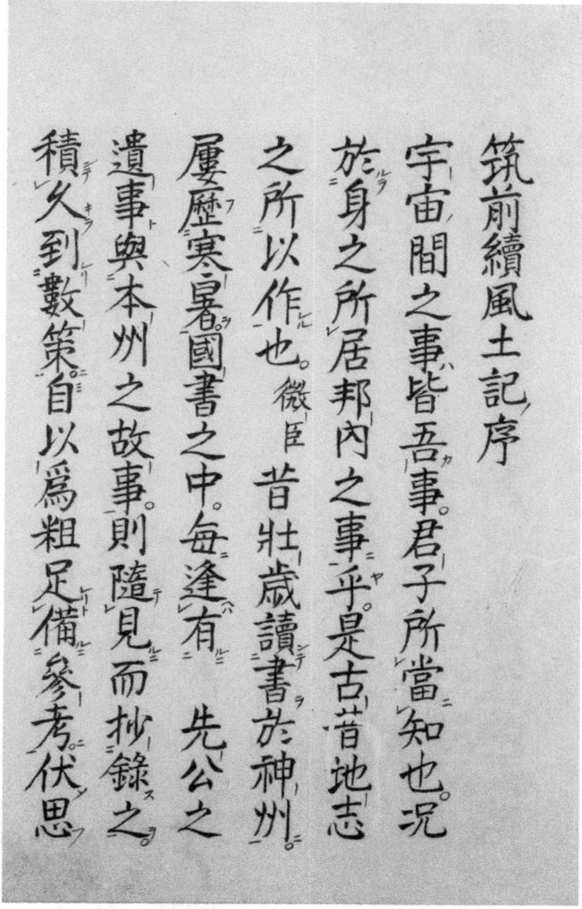

筑前續風土記序
宇宙間之事皆吾事君子所當知也況
於身之所居邦內之事乎是古昔地志
之所以作也。微臣昔壯歲讀書於神州。
屢歷寒暑圖書之中每逢有　先公之
遺事與本州之故事則隨見而抄錄之。
積久到數策自以爲粗足備參考伏思

FIGURE 2.3. "Preface" (*Jo*). This is the second preface to *Zoku fudoki*. Courtesy of Fukuoka Prefectural Library, Local Materials Division, Takeda Collection.

his narrative of various historical events makes this topographic text entertaining and draws the reader into the imagined past of Chikuzen. For instance, Ekiken starts with an explanation for the name Tsukushi in the brief historical background of the whole province. It starts as follows:

This province was named Tsukushi because in antiquity Chikuzen and Chikugo together constituted one province, and together they were called

筑前國續風土記卷之一

貝原篤信撰定

貝原好古編緣

竹田定直校正

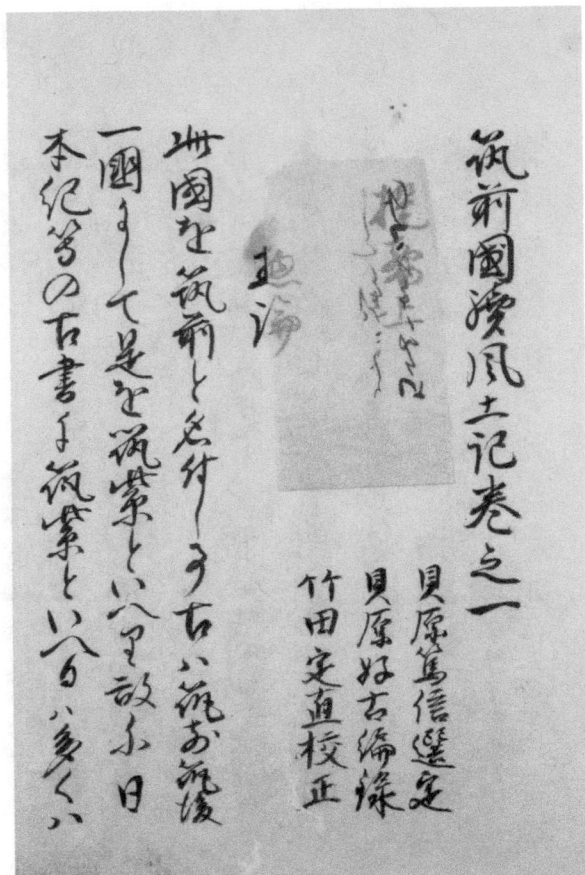

FIGURE 2.4. "General Remarks" (*Sōron*) in *Zoku fudoki*, vol. 1. Courtesy of Fukuoka Prefectural Library, Local Materials Division, Takeda Collection.

Tsukushi. Therefore, references to Tsukushi in the ancient documents, including *Nihon shoki*, often mean both provinces, i.e. Chikuzen and Chikugo. There was a period when all nine provinces (*kyūkoku*) [in Kyūshū of Chikuzen, Chikugo, Hizen, Higo, Buzen, Bungo, Hyūga, Ōsumi, and Satsuma] constituted Tsukushi. There were also times when provinces other than Chikuzen and Chikugo were called Tsukushi because the provincial office (*kanpu*) was located in Chikuzen in ancient times. The provincial office administered the nine provinces in Kyūkshū and the two islands (*Kyūshū nitō*) [of Tsushima and Iki]. That is why all nine provinces were referred to as Tsukushi. This is the same as the whole of Japan being called Yamato when the imperial capital (*teito*) was located in Yamato province.[43]

This clarification reminds us of the similar efforts we observed in Hoshina Masayuki's *Aizu fudoki* in the previous chapter. Like Masayuki, Ekiken clarified the name of Tsukushi to demonstrate the existence of different administrative practices in his time and to establish that over time *Chikuzen* had referred to different parts of Kyūshū. By drawing on four more sources, *Shoku Nihongi*, *Fudoki of Chikugo Province* (*Chikugo no kuni fudoki*), *Commentary of Leaves from a Forest of Words* (*Shirin saiyōshō*), and Sengaku's *Commentary on Man'yōshū* (*Man'yōshō*, or also known as *Man'yōshūshō*), Ekiken attempted to determine how the name Chikugo came into being. The next one and a half pages represent his attempt to validate the story of each account, but none turns out to be true following his reference to lengthy quotations from official history records. Then, Ekiken reveals his original thoughts by quoting a poem found in a fifteenth-century text from Korea, *The Record of Various Countries Located in the Eastern Sea* (*Kaitō shokokuki*). He verifies the poem by referencing an official document issued by the Hōjō family during the Kamakura period (1185–1333). Reading and analyzing these sources, Ekiken states:

> In the ancient past, people built numerous stonewalls in the northern sea close to Chikuzen province to prevent barbarian invasions. These stones of "*tsuku-ishi*" (stones that were piled up), which was abbreviated to Tsukushi, are the origin [of the name Tsukushi]. Miscellaneous accounts include a number of stories of invasions of Japan from countries in the west in the ancient past, and, indeed, Emperor Chūai [149–200, r. 192–200] was killed by an arrow fired by such invaders.[44]

The passage continues by offering more accounts of stonewall building projects in Chikuzen and explains that the province constantly needed to guard itself against foreign invasion throughout its history. Coastal defense had been an important responsibility of the political authorities

43. Kaibara E., "Chikuzen no kuni zoku fudoki," 6.
44. Kaibara E., "Chikuzen no kuni zoku fudoki," 8.

in Chikuzen, and it brought about its long-term political stability and prosperity. Ekiken noted that it was not possible to confirm the validity of this claim, but the rest of his narrative is based on this origin story. In fact, he made various references to the stone barriers and the role of stones throughout *Zoku fudoki*.

Bruce Batten confirms that Chikuzen was historically a vital defense point against invaders, especially during the seventh and eighth centuries. He argues that an awareness of foreign threats at this time compelled a new sense of "borders" in Japan.[45] After a united army consisting of Japanese and Kudara Korean soldiers was defeated by the joint army of the Tang Chinese and Shiragi Korean forces at the Battle of Hakusukie in 663, the northern parts of Kyūshū became the strategic defense point for the territory. Batten further argues that the end of the battle promoted additional diplomatic contact with Chinese and Korean imperial envoys, making Tsukushi a site of foreign interaction. At the same time, the imperial court built a number of military facilities, such as castles, levees (*tsutsumi*), and checkpoints, and deployed guards called *sakimori* and *susumi* to enhance its defenses in northern Kyūshū. Ekiken devoted significant space in *Zoku fudoki* to Mizuki village in the county of Mikasa. For example,

The *Nihongi* writes about [the village of] Mizuki as follows: Emperor Tenji [626–72, r. 668–72] spent three years in the province of Tsukushi building a big dike to accumulate water, and this is how the place came to be called Mizuki ["water castle" to hold water]. I assume that the emperor built this as a stronghold for Dazaifu. The *Chronicle of Japan Continued (Shoku Nihongi)* documents that Emperor Shōtoku [718–70, r. 764–70] in the first year of Tenpyō shingo (1425) named a female official of Dazaifu (*dazai shōni uneme ason*), Kiyoniwa, and designated her specifically to be in charge of repairing the water dike. When we look at the dike today, the height is five *ken* [9.8 yards], the root is twenty-seven *ken* [53.1 yards], and the length from east to west is about eight *chō* [954 yards]. Today, about one *chō* [119 yards] of the dike is gone and has no bank, and inside the dike there are rice paddies; it does not hold water anymore. In the twelfth year of Genroku (1699), when the rice paddies were made along the dike, two big trees

45. Batten, *Kokkyō no tanjō*, 50–51.

were dug out of the earth. They were about three *ken* [5.9 yards] in length with the cut end being a little over two *shaku* [24 inches]. One was a cedar tree, and the other was unidentifiable. They must have been the trees that existed when Mizuki was originally built.[46]

The historical background on Mizuki offered here conveys a sense of continuity and the authenticity of the place, even though the dike no longer held water. By focusing more on the prosperity of Mizuki in Tsukushi's history, Ekiken's analysis validated how the place became an important site, which was also known as the Checkpoint of Mizuki (Mizuki no seki) and visually demarcated by a gate and large foundation stones. Ekiken did not highlight the strategic background of Mizuki, although his description of its prosperity as a hub near Dazaifu, the regional government for the entire Kyūshū region, might imply the region's political and cultural liveliness.[47]

In addition to the historical origins of each site and information about the commercial and cultural development of the places in Chikuzen, *Zoku fudoki* introduces almost all the counties in the province by reference to their connections with local shrines and temples. *Zoku fudoki* is organized in a way that initially offers a brief overview of the origins of the county and the village and then explores the relationship with local shrines and temples, which often reaches back in time to the age of the gods. Indeed, many of the local shrines have divine connections to the gods, and Ekiken carefully traces such historical connections by referencing the official history texts, such as *Procedures of the Engi Era* (*Engishiki*, 927), *Wamyōshō*, *Shoku Nihongi*, and other temple records.[48] For instance, the account of

46.   Kaibara E., "Chikuzen no kuni zoku fudoki," 187. One *ken* is about 6 *shaku*, which is about 1.8 meters (6 feet), and 1 *chō* is about 109 meters (120 yards).

47.   Batten, *Kokkyō no tanjō*, 82–87.

48.   Ekiken owned these reference texts, and he probably used them to verify the historical origins and background of the places through reference to them. The catalog of Ekiken's personal library shows that he owned maps of various parts of Japan, such as *Nihon bunkeizu* (a map of divided Japan); *Nihon kakkokuzu* (a map of the provinces in Japan), which consisted of sixty-eight images; and others, as well as *Kanbun inchishū* (A Collection of the Territory Documents that were issued in the fourth year of Kanbun, 1664). Maps and *Kanbun inchishū* are likely to have helped depict directions, the detailed network of villages, and the exact annual rice yields of the village as he composed these spatial narratives. Kyūshū Shiryō Kankōkai, "Ganko mokuroku," 4–39.

Mikasa county in volume seven of *Zoku fudoki* begins with a passage from *Nihon shoki* that narrates how Empress Jingū lost her bamboo hat (*kasa*) during her hunting trip to the area. This incident gave birth to the name Mikasa, which literally means "her majesty's hat."

There are eighty-six villages within Mikasa county, and Ekiken records each one using the correct characters and readings, while also describing each place and its historical significance. Obviously these names and readings of the county and villages were officially registered with the shogunate, as a result of the land distribution process that we observed in chapter one.[49] The entry for Mikasa county starts with a mountain called Kamado and Kamado Shrine, located on top of Kamado Mountain. The mountain is located about six *ri* [14.6 miles] away from Fukuoka, fifty *chō* [2.8 miles] away from Dazaifu, and twenty-two *chō* [1.5 miles] away from Yūchisan village.[50] The descriptions read as follows:

> This mountain is located in the center of the province and is very high. This is where the marvels of the changing phenomena of the universe (*zōka shinshū*) gather together and the divine spirits (*shinrei*) reside. This is why Kamado Mountain is called the ultimate guardian god (*sō chinshu*) of Chikuzen province. There are many mountains within our land (*kokudo*) that have become the guardian gods (*chinshu*), which are known as *chinzan* (guardian mountain). The divine spirits (*shinrei*) gather in such mountains and pacify the country. Atago, Hiei, and Ibuki mountains in the provinces of Yamashiro and Ōmi are also guardian mountains. . . . In these mountains, the divine spirits reside, which makes them essentially different from other mountains.[51]

This passage explains why Ekiken started with the special mountains when introducing the life of the county. These mountains, called *chinzan*, protect the region, so they constitute a central importance in the life of

49. Ekiken owned a copy of the twenty-five-volume *Kanbun inchishū*, so it is likely that he validated each village and county name in the compilation of *Zoku fudoki*. Kyūshū Shiryō Kankōkai, "Ganko mokuroku," 26. Also, Ekiken incorporated official documents regarding the land surveys (*kenchi*) of temple property (*jiryō*) and other Buddhist temple documents. Kaibara E., "Chikuzen no kuni zoku fudoki," 150–51.

50. Kaibara E., "Chikuzen no kuni zoku fudoki," 146.

51. Kaibara E., "Chikuzen no kuni zoku fudoki," 146.

the community. They are different from other mountains because divine spirits, *shinrei*, reside there and protect the people. Ekiken calls the divine spirits *shinrei*, not *kishin*, *yin*, or *yang*, but clearly this excerpt is inspired by *kishin* discourse.

By closely following *kishin* discourse, Ekiken presents the guardian mountains as the realm of divine spirits, thereby making the mountain a sacred space. He further characterizes *chinzan* as "standing high" and "covered in mists and haze."[52] In his description of Kamado Mountain, Ekiken points out the profuse haze that appeared like smoke from a cooking stove (*kamado*), as well as other mysterious mists and haze that filled the mountainous space in the form of thick fog. He states that these vapors were there to hide the presence of the divine spirits (*shinrei*), which were invisible to the naked eye. At the same time, drawing the reader's attention to the beauty of Kamado Mountain, Ekiken discusses its special features, with its sharp, granite-like rocks and the cool feel of the rocks in the clean air. He describes it as follows:

> Truly, this place makes one feel absolutely amazed (*kizetsu*). I have visited beautiful mountains in various provinces, but I have never been to a place like this. . . . From the top of the mountain, one can see afar, to where other mountains appear, seeming smaller than their actual size. One can overlook Kyūshū and the vast expanse of the neighboring provinces. To the northwest, one can see Iki and Tsushima Islands in the distance. On a clear day in the fall, one can vaguely see the mountains in the unknown land of Korea (*Shinra*). It is indeed a view of vast expansiveness. The mountains have many cherry trees in the spring and Japanese maples in the autumn. It is absolutely amazing to see. This place presents other beautiful sights throughout the four seasons, and the striking changes that the mountain experiences seasonally are beyond description.[53]

Summarizing his experience of being in Kamado Mountain in this way, Ekiken tries to convey the otherworldliness of the mountain by focusing on what he has seen and sensed there, such as the pure, clean air and the natural features that generate a sense of sacredness and beauty. These

---

52. Kaibara E., "Chikuzen no kuni zoku fudoki," 147.
53. Kaibara E., "Chikuzen no kuni zoku fudoki," 147.

visual and sensory observations, combined with the mystic mist and haze, enhance a sense of the sacredness of the tall mountains of *chinzan*. The spiritual experience in Kamado Mountain is made possible precisely because of the intricate workings of *yin* and *yang* and the *kishin*, which are both characteristic of *chinzan*, even though he never uses the term *kishin*.

Ekiken's focus on the origins of Kamado Shrine reveals on one hand the wondrous effects of *ki*, but on the other hand, the actual history of how the shrine came into being. Citing the *Engishiki*, Ekiken states that "Kamado Shrine in Mikasa county has one big space for a *myōjin* (manifestation of the deity), as recorded in the "Book of the Gods' Names" (*Jinmyōchō*) [in volumes nine and ten] of *Engishiki*."[54] Furthermore, the details of the shrine identify the local deities that emerged there, as described below:

> Kamado Shrine enshrines a goddess, Tamayori hime (Princess Tamayori) of the sea, a wife of Ukaya fuki awasezu no mikoto [who is the father of Emperor Jinmu, the first emperor of Japan]. Perhaps, after giving birth to Emperor Jinmu in Mt. Takachio in Hyūga province [present-day Miyazaki and partially Kagoshima prefectures], she entered Kamado Mountain. There are two seats for the deities in the shrine precinct—the left is for Empress Jingū and the right is for [her son] the Hachiman ōkami (Great God Hachiman). There are reasons why the divine spirits enter a mountain like this, but if the mountain is the residence of ancestral gods, the divineness [of the mountain] must become far more significant to attract other divine spirits. And, the *reigen* (miraculous power) of these divine spirits must also become ever more exceptional.[55]

This excerpt identifies the deities, starting with the primary one, Princess Tamayori of the sea. It demonstrates this locale's connections with the deities, such as Tamayori and her husband, Ukaya fuki awasezu no mikoto, who is the father of the first human emperor, Jinmu. Ekiken does not explain who these gods were or their relationships to one another, but my research shows that the Hachiman ōkami is believed to be the divine spirit of

54. Kaibara E., "Chikuzen no kuni zoku fudoki," 147.
55. Kaibara E., "Chikuzen no kuni zoku fudoki," 147.

Emperor Ōjin, whose mother, the legendary Empress Jingū, successfully led an invasion army in Korea according to *Nihon shoki*. These details indicate Chikuzen's ties with the local gods that have a divine connection with the past, thus enhancing the idea that Japan was created by the deities.

Ekiken's descriptions of the landscape of Chikuzen are inspired by *kishin* discourse, but *kishin* is hidden in his meta-narrative because Ekiken's narrative is dominated by the series of local Japanese deities he presents, along with their divine spirits of *shinrei* and *reigen*, and the haze and fogs that surround the mountains. The *kishin*-inspired storyline is merged with Japan's genesis accounts and the actual landscape that preserves these features. Ekiken narrativizes the presence of divine spirits as if they had been residing in the natural environment and the spaces of shrines, rewarding the people who worshiped them with blessings of stability, peace, and prosperity. Bestowing significance on stones and rocks in the history of Chikuzen and on the religious events and rites that had taken place in Kamado Mountain since the classical period, Ekiken highlights expressions of the divine power as well as rituals and the popular celebrations. By unveiling layer after layer of the divine histories inscribed in the place, *Zoku fudoki* shows how the people in Chikuzen secured a prosperous future by furthering the relationship with the land that had historical ties with the divine spirits. By equating divine qualities to the natural environment, such as the clean air, pure water, and mysterious vapors in the mountains, Ekiken ascribes sanctity to the natural landscape.

In his essay "Jingikun," Ekiken lists the *chinzan* of Japan and explains how these mountains housed the guardian gods by taking them to the place they favored, such as the shrines (*shinshi*) that stood within the beautiful sacred mountains (*meizan reishū*).[56] In *Zoku fudoki*, he produces

---

56. Ekiken lists numerous mountains known as *chinzan* following this remark. For example, the home provinces have Mt. Atago, Mt. Hiei, and Ibukiyama Mountain. He lists beyond the home provinces: Chichibu Mountain in Musashi, Hakuhō Mountain in Kai (present-day Yamanashi), Mt. Asama in Shinano, Hakusan Mountain in Kaga, Tateyama Mountain in Ecthū, Mt. Daisen in Hōki (present-day western Tottori), Kirishima Mountain in Hyūga (present-day Miyazaki), Mt. Aso in Higo (present-day Kumamoto), Hiko Mountain in Buzen (present-day eastern Fukuoka), and Mt. Yufu in Bungo (present-day Ōita). He notes that divine spirits reside in these mountains, and humanity's awe, sincerity, and rituals shall be given to the deities at these mountains. Kaibara E., "Jingikun," 684.

a narrative of Chikuzen as a region protected by the divine spirits by framing it in the spatial theory that Japan's location had a plentiful supply of *yang ki*. At the same time, highlighting the actual shrines and temples in many of the sacred mountains, Ekiken emphasizes how physically the Japanese archipelago adhered to the idea of *shinkoku*. Many mountains function as anchors, appeasing evil and negative forces to pacify the country. Traces of the gods are naturalized as parts of the natural landscape, and the earth of the Japanese archipelago gradually acquires magical powers.

Japan as "Shinkoku," the Way of Japan as "Shintō"

By defining Japan as *shinkoku*, Ekiken successfully attributes a distinct quality to Japan and represents it as a separate entity from China. As we have observed, by contrasting *shinkoku* Japan with Chinese *seijinkoku*, Ekiken claims that people who were born into the Japanese archipelago knew the way of the gods (*shintō*). Yet it was difficult to discern what exactly the way of Japan was, apart from using expressions like "the way of *shinkoku*." Ekiken once wrote:

> The way of the gods (*shintō*) is, indeed, the way of heaven (*tendō*). Its teaching is vast and deep, but since there is one principle (*ichi ri*) in heaven, it was always clearly practiced in people's daily lives. Thus, easy aspects (*kinsho*) of the teaching are simple and have a clear principle, and they are simple to understand even for an unrefined ignorant couple. . . . Even though there is no teaching [of *shintō*] in a written format (*kotoba no oshie nakere domo*), people were capable of learning *shintō* by heart (*shinshū*) and practiced it naturally without being taught. . . . Thus, *shintō* is a simple principle and unwritten teaching (*fugen no oshie*).[57]

Fully admitting that *shintō* teaching was unwritten and that no one in his time knew exactly what it was, Ekiken criticized those who identified the three historical texts (*shisho*) of *Chronicle of Old Events in the Previ-*

---

57.   Kaibara E., "Jingikun," 641–42.

ous Ages (*Kujiki*, also known as *Sendai kuji hongi*), *Kojiki*, and *Nihon shoki* as records of the ancient past (*jōko*) and the canonical texts (*kyōten*) of the way of the gods.[58] In Ekiken's view, they did not see the significance of the simple unwritten teachings of *shintō* and, instead, tried to invent these texts as a valuable record of *shintō* teachings, without backing them up with historical evidence. While Ekiken accepted these texts as indispensable historical documents that recorded matters relating to *jōko*, he insisted that these texts, *Kojiki* and *Nihon shoki,* were not written in the language (*gen* or *koto*) of the *jōko*, and that they were not, therefore, the teachings of the *jōko*.[59] Ekiken emphasized that *shintō* was all about having a sincere heart, and it was never intended to uphold the five Confucian virtues (*gojō no sei*) of benevolence (*jin*), righteousness (*gi*), propriety (*rei*), wisdom (*chi*), and sincerity(*shin*) or the five moral relationships (*gorin no michi*).

Even so, because there was a need to identify and explain what *shintō* was and spread the teaching through words at his time, Ekiken suggested in "Jingikun" that the best way to do so was to borrow the Four Books of Confucius and the Five Classics (*shisho gokyō*) of Zhu Xi that recorded the ultimate way of the Chinese sages.[60] He argued that the teaching of the sages was exactly the same as *shintō* teaching because there was only one way, "heaven's way," between Heaven and Earth, and that the way of the Chinese sages was historically practiced as the way of heaven. If the way of the sages was the same as heaven's way, it could also be the way intended for Japan. Evoking *yin, yang,* and other conceptualizations of the Neo-Confucian metaphysics, Ekiken concluded that *shintō* was practiced in the same space that created the eternal principle of *yin* and *yang* (*in yō zōke no jōri*), which generated all things and phenomena.[61] He nativized Confucianism into Japan's teaching of *shintō* by insisting on the idea that there was only one way in Heaven and Earth. This understanding of sharing the heavenly way with China and the rest of East Asia explains why Ekiken could not distinguish Japan from China when he tried to attribute distinct qualities to Japan. He could only point to

58. Kaibara E., "Jingikun," 642.
59. Kaibara E., "Jingikun," 654.
60. Kaibara E., "Jingikun," 642.
61. Kaibara E., "Jingikun," 643.

the longer life expectancy of Japan's people and their honesty as distinguishing features because, after all, the two countries shared a concept of the way of heaven.

Ekiken's nativization of Confucianism was not unique to him.[62] Hayashi Razan also wrote about the decline of *shintō* in Japan by blaming Prince Shōtoku for eliminating the future possibility of *shintō* after the seventh century.[63] Razan is well known as a Neo-Confucian scholar in historiography, a man who worked for Tokugawa Ieyasu and introduced Neo-Confucian scholarship into Japan from Korea and China, but he devoted a considerable amount of time to the study of various local deities in Japan.[64] For example, Razan's *On Shrines in Our Country* (*Honchō jinjakō*) offers an explanation for the spread of shrines throughout the archipelago. The book starts by explaining the establishment of the first "twenty-two shrines" (*nijūni sha*) in the capital region and moves on to discuss other major shrines in the province.[65] In his preface to *Honchō jinjakō*, Razan explains that the shrines were registered in volumes nine and ten of the *Engishiki*, specifically in the volumes known as "Jinmyōchō," which list the shrines that had been registered by the time of the production of the *Engishiki*. He writes that these twenty-two shrines were mixtures of big, small, and medium shrines in Japan, and that a total of 3,132 deities were enshrined within them.[66] There were also deities outside of these shrines, which are called *shikige no kami* (deities that were not listed in *Jinmyōchō*), whose shrines include Iwashimizu, Yoshida, Gion, and Kitano.

62.   See, for example, Kobayashi, "Kinsei ni okeru chi no haibun kōzō"; Uranishi, "Edo jidai chūki no ichi shintō-ka."

63.   Ekiken also blamed Prince Shōtoku for protecting Buddhism and identified his patronage as the cause of the decline of shintō in Japan. Kaibara E., "Jingikun," 671–73.

64.   Ishida and Takahashi, "Kaidai," 54. For Razan's relationship with the Tokugawa shogunate, see, Ooms, *Tokugawa Ideology*.

65.   These twenty-two shrines are Ise, Iwashimizu, Kamo, Matsuo, Hirano, Inari, Kasuga, Ōharano, Ōmiwa, Isonokami, Yamato, Hirose, Tastuta, Sumiyoshi, Hie, Umemiya, Yoshida, Hirata, Gion, Kitano, Niukawakami, and Kifune. Apart from Ise, they were all located in the home provinces. Japan Knowledge, *Kokushi daijiten* <https://japanknowledge.com/library/en/>.

66.   Hayashi, "Honchō jinjakō," 31.

Razan's preface explains several annual events that took place in the shrines and how deities were worshiped throughout the year in his time. He made remarks by using the familiar expression used by Ekiken that Japan was *shinkoku*.

> Our country, Japan, is the country of deities (*shinkoku*). Emperor Jinmu succeeded the heavenly sovereign (*ten ni tsugu*) and established *kyoku* (or *chi*) [the origin of all things in the universe in Zhu Xi Neo-Confucianism]. Therefore, the royal succession (*kōcho*) was never disrupted and the "royal way" (*ōdō*) was widely spread. This was "the way" that our deities in heaven (*tenjin*) had given to us. However, in the late classical period Buddha (Busshi) took a chance and transmitted the law of India (*saiten no hō*), which changed the manners and customs (*zoku*) of our eastern region (*waga tōiki*). The royal way eventually declined, and the way of the gods (*shintō*) gradually ceased to exist. However, the heresy (*itan*) could not stand on its own, so the heretical theory (*sadō no setsu*) established Izanagi and Izanami in Sanskrit, and Sun Goddess [Amaterasu], became Dainichi [shortened version of Dainichi nyorai, who is the supreme Buddha of the Cosmos in Shingon esoteric Buddhism].[67]

The passage shows Razan's understanding and knowledge of local *shintō* practices and explains how "the way of our heavenly deities" came to decline in the classical and medieval periods. The shrines were initially registered in the tenth-century official record of *Engishiki* as those that had relationships with local deities. During the medieval period, however, Buddhism, in particular Esoteric Buddhism, obtained much support from the court and powerful regent families, and the *shintō* shrines' connections with the Buddhist temples and the court became more powerful.[68] Razan accused Buddhism of overwhelming *shintō* deities to the extent that it changed the identity of *shintō* gods.

---

67. Hayashi, "Honchō jinjakō," 31.
68. Often, through the mediation of the court and courtiers, the temples provided the shrine with monetary and material support and land donations, in return for dominating the rituals and other events to maximize the benefits to be gained from the deities.

His purpose in writing *Honchō jinjakō* was clearly to regain the minds and the manners of Japanese people before they were "corrupted by Buddhism." Razan states:

> Now in my study of the shrines (*jinjakō*), I examine the existing writings on the shrines (*jinja*), ask older people, study the history of the temples (*engi*), and validate the research findings through various records (*shosho*), such as *Kujiki, Kojiki, Nihongi, Shoku Nihongi, Engishiki*, excerpts from *fudoki, Kogo shūi* (Gleanings from Ancient Stories), *Monzui* (Literary Essence of Our Country), *Jinnō shōtōki, Kuji kongen* (Sources of Official Matters). . . . My only wish is that people (*sejin*) will worship our gods (*waga kami*) and eliminate foreign Buddha (*kano hotoke*). Then, it might be possible for the purity and honesty (*junchoku*) of the ancient past (*jōko*) to be restored in our country (*kokka*), cleansing the impurity that exists both inside and outside our people (*minzoku*).[69]

The various records that appear in the excerpt, such as *Nihon shoki, Engishiki, Jinnō shōtōki*, and others, are official history texts, showing that Razan meticulously collected "the facts" about the local shrines to present their authenticated historical origins. Moreover, the *Honchō jinjakō* includes phonetic glosses in *kana* to allow readers to read the quoted passages in "Japanese words" (*yamato kotoba*). For instance, the very first section of the text is on Ise Shrine, and it reads: "*Yamato fumi* (*Nihongi*) writes that Izanagi and Izanami together gave birth to the Sun Goddess, who came to be called Ōhirume no muchito." Without this explanation, readers would not know that Ōhirume no muchito was a Japanese name for the Sun Goddess Amaterasu (who is also known as Ōhirume no mikoto, Ōhirume no muchi no kami, or simply Ōhirume). Even though Razan skimped on the details, he provided *kana* reading for every word in the sentences, clearly instructing the readers to pronounce each word in *yamato kotoba*.[70] The *kana* readings indicate that he referenced *Nihon shoki* and verified the pronunciation of the names of the deities and places by locating the Japanese equivalent of *Yamato fumi* in *Nihon shoki*. Thus,

---

69. Hayashi, "Honchō jinjakō," 32. Scholars mostly agree that *jōko* is a period of time concluding with the year 645.

70. Hayashi, "Honchō jinjakō," 34.

like Ekiken, Razan sought to verify the connections of the deities to the various local shrines from the age of the gods to his own time.[71] He tried to demonstrate the original state of the establishment of *shintō* shrines in Japan before their encounter with Buddhism.

Ekiken and Razan examined the histories of local places, especially the shrines and temples, to validate the origins and clarify the divine connections between the land and the deities from the ancient past. They did so as a way of proving that Japan was the country of deities. They used the conceptual framework of Confucianism and Neo-Confucianism as the foundation when structuring and representing the history of Japan, Japan's spiritual nature, and its practices, even though none of the canonical texts stated these "facts." By drawing on major values and morals outlined in Confucian and Neo-Confucian texts, they delineated the discursive boundaries of Japan's *shintō*, which was proven to be flexible, transferable, and universal because *shintō* was the *tendō*. By systematizing the history of local shrines through Confucian conceptualization, Razan and Ekiken generated a discourse of Japan as the original country of the deities.

Their work reflects the rising scholarly interest that existed in the seventeenth century in mapping the space of Japan and developing a discourse of Japan as a separate entity from China. By employing the metaphysics of *yin* and *yang*, Tokugawa scholars began mobilizing a discourse of Japan as *shinkoku*, which came to naturalize the idea that the Japanese landscape was where the deities resided, an idea that resonated in the following centuries. The next chapter examines how Ekiken disseminated the idea of *shinkoku* Japan through the commercial publication of guidebooks.

71. Razan researched the development of local *shintō* beliefs, traditions, and secret rituals and teachings besides the histories of the *shintō* shrines. See, for example, *Transmission of shintō* (*Shintō denjushō*, better known as *Shintō denju*), *Important Terms in Shintō* (*Shintō yōgo*), *Correspondences between the Way of Gods and the Way of Deviation* (*Shin'eki gōkan*). Taira estimates that *Honchō jinjakō* was written at Razan's intellectual prime, between 1638 and 1641, when Razan was particularly interested in various *shintō* shrines and their secret teachings. Taira, "Kaisetsu: kinsei no shintō shisō," 510–19.

CHAPTER 3

Mapping the Capital

"Ekiken books" (Ekiken-bon) occupied . . . 7 percent of the entire collection, sixteen books out of a total of seventy-one, to be exact, in the Mita family library. The collection includes Ekiken's didactic books written in Japanese script (*wabun*), his dictionaries, such as *Numerical Categories in Japan and China* (*Wakan meisū*, 1678), and *Everyone's Treasures: Record of Trivial Matters* (*Banpō hijiki*, 1705), as well as medical texts, such as *Precepts for Nurturing Life* (*Yōjōkun*, 1713) and *A Collection of Life Principles* (*Isei shūyō*, 1714), and the gardening books *Genealogy of Flowers* (*Kafu*, 1698) and *Genealogy of Greens* (*Saifu*, 1714). . . . More than a quarter of the entire collection of the Mori family library consists of Ekiken books. Clearly, [Mori] Nagaemon was a big fan of Ekiken . . . . There was a wide audience for Ekiken's books, including village headmen (*shōya*) and higher ranking farmers (*jōsō nōmin*), not just the warrior classes as previously assumed by historians.

— Yokota Fuyuhiko, "Ekiken-bon no dokusha"

Kaibara Ekiken's scholarship and scholarly contributions have long attracted a good deal of attention in both English- and Japanese-language scholarly circles. Mary Tucker, for instance, suggested a few decades ago that Ekiken sought to transmit the way of the ancient sages to spread "the universal elements of Neo-Confucianism" in Japan.[1] Similarly, Japanese historians have identified Ekiken as a "Confucian Shinto" (*juka shintō*) scholar who "applied" Neo-Confucian learning to Japan, claiming that this eventually led to the formation of an indigenous Japanese thought, culminating in Yamazaki Ansai's *Suika shintō*.[2] According to

1. Tucker, *Moral and Spiritual Cultivation*, 3.
2. Abe A., "Juka shintō to kokugaku," 498–99; Araki, "Kaibara Ekiken no shisō"; Ishida, "Zenki bakuhan taisei no ideorigī"; Okada T., "Kaibara Ekiken," *Edoki no ju-*

this argument, Ekiken, Hayashi Razan, and other *juka shintō* scholars borrowed the concepts of Neo-Confucianism as a means of reconfiguring existing Shinto discourses in Japan, paving the way for Ansai's school of thought and the rise of Nativism (Kokugaku) in the late eighteenth century.

As highlighted in the previous chapter, Ekiken's and Razan's scholarly efforts were not necessarily aimed at the establishment of either a Neo-Confucian or *shintō* school of thought in Japan. Instead, they sought to map the space of Japan in relation to China and produce an independent discursive entity centering on the idea that Japan was the country of the deities. Therefore, I reject the thesis of the "Japanization of Confucianism" (*jugaku no Nihonka*), which asserts that "Confucian Shinto" scholars were merely importing foreign concepts to systematize the existing knowledge structure in Japan.[3] Precisely because Ekiken and Razan endeavored to make Japan recognizable by reference to the cultural authority of China, they used the identical conceptual framework to make *shinkoku* Japan look exactly like the sagely country of China. As part of this process, they identified the way of the deities as the way of Japan, but this delineation of *shintō* was not the same as the popular worship of local deities in the medieval era. Even though such practices existed, they did not necessarily form the domain of knowledge referred to as *shintō* in the medieval era.[4] Such a domain emerged only in the seventeenth century as scholars like Razan and Ekiken tried to define the nature of Japan.

This chapter moves on to discuss the dissemination of Ekiken's *shinkoku* narrative and demonstrates how he tried to educate his readers about the distinct qualities of the Japanese *fūdo*. As the recent burgeoning

---

gaku, and *Yamazaki Ansai to Ri Taikei*; Taira, "Kaisetsu: kinsei no shintō shisō," 507–58; Tajiri, "Kinsei Nihon no 'shinkoku'ron"; Takahashi M., "Kinsei juka shintō no itanron."

3. Watanabe H., *Sōgaku to kinsei Nihon shakai*, 201.

4. It is beyond the scope of this chapter to lay out the phenomenon of Shinto and its genesis. Mark Teeuwen, for example, argues that a concept of "Shinto" that focused on the veneration of local gods of ancient origin, reveals the first signs of development in the late medieval period. He traces it to the writings of Yoshida Kanetomo (1435–1511) in the fifteenth century. For more on the origins and development of the term *Shinto*, see Teeuwen, "From Jindō to Shinto."

literature on Japanese spatial imagination has shown, Ekiken's topographic writings played a critical role in popularizing both travel and travel literature (*kikōbun*). He wished to show his readers Japan's position in the broader universe by publishing commercial guidebooks because he was convinced that Japan was fundamentally blessed with superior qualities compared with other countries, due to its privileged location. I argue that Ekiken used the print culture to disseminate the message of *shinkoku* Japan, but I disagree with the conventional categorization of his topographic writings as works of travel literature. Instead, I treat his guidebooks as cultural representations that instantiated the *shinkoku* claim and reveal how his promotion of learning about the country implicitly aligned with the traditional *kishin* discourse. Through my analysis of one of his published guidebooks, *The Excellent Views of the Capital* (*Keijō shōran*, 1706), I show that Ekiken's goal in permeating the *shinkoku* claim was to pacify the divine spirits drifting in the mountainous space of the capital and turning the idea of *shinkoku* Japan into the center of Japanese identity.

The Rising Publishing Industry and Ekiken's Writings

Ekiken is famous for widely publishing educational texts, and his didactic texts of the "Ten Precepts Books of Ekiken" (*Ekiken jikkun*) and "Ekiken books" (Ekiken-bon) were popularly used as textbooks in temple schools (*terakoya*) and private schools that taught reading and writing (*tenarai juku*).[5] Besides the moral teachings of Confucianism, he energetically published books on medicine, dictionary-like reference books, and topographic texts as travel guides for popular audiences. He wrote many books on local topography, but only a handful were published in his lifetime:

5.　*Terakoya* education was conventionally understood as the acquisition of practical skills, but recently scholars have demonstrated that children at these private schools were engaged in more advanced skills, involving sophisticated cultural and artistic techniques (*kōyō*), such as Noh chanting (*utai*), in addition to the basic reading and writing skills. See, for example, Koyasu, "Shushigaku to kindai Nihon no keisei," 92–93; Tsujimoto, *Kinsei kyōiku shisōshi no kenkyū*; Umemura, "Kinsei ni okeru minshū no tenarai."

A Tour of the Province of Yamato (*Washū junranki*, 1696), *The Excellent Views of the Capital* (*Keijō shōran*, 1706), *A Record of the Arima Hot Springs* (*Arima no yama onsenki*, 1711), *A Record of the Kiso Road* (*Kisoji no ki*, 1713), *A Tour of Several Provinces* (*Shoshū junranki*, 1713), and *Scenic Views of Nikkō* (*Nikkō meishōki*, 1714).

Ekiken teamed up with one of the two most successful booksellers of the time (*shoshi* or *hon'ya*) in Kyoto, and his books brought the second master, Ogawa Tazaemon, with a considerable profit.[6] Known by their business name (*yagō*), Ogawaya, every master in the bookshop carried the same name: Tazaemon.[7] The popularity of the books allowed Ogawaya to publish Ekiken's guidebooks even after Ekiken's death, and titles such as *A Record of the Eastern Road* (*Azumaji no ki*, 1721) and a new guidebook series of *The Scenic Views of Japan* (*Fusō meishōzu*, 1713–28) brought additional fortune to the publishing house.[8] The publishing of the *Fusō meishōzu* series involved making a number of changes due to the author's death. Nevertheless, the series that identified Amanohashidate in northern Kyoto prefecture, Itsukushima in Hiroshima, Matsushima in Miyagi, and a renowned cherry blossom spot, Yoshino, as the most scenic spots in Japan was successful.[9] The first three of these are still known as the Three Scenic Views of Japan (*Nihon sankei*), a designation first used by Hayashi Gahō, the author of *On the Matters and Places of Japan* (*Nihonkoku jisekikō*, 1714).

---

6. Ogawa Tazaemon was not one of the ten publishers known as "The Excellent Ten" (*Jittetsu*) Confucian bookstores, but he was famous and almost exclusively published Ekiken's work, the books of Nishikawa Joken (1648–1724), and the major works of the Mito domain. There were seventy-two prestigious bookstores in Kyoto at this time. Wakimura, *Tōzai shoshigai kō*, 10–12; Yokoyama, "Tatsujin e no michi," 57.

7. Ryūshiken is the bookshop name (*kengō*) of Ogawa Tazaemon, and it remained powerful in Kyoto until the Meiji period, when they opened another shop in Tokyo. Their real last name was Ibaraki, so Tazaemon was also called Ibarakiya. Kawahira and Katsumata, *Fusō meishōzu-kō*. See also Yokota, *Nihon kinsei shomotsu bunkashi no kenkyū*, 437–68.

8. For information about the popularity of Ekiken's books, see also Inoue T., *Kaibara Ekiken*; Konta, *Edo no hon'ya san*, 71–74; Tsujimoto, "Moji shakai no seiritsu to shuppan media," 138–40; Yokota, *Nihon kinsei shomotsu bunkashi no kenkyū*, 437–41. Also, this series of *The Scenic Views of Japan* employed a folded booklet style called *orijō shitate*. The format is reflective of the booksellers' desire to find a convenient style for viewing the images panoramically while allowing the reader to look at the written text.

9. Ekiken identified *Nihon sankei* as Matsushima, Amanohashidate, and Itsukushima. Kaibara E., "Wakan meisū," 825.

Ogawa Tazaemon's success as a bookseller and his ensuing support for Ekiken's works paralleled the growing publishing industry in the late seventeenth and eighteenth centuries. As Wakao Masaki (among others) argues, the robust publishing business in the eighteenth century depended on popular demand, and the readers' intellectual energy sustained the activities of writing, reading, and publishing.[10] The basic principle for publishing was therefore profitability, and the remarkable sales of Ekiken's works are evidence of their high value.[11] Historians speculate that one of the appeals of Ekiken's writings was the "new seeing" approach in his local topography texts, which dramatically changed how travel literature was written.[12] Filled with a "scientific accumulation of information about all parts of Japan," Ekiken's accounts conveyed a special sense of the attachment that local people had with a place to a wider audience.[13] In later years, his guidebooks also profoundly influenced a number of important scholars, including Motoori Norinaga (1730–1801).[14] Norinaga not only used Ekiken's topographic writings for his own research, he also wrote a tour guide to his hometown, *The Excellent Views of Matsuzaka* (*Matsuzaka shōran*), directly inspired by Ekiken's 1706 guidebook of the capital, *Keijō shōran*.

The relationship between Ekiken's books and the rise of the publishing industry illustrates the increasing power of popular curiosity that influenced social and cultural trends, which in turn directly affected the profits of the bookselling business. The analysis of the broader social and intellectual changes that surrounded the publishing business reveals the factors that made Ekiken's travel guidebooks considerably popular. In this regard, the perception of his topographic writing as travel literature in

---

10.   Wakao, "Sōron: shoseki bunka to sono kitei," 18.

11.   Takagi G., "Shoshi, kashihon'ya no yakuwari," 248.

12.   Plutschow, *Reader in Edo Period Travel*, 32–45. See also Itasaka, "Chihō no bungaku"; Suzuki T., *Kinsei kikō bungei nōto*, 9; Traganou, *Tōkaidō Road*, 97; Yonemoto, *Mapping Early Modern Japan*, 48.

13.   Keene, *Travelers of a Hundred Ages*, 324–25; Yonemoto, *Mapping Early Modern Japan*, 56.

14.   Norinaga made reference to Ekiken's *Yamato meguri* in his *Sugagasa no nikki* (The Sedge Hat Diary) written in 1772. Marra, *Poetics of Motoori Norinaga*, 220. See also 61 and 113–14.

the existing historiography is misleading.[15] Travel literature originates with the accounts of travel in the Heian period (794–1185), most notably the *Tosa Nikki* (The Tosa Diary) by a male courtier, Ki no Tsurayuki (884–936), who authored this piece in the Japanese *kana* syllabary by pretending to be a female writer. He punctuated the prose account of the journey between the capital and Tosa province with Japanese *waka* poems. Written in the style of a diary with the evocative language of poetry by the hand of "female" writer, *Tosa Nikki* became the most notable model of the diary as literature, and the genre of travel literature had become a literary style of belles-lettres by the mid-fifteenth century.[16] The major purpose of classical and medieval travel literature was to make aesthetic observations, such as reflective moments and the author's various feelings during the journey.[17] The development of travel literature from classical through medieval to early modern shows a number of changes over the period, but the fundamental focus on capturing the aesthetics of travel remained unchanged.

The features associated with Ekiken's writings on local topography, by contrast, were fundamentally different from those found in travel literature. In spite of the difference, scholars still place his works in this category and evaluate his writings for their aesthetic quality. For example, Itasaka Yōko assessed Ekiken's writings as "dry and tasteless" (*mumi kansō na*) and lamented the lack of culminating emotions in his essays.[18] She argued that he could have written in a more literary manner by following the example of *Pillow Book* (*Makura no sōshi*) or the *Tale of the Heike* (*Heike monogatari*), but Ekiken's sensibilities were only represented in

15.   Itasaka, "Kaisetsu," "Kaibara Ekiken *Azumaji no ki*," "Kaibara kazō 'Azumaji no ki' no hen'yō," and "Meisho zue rui no fūkei byōsha"; Keene, *Travelers of a Hundred Ages*, 323–27; Plutschow, *Reader in Edo Period Travel*, 32–45; Suzuki T., *Kinsei kikō bungei nōto*, 9; Traganou, *Tōkaidō Road*, 97; Yonemoto, *Mapping Early Modern Japan*, 44–68.

16.   *Utamakura* is a category of poetic words, often involving place names mentioned in some of the imperial anthologies. *Utamakura* works like a code in which special meanings, involving mood, season, or other references, are implied. Kamens, *Utamakura, Allusion, and Intertextuality*.

17.   Carter, "Sōgi in the East Country," 170.

18.   Itasaka, "Kaibara Ekiken to kikōbun," 24.

his adventurous spirit, curiosity, and a desire to learn about local people's customs in the villages he visited.[19]

Although some of Ekiken's topographic writings have *kikō* in the title, as in the case of *A Record of the Travel in the Year of Jinshin* (*Jinshin kikō*), *A Record of the Journey to the Northwest* (*Seihoku kikō*, 1713), and *A Record of the Journey to the South* (*Nan'yū kikō*, 1713), my analysis suggests that these writings were his attempt to delineate and create the representation of the space of Japan to express the significant sense of place as evidence for his *shinkoku* claim. Importantly, Ekiken did not intend all his topographic writings to be treated equally, and those that were unpublished were more or less personal notes to himself.[20] One of his unpublished works, *A Record of the Kumano Road* (*Kumanoji no ki*), which he completed in 1694, was written even though he never traveled to Kumano. He had a strong desire to visit Kumano once in his lifetime, and this prompted him to gather relevant materials.[21] Based on the various topographic and historical reports on Kumano he had read, he wrote the essay without having seen the actual topography. Even so, he described Kumano as "sticking out from the southern part of Kishū province, and the climate (*fūki*) is warm and mild (*onwa*)" in the beginning of the essay. He continued, stating that abundant beautiful views were available and:

> Kumano is said to be the most scenically beautiful (*meishō*) place in Japan. Zen monk Zekkei [(1336–1405)] (Ekiken later corrected the monk's name from Kyōkai to Zekkei, which is marked in the text) crossed the sea from here to Ming China and met Emperor Zhu Yuanzhang [(1328–98, r. 1368–98)]. Then, he asked the emperor about the shrine [in Kumano] that is related to Jofuku [Xu Fu in Chinese. He was sent twice to the eastern

---

19.   Itasaka, "Kaibara Ekiken no *kikōbun*."

20.   *Jinshin kikō*, *Record of the Travel to Bungo Province* (*Hōkoku kikō*), *Record of the Travel to the Eastern Shore of Ōmi Province* (*Kōtō kikō*), and *A Record of the Kumano Road* (*Kumano ji no ki*) were not published in his lifetime, but much later in modern times in the form of an anthology. Kaibara E., "Jinshin kikō" and "Hōkoku kikō"; Kaibara T., "Honkoku Ekiken shiryō."

21.   Itasaka, "Kaibara Ekiken no *kikōbun*," 38–39. According to Itasaka, *Kumano ji no ki* is only available today in the handwritten manuscript copy made by Ekiken's wife, Tōken, housed in the library of the Kaibara family.

seas by Emperor of Qin, Shi Huandi, to search for the elixir of life]. Zekkei composed a poem, saying: "In response to the order of Emperor Zhu, I read a poem about the three sacred mountains [legendary three mountains, *Sanshenshan*, in China]." Emperor Zhu responded by *heyunshi* [a style of Chinese poetry]. These are the stories about Kumano.[22]

It is interesting to learn that someone could write in such detail without having visited Kumano. Clearly, Ekiken found references to the Zen monk Zekkei and the story about him in reference books. When the essay describes the topography, it sounds as if Ekiken had actually been there and had appreciated these views. The following places were to be found along the path to the grand shrine (*hongū*) of Kumano when traveling from Osaka:

- Kimiidera Temple calls itself Kongōbuji [temple of the Diamond Mountain, the head temple of the Shingon Buddhism at Mt. Kōya]. The temple connects to Saika no ura [which is a beach, and Saika no ura was mentioned in poems in *Man'yōshū*]. (The text annotations that Ekiken later added include the following: The shrine is located on higher ground, looking down on the beautiful bay that is frequently mentioned in *waka* poems. The view is absolutely beautiful, *zekkei*.)
- Kuroi village, Hikata [village]: These two villages produce Japanese maple trees (*momiji*), and even Shinmachi in Kyoto buy these *momiji* from here to coat [their lacquer work]. . . .
- Dōjōji Temple is located fifteen *chō* [almost a mile] away [from the major road]. (The text indicates that he later added the following: This temple exists today at the same location, and the bell that belongs to this temple is mentioned in *Japan's First Comprehensive History of Buddhism* [*Genkō shakusho*] [a thirty-volume text from the Genkō era, 1321–24]. The temple is also referred to in *sarugaku* [performance], so I will not write about it here.)[23]

As seen in the annotations on the essay, this draft illustrates the process by which Ekiken added more information, such as the Saika no ura bay

---

22. Kaibara T., "Honkoku Ekiken shiryō," 84.
23. Kaibara T., "Honkoku Ekiken shiryō," 84.

that was mentioned in the *Man'yōshū*, and a reference to the bell at Dōjōji Temple in *Genkō shakusho*. To complete these essays on local topography, Ekiken verified the direct quotations, historical information, and information on local industry and manufacturing. The inclusion of Zekkei's poem to Emperor Zhu suggests that Ekiken had access to the *gozan* literature, as the poem had been preserved in the anthology of Zen poetry by the *gozan* monks.[24]

Unlike the unverifiable sections that remained in the manuscript of *Kumanoji no ki*, Ekiken's published materials were all carefully validated by his observations. His objective in producing the published topographic writings was to provide readers with accurate representations of a space, whether it was the capital, Kyoto, the ancient capital of Nara, or somewhere else. Thus Ekiken excluded any self-reflective remarks and identified the sources to validate his claims, following the Kōshōgaku (evidential studies) method. He also made a clear gesture toward clarifying the fame of the place. In the published works, for instance, he used the term *meisho* specifically to mean the "place with a name" or the "place that has a name" that derived from *nadokoro* (or *na no aru tokoro*) in Japanese *waka* poetry. These poetic sites became famous after attracting poetic and aesthetic travelers who visited to experience the feelings of the poet who had written about the site.[25] Some of these places were scenic, but not all of them were. Ekiken drew a distinction between places of scenic beauty and poetically famous places by using the terms *shōkyō, meishō, kakyō,* and *shōran* to highlight scenic beauty. He explained the origin of the fame attached to the places by citing military tales, historical events, religious causes, or otherwise to clarify the origins of the place name. This careful verification process, based on empirical information, inevitably rendered the narrator useless. Without a narrator who is willing to share sentiments and views with the reader, the published essay becomes nothing more than a series of facts, such as dates, numbers, directions, and things one

---

24. Kageki, *Shōken Kō zenchū*, 142–46.

25. In *Fusō kishō* Ekiken writes about the confusion about places that later became famous. According to him, poets tended to write poems based on the feelings and emotions attributed to the place, even though they had not actually visited the site. Consequently, many places became famous by mistake, lacking the topographic features the site was said to have possessed. Kaibara E., "Fusō kishō," 319. See also Nenzi, *Excursions in Identity*; Suzuki S., *Edo no meisho to toshi bunka*, 28–48.

is likely to see there. The narrative simply follows the beginning, middle, and end of the journey, and the writing often sounds dry and bland.

The following excerpt from Ekiken's *A Tour of Yamato Province* (*Washū junranki*, 1694) suffices to illustrate this point. The excerpt shows that Ekiken wove numerous official history texts in order to reveal historical connections to previous rulers and introduce some points of interest that could be verified empirically.[26] This section concerns the imperial burial mound of Empress Jingū, a legendary figure, which is one of the landmarks in the area called Utahime in Nara.

The burial mound of Empress Jingū is located a little over five *chō* [0.3 miles] southwest of Utahime. People in the village call the mound "Empress's Tomb Mountain" (Omihaka yama) or the "Great Palace" or the "Sovereign's Palace" (Ōmiya), but it is a small mountain (*koyama*). There are old pine trees growing there. This mound is what is referred to, in *The Chronicles of Japan* (*Nihongi*, another name for *Nihon shoki*), as a royal burial mound, whose shape resembles the pattern of a series of shields, and it is located above a pond (*saki no tatanami no ike no e no misasagi*). There is an empty moat (*karahori*) around it. At the northern end of the mound, there is an ascending path. And, there is a big stone mound (*ishizuka*) to the west of Empress Jingū's tomb. A small number of small pine trees grow there. To the southwest of the stone mound, there is the village of Misasagi-mura (village of the royal grave). The leader of the village elders (*rirō*) says that Omihaka yama is the burial mound of Empress Jingū, but he does not know to whom the *ishizuka* belongs. *Engishiki* mentions the burial mound for Emperor Seimu as being behind the pond of the royal burial mound, whose shape resembles the pattern of a series of shields (*saki no tatanami no ike jiri no misasagi*) in Yamato. Thus, this stone mound should be regarded as Emperor Seimu's.[27]

26. According to the Comprehensive Catalogue of Japanese Rare Books, produced by the National Institute of Japanese Literature, *A Tour of Yamato Province* is officially known as *Yamato meguri*. However, there is an alternative pronunciation for the title, especially when written in nonphonetic Chinese characters that have several different possible readings. In Chinese characters, a reading of "Washū junranki" is possible as well as "Yamato meguri," but in the phonetic *kana* syllabary, the title is unequivocally read as "Yamato meguri." Kaibara E., "Washū junranki."

27. Kaibara E., "Washū junranki," 48. One *ri* is about 36 *chō*, which is 3.927 kilometers. One *chō* is about 60 *ken*, 109 meters. One *ken* is about 6 *shaku*, which is about 180 centimeters. As for directions, Ekiken uses both the Eastern twelve zodiac sign–based direction system and the Western four cardinal point system.

Ekiken would have been able to obtain information about Omihaka yama, the Ōmiya, the village of Misasagi, and the imperial mounds from the *Nihon shoki* and *Engishiki*, but he would have needed to see the location of the pond in relation to the tombs to deduce whose tombs they were. We know he owned a copy of *Nihon shoki* and *Engishiki*, among other items, and he verified that the Utahime area was mentioned in these texts and how the village Misasagi-mura had come to assume its name.[28]

By presenting the facts, Ekiken's narration has the effect of reviving the view of the actual local landscape. This mode of writing allows the reader to picture the landscape through reference to a brief yet extracted body of information, which provides an explanation of the site. I refer to this navigational narrative as a narrative map, which becomes an effective narrative device when combined with his narration, punctuated by information about distances and directions. Ekiken rarely used pictorial maps in his guides to local places, but with the narrative map, his readers had the essential information to help them orient themselves spatially and horizontally when traveling with Ekiken. Containing only minimal information about the significance of each place, Ekiken's narration had the capacity to stimulate visual images of the natural scenery, often accompanied by the sound of streams and waterfalls.

Ekiken's narrative map enhanced the travel experience. There was a long tradition in East Asia of enjoying imaginary journeys called *gayū*. This was achieved by looking at a painting of mountains and rivers, which allowed the observer's thoughts to travel into a dream world, the same way one might day dream while sitting at one's desk.[29] The imaginary journey experience was further developed in the early modern era through a robust print culture, as Robert Goree vividly demonstrates in his study of the eighteenth-century guidebook series called *meisho zue*.[30] Ordinary travelers studied the historical background or contemporary significance of a place before actually embarking on the journey. Thus, the growing reading public was increasingly well educated and in favor of more empirical observations. A cohort of sophisticated readers was precisely what was needed to

---

28.   Kyūshū Shiryō Kankōkai, "Ganko mokuroku," 5.

29.   Idemitsu, "Ike Taiga hitsu Manpukuji tōhōjō fusumae," 276.

30.   Goree, "Fantasies of the Real." See, also, Nenzi, *Excursions in Identity*.

ensure that fact-based guidebooks such as Ekiken's became fashionable.[31] As shown for Kumano, abundant information existed for travelers and enthusiasts on various tourism-worthy destinations—whether they were embarking on a real trip or imagining the tour of their dreams—and travel became a way of learning about places in Japan.[32] The amount of available information is a testament to the increase in popular interest in various local places, and popular demand itself influenced the nature of books on the market.

In turn, the reader's preference for empiricism affected the writing of Ekiken and others.[33] Unlike publishing trends that targeted the tastes and needs of scholars in the sixteenth century, since the mid-seventeenth century readers began to include a broad swathe of society, thus popularizing the book industry.[34] Reflecting these changes, Ekiken began to act on the advice of publishers, who advocated writing in a simpler and more playful tone to reach a wider audience. For instance, the publisher hesitated over Ekiken's *Annotations on Great Learning* (*Daigaku shinso*), fearing the book was too difficult for the new generation of readers. Even though Ekiken believed that the annotations written by Chinese scholars on Zhu Xi's commentaries on *Great Learning* would be extremely valuable, no publisher (*shoshi*) shared his enthusiasm, concluding that this book would fail to attract enough readers.[35]

By the eighteenth century, the serious works of erudite scholars no longer occupied a privileged place in the publishing market, and scholarly writers needed to soften their difficult style of writing and adopt a lighter vocabulary to meet the needs of amateur readers (*shirōto*). Publishers encouraged Ekiken to use Japanese *wabun* and write more casually

31.   Yokota, "Kinsei minshū shakai," "'Rōnin hyakushō' Yoda Chōan," and "Edo jidai minshū no dokusho"; Yokoyama, "Tatsujin e no michi," 25–26.

32.   Mary Elizabeth Berry has called this state of information "the library of public information." Berry, *Japan in Print*, 13–53.

33.   Itasaka writes that Ryūshiken found Ekiken's writings particularly appealing because they were empirical, excluding personal sentiments and lacking emotional reflective moments. Itasaka, "Kaibara kazō 'Azumaji no ki' no hen'yō," 177, 184–89.

34.   Fujizane, "Santo no hon'ya nakama," 35–36; Yakuwa, "Kinsei minshū no ningen keisei," 226–29; Clements, "Rewriting Murasaki."

35.   Tsujimoto, *Shisō to kyōiku no mediashi*, 99.

to appeal to a pleasure-seeking readership.[36] These stories illuminate the changing trends in learning and the subsequent broadening of the various audiences of the reading public. Within this context, Ekiken's guidebook of Japan's capital emerged and captured the attention of a wide popular audience. I now analyze how he enabled readers to experience the capital by traveling through the landscape.

Ekiken's Guidebooks as Educational Tools

Keijō shōran provides readers with seventeen-day tours of the capital. The itineraries occasionally involve a river crossing by boat, but primarily they are walking tours. Every day, the tour leaves central Kyoto and ventures into one section of the capital (*rakuchū*) or suburb of the capital (*rakugai*), and each tour is filled with scenic beauty spots, such as waterfalls, blossoming flowers, and beautiful trees, including cherry blossom, plum trees, camellias, and maples, plus sites of historical significance from the recent and ancient past (see tables 3.1–3.3). Mary Elizabeth Berry has translated the title of this guidebook as *The Excellent Views of Kyoto* and has highlighted the author's educational contribution in relation to the emerging sense of community. She argues that Ekiken offered his readers "cultural custody of the landscape of Kyoto in exchange for cultural literacy."[37] She goes on to argue that by understanding the "cultural literacy" of Kyoto and identifying "Kyoto's codes," Ekiken's goal for this tour was to enable the reader to understand the centrality of Kyoto in relation to the wider Japanese community. Berry has also pointed out that the tour provided the reader with a degree of cultural literacy about Kyoto by controlling the contents of the tour in a rather strict way, acting as the "custodian of culture."

36.   Inoue T., *Kaibara Ekiken*, 132–35. See also Yokota, *Nihon kinsei shomotsu bunkashi*, 457–61, and *Nihon no rekishi*, vol. 16, *Tenka taihei*, 345–51. Some letters of correspondence between him and various publishers are preserved in volume 5, *Ekiken shiryō: shokanshū*. They include instructions from the publisher, such as changes to Ekiken's original draft that were translated from classical Chinese to Japanese (*kokuji*) to meet the needs of a popular audience (*minzoku*), which was more likely to understand a Japanese colloquial version more easily (*zokugo*). Kyūshū Shiryō Kankōkai, *Ekiken shiryō: shokanshū*, 98.

37.   Berry, *Japan in Print*, 185–87, 208.

Although I am unable to state exactly why Ekiken divided the tour into seventeen days, a Chinese authoritative topography book of the time, *The Excellent Views of the Realm* (*Fangyu shenglan* in Chinese, *Hōyo shōran* in Japanese, 1239), seems to be in implicit harmony with *Keijō shōran*. It was written by a Chinese author, Zhu Mu (d. 1255), who compiled a *fudoki*-like topographic record of the entire Southern Song dynasty by dividing the realm into seventeen provinces (*lú*). He organized the book's contents, such as information about local history, special products, topographic and historical features, famous people and poetry, within the framework of the seventeen *lú*. The combination of spatial information and poems about local places led to this text being used more as a tour guide of scenic spots in Southern Song than as a gazetteer.[38] Many men of culture in seventeenth-century Japan, including Tokugawa Ieyasu and Emperor Goyōzei (1572–1617, r. 1586–1611), read this book and were fascinated by it. Emperor Goyōzei even commissioned a poetry anthology, to which he gave the title *The Excellent Views of the Realm in the World of Japanese Poetry* (*Waka hōyo shōranshū*).[39] Ekiken's *Keijō shōran* assumes a similar format, comprising seventeen-day tours and a supplementary section called *Shūi* (gleanings), with the segments allowing readers to experience the excellent views and milieu of the capital. The *Shūi* section lists additional sightseeing spots for those who had more time during or after the seventeen days. Considering that Ekiken wanted to produce advanced scholarship and historiography in Japan, it is reasonable to assume that he was influenced by some aspects of the structure of this renowned Chinese topographic text when producing his tour of the capital.

It is also noteworthy that Ekiken's gesture of inviting readers to join his tour is remarkably friendlier than previous "guidebook" texts that had appeared in Japan. For example, before *Keijō shōran*, popular texts on Kyoto included Nakagawa Kiun's *A Child of Kyoto* (*Kyō warabe*, 1658), Yamamoto

38.   For the impact and use of Zhu Mu's text, see, for example, Tian, *Tao Yuanming and Manuscript Culture*, and Bol, "Rise of Local History," 62–63.

39.   Requesting the compilation of a poetry anthology was historically a gesture demonstrating one's supreme authority through the medium of poetry. By selecting the best poems expressing a certain aesthetic sensibility, the emperor and courtiers produced collections of superior poems, which symbolically promoted their aesthetic sensibilities as superior. See, for example, Sakai S., *Kinri-bon kasho no zōshoshiteki kenkyū*; Ogawa and Yoshioka, *Kinri-bon to kotengaku*.

Taijun's *A Collection of Places of Fame in the Capital* (*Rakuyō meishoshū*, 1658), and Matsuno Genkei's *A Record of the Capital in Japan* (*Fusō keikashi*, 1665). These texts are called "records of famous places" (*meishoki*), and offer comprehensive information about various places in the form of a list. These texts can be used as guidebooks, but they are more useful as reference material. In my view, their structure, which involves laying out information without a developmental framework, is much closer to *fudoki*, even though *meishoki* texts are often introduced as guidebooks in historiography.[40] The structure of *meishoki* is a collection of countless places, with the purpose of introducing, one by one, their topographic details, their special local products, and histories to the readers while following the classificatory system of similar Chinese texts.[41] The information is exhaustive and sometimes redundant, with one place listed under more than one subject heading. By contrast, *Keijō shōran* takes the form of a progressive tour that starts at one place and reaches its destination by the end of the day. This structure allows him to give readers a sense of completion by moving from one place to the next and from one day to the next for seventeen days. By strategically crafting such a progressive tour, Ekiken achieves his objective of informing the reader of the feel of the capital, based on a style that is superior to others.

In fact, Ekiken's preface to *Keijō shōran* explains his motives that guide the making of this travel book. Specifically writing about his desire to nurture a popular understanding of the capital, he stresses the need to build a shared understanding of Japan's political and cultural center. The preface begins as follows:

Heianjō is located in the village of Uda in Atago country of Yamashiro province. After Emperor Jinmu (711–585 BCE, r. 660–585 BCE) founded

40. Indeed, Matsuno Genkei wrote in his preface to *A Record of the Capital in Japan* (*Fusō keikashi*) that he aimed to replace the original *fudoki* of Yamashiro province, *Yamashiro no kuni fudoki*, so that the style of *Fusō keikashi* resembles *fudoki* and it became a smaller-scale version of it. Matsuno, "Fusō keikashi," 1.

41. *Fusō keikashi*, for example, adopts the headings from *The Record of the Great Ming* (*Da Ming Yitong zhi*) and structures the book within the sophisticated classificatory system of Ming China, ranging from the capital (*keijō*), shrines (*jinja*), mountains and mountain peaks (*sangaku*), to checkpoints and bridges (*sekiryō* or *kan'ryō*). Matsuno, "Fusō keikashi."

a capital of Kashihara in Yamato province for the first time, subsequent emperors established thirty-five royal places (*miyadokoro*) and changed the location of the capital over forty times. . . . This capital, Heianjō, is tranquil and peaceful. The capital was named through reference to the number of people who happily celebrated it . . . Our Japan (*waga hi no moto*) has good manners and customs (*fūki*); the earth (*tochi*) is deep and fertile, and the people are noble. Additionally, there are abundant harvests and a good living environment. Japan is superior to other countries in many aspects, but our people do not know this. They do not know anything at all about how the ancient people came to name our country *Toyo Akitsushima* (Islands of abundant harvests in the autumn), or how the Chinese people came to respectfully call Japan a "country of men of virtue" (*kunshikoku*), a "country that never dies" (*fujikoku*), or why Chinese people spoke highly of Japan.[42]

The preface goes on to state that if those who live in the capital (*miyako*) know so little about the extraordinary aspects of the city, those who live outside surely know nothing about it. Ekiken insisted one had to feel that one was part of this capital and this was "the earth of my land" (*waga tsuchi*).[43] What motivated him to write this book was therefore his desire to inform readers about the outstanding quality of the *fūdo* of the capital (*miyako no fūdo*), allowing them to experience it. By publishing this book, Ekiken aimed to foster a shared understanding of the capital of the country, and he stated that he had selected the sites for the visitors to see (*miru beki tokoro dokoro*) by carefully focusing on the sense or feeling of a place, based on the *fūdo* of the capital and the feeling of "earth."

In his understanding, it was only natural for a royal capital to be built in the location of Heianjō because it was topographically an ideal place, a "heavenly capital" (*tenpu no kuni*), surrounded with unbeatably beautiful and rich nature (*sansen suido*), one that yielded abundant autumn harvests.[44] The area had a river to the east, a broad avenue to the west, a basin to the south, and a hill to the north, and it was perceived as being "more perfect" than the international capital of Chang'an in ancient China. The Japanese planners from the capital worked to actualize the

---

42. Kaibara E., "Keijō shōran," 1–2.
43. Kaibara E., "Keijō shōran," 2.
44. Toby, "Why Leave Nara?"

ideal space at this site in Heianjō.[45] It was explained that Emperor Kanmu (737–806, r. 781–806) moved the capital to Heianjō in 794 because the area was protected by the four guardian gods of the Blue Dragon (*seiryū*) in the east, the Scarlet Bird (*suzaku*) in the south, the White Tiger (*byakko*) in the west, and the Black Tortoise (*genbu*) in the north, perfectly corresponding with the four gods (*shijin sōō*).[46] Even though the terrain was already ideal, the emperor built another guardian of *shōgunzuka* on top of the Higashiyama mountain range to protect the capital.[47] As Ekiken explains, the spatially perfect correspondence between the capital city and the four gods was the reason for the abundance of crops and the extraordinary sense associated with the capital.

Here, we no longer find references to the preeminence of the east and it being the location of abundant *ki* (chapter 2). The idea of the topographic perfection of the capital prioritizes topography over history, but the idea of *shijin sōō* privileges the divine connections to the land, not metaphysical relations or the movement of *ki*. Based on the idea of the *shijin sōō* as the sign of supremacy of the *fūdo* of the capital, Ekiken divided the space associated with the capital into eight segments, following the twelve-sexagenary cycle that determined the time of day (*jikoku*) and the four major points of the compass (*hōi*) (figures 3.1 and 3.2). The first day of the tour begins with an exploration of the eastern suburbs of the capital and progresses clockwise from there over the next nine days. Ekiken adhered to the idea of the East as the place where things began in his tour of the capital. However, when the journey reaches the northwestern part of the capital, in the area called Sannoo, it takes a surprising turn, heading back south, north, and again south, and then on to the neighboring province of Ōmi. This route goes back and forth between

45. Berque, *Japan: Cities and Social Bonds*, 50. Chang'an was not set in a perfect terrain because the "Wei River flowed to the north," not toward the south.

46. Kaibara E., "Zoku wakan meisū," 867. Takei and Keane, *Sakuteiki*, 83–84. The belief in *fenshui* influenced the idea of *Shijin sōō*, an ideal topography for the four Taoist gods.

47. *Kyō warabe* also lists *shōgunzuka* as one of the places to see. The description in *Kyō warabe* is very similar to Ekiken's, stating that *shōgunzuka* was built during the reign of Emperor Kanmu as a protective deity (*shugoshin*) for the capital. It was an eight-*shaku*-long (about eight feet) clay statue (*dogūjin*), with a bow and arrows. Whenever disturbances occurred in the realm, it is said that the *shōgunzuka* shook the ground. Nakagawa, *Kyō warabe*, 28–29.

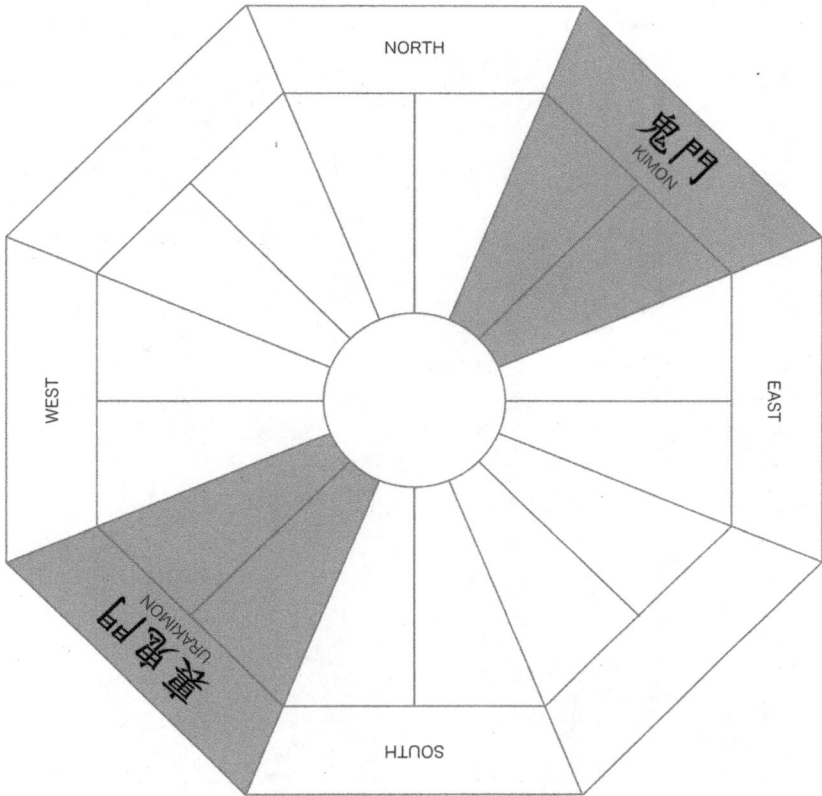

FIGURE 3.1. Direction chart. This chart indicates the two unlucky quarters of the "demon's gate" (*kimon*) and the "reverse demon's gate" (*urakimon*). The directions of northeast (*ushi tora*) and its symmetrical other, southwest (*hitsuji saru*), were commonly perceived to be the entry points of evil spirits. Although the twelve zodiac signs of the rat, the ox, the tiger, the rabbit, the dragon, the snake, the horse, the goat, the monkey, the rooster, the dog, and the pig represented time that corresponded with the hour, month, and year cycle, they also signified the direction. Created by Yoh Kawano.

south and north and appears to be random, but if we conceptualize two parts in the seventeen-day tour, they seem to progress in a logical fashion: the first nine days follow a clockwise direction, whereas the second half is devoted to the exploration of the northeast section.

Although we cannot know Ekiken's intentions in relation to this route or the reason for breaking down the capital into eight spaces, my hypothesis is that, considering the strange route, Ekiken relied on divination

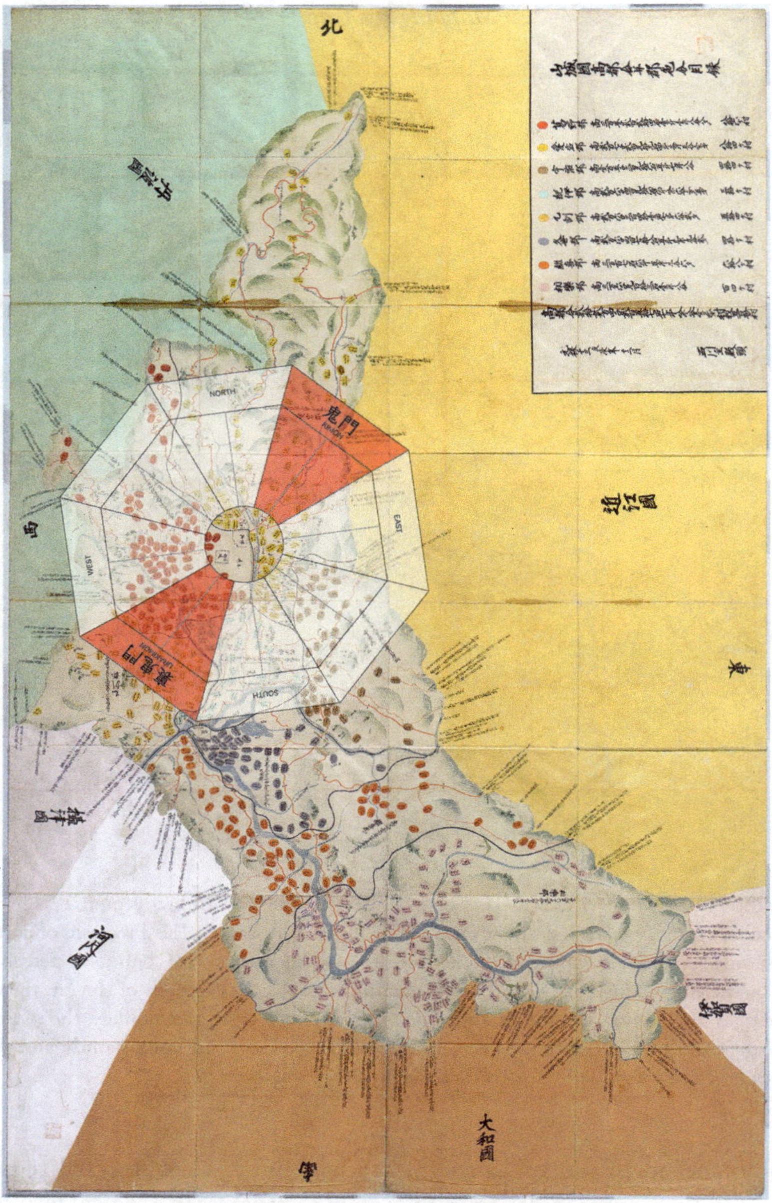

FIGURE 3.2. Topography of the capital of Japan. If figure 3.1 is imposed onto the provincial map of Yamashiro, it becomes clear that the capital adhered to the ideal topography, with four corners secured by four gods (*shijin sōō*). The direction of northeast is guarded by the most sacred mountain in early modern Japan, Mt. Hiei, while Mt. Yawata and the Iwashimizu Hachimangū Shrine are located in the opposite direction (*urakimon*) to protect the capital. Created by Yoh Kawano.

knowledge, which was popular in the eighteenth century.[48] As historians in Japan have amply demonstrated, the use of fortune-telling was prevalent in the early modern era, and information about it was spread via popular encyclopedic reference books, such as the *setsuyōshū* and *The Book of Divination* (*Ōzassho*), which encouraged people to avoid unlucky times and directions.[49] These books offered an explanation for how to determine good directions for a certain event and how to predict the appropriate time and day for an activity by providing numerous illustrations and charts. These lucky or unlucky measurements originated in the practice of the "way of *yin* and *yang*" (*on'yōdō*) and were used in the imperial court during the Heian period. However, as Umeda Chihiro argues, by the early eighteenth century the knowledge of *on'yōdō* consisted of various portions of knowledge in relation to "calendar and astrology" (*rekisen*).[50] Along with astronomy (*tenmon*), fortune-telling, which sought to read people's palms and faces (*sōhō*), and other methods, books like *Ōzassho* standardized the popular practice derived from the *yin* and *yang* knowledge in everyday life.[51]

The steady sales enjoyed by these books implies that ordinary people were involved in predicting the future so as to avoid ominous things that might occur in everyday life. Yokoyama Toshio's study highlights the tenacious and steady proliferation of *ōzassho*-based knowledge over the 200 years after the seventeenth century. In spite of scholarly opinions, including that of Ekiken, who criticized the "rootless," illogical," and "false" information that originated in *ōzassho*-like books, commercial publications flourished.[52] Ekiken often expressed his suspicion of the recommendations made in *ōzassho* books, but intriguingly, his tour of the capital seems to integrate knowledge about how to avoid unfavorable times and spaces.[53] Given his

48. Kawase, *Shoshigaku nyūmon* and *Zōho Kokatsujiban no kenkyū.*

49. Hashimoto Manpei, "Kaisetsu: 'Ōzassho' no keitō to tokushoku," 147–62; Mizuno, *Eki, fūsui, reki, yōjō, shosei*, 10; Yamada, *Hōi yomitoki jiten*; Yokota, "Shomotsu o meguru hitobito," 2–8.

50. Umeda, "Rekisensho no shuppan to ryūtsū," 111.

51. Endō K., *Kinsei on'yōdōshi no kenkyū*, 528–33; Kawasaki, "Kinsei shakai ni okeru rekisen no jittai"; Morita T., "Daizassho kenkyū josetsu." See also Ōno I., *Ganzan Daishi mikuji-bon no kenkyū*; Suzuki I., *On'yōdō.*

52. Yokoyama, "Ōzassho kō," 30–31.

53. For example, in *A Collection of Life Principles* (*Isei shūyō*, 1714) Ekiken wrote that *Ōzassho* includes many theories about dietary restrictions that draw on the theories of *yin yang* scholars. However, those theories cannot be verified with the information in

scholarly authority, this might perhaps be a gesture to describe the "logical" and proper way of touring the capital, during which one might run into unlucky spirits, precisely because the capital lay on topographically perfect ground in relation to the four gods.

Here it is appropriate to provide today's readers with a visualization of the tour, even though *Keijō shōran* offers no maps because Ekiken uses the navigational method of the "narrative map." The daily maps associated with the tour (figures 3.3–3.16) help us better grasp the itinerary, routes, and scale. The basemaps I have used for these daily maps are contained in the *Genroku kuniezu* for Yamashiro province and Ōmi province, selected to take advantage of the contemporaneous information contained in the map and Ekiken's guidebook. *Genroku kuniezu* allows us to see the locations of temples and shrines, plus rivers and mountains, in the way Ekiken saw them as he traveled throughout Yamashiro and Ōmi provinces. Indeed, his tour covers most of the places marked in the area of Yamashiro and Ōmi *kuniezu*, which indicates his attempt to verify the place names, locations, and historical background of all the places, as depicted in the official maps.[54] His diary shows that he had occasion to look at the provincial maps that were kept in the domain's library.[55]

---

the books of fauna and flora (Honzōgaku) of the ancient past. Kaibara E., "Isei shūyō," 815–16. At the same time, we find that Ekiken was intrigued by the presence of *yin yang* scholars, and he made a special note about three scholars in Nakabaru village in Onga country in Chikuzen. He added that there were about fifty *yin yang* scholars throughout the country. Kaibara E., "Chikuzen no kuni zoku fudoki," 327–29.

54. As mentioned more than once in this study, the capital was burned to the ground as a result of the destruction during the Sengoku period, and many sites were in the process of being reconstructed or fully restored in the seventeenth century. Ekiken made reference to these historical changes in his guidebooks. For example, in *Washū junranki* he made a very specific reference to the statue of Buddha in Tōdaiji. Today, the big statue of Buddha is housed in the Daibutsu Hall (*daibutsuden*) in the Tōdaiji, but Ekiken recorded that the Buddha statue stood directly on the ground, without a roof to protect him from the rain and wind. The *kuniezu* of Yamato province indicates an empty square labeled "Daibutsu," without the inclusion of a hall, indicating that the Buddha statue stood outside, just as he described.

55. The catalog of Ekiken's library shows that he owned a copy of an "Atlas of Japan" (*Nihon bunkei-zu*); a "Map of Provinces of Japan" (*Nihon kakkoku-zu*), which consists of sixty-eight provinces; forty-three maps of "Map of Japan" (*Nihon kokuzu*); three big and small maps of "Map of Japan" (*Nihon-zu*); and one map of each of the following:

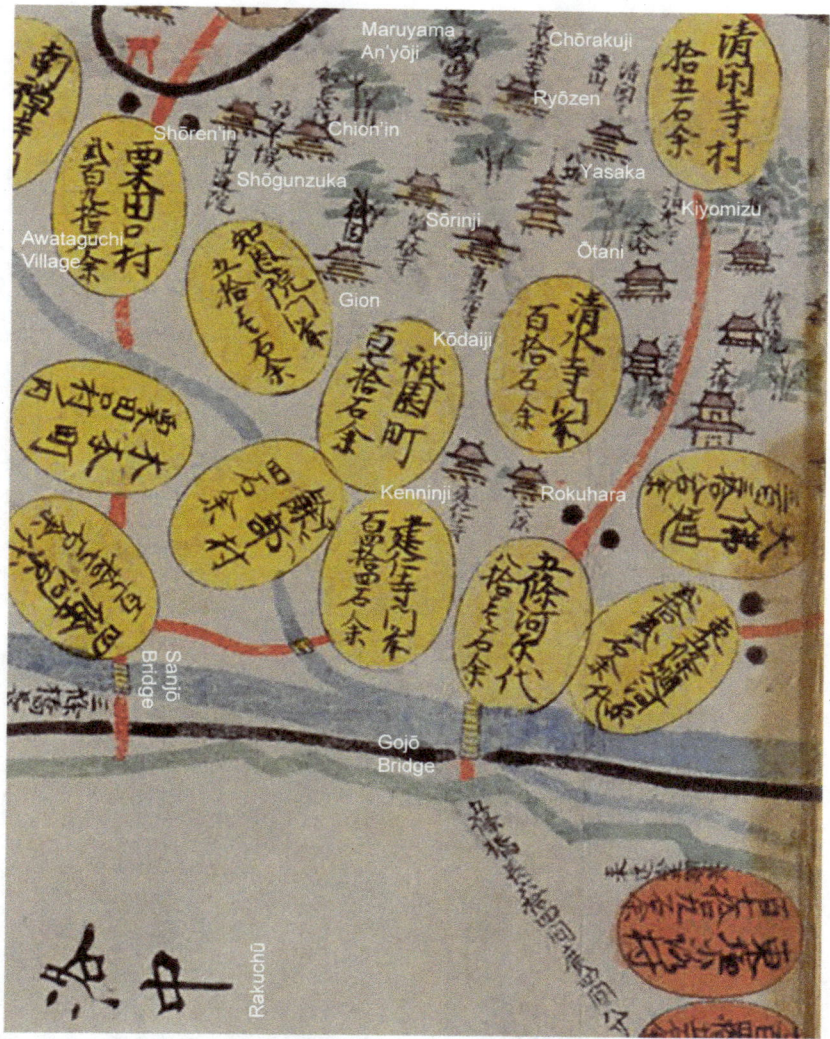

Maruyama
An'yōji

Chōrakuji

Ryōzen

Shōren'in

Chion'in

Yasaka

Shōgunzuka

Kiyomizu

Awataguchi
Village

Sōrinji

Ōtani

Gion

Kōdaiji

Kenninji

Rokuhara

Sanjō
Bridge

Gojō
Bridge

Rakuchū

FIGURE 3.3.   Day 1 of the tour. This map shows a path from Sanjō Bridge in the center of the capital to the eastern part of the suburb. Ekiken writes that the first day takes "a path from Sanjō through Nawate village, and then to Kenninji, Rokuhara, Kiyomizu, and Awataguchi." The full distance is about four *ri* (ten miles). For figures 3.3 to 3.16, I added labels to the *Genroku kuniezu* of Yamashiro province. Courtesy of the Digital Archive of National Archives of Japan.

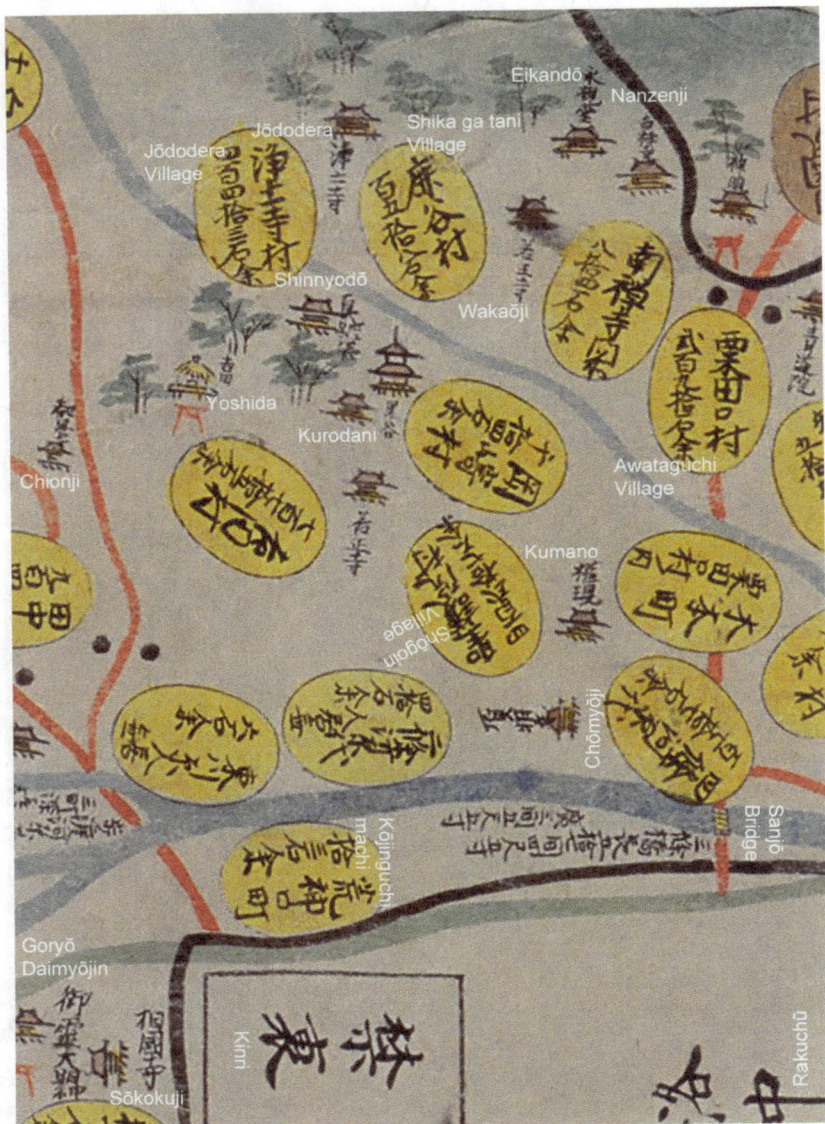

FIGURE 3.4. Day 2 in the eastern part of the suburb, centering on Nanzenji to Ginkakuji, Yoshida, and Shōgoin. The entire distance is about 4.5 *ri* (eleven miles).

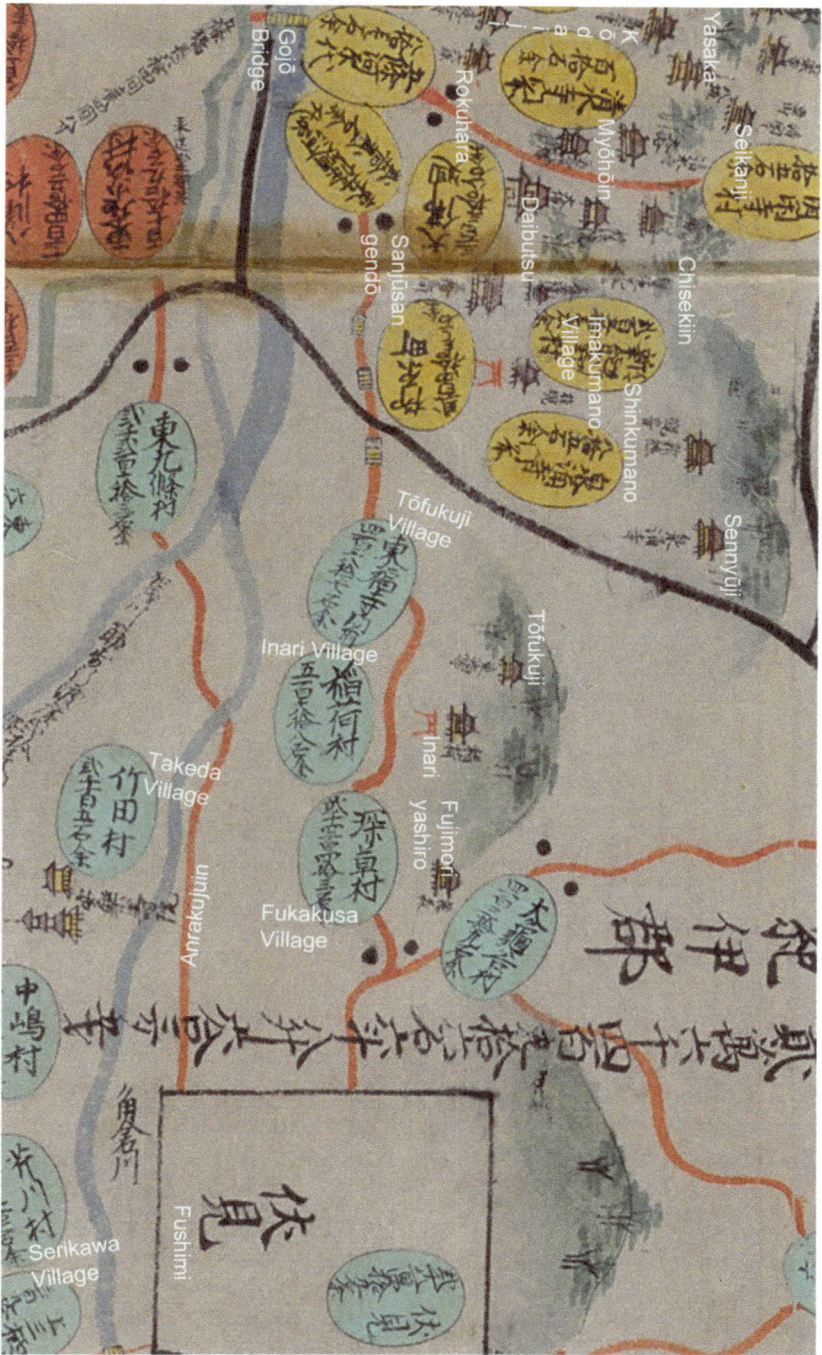

FIGURE 3.5. Day 3 in Fushimi. The entire distance is about 6.5 *ri* (sixteen miles), and Ekiken advises that it is necessary to "leave early in the morning."

FIGURE 3.6.   Day 4 in Kami no daigo, in the southeastern part of the suburb. The entire distance is over seven *ri* (seventeen miles), and again he advises that one must "leave early in the morning."

The itinerary of the tour reveals a number of anomalies. First, on days 8, 10, and 11, there is a narrow focus on a single destination: a mountain. Even though the number of sites to visit on each day varies, the tour generally focuses on sites such as shrines and temples, villages, bridges, moun-

"Map of Kyoto" (*Kyō-zu*), "Map of Edo" (*Edo-zu*), "Map of Ise Province" (*Ise-zu*), "Map of Osaka" (*Osaka-zu*), "Map of China" (*Chūka yochizu*), and "Map of Mt. Yoshino" (*Yoshinoyama-zu*). Kyūshū Shiryō Kankōkai, "Ganko mokuroku" and "Kazōsho mokuroku," 23, 25, 42, and 55.

FIGURE 3.7. Day 5 in Uji. The entire distance is about eight *ri* (twenty miles), and he gives the same advice regarding the need to leave early in the morning.

Table 3.1

Places Mentioned during the 17-Day Tour of the Capital, Days 1–5

	Day 1	Day 2	Day 3	Day 4	Day 5
Bridges	Sanjō kobashi Sanjō ōhashi Shirakawabashi Yamatobashi		Gojō no hashi		Bungobashi Ujibashi
Fields				Ogurusuno	
Forests/mountains	Otowayama Mt. Ryōzen/Washi no oyama	Nyoigatake Shōgoin no mori	Amidagamine Jōnan kami no mori	Kasadoriyama Kazan Ōsakayama Otowayama Ura no nakayama	Asahiyama Ōbakusan Yashimatōge
Gongen/Myōjin	Jishu Gongen	Kasuga shisho Myōjin Kumano Gongen Ryūraku no ike	Kumano Gongen	Kiyotaki Gongen	
Lakes/ponds		Ginkakuji no sensui			A large pond at Maki no shima
Mounds	Chikushōzuka Shikamazuka Shōgunzuka		Mimizuka in front of Hōkōji	Shigehira no kubizuka	

Rivers	Kamogawa Shirakawa Takasegawa		Kamogawa Takasegawa		Ujigawa Yamabuki no se
Rocks/stones	Mekura ishi at Jishu Gongen			Fujito no ukisu no iwa Kamo no Chōmei no ōishi at Hino	
Shrines	Amaterasu daijingū Jishu Gongen no yashiro Somin shōrai no yashiro	Kasuga Myōjin no yashiro Kumano Gongen no yashiro/ Wakaōji Yoshida	Fujimori no yashiro Gokō no miya jinja Inari taisha Shinkumano	Kiyotaki Gongen no yashiro Miyaji no Iyamasu no yashiro Usa hachiman no yashiro	Ama no oshihomimi no mikoto no yashiro Fuji no mori no yashiro Hashi hime no yashiro
Springs	Reisen at An'yōji	Banmuji no seisen Ginkakuji no sensui			
Teahouses		Hyakumanben Nanzenji Shinnyodō The first tea room at Tōkyūdō		Kanshuji	Rokujizō village Uji Kōshōji

(continued)

Table 3.1
(continued)

	Day 1	Day 2	Day 3	Day 4	Day 5
Temples	An'yōji	Banmuji	Anrakujuin	Daigoji (Kami Daigo)	Bukkokuji
	Aragoji	Chionji	Chisekiin	Daigoji (Shimo Daigo)	Byōdōin
	Chion'in	Chōmyōji	Hōkōji	Gankeiji	Daihōji (perished)
	Chōrakuji	Eikandō/Zenrinji	Hōtōji	Iwamadera	Eshin'in
	Gion Kanjin'in	Ginkakuji	Manjuji in Tōfukuji	Kanshuji	Manpukuji
	Higashi honganji	Hiden'in	Myōhōin	Sanpōin	Mimurodoji
	Hōkanji	Konkai Kōmyōji	Ōtani	Seikanji	Tani no yakushi
	Isshin'in	Kōunji	Rengaōin/33-gendō	Zuishin'in	Uji Kōshōji
	Jōjuin	Nanzenji	Sennyūji		
	Kenninji	Shinnyodō	Shinkumano Kannon		
	Kenshōji		Tōfukuji		
	Kiyomizudera				
	Kōdaiji				
	Kōshindō/Zenkōin				
	Kyōkakudō				
	Oku no in				
	Rokuharamitsudera				
	Shōbōji				
	Shōren'in				
	Sōrinji				
	Taisanji				
	Tamuradō				
	Yasui Shinshōji				
	Zuisenji				

Tombs	Hideyoshi's wife's tomb at Kōdaiji		Hideyoshi's tomb near Hōkōji Imperial tombs at Sennyūji Monk Shinran's tomb at Ōtani Retired Emperor Toba's mausoleum at Anrakujuin	Emperor Daigo's in Shimo Daigo Emperor Suzaku's in Shimo Daigo Retired Emperor Kōsō's mausoleum near Seikanji Tamuramaru's tomb in Ogurusu	Tang Monk Ingen's tomb at Manpukuji
Valleys		Dangōtani Shikagatani	Kasumi no tani	Kasadori no tani Komatsudani Shirudani	
Waterfalls	Otowa no taki	Komagataki Nyoigataki The Heike's last battle at Nyoigatake			
Other sites	Cherry trees in Chion'in, Gion Kanjin'in, and Jishu Gongen	Shōgoin's yaezakura	Hideyoshi's old castle in Fushimi Jōnan rikyū site in Takeda Maples at Tōfukuji's Tsūtenkyō bridge Peach trees in Fushimi	Cherry trees in Shimo Daigo Maple trees in Kasadori Misasagi village in Yamashina Plum trees in Hino	Yoshimasa's suicide at Ōgi no shiba Cherry trees at Uji Kōshōji and Daigo Fireflies in Uji Kōshōji Tea masters in Daihōji and Uji

Table 3.2

Places Mentioned during the 17-Day Tour of the Capital, Days 6–11

	Day 6	Day 7	Day 8	Day 9	Day 10	Day 11
Bridges		Togetsukyō	Kiyotakigawa no hashi	Takahashi	Kinbashi Yodo no kobashi Yodo no ōhashi	
Fields	Ōharano	Uchino				
Forests/mountains	Oshioyama	Arashiyama Kameyama Ogurayama	Atagoyama	Gochisan Makinoosan Narabi no oka Ōuchiyama Takaosan Toganoosan	Horagatōge Otokoyama/ Yawatayama	Hieizan/ Tendaisan Shimeigahora
Gongen/Myōjin	Kasuga Myōjin Mukō Myōjin	Konoshima Myōjin Matsuo Myōjin Zaō Gongen		Hirano Myōjin		
Lakes/ponds	Saeno no numa	Ōsawa no ike		Daidō Hōshi ga ashigata ike Kōtaku no ike Obitoriike Ryūanji no ike		
Mounds	Yotsuzuka				Onnazuka Otokozuka	

Rivers	Katsuragawa Mukōgawa/ Kitsunegawa Ōigawa	Kadonogawa Katsuragawa Ōigawa	Kiyotakigawa	Kamiyagawa Kiyotakigawa	Hōjōgawa Kinkawa Yodogawa
Rocks/stones				Awasedo ishi from Gochisan Kinkakuji's ishi fudō Sazare ishi	
Shrines	Kanjin no yashiro Kasuga Myōjin no yashiro Kisshō tennyo no yashiro Mukō Myōjin no yashiro	Ichiidani no jinja Konoshima Myōjin no yashiro Matsunoo/Matsuo yashiro No no miya Umemiya Zaō Gongen no yashiro	Atago jinja	Fukuōji no yashiro Fune no yashiro Hirano no yashiro Kitano tenmangū Tenjin no yashiro Tokihira Daijin no yashiro	Iwashimizu hachimangū Kōra no yashiro Yahatagū
Springs		Seisen at Konoshima Myōjin			
Teahouses	Mukō Myōjin no yashiro	Hōrinji Rinsenji		Kitano tenmangū	

(continued)

Table 3.2
(continued)

	Day 6	Day 7	Day 8	Day 9	Day 10	Day 11
Temples	Kisshōin	Chōfukuji	Tsuki no wa	Asahidera	Iwashimizu Gokokuji	Enryakuji
	Nishi Iwakura	Daihikaku		Higashi mukai no Kannon	Tōji	Jizōdō
	Sankoji	Daitokuji		Jizōin		Kazōin
	Shōjiji	Hachiokadera/ Kōryūji		Kinkakuji/ Rokuon'in		Kōdō
	Tōji	Hōrinji		Kōzanji		Konpon chūdō
	Yoshiminedera	Myōshinji		Myōkōji Hannyadera		Kurodani
		Ninnaji		Ninnaji		Monjurō
		Nison'in		Rengeji		Monk Jien's Hall
		Ōjōin		Ryūanji		Mudōji
		Rinsenji		Saimyōji		Sōrindō
		Sanpōji		Saionji		
		Seiryōji/Saga no Shakadō		Sanpōji		
		Tenryūji		Sanson'in		
				Takaodera		
				Tōjiin		

Tombs		Tang Monk Chōnen's in Saga	Emperor Seiwa's in Mizunoo	Emperor Kōkō's near Ninnaji	
				Kitano Tenjin's mother's tomb	
Valleys		Ichiidani			
Waterfalls		Nakoso no taki (trace)	Higurashi no taki		Otowa no taki
		Tonase no taki			
Other sites	Nagaokakyō site near Kuze	Arashiyama's cherry trees	Views from Mt. Atago	Takaodera's bell (Takao no sanzetsu)	
	Shōjiji's maple and cherry trees	Ninnaji's yaezakura		Umegahata's plum trees	
	Yoshiminedera for cherry trees and eye medicine	Rinsenji's garden			
		Tenryūji's garden			

Table 3.3

Places Mentioned during the 17-Day Tour of the Capital, Days 12–17

	Day 12	Day 13	Day 14	Day 15	Day 16	Day 17
Bridges	Koeda no hashi				Sanjō no ōhashi Seta no hashi Shirakawabashi	Senzoku no hashi
Fields			Ōhara/Ohara		Awazu no hara	Miareno Murasakino Rendaino
Forests/ mountains		Kuramayama		Hiranogatake	Kagamiyama	Funaokayama
				Kagamiyama Kiryūyama Mikamiyama	Kōjin'yama Ōsakayama Ushioyama	Hieizan Kataoka no mori Kōyama Mikageyama Tadasu no mori Takagamine Ukita no mori
				Nagarasan		
Gongen/Myōjin	Kawakami Myōjin Yodo hime Myōjin	Yuki Daimyōjin		Karasaki Myōjin Shinra Myōjin	Shoha Daimyōjin	Kamo no Myōjin
Lakes/ponds		Mizoroike		Lake Biwa	Lake Biwa	
Mounds	Toba no koizuka					
Rivers	Kamogawa Katsuragawa Yodogawa	Minamikawa	Kamogawa	Kamogawa	Setagawa Shirakawa Tagamigawa	Kamogawa Kōyagawa Mitarashigawa (Nara no ogawa)

Rocks/stones	Fugo oroshi no ishi Sōjō ga dani no ishi		Butsuzō no ōiwa at Sennichidera Rock production in Shirakawa village Stone rooms (anashitsu) in Hyakugōin		A small hill in Takagamine (iwakage) Kagami ishi in Takagamine A rock pillar (ishi no hashira) at Senzoku Bridge
Shrines	Rikyū hachiman Tennō no yashiro Yodo hime Myōjin no yashiro	Emon no yashiro Kifune no yashiro Yuki Daimyōjin no yashiro Kajii no miya Okage no yashiro	Hachiōji no yashiro Karasaki Myōjin no yashiro San'ō/Hiyoshi no yashiro Shinra Myōjin no yashiro Tōshōgū	Ryūō no yashiro Shinmei no yashiro Shoha Daimyōjin no yashiro Tatebe hachima no yashiro Tawara Tōta Hidesato no yashiro	Hashimoto no yashiro Imamiya Iwamoto no yashiro Kamigamo jinja Kawai no yashiro Mikage no yashiro Mioya no yashiro Nara no yashiro Shimogamo no yashiro Ukita no yashiro

(continued)

Table 3.3
(continued)

	Day 12	Day 13	Day 14	Day 15	Day 16	Day 17
Springs			Oboro no shimizu Zegai no mizu		Hashirii no kiyoki izumi Keage no mizu Seki no shimizu	Seisen near Mitarashigawa
Teahouses	Rikyū's tearoom in Yamazaki	Kurama village		Karasaki	Hashirii Matsumoto	Imamiya
Temples	Hōshakuji Kannonji Renchōji Takaradera Tōji	Bishamondō Fudarakuji Kuramadera Myōjuin Sainenji	Jakkōin Shōkō no Amida	Hyakugōin Jigen Taishi no tera Miidera/Onjōji Sennichidera Shōgun jizōdō Taka Kannon/Junrei Kannon Taka Kannon in southern Ōmi	Genpōji Ishiyama Kannondō Jūzenji Miidera Sekidera Taka Kannon	Imamiya Daitokuji Jinkōin Jōkyōdō/Jōshōji Nichiren dansho temple Reigenji Senbondera Shōdenji Unrin'in
Tombs	Monk Mongaku's wife's tomb (Koizuka)	Ono no Komachi's tomb at Fudarakuji	Kenreimon'in's small mausoleum near Jakkōin		Emperor Tenji's mausoleum in Kagamiyama	Emperor Ichijō's mausoleum in Takagamine

Valleys		Rōeidani Sōjōgatani	Nishi no tani Ryūkokudani			
Waterfalls		Ryūō no bakufu	Otonashi no taki		Otowa no taki	
Other sites	Aki no yama garden at Kamitoba Imperial visits to Serikawa village Yodo Castle	Armor of Benkei and Yoshitsune in Kurama Fujiwara no Kintō read poems at Rōeidani Saigyō's home at Sainenji Sōjōgatani is Tengu's home	Kamaburo treatment in Yase	Karasaki no ippon matsu Sakamoto's many stone bridges	Imai Kanehira's tomb in Awazu no hara Kiso Yoshinaka's tomb in Zeze Hinooka execution ground (haritsukeba) Murasaki wrote *The Tale of Genji* at Ishiyama Kannondō Zeze Castle	Tombs of Murasaki and Ono no Takamura in Senbondera An old castle at Funaokayama Gardens in Tadasu no mori Karasukiga hana, east of Mt. Funaoka

tains, poetic places, and the like, except for these three days (see tables 3.1–3.3). Second, another abnormal aspect of the itinerary is the inclusion of Ōmi province. If this tour is truly "the Excellent Views of Kyoto," as Berry has translated it, it is certainly misleading because Ōmi was not part of Kyoto or Yamashiro province and not even one of the five home provinces (*gokinai*) of Yamashiro, Yamato, Kawachi, Settsu, and Izumi. The assumption is that the capital in Ekiken's mind was more conceptually shaped, not bounded by geographic borders. Finally, the most peculiar aspect of the itinerary is the irregular direction, which avoids the south during the first nine days, as mentioned earlier. The tour returns to visit Mt. Yawata in the south on day 10, and the second part of the tour heads mostly toward the northeast area of the capital, Mt. Hiei, on day 11; the northern mountains of Kurama and Kifune on day 13; Ōhara on day 14; and then the neighboring province of Ōmi, which is directly behind Mt. Hiei. The tour returns to the southern area on day 12 to visit Yamazaki before veering toward the northern mountainous area. Notably, the two irregular visits to the south are inserted between visits to the north, which have the sacred mountainous areas surrounding Mt. Hiei, standing guard over the direction of the "demon's gate" (*kimon*), a place where evil spirits were believed to enter the capital.

The order of the journey is confusing for today's readers, but considering that the direction of Mt. Yawata is what is known as a "reverse demon's gate" (*urakimon*), another gateway for evil spirits, we can well imagine that this location and the direction of *kimon* were highly charged with supernatural forces. Both are locations where the divine deities were believed to have fought off evil spirits as they defended the capital. The journey appears to avoid this direction by "going underground" (*kuguru*) and resurfacing in the western region on day 6 to continue its clockwise movement until day 9. When the first part of the journey is over, the trip returns to the south, where Mt. Yawata is located. Day 11 is when the tour heads up to Mt. Hiei, the most sacred area within the capital. By perceiving this move to be a symbolic act of "going under," the traveler is seen as being cleansed into a purer being before going on to visit Mt. Hiei. Hattori Yukio explains that in traditional theater performances, this act of "going underground" is associated with a gesture indicating a movement out of this world (*zokkai*) and the entrance as a purified being into a world of different dimensions (*ijigen no sekai*).[56] Together with the standardization of practice on avoiding bad directions in daily life, it might be plausible to assume that Ekiken's tour incorporated this idea by conceptualizing the area of *urakimon*, where Mt. Yawata stands, as a guardian mountain (*chinzan*), a supernatural space to cleanse oneself before entering the world of different dimensions. The journey would go smoothly as long as the traveler had been cleaned by visiting *urakimon* on days 10 and 12, that is, prior to visiting the most sacred space within the capital, the focus of the second half of the journey.[57] If we follow this hypothesis, Ekiken's tour embodied the increasing popularity of fortune-telling and his wish to educate his readers with fact-based knowledge. As he emphasizes in his preface, this tour selected the places to see in the capital to understand its *fūdo*. It is possible that he presented them in the correct order to convey the distinct quality of the capital of *shinkoku* Japan.

Narrativizing the Capital of "Shinkoku" Japan

Ekiken's tour generally starts somewhere in central Kyoto, either Sanjō Bridge, Tōji Temple, or Gojō Bridge, then heads toward specific destinations and at the end of the day returns to central Kyoto. Notably, on the tenth and eleventh days, the tours do not start in central Kyoto but originate near the mountains, as if the traveler was supposed to know how to start the day at Mt. Hiei and Mt. Yawata, hence they were omitted from

56.   Hattori Y., *Ōinaru koya*, 110–21. Elsewhere in the book, Hattori writes about other symbolic meanings attributed to certain places in early modern Japan, such as the pleasure quarters, the bath-houses (*yudono*), and the theaters, in addition to shrines and temples. The visitor made an emblematic gesture to travel to these sites via bridge or boat across the river, lakes, or sea, or narrow path or gate. Similar to the religious architecture, the sites of pleasure in the medieval eras were viewed as spaces that were extraordinary (*hinichijō*) and out of this world (*ijigen*). This sense of otherworldliness sometimes made the spaces of pleasure sacred.

57.   The most sacred area of Mt. Hiei is Shimeigahora (the peaks of Mt. Shimei), whose name originates in the mountain peaks of Simingshan of Tiantai Buddhism in Tang China. Japan knowledge, *Nihon rekishi chimei taikei*, https://japanknowledge.com /library/en/.

the text. The lack of departure points on these days may indicate that *Keijō shōran* was not written as a document to be carried; alternatively it might suggest that the readers might easily obtain travel and accommodation information in the areas near Mt. Hiei and Mt. Yawata.[58] Overall, the seventeen-day tour features the site of the former imperial court, including the ancient capitals, the locations of imperial villas, and the imperial tombs and burial grounds, all of which are spread around Yamashiro province and beyond. The tour highlights temples and shrines, natural features, poetically and historically famous sites, and others, but there is no explanation for privileging these sites in relation to others. Rather, the in-depth detail relating to the identity of the deities; the historical background of the shrines, temples, and their festivals; and the extraordinary scenic beauty that Ekiken reported deep in the mountainous area signal that the implicit story line of his narration is to highlight the presence of the divine spirits.

For example, the itinerary for day 6 is filled with visits to temples and shrines in the spirit-rich areas known as Ōharano and Mt. Oshio in the western suburbs, which was the home of Emperor Junna (786–840, r. 823–33), his burial site being in Mt. Oshio (figure 3.8). The tour for day 6 sets out from Tōji Temple and leads down to Kuze village, introducing the reader to the former capital of Nagaokakyō, before eventually moving down to Yamazaki (figure 3.9). Yamazaki was the former capital of Nagaokakyō, and it housed an imperial villa during the reign of Emperor Saga (786–842, r. 809–23).[59] In addition to the legacy of the liveliness and prosperity of the ancient capital, the reader learns more about how this area was historically connected with the deities. The concentration of temples and shrines in the area indicates the existence of various divine spirits, as outlined here:

58. At the same time, I point out that Miyamoto Tsuneichi argues that Ekiken's guidebooks were important canonical texts for travelers, who referenced them closely and carried them during the trip. For example, Yasuda Airō from Tosa traveled to Nara in 1838 and toured the province by following Ekiken's *Yamato meguri.* Yasuda A., "Yamato meguri nikki." See also Miyamoto, "Tanken, kikō, chishi: saigoku hen: jo," 3.

59. Kurokawa, *Yōshū fushi,* 35. In this work, Kurokawa paired Yamashiro province with the region of Yōshū in China, where the ancient capital, Chang'an, was located. See also Tachikawa, *Kyōtogaku no koten Yōshū fushi.*

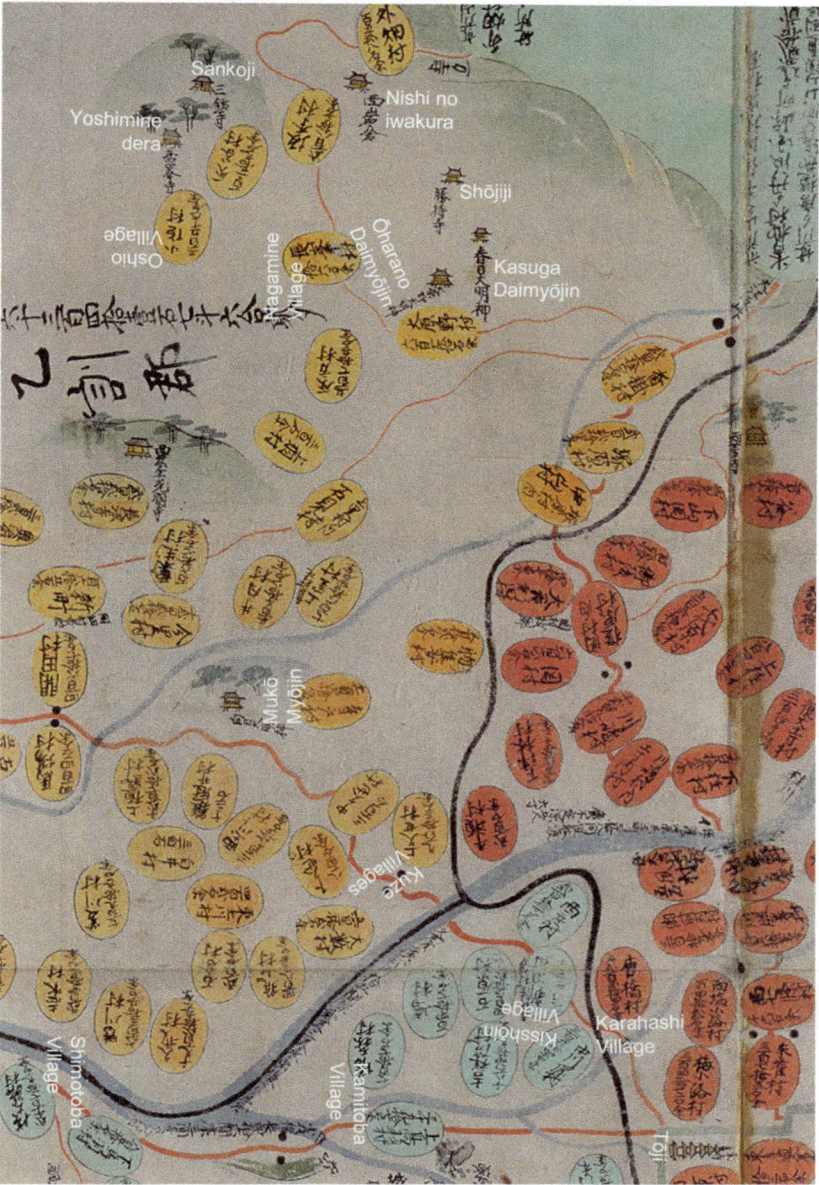

FIGURE 3.8. Day 6 in Ōharano and Oshio. The entire distance is over five *ri* (twelve miles). River crossing by boat (*funa watashi*) is available at Katsura River.

- Ōharano: There is a shrine here dedicated to Kasuga Myōjin. There is also a temple called Shōjiji, which has a votive tablet (*gaku*) written by Michikaze [Ono no Michikaze (894–966), a renowned calligrapher]. There are many Japanese maple (*momiji*) trees, and also cherry blossom trees called Saigyō zakura [a monk/poet Saigyō (1118–90)'s cherry blossom trees]. People call this temple a temple of flowers. There is a pond in front of the temple, known as Saeno Pond. It is a *meisho*.
- Mt. Oshio is a mountain that stands above the Ōharano fields.

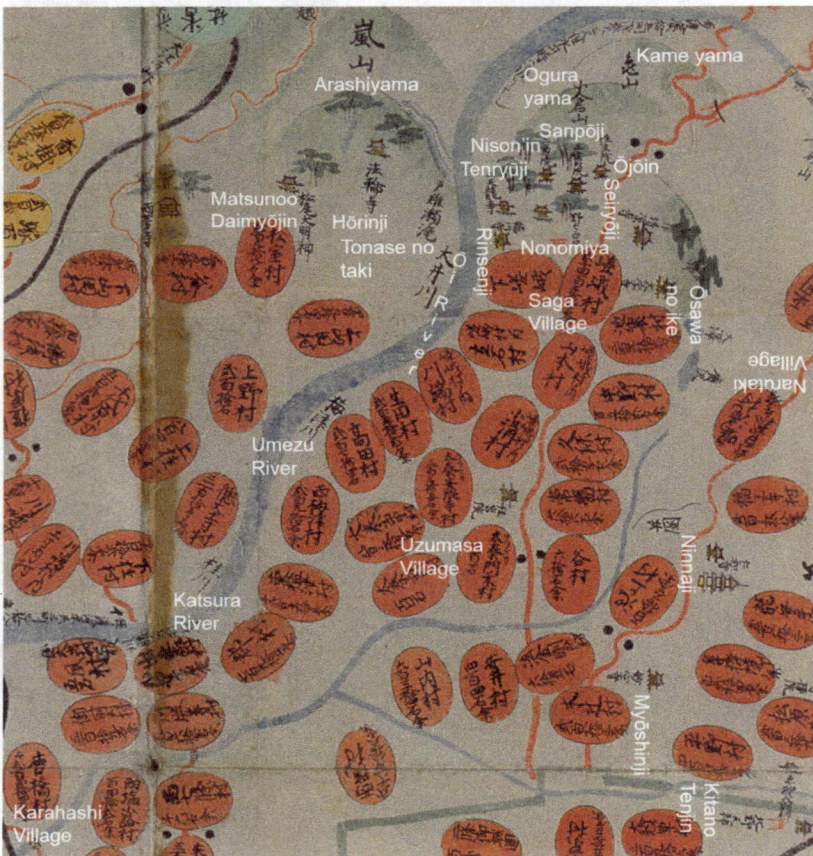

FIGURE 3.9. Day 7 in Saga, the western part of the suburb. The entire distance is over 5.5 *ri* (fourteen miles). At Matsuo, river crossing by boat is available.

- Yoshimine Temple stands on top of Mt. Oshio. There are many cherry blossom trees along the slope leading to Mt. Oshio. This temple produces eye medication (*megusuri*). It is their special product (*meisan*).
- Nishi no iwakura is located north of Sankoji Temple.
- Sankoji Temple stands further above Yoshimine Temple. No women are allowed here.[60]

Ekiken mentions only Kasuga Myōjin by name, but Emperor Kanmu brought the deities of Kasuga Shrine to Nagaokakyō when he built the capital in Nagaoka. When the emperor later moved the capital to Heiankyō, he brought these deities to act as protectors of the royal capital and built the Ōharano Shrine to house the Ōharano Daimyōjin.[61] The deities at Ōharano Shrine obtained the same prestige and status as the deities in Kasuga Shrine in Nara, which is one of the most prominent shrines in Japan along with the Ise and Iwashimizu Shrines.[62]

Ekiken's description of the field of Ōharano mainly consists of a list of temples, but because he only offered limited explanations about them, his narration does not inform the reader of their spiritual significance. My research indicates that Yoshimine Temple was a designated site of the Saigoku Kannon pilgrimage (*Saigoku sanjūsan-sho junrei*), with Emperor Kanmu building Konzōji in 718 and designating it as a form of protection to defend the capital when he built Heianjō. Because Konzōji was the furthest west of all the temples in the capital, in 729 the emperor buried

---

60. Kaibara E., "Keijō shōran," 21.

61. Kasuga Shrine in Nara enshrines the tutelary deities (*ujigami*) of the Fujiwara family, namely, Take mikazuchi no mikoto, Iwainushi no mikoto, Ame no koyane no mikoto, and Hime no kami. The wife of Emperor Kanmu was from the Fujiwara, and when the emperor moved the capital from Nara to Nagaoka, he moved the deities of the Kasuga Shrine to Kyoto as the protective deities of the capital and the tutelary deities of the Fujiwaras in Kyoto. Nagashima, *Nara bunka no denryū*, 220–34.

62. Myōjin, also read as Akitsukami, is often explained as the manifestation of a deity. *Kojiruien* explains it as the "true deities" (*makoto no kami*) who were supreme (*suguretaru kagiri*) among the deities, such as Kasuga Daimyōjin and Matsuo Daimyōjin. The shrines that house these myōjin throughout the archipelago were given an equally high rank and were served by the eminent shrine priests. They often received offerings from the imperial court. Jingūshichō Kojiruien Shuppan Jimusho, *Kojiruien*, 143–58.

important Buddhist sutras in the temple and made Konzōji the "stone warehouse" (*iwakura*) of the west, a shield against the evil spirits trying to enter the capital.[63]

In this way, the reader learns that the regions of Oshio and Ōharano are profoundly spiritually connected with the places that house divine spirits.[64] Yoshimine Temple, Konzōji, and Sankoji were designated as *fudasho* for the Kannon pilgrimage of the western hills (*nishi no oka* or *Saihoku no oka sanjūsan-sho junrei*) when the practice was later revived in the eighteenth century. The pilgrimage started out as a smaller version of the Saigoku Kannon pilgrimage in Shikoku, created for those who were unable to tackle the longer pilgrimage, and it reached its climax in the mid-Muromachi period (1336–1573). Following the Sengoku period, people revived this pilgrimage within the capital, regarding the western hills as the pure land of the East (*saihō jōdo*).[65] In the mid- to late seventeenth century, those in the western suburbs of the capital revitalized the pilgrimage, and devoted travelers quickly popularized the region as the western hills pilgrimage. This is an implicit example of the Japanese revering and celebrating the deities throughout history, with the inclusion of these temples and shrines highlighting the significance of popular spirituality, as if to confirm that the great peace was sustained because of the practice of popular worship.

Indeed, the integration of local deities into the landscape and the presentation of the spiritual landscape of the western hills highlight the widespread practice of popular worship in the region. This is a recurring motif of Ekiken's tour of the capital, which he underscored when it approached the most holy place in the capital, Mt. Hiei, on day 11; the mountainous area of Kurama and Kifune on day 13; and Kōya village, which was located in the western foothills of Mt. Hiei, on day 14. Ekiken stressed the natural beauty of the sacred mountains on these days and carefully described the clean air, pure water, and sound of the waterfall and streams for his readers. He depicted the clear view of Awaji Island, the Seto Inland Sea and Shikoku Island, Lake Biwa, and Otowa no taki waterfalls, located in the

63. Takemura, *Shinsen Kyoto meisho zue*, 158–59.

64. Kyoto Shinbunsha, *Rakusei no Kannon san*, 6–13, 22–25; Kyoto Shiseki Kengakukai, *Kyoto rakusei rakuhoku sanpo*, 46–48.

65. Haruno, *Kyoto rakusei sanjūsan*, 12.

deep mountains, on one hand, while drawing the reader's attention to the presence of the priests, monks, and ordinary devotees who visited Mt. Hiei, on the other. Describing how Mt. Hiei attracted many religious people to the area of its quiet mountainous interior, Ekiken sought to articulate the feeling of being in the mountains by describing the view in a series of short sentences, such as the view being "excellent" (*sugure tari*) and "extraordinary" or "foreign" and "unfamiliar" (*koto naru*).[66] These adjectives capture the extraordinary feelings that might result from the mixture of scenic beauty, the silence in deep mountains, and the lively spirits of pious people.

On days 15 and 16, he took the readers to the province of Ōmi, on the other side of the holy space of Mt. Hiei. Ōmi was not one of the five home provinces, but it is divided from Yamashiro only by the chain of mountain peaks. In other words, the western edge of Ōmi province is equally as "spirited" as the extension of the space associated with the Mt. Hiei community, and the map of Ōmi confirms this point (see figure 3.14). The *Genroku kuniezu* marks the western border of the province with "Dai Hieizan *meisho*" (*meisho* of Big Mt. Hiei) and "Shō Hieizan *meisho*" (*meisho* of Small Mt. Hiei), explaining the sacred space of Mt. Hiei as it continues beyond the provincial border. For Ekiken, the capital was a place protected by the divine spirits and populated by people who gathered at the temples and shrines. The divine space of Mt. Hiei is continuous, as witnessed in the presence of a string of shrines and temples, namely, Hakugōin, Shinra Myōjin no yashiro, and Karasaki Myōjin no yashiro. The deities reside in the sites of shrines and temples, in mountain ranges where the view is most amazing.

The spiritual area that extends across Ōmi province presents scenic views and popular worship that is complimentary. For example,

- Miidera Temple: Also known as Onjōji. There are many *waki dera* (branch temples). There is a well. There is a bell. Women are not allowed here. The mountain above is Mt. Nagara. It is a *meisho*.
- Taka Kannon: Stands in a higher place. A view overlooks the lake [Lake Biwa] afar, and it is beautiful. Also known as *junrei kannon* (the site of a Kannon pilgrimage). It is one of the thirty-three sites associated with

66. Haruno, *Kyoto rakusei sanjūsan*, 30.

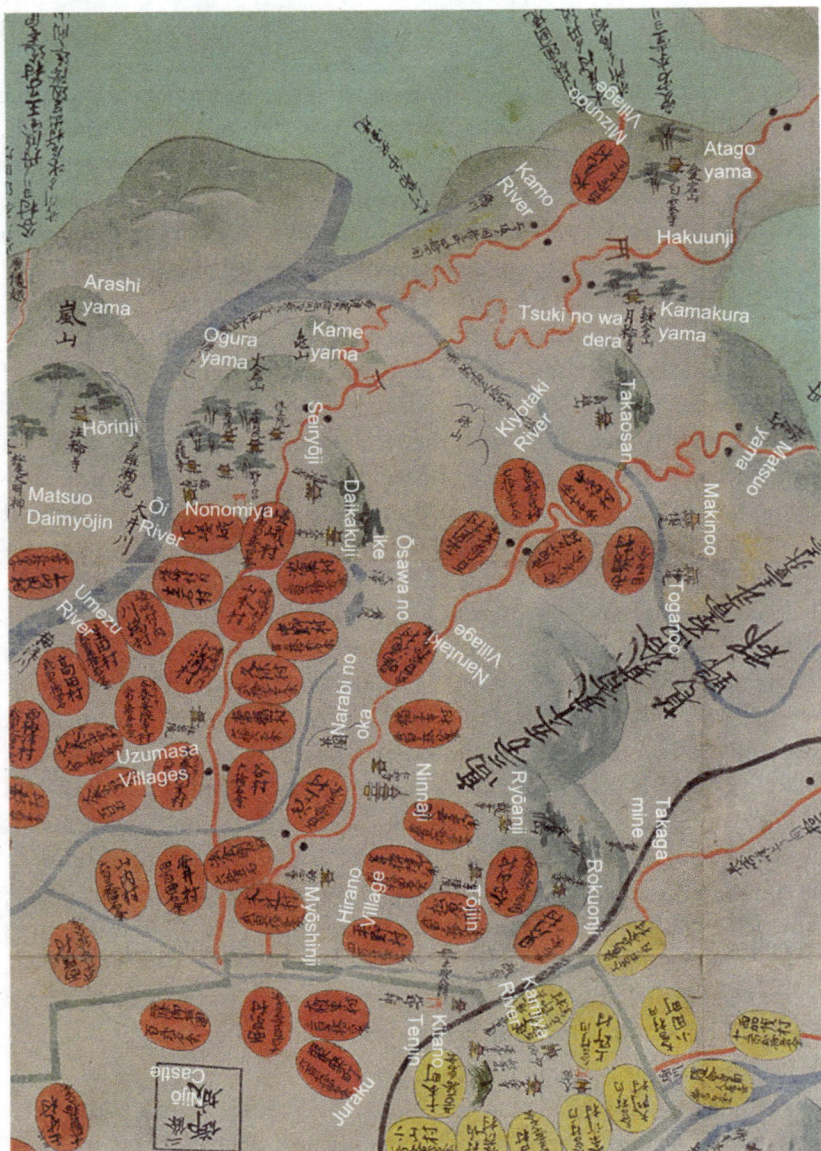

FIGURE 3.10. Days 8 and 9 in the western and northwestern suburbs. On the eighth day, the tour follows a path to Mt. Atago. The entire distance is about eight *ri* (twenty miles). Day 9 covers Takao, Makinoo, and Toganoo. The entire distance is over five *ri* (twelve miles).

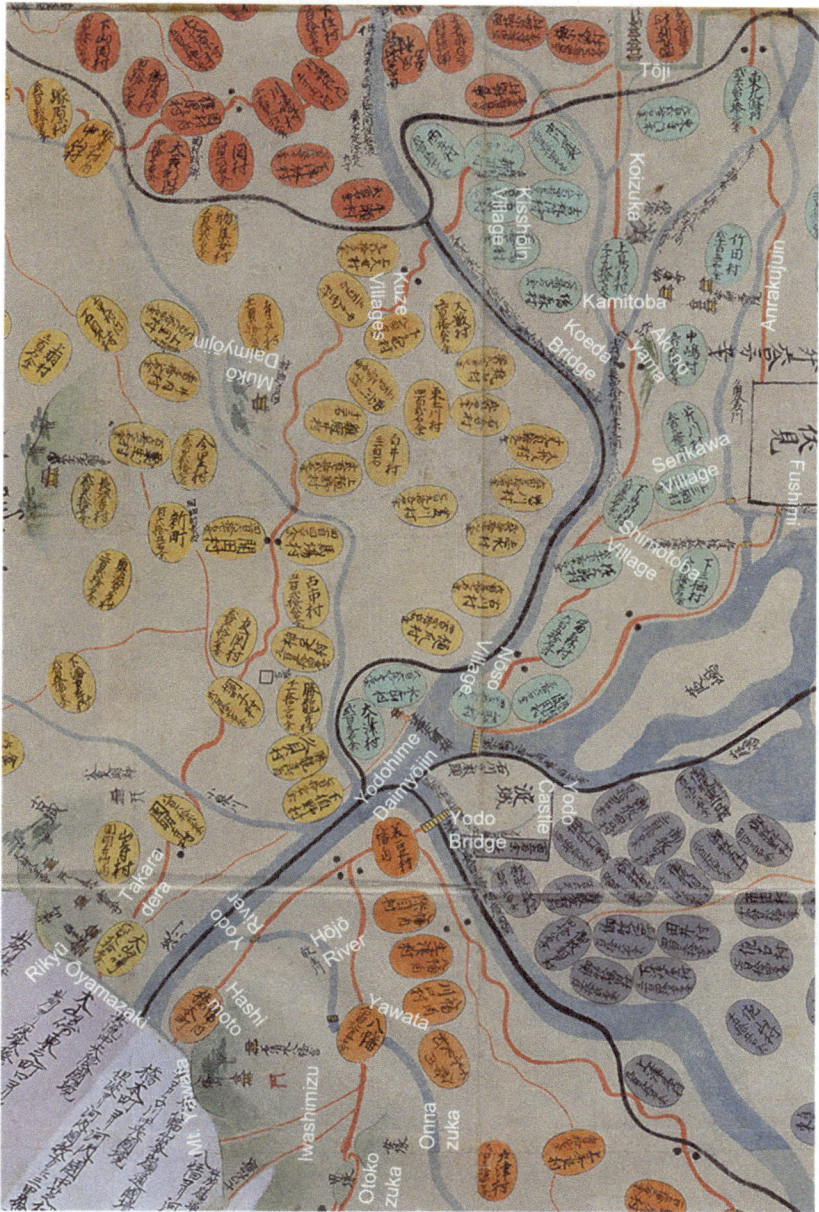

FIGURE 3.11. Days 10 and 12 in the southwestern suburb. Day 10 covers Mt. Yawata, the reverse unlucky quarter. The entire distance is eight *ri* (twenty miles). Ekiken suggests that the reader needs to take boats from Fushimi and Yodo. On day 12, the tour goes further south to reach Yamazaki. The entire distance is eight *ri* (twenty miles), and river crossing is available at Katsura River.

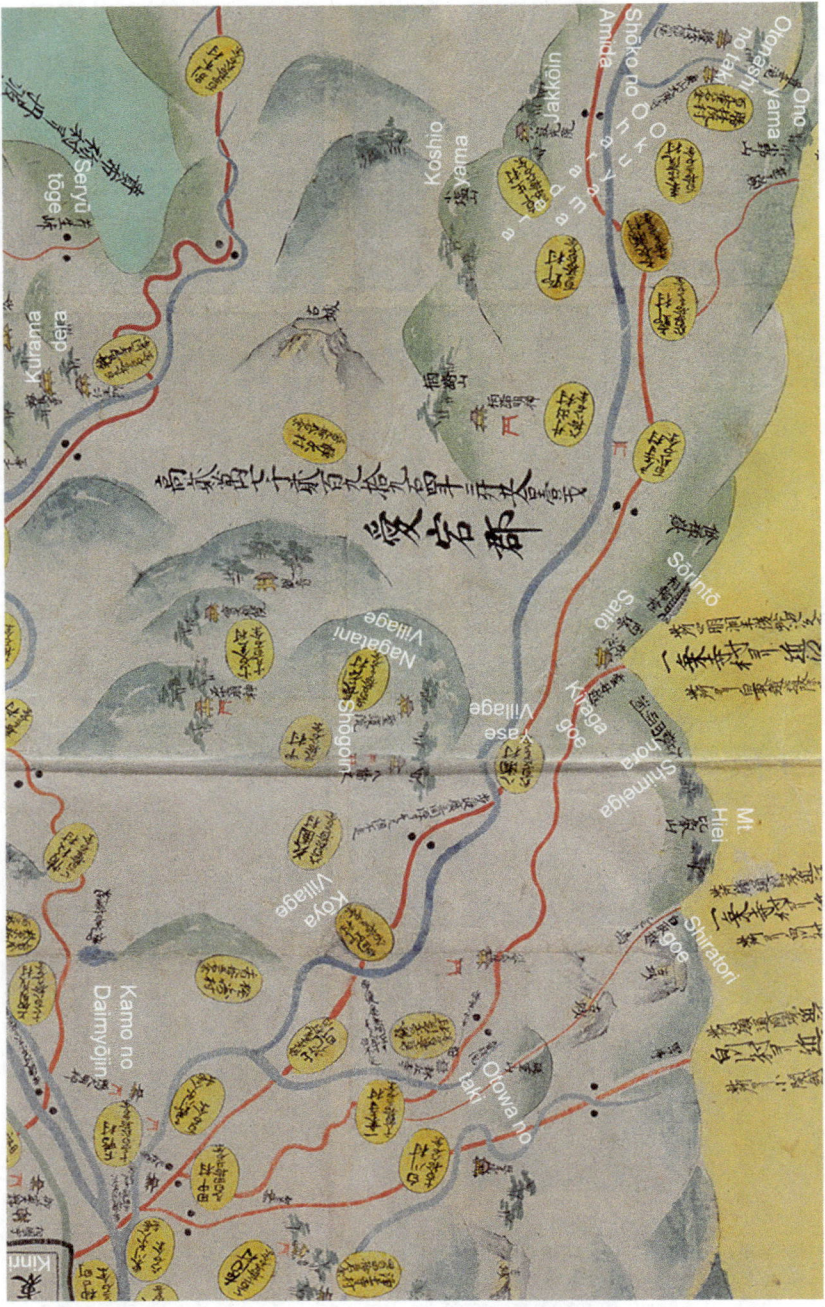

FIGURE 3.12. Days 11 and 14 in the northeast. On day 11, the tour heads toward Mt. Hiei. The entire distance is eight *ri* (twenty miles). Day 14 covers Ohara, the entire distance being over seven *ri* (seventeen miles).

FIGURE 3.13. Day 13 in Mt. Kurama. The entire distance is about six *ri* (fifteen miles).

FIGURE 3.14. Day 15 in Higashi Sakamoto in Ōmi province. The entire distance is eight *ri* (twenty miles).

the Saigoku Kannon Pilgrimage. There is another Taka Kannon in the south of Ōtsu. This one is also located on the high ground, and the view from there is also incomparable. Ōtsu looks down the lake [Lake Biwa], and one can see Mt. Kagami [in the east], Mt. Mikami [in the east], Shiga in the north, Karasaki [in the west], Hira no ga dake mountain peak [in the west], and all other [noteworthy] sites of Ōtsu.[67]

These excerpts differ slightly from figure 3.15, which shows Miidera and a Junrei Kannon located on one small hill, while depicting the Taka Kannon and Seki Temple (Seki no Myōjin) on another hill. Both locations are close to Sekidera village, and Ekiken's explanation seems to link these Kannon halls and temples and the Miidera complex. He does not mention it, but Miidera was also one of the thirty-three Saigoku Pilgrimage sites and the main temple for one of the Tendai Buddhism sects (Tendai *jimon*). Ōtsu had, in fact, been the capital of Emperor Tenji (626–72, r. 668–72) since 667. The inclusion of Ōmi in Ekiken's tour allows him to demonstrate that the divine spirits hover around the mountainous area to the north and northeast of the capital. In so doing, the natural beauty, popular spirituality, and reigns of the emperors are fused together. Ekiken linked these natural features of high mountains and lakes with the dead and the living, thus creating the religious, spiritual landscape of the capital.

The last day of the tour focuses on the northern part of the capital. The tour takes the reader to the ultimate sites of the divine spirits, located to the north of the imperial palace. This area is depicted as being the symbolic reservoir of the spirits, where the Shimogamo and Kamigamo shrines are located, as well as the shrine called Mikage no yashiro, the site where the deity of Shimogamo first appeared. Ekiken drew attention to the position of this site, which was directly west of Mt. Hiei so that it would receive spiritual waves from the tall mountain via the wind. By emphasizing the serenity of nature, such as the pure water of Mitarashi River and the Tadasu no mori forests, Ekiken described the shrine compound of Kamigamo and Shimogamo as being absolutely beauti-

67. Haruno, *Kyoto rakusei sanjūsan*, 35.

FIGURE 3.15. Day 16 in Ishiyama in Ōmi province. The entire distance is nine *ri* (twenty-two miles).

ful, surrounded by gardens (*rinsen*) and other beautiful spaces.[68] In his description of the environment, he mentions that the field called Mirareno that spreads around the north of Kamigamo Shrine was where

---

68.   The Kamo shrines obtained their status as second only to the Ise Shrine from Emperor Kanmu in 807, receiving much support from the imperial court and maintaining strong connections with it. Japan Knowledge, *Nihon rekishi chimei jiten*, https://japanknowledge.com/library/en/.

Kamo Myōjin of the shrine first appeared. Claiming that even foreigners had heard about the extraordinary divine ambience of the Kamo area where Kamo Myōjin lies, Ekiken cited a Chinese text from the *Encyclopedia of Imperial Court* (*Huang chao lei yuan*, *Kōchō ruien* in Japanese) that outlined the details of this deity.[69] Mirareno field extends from Kōya village to below Mt. Hiei, where the deity of the Shimogamo Shrine appeared, and Ekiken remarks that this area was "an extraordinarily spiritual land (*reichi*), where truly divine *ki* energies gather (*jinshū no ki atsumaretaru*)."[70]

What he was describing here was the northern area of the capital from Mt. Hiei to the western edge, reaching Mt. Funaoka and Takagamine peaks in the northwestern suburbs. These mountains, in the northwest near the provincial border with Tanba, were historically where the spirits of the dead gathered because the dead were buried here.[71] Although he never mentioned that the dead would rise up and float around the high mountains, the association between the dead and the mountainous regions is reminiscent of the traditional discourse of *kishin*. Indeed, without ever using the term *kishin*, Ekiken highlights the festivals on this tour, such as the precelebration for the Kamo matsuri (Kamo Festival), the Mikage matsuri (Mikage Festival), and the Iwashimizu Hōjōe festival in Mt. Yawata, by describing the lively imperial emissary from Kyoto.[72] In his depiction of these festivals, he offers details of the elaborate processions along the route from shrine to shrine, accompanying the imperial envoy, shrine priests, and musicians, while focusing on the expressions of the people who are celebrating and revering the deities that emerge

---

69. Kaibara E., "Keijō shōran," 39.
70. Kaibara E., "Keijō shōran," 39.
71. Gotō and Yamao, *Rakusei tanbō*, 83.
72. According to Priest (*shōnegi*) Kamo no Toshiharu (1734–85), the procession's objective is to transfer the *shinrei* (divine spirits) from Mt. Mikage to Kamigamo Shrine, and the procession itinerary starts at Shimogamo Shrine, pays a visit to Mikage Shrine to perform the ritual, and carries the *shinrei* to Kamigamo Shrine. This new route was established during the Genroku period (1688–1703); another theory claims that originally the procession began at Kamigamo Shrine, with the *shinrei* being carried to Mikage Shrine. Kamo no Toshiharu, "Kamosha nenjū gyōji," 145–46.

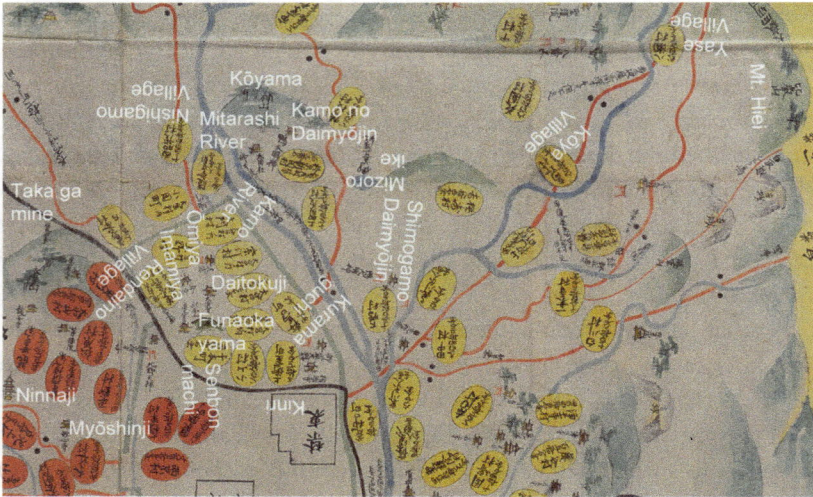

FIGURE 3.16.   Day 17 in the north of the capital, from Tadasu no mori to Kamigamo. The entire distance is about 4.5 *ri* (ten miles).

from the very landscape of the capital.[73] He skips the complex historical details, emphasizing the happy and cheerful atmosphere to draw attention to the popular worship of the deities. His tour sought to celebrate the deities of the country because celebrations of the gods had been the rule in Japan.

Intriguingly, on day 16, Ekiken mentions that a woman writer of the Heian period, Murasaki Shikibu, wrote the *Tale of Genji* at Kannon Temple in Ishiyama in Ōmi province.[74] Pointing out the temple houses, two poems

73.   These prefestival events were very important and before the outbreak of the Ōnin War in 1467, the procession included the Kamo no Saiō or Saiin, who was a chosen unmarried daughter of the emperor. Kamo no Saiō was of central importance to the rituals involved in the Kamo festival, for which she had to prepare herself for about two years to completely remove impurity. The procession of Saiō, followed by the imperial emissary and envoys, attracted large crowds, as depicted in the *Tale of Genji*. "Kamigamo jinja" in Japan Knowledge, *Nihon rekishi chimei jiten*, https://japanknowledge.com/library/en/.

74.   Murasaki's popularity had much to do with a growing readership in the peaceful Tokugawa era. Meeting the needs of new readers with limited levels of literacy, publishers provided simple commentaries, digests, and illustrated editions of the classic texts, offering educational and aspirational reading experiences to a new generation of readers. Clements, "Rewriting Murasaki."

written by Murasaki, her statue, and other objects she owned, including her hand-copied Buddhist sutra of *Daihan'nya*, Ekiken encourages his readers to ask the Buddhist priests to display these objects when they go to Ishiyama.[75] The casual references to Murasaki's literary genius in Ishiyama and Kiso Yoshinaka's tomb in the village of Zeze were appropriate when the popularization of masterpieces and historical figures was on the rise.[76] Ekiken used these popular figures as a means of enticing his readers to travel and learn more about their country.

With the culmination of the tour at the most spiritual area of Kamo, Ekiken's view of the city was able to embrace the idea of *shinkoku* Japan that adhered to the topographic perfection of *shijin sōō*, and he reinforced the idea that the capital was surrounded by the powerful presence of divine spirits who protected and stabilized the country. In contrast with the previous chapters, where his conceptualization of the space used Neo-Confucian metaphysics, his guide to the capital is almost completely shaped by the idea of local deities and the popular worship of them. Only rarely do his descriptions of the scenic beauty of the mountains evoke the power of *yin*, *yang*, or *ki*; instead, he is concerned almost exclusively with conveying the divine ambience of the city that originated from *shijin sōō* topography. Considering that his goal in developing the tour was, as specified in the preface, to allow readers to feel the *fūdo* of the capital, the question of whether to conform to the pacification of *kishin* in the traditional sense became irrelevant. Instead, his depiction of *miyako no fūdo* spread awareness of celebrating the auspicious origins of the country, while his tour of the capital was a prayer of supplication for the eternal presence of divine rule.

The power of Ekiken's prayers did not last, and the spirits that were once discursively contained in the medium of *ki* reemerged with the rise of Nativism in the late eighteenth century. Unlike the ancient China's *kishin* discourse, *kishin* returned to the intellectual landscape of Japan as the protector of community. As the country experienced a number of

75. Kaibara E., "Keijō shōran," 32–37. These objects are housed in the Ishiyama Kannon hall. During the tour, Ekiken mentions other popularly inspired sites, such as the house of Minamoto no Yoshitsune (1159–89) in the Kurama Temple, along with his warrior helmet (*kabuto*) and Benkei's *tachi* sword.

76. Mizutani, *Shinsen retsudentai shōsetsushi*, 87–91.

ideological threats and political instability, Hirata Atsutane presented an ideal vision of society in which "all things past and present—spirits, ancestors, and the living—were held together" in the divine land.[77] The next chapter explores the resurfacing of *kishin* discourse and its transformation in the ensuing time of crisis.

---

77. Harootunian, *Things Seen and Unseen*, 27. See also Katsurajima, *Bakumatsu minshū shisō no kenkyū*, 3–7.

CHAPTER 4

Transformation of the Spirits

> When textual and intellectual production is seen as a process, the text, because it has been produced, must be apprehended as a component of the general system of production and the "real" must be understood not as its object to reflect but as its institutional conditions of existence. Because textuality is a productive activity, its own components—texts—must be seen as distinct practices of signification, which are related . . . to other practices of signification.
>
> —Harry Harootunian, *Things Seen and Unseen*

The previous chapters discussed scholarly production and the circulation of the narrative of Japan as the country of the deities since the seventeenth century. Kaibara Ekiken was one of those who avidly spread the idea that the Japanese archipelago had divine connections and the landscape was the realm of the spirits, doing so by writing *fudoki* and publishing commercial guidebooks. The traces of *kishin* discourse, initially inspired by the traditional notion of the spirits of the dead in East Asia, was replaced with the Japanese terms Ekiken used, such as the "divine spirits" (*shinrei*), "spirited land" (*reichi*), and "spirits and souls" (*reikon*). The disappearance of *kishin* in Ekiken's *shinkoku* Japan paralleled the expanding scholarship prompted by the new availability of historical texts about the deities in the ancient past, including the *Kojiki* and *Nihon shoki*. The evidential studies on local topography that revealed the presence of various deities prompted new research that sought to validate the identities of these deities, their roles in relation to the creation of the country, and how they related to *kishin* discourse.

This chapter analyzes how these findings amplified the discussions on the spirits and *shinkoku* narrative as they engaged with other discourses in the changing social and political contexts of late eighteenth-century Japan. Large-scale popular anxieties in late eighteenth-century Japan gave rise to a particular school of thought, Nativism (Kokugaku), and *kishin* discourse experienced a shift in focus and became the vital element of the discourse of Japan. Kokugaku scholars, who were "profoundly implicated in questioning the distribution of power within their society," saw the need to clearly define the conceptual borders of Japan and produce the cultural unity of their imagined community.[1] What the discourses on *kishin* and *shinkoku* Japan had in common was a deep sense that the presence of the spirits was a defining feature of the country. Most notably, one of the great men of Kokugaku, Hirata Atsutane (1776–1834), wrote a *New Theory of Kishin* (*Kishin shinron*) in 1805 by referencing Arai Hakuseki (1657–1725), Ogyū Sorai (1666–1726), Motoori Norinaga (1730–1801), Confucius, and a variety of Confucian and Neo-Confucian scholars who engaged in the debate about *kishin* before Atsutane.[2] Declaring all previous theories on *kishin* to be false and hypothetical, while confirming the existence of *kishin* in traditional metaphysics, Atsutane's theory replaced *kishin* with *kami*. He argued that all things in this universe could not be ascribed to the fine workings of *yin, yang,* or *ki* but to the *kami,* the deities of Heaven and Earth (*amatsu kami kunitsu kami*), who had been present in the Japanese archipelago since time immemorial.

The resurfacing of *kishin* in Atsutane's theory stood as an extension of the scholarly discoveries of Motoori Norinaga, who dedicated thirty-five years of his life to reading and making annotations on the *Kojiki,* eventually producing the *Commentaries of Kojiki* (*Kojikiden*) in 1798. As is well known, the *Kojikiden* established the *Kojiki* as the "earliest extant text written in Japan," which "recorded oral transmissions handed down from the formative moment" and articulated the names, identities, and roles of the deities in the divine age (*kamiyo*).[3] Based on Norinaga's findings of the experience of *kamiyo,* Atsutane valorized the deities of Heaven and Earth as the creators of Japan and the whole universe, claiming that all activities associated with *kishin* were actually the activities of the deities in *shinkoku* Japan.

---

1. Burns, *Before the Nation,* 5–34; Haga N., *Kokugaku no hitobito,* 60–67.
2. Atsutane's *Kishin shinron* dates from 1805 but remained unpublished until 1820 when *Shin kishinron* appeared with some revisions made to the 1805 version. Asano, "Kaisetsu: Hirata Atsutane to *Kishin shinron*"; Tahara, "Kaisetsu: Tamano mihashira igo."
3. Burns, *Before the Nation,* 1.

Thus far, I have discussed several scholars without clearly identifying them as *shintōists*, Neo-Confucianists, Buddhists, or otherwise in an effort to avoid an arbitrary and ahistorical categorization. In their attempt to pose Japan as an independent entity, many Tokugawa scholars imaginatively used more than one methodology, and consequently their method of producing the images and ideas to represent Japan in relation to China cannot be easily characterized as "Confucian" or "*shintō.*" Considering that their intellectual activities took place independently and before the rise of Nativism, and that their attempts were each shaped by specific conditions, it is not accurate to call them pre- or proto-Kokugaku or in any other way indicate a progressive linear development. Their narrativization of *shinkoku* Japan was one of many competing discourses that formed the context within which *kishin* became the central narrative thread for the representation of Japan in the nineteenth century. Therefore, without appealing to a particular school of thought, this chapter examines the process by which a unifying narrative of a community emerged through *kishin* discourse, while shedding light on the broader issues that concerned various scholars in the latter half of the Tokugawa era.

The Rise of Kokugaku

Late eighteenth-century Japan witnessed an increasing number of uprisings, natural disasters, and other kinds of social and political upheaval that caused intense levels of popular anxiety.[4] Most recently, Hirano Katsuya has shown that signs of disquiet translated into the shogunate's inability to deal with the changing social and economic problems, and the mounting discontent was represented in popular literature mocking the moral and political authority of the shogunate.[5] Believing that the contact with Chinese culture in the eighth century represented the beginning of the corruption of the Japanese way of life, Kokugaku scholars cast a critical eye on the source of the moral authority of the shogunate. They argued that it was necessary to remove the influence of Chinese culture

---

4. See, chapter 1 of Burns, *Before the Nation*, 16–34.
5. Hirano, *Politics of Dialogic Imagination*; Endō J., *Hirata kokugaku to kinsei shakai.*

from Japan's political and legal structures, moral codes, and economic activities, as well as spiritual and other practices. Holding that the *Kojiki* recorded the ancient way of the gods from the divine age, Motoori Norinaga was determined to interpret the text and reveal the ancient way (*inishie no michi*) of *kamiyo*.

At his mother's suggestion, Norinaga initially studied medicine in Kyoto from the age of twenty-three to become a physician.[6] Studying in the cultural capital, he interacted with various scholars and became deeply involved in studying Japanese *waka* poetry (Kagaku). In 1752, he joined the school of Morikawa Akitada (dates unknown) and became a disciple of Aruga Chōsen (1712–74). Profoundly influenced by the established Nijō School of poetry that had inherited a tradition called the Teachings of Poems Now and Then (*kokin denju*), Norinaga also read the poetic theories of Keichū (1640–1701), among other Kagaku theories.[7] His reading of these theories prompted him to seek a meeting with Kamo no Mabuchi (1697–1769), one of the most renowned scholars of Kagaku at that time. When Norinaga actually met Mabuchi in Matsuzaka in 1763, he was told that one could obtain the real "heart of the ancient" (*inishie no kokoro*) by studying poems in the *Man'yōshū* and could understand the "historical records of the gods" (*kami no mifumi*) by reading the ancient words (*inishie no koto*) of the *Man'yō*.[8] Ōno Susumu emphasizes the profound impact of Mabuchi's poetics on Norinaga's thought and the way Norinaga read and apprehended *Kojiki*.[9] As recorded in the story of "A Night in Matsuzaka" (*Matsusaka no ichiya*), Norinaga's dramatic meeting with Mabuchi was the start of his serious study of poetry.[10] Norinaga once wrote that *waka* poetry was capable of moving even *kishin*, and good poems embodied the heart of poets who had perfected their skills.

6.   Matsumoto, *Motoori Norinaga no shisō to shinri*, 156.

7.   Marra, *Poetics of Motoori Norinaga*, 3–4.

8.   Koyasu, *Norinaga to Atsutane no sekai*, 19–21.

9.   Ōno S., "Kaidai."

10.   Sasaki Nobutsuna (1872–1963) wrote about the dramatic meeting of Norinaga and Mabuchi under the title "Matsusaka no ichiya" for an elementary school (*jinjō shōgakkō*) textbook on Japanese (*kokugo*). It was compiled in the eleventh volume of the textbook that dates to 1918. Museum of Motoori Norinaga, http://www.norinagakinenkan .com; Koyasu, *Norinagagaku kōgi*, 65–72.

Norinaga's study of poetry nurtured a strong belief that the *Kojiki* narrated everything about life in *kamiyo*, although he regarded the *Nihon shoki* as a more complete historical document.[11] Considering that there was no written language in antiquity and the oral tradition was the rule by which history was recorded, Norinaga privileged the *Kojiki* as the supreme text of the gods (*kami taru fumi*), claiming that it revealed truths about the divine age of Japanese history.[12] Norinaga wrote about the centrality of poetics of the *Man'yōshū* in "First Steps Up the Mountain" (*Uiyama bumi*, 1799), an essay by which his students could learn about the ancient (*inishie no manabi* in Norinaga's term, also known as Kogaku) at his school. For example, it states:

> Study the *Man'yōshū* well. This book is a collection of poems, but it is very valuable in our attempt to understand "the way" in addition to the two chronicles (*futa mifumi*) of *Kojiki* and *Nihon shoki* . . . . According to my teacher Mabuchi, to understand the "way of the ancient" (*inishie no michi*), we should study the poems of ancient times, read the poems in that manner (*inishie fū*), learn the prose (*fumi*) that is written in that style, compose the prose in the ancient style and manner, and familiarize ourselves with the ancient word (*inishie no koto*). We should read *Kojiki* and *Nihongi* well because, without knowing the ancient words, one will never learn the ancient meanings (*inishie no i*). Without knowing the ancient meanings, one will never learn the ancient way (*inishie no michi*) . . . because, in general, words (*kotoba*), technique (*waza*), and heart (*kokoro*) correspond with the manner (*sama*) of the person. For example, people with an awe-inspiring heart (*kokoro no kashikoki hito*) speak and act in just the same way as their heart.[13]

The last part of the excerpt sheds light on Norinaga's understanding of words and how meaning is produced. The idea that an utterance is the reflection of the speaker's heart, and written or spoken words capture the real meanings of the person who is writing, suggests the value of studying the written texts carefully so as to draw more information from the

---

11.   Asukai, *Nihon kindai seishinshi no kenkyū*, 79.

12.   Koyasu, 'Norinaga mondai' towa nanika, 72. For background information concerning the production of *Nihon shoki*, see Sakamoto, *Six National Histories of Japan*, 30–89.

13.   Motoori, "Uiyama bumi," 17.

written word. These ideas recur in Norinaga's writings, and his theorization of the aesthetic sensibility called *mono no aware* shares these ideas. He wrote that the essence of Japanese *waka* was to express this *mono no aware* in words within the poetic context in his unpublished essays "A Small Boat amidst the Reeds" (*Ashiwake obune*) and "Personal Views on Poetry" (*Isonokami sasame goto*).[14] He thought it possible that by studying *mono no aware*, the students of *waka* would be able to understand how the poet expressed not only his or her feelings (*kokoro*) but also the context or events (*koto*) that generated these feelings. *Waka* poetry was therefore the embodiment of *mono no aware* and the context that generated the feelings that were expressed in words (*kotoba*).

Based on this premise, Norinaga was devoted to reviving the content of the *Kojiki* and annotated the record that documented the matters of the divine age (*kamiyo no koto*).[15] His insistence on understanding the ancient words correctly related to this meaning-making process, and the person who wished to read the poems from the *Man'yōshū* had to master this way of meaning making to decipher how the gods spoke and what they were saying (*kami no monoii*).[16] The ability to understand this way of articulating the meaning had the potential to enhance one's ability to comprehend the heart of *kamiyo*, which excluded the presentist conceptions that were mostly shaped by foreign teachings of Buddhism and Confucianism (*adashi kuni no jufutsu nado no oshiegoto*). The ability to understand the original contexts of *Kojiki* in the original words of Japan (*yamato kotoba*) uttered by the deities was extremely important. As the *Kojiki*'s preface stated, Hieda no Are (dates unknown) read the words of Emperor Tenmu (631–86, r. 673–86) aloud, while Ōno Yasumaro (d. 723) wrote down his utterances, which made the *Kojiki* essentially a record of Emperor Tenmu's voice. Because the *Kojiki* was initially read out by Hieda no Are, even though Ōno Yasumaro wrote in the mediation of Chinese characters, Norinaga claimed it was possible to retrieve the meanings and contexts by attributing the "correct" reading. Setting aside the question

14. Koyasu, *Norinagagaku kōgi*, 26–32. *Ashiwake obune* was written in 1757 and remained unpublished until modern times. Norinaga wrote *Isonokami sasame goto* in 1763, and it was published in 1816.

15. Koyasu, *'Norinaga mondai' towa nanika*, 84–86.

16. Motoori, "Kojikiden ichi no maki: Yomizama no koto," 33.

of who could decide which way of reading was correct, the completion of the *Kojikiden* and its establishment as the divine record of the ancient past by default determined that Norinaga had read it correctly and that he had retrieved the original *yamato kotoba*.

Considering that in the seventeenth century Kaibara Ekiken and Hayashi Razan were skeptical of the historical validity of the *Kojiki* and *Nihon shoki*, Norinaga's designation of these texts as the record of the way of the gods (*kami no michi*) indicates both ruptures and continuities with the discourse of *shinkoku* Japan. Identifying the ancient way in the *Kojikiden*, Norinaga privileged the way of antiquity as the fundamental way of Japan, turning the Kogaku of ancient learning into the Kokugaku (learning of the country) of Japan. He wrote that knowing the ancient way was fundamental to Kokugaku. In the essay "Uiyama bumi," Norinaga positioned the way of the antiquity as the way of all learning in the following manner. He wrote:

There are various ways of learning (*mono manabi no suji*) in this world. Let me list some of the texts that show the way. The first book is the "Record of the Age of the Gods" (*Jindaiki* or *kamiyo no fumi*) [in *Nihon shoki*], which should be central. To those who wish to learn the way, their endeavor is called the learning of the deities (*kami no manabi*), and those who wish to learn this knowledge are called the learners of *kami no manabi* . . . there is also learning of poetry (*uta no manabi*), and there are two kinds of this. The first part is to compose poems. The second part is to interpret the texts of poetry collections and tales . . . what one should study most is the learning of the way (*michi no gakumon*). First of all, this way is the way of the Sun Goddess, Amaterasu (*Amaterasu ōmikami no michi*), and it shows the rule of the heavenly sovereign (*tennō*). This way has been practiced in all directions [under Heaven] and in all countries, and this is the true way (*makoto no michi*). This way was only transmitted to one country [Japan]. What is this way like? This way is recorded in the two history records (*futa mifumi*) of *Kojiki* and *Nihon shoki*, which are concerned with various historical events in the age of the gods and the early history of Japan. Therefore, read and look at these two chronicle texts carefully and repeatedly.[17]

17. Motoori, "Uiyama bumi," 3–5.

The excerpt clearly positions the way of the gods in *kamiyo* as being central to the way of all learning, while also identifying the *Kojiki* and *Nihon shoki* as the privileged historical records that embody the way, referred to as *kami no michi*. These texts became the basis of "learning of our country" (Kokugaku) and were studied in Norinaga's academy, Suzunoya, in the years that followed. The excerpt continues to encourage students to study Norinaga's other essays, such as "Correct Words of the Age of the Gods" (*kamiyo no tadashiki kotoba*), so as to understand the manner of the ancient language (*inishie no kotoba no yō*). If students were willing to learn in this way, their Japanese soul (*yamato tamashii*) would be strengthened, preventing them from falling into the mode of the Chinese heart (*kara gokoro*). As Koyasu Nobukuni has argued, it was Norinaga who first equated the deities of the divine age with the notion of *kami*, which included spirits and supernatural beings, and produced the definition of the deities that corresponded with the mythology of the divine creation of the Japanese archipelago.[18]

Given that Norinaga was critical of the artificiality of Confucian and Buddhist teachings and valued the unwritten nature of the way of the gods, it seems contradictory that he came to position the two chronicles as the valid and canonical historical records of the gods (*kami no futa mifumi*). On the other hand, in his discussion of the way in "The Rectifying Spirit" (*Naobi no mitama*) in the *Kojikiden*, he remarked that there were no written teachings of any kind in Japan, and that was precisely the way of Japan.[19] Even while he was excavating the text of the *Kojiki* to articulate the deities, Norinaga defined the deities rather ambiguously, writing:

I am still unable to understand what is meant by the name *kami* (*kami to mōsu na no kokoro*). Generally speaking, *kami* are various deities of Heaven and Earth that appear in the ancient records (*inishie no mifumi domo*). *Kami* are also spirits (*mitama*) that are enshrined in shrines (*yashiro*). *Kami* also include people, birds and animals (*tori kemono*), trees and plants and others (*sōmoku no tagui*), as well as oceans and mountains (*umi yama*) that possess the virtuous (*koto*) things beyond this world (*yo no tsune*) and the awesome things (*kashikoki mono*) that inspire us.[20]

18. Koyasu, *Norinagagaku kōgi*, 148.
19. Motoori, "Kojikiden ichi no maki: naobi no mitama," 58.
20. Motoori, "Kojikiden san no maki: kamiyo no hajime no maki," 125.

Norinaga presented a definition of *kami* that comprehensively covered the various forms of the deities, but in terms so abstract that it was reminiscent of Zhu Xi's discussion of the fine workings of *yin* and *yang* in relation to *kishin*: that is, that *kishin* lived everywhere in the form of *yin* and *yang*. Norinaga continued to list good and bad *kami*, as well as respectful ones and mean spirits, in this section of "Naobi no mitama," prompting the question as to what *kami* really were. He explored the relationship between the deities of Heaven and Earth and the mountains, rivers, trees, and the like, as well as identifying their places of residence.

To be sure, Norinaga's ambiguous discussion on the idea of *kami* elicited much discussion among his followers and other Kokugaku scholars. For our purposes, it suffices to point out that Norinaga's priority was not to generalize about the overarching qualities of the deities. Instead, he sought to reveal the experiences of *kamiyo* and take note of the contributions made by each deity in *Kojikiden*, whether they were bad, good, respectful, or mean-spirited. By preserving the original nature of the deities, Norinaga stayed away from the dynamics of Chinese learning that used the notion of cosmology, *yin*, *yang*, five phases, and the like. As he repeatedly asserted, people in his time might be familiar with such conceptualizations as being the original principles of Heaven and Earth (*tenchi no onozukara no kotowari*), but the divinity of the deities was completely different and simply unexplainable. The impossibility of describing their divinity was what made the acts of the gods (*kami no mishiwaza*) mysterious and marvelous. Norinaga's position was summarized well in the following statement: "Heaven is just Heaven, men and women (*metsu*) are simply men and women, and fire and water are nothing but fire and water."[21] Without seeing the deities as analogous to *kishin*, Norinaga's intention was to strengthen *yamato tamashii* to maintain the mode of understanding and learn to maintain the Japanese heart.

If we recall that the *kishin* discourse was mostly popular with members of a circle who identified themselves as Confucian scholars, this explains why we rarely see the term *kishin* in Norinaga's theorization of the deities in antiquity. However, as we will now see, Hirata Atsutane published vigorously on the topic of the spirit, transformations of the spirit, and other aspects of supernatural phenomena, and his list includes *Strange*

21. Motoori, "Kojikiden ichi no maki: *Shoki* no agetsurai," 10.

Tales of the Land of Immortals (*Senkyō ibun*), *Kishin shinron*, *The True Pillars of the Spirit* (*Tama no mihashira*, 1813), *On the Supernatural World of Now and Then* (*Kokon yōmikō*, 1828), and *Things Written and Heard about the Rebirth of Katsugorō* (*Katsugorō saisei kibun*). Given that his 1805 theory of *kishin* was composed in response to his students' questions about *kishin*, the spirits were, in fact, widely discussed beyond the circle of Confucian scholars. Atsutane brought together the *kishin* discourse of Confucian scholars and the popular fascination with the spirits of the dead, and his new theory of *kishin* changed the scholarly trend with regard to debates about the spirits.

Hirata Atsutane and His Theory of "Kishin"

Born into a warrior household in Dewa (present-day Akita) province in 1776, Atsutane studied Confucianism and medicine beginning in his childhood. We learn some details about his youth in *Short Story of Great Hirata Atsutane's Life* (*Taigakukun goichidai ryakuki*), which was written by his adopted son, Hirata Kanetane (1799–1880). Scholars generally agree that Atsutane had an unfortunate childhood up to the point he left his hometown of Akita for Edo.[22] Arriving in Edo at the age of twenty, he was adopted into the Hirata household; his adoptive father was a teacher of military tactics (Heigaku). Atsutane believed the Hirata house was descended from the Taira family from the Heian period, and he wrote his name as Taira Atsutane in many of his essays. In 1801, at the age of twenty-six, Atsutane read Norinaga's works for the first time, and from then on he began to study Kogaku, strongly believing in an intellectual bond with Norinaga.[23] By 1804, Atsutane opened a private school, Ibukinoya, in Edo, and became a student of Norinaga's son, Motoori Haruniwa (1763–

22. For a detailed overview of Atsutane's difficult childhood, see the first chapter of Yoshida M., *Hirata Atsutane: reikon no yukue*, 16–42.

23. Motoori Ōhira (1756–1883), heir to Suzunoya, gave one of the three objects that his students kept in memory of Norinaga to Atsutane when he came to visit Suzunoya in 1805. Koyasu, *Norinaga to Atsutane no sekai*, 53; Muraoka, "Hirata Atsutane ga suzunoya nyūmon no shijitsu"; Matsumoto, *Motoori Norinaga no shisō to shinri*, 163.

1828) in June 1805.[24] In December of the same year, Atsutane completed the *Kishin shinron* and claimed to be the true successor of Norinaga.[25]

It is intriguing that Atsutane, who lacked Norinaga's deep knowledge of philology, cast himself as the scholarly successor to Norinaga and had numerous followers and supporters across the country. Unlike Norinaga's practice of scholarship that centered on the investigation of textual exegesis, philological study, grammatical explication, and other aspects of language and textuality, Atsutane's scholarly style was closer to the Confucian evidential study of Ekiken and Razan, which validated "facts" through textual references from various official history texts, poetry, and other sources.[26] Therefore, Atsutane's new theory of *kishin* seemed insignificant to Norinaga's students, largely because *kishin* discourse was almost exclusively associated with scholars of Chinese learning (Kangaku).[27] One of the Kokugaku scholars at Norinaga's Suzunoya, Ban Nobutomo (1775–1846), for example, told Motoori Ōhira (1756–1883), who was the heir to Suzunoya, that Atsutane's *Kishin shinron* was not impressive as the work of someone claiming to be Norinaga's successor, but he suggested it might help Kangaku scholars because the theory demonstrated the existence of the heavenly deities (*tenjin*) and other deities even in ancient China.[28] Because deities were not believed to be innate in China, Kokugaku scholars found Atsutane's theory confusing and irrelevant. Similarly, when his *Tama no mihashira* was published in 1813, it led to even more intense inquiries being made by Norinaga's students.[29]

Why did Atsutane choose to draw from the Confucian discourse of *kishin* as he sought to enhance his theory of how to strengthen the Japanese heart as the valid successor of Norinaga?[30] Considering that Atsutane

24.   Asano, "Kaisetsu: Hirata Atsutane to *Kishin shinron*," 287.

25.   Asano, "Kaisetsu: Hirata Atsutane to *Kishin shinron*," 288.

26.   Burns, *Before the Nation*, 2.

27.   Koyasu, *Edo shisōshi kōgi*, 145–79. See, for example, Motoori Ōhira's preface to Atsutane's *Kishin shinron*, "*Kishin shinron* no jo," which is compiled with Atsutane's work. Hirata, "Kishin shinron," 2.

28.   Watanabe K., *Hirata Atsutane kenkyū*, 113.

29.   Tahara, "Kaisetsu," 566–67; Koyasu, "'Kōsetsuka' Atsutane no tōjō."

30.   For a critical analysis of the representative scholars who spoke about *kishin*, see Koyasu, *Kishinron*.

studied Confucianism from childhood, it is no surprise that he was familiar with the discourse of *kishin* and how the spirits of the dead floated around the space of the living as the ancient Chinese discourse of *kishin* claimed. I am inclined to believe that when Atsutane became aware of Norinaga's teachings about strengthening the heart of the Japanese by eliminating *kara gokoro*, he might have thought of a potential way of blending the *kishin* of Confucian discourse and Norinaga's discoveries of the deities of Heaven and Earth.[31] Thus, he redirected the function of *kishin* to strengthening the *yamato tamashii* and countered the contradictions in the perceived reality of the nineteenth century. To produce a narrative of Japan to enliven declining public morale, Atsutane was guided by the scholarly framework of *kishin* discourse and tried to perfect his teaching of Kokugaku as a similar system of knowledge for his followers, who were desperately seeking moral and spiritual support.

One of the Confucian scholars Atsutane repeatedly quoted in his *Kishin shinron* was Arai Hakuseki, who was interested in ideologically shoring up the shogunate's position within the existing power structures sharing legitimacy with the imperial court.[32] First and foremost as a Confucian lecturer to Lord Tokugawa Tsunatoyo (1662–1712) of Kōfu domain, who later became the sixth shogun, Ietsuna (r. 1709–12), Hakuseki had a deep understanding of the traditional political philosophy of East Asia and Confucian historiography.[33] Among other things, he studied the reason various rituals and religious rites had come to be performed in the imperial court in the ancient past, and he tried to reassert shogunal power by enhancing the shogunate's ceremonial roles. His *Kishinron*,

---

31.   In this regard, I acknowledge a chapter by Numata Satoshi, who reevaluated the significance of *kishin* in Atsutane's thought. I came across this essay at the very end of this current project, but his reappraisal of the Atsutane's belief in the existence of supernatural beings confirms my argument outlined in this chapter. Numata, "Kishin, kaii, yūmei." See also Endō J., "Hirata Kokugaku to yūmei shisō" and Yoshida A., *Kōkyō suru shisha.*

32.   For example, Hakuseki gave the shogun a new title, the "great prince" (*taikun*), and involved himself in important decision-making activities concerning matters of the economy, foreign relations, and local governance. See Nakai, *Arai Hakuseki no seiji senryaku,* 82–121; Toby, *State and Diplomacy,* 69–85.

33.   Asano Sanpei writes that even though the official date of publication of *Kishinron* is 1800, the completion of the manuscript was much earlier, sometime in the Shōtoku period (1711–15) when Hakuseki's writing was prolific. Asano, "Kaisetsu: Arai Hakuseki to *Kishinron,*" 275–79.

along with his *On Rituals* (*Saishikō*), reflects his attempt to renew shogunal power by intervening in matters of rituals based on practices in
ancient China. For example, the beginning of Hakuseki's *Kishinron* starts
as follows:

> It is truly difficult to comment on the matter of *kishin*. The difficulty is
> not simply about commenting (*iukoto*), but hearing (*kikukoto*) *kishin* is also
> very difficult. Not just hearing it, but believing (*shinzurukoto*) in it is
> also very difficult. The difficulty in believing in *kishin* is caused by the
> difficulty in learning about (*shirukoto*) *kishin*. And yet, it will be possible
> to hear *kishin* if one believes in it. Likewise, it will be possible to believe in
> *kishin* after one learns well about *kishin*.[34]

This excerpt shows the difficulty of dealing with the topic of *kishin*, and
it also explains how one could talk about *kishin* and learn and understand
what they were. The goal of this essay was therefore to prove that it was
possible to master what *kishin* were, and Hakuseki introduced numerous
references from classical works on the sages to inform readers about the
discourse of *kishin*. By exhaustively citing the remarks made by former
Confucian scholars from ancient China onward, Hakuseki presented
himself as an expert with the authority to speak about *kishin*.

Following this, and drawing on *The Rites of Zhou* (*Zhouli* in Chinese,
Shūrei in Japanese), Hakuseki defined *kishin* as the deities in Heaven
(*kami*), the deities on Earth (*gi*), and demons in person (*oni*). In spite of
the different names, *kami*, *gi*, and *oni*, Hakuseki stated that there were
in truth two spirits of *ki* (*kirei*)—*yin* and *yang*—and they were therefore
called *kishin*. This definition echoes what we observed in chapter 2 in
relation to the existing understanding of East Asian cosmology. Hakuseki
went on to explain how *kishin* related to the rituals. By referencing *The
Rites of Zhou*, he wrote as follows:

> When people die, the soul (*tamashii*) ultimately returns to heaven, and the
> body returns to earth. Because the soul and body of a person return to
> heaven and earth, the person then becomes *oni*. The ancient sages (*sen'ō*)
> came to control *oni*. *The Rites of Zhou* states that when the ancient sages

34. Arai, "Kishinron: genshū," 1.

became rulers, they made certain they performed rituals to worship the deities in Heaven, on Earth, and in the person. The books concerning the rites (A *katchū* starts here, explaining that these books describe how to celebrate the deities of Heaven and Earth.) discuss, in detail, [because the deities live in them] the sun, the moon, the stars, the cold and heat, the floods and drought, the mountains, the forests, the rivers, the valleys, and hills [the deities can] generate clouds and, furthermore, wind and rain. These books also mention that the ancient sages built grand shrines (*taisha*) for regional lords (*gunsei*) and royal shrines (*ōsha*) for the sages themselves to worship the deities on behalf of their organic community (*shashoku*). (Another *katchū* starts here, explaining that these rituals are associated with the worship of local gods and the gods of five grains.) Also, the ancient sages founded seven rites for . . . [35]

This excerpt goes on to illuminate what the ancient rulers of China did when they assumed power by inserting several *katchū* notes offering annotations to the sources. First and foremost, the ruler pacified the spirits in various spaces by performing rituals to worship the spirits in Heaven and on Earth, plus the ancestors. By stipulating the occasion and purpose of each ritual, Hakuseki articulated the connections between rituals and specific spirits and explained why certain prayers and ceremonies were deemed necessary for the region and the broader community of the country. In *"Saishikō,"* Hakuseki clarified the purposes behind these ritual performances in a more detailed way by referencing the rationale of the sages. For example, he stated,

No matter how virtuous the deity was, if *ki* between Heaven and Earth (*tenchi no ki*) was not harmonious, the deity could not engender harmony among the people (*tami no wa*). Even if *oni* intended to do vicious harm to people, *oni* would not be able to do any harm to people if the *ki* between Heaven and Earth was harmonious (because *oni* had no one to cling to). In other words, it depends on the *ki* between Heaven and Earth as to whether one might either receive blessings from the deities or misfortune from *oni*. Because the impact of *ki* between Heaven and Earth on the lives of the people is so significant, the ancient sages performed rituals. They enlightened the people and celebrated *kishin* to receive their assistance . . . in

35. Arai, "Kishinron: genshū," 2.

the ancient past in our country the imperial court followed these rituals exactly (see my earlier annotations). The national histories (*kokushi*) of different generations record in detail how the imperial court ruled the country by following the system of rituals and celebrations (*reiraku seido*) . . . and called itself the country of the deities (*shinkoku*). However, the tradition began to decline and people started to celebrate *kishin* that were not supposed to be celebrated.[36]

This passage illustrates the point that the metaphysical balance between Heaven and Earth affects the behavior of the spirits, whether they are the spirits of Heaven or people, and Hakuseki highlighted the value of ritual as a way of maintaining the harmony of *ki* between Heaven and Earth. Hakuseki argued that the celebration of the wrong deities and spirits had caused the imbalance of *ki* between Heaven and Earth, and the synchronization of *yin* and *yang* was essential for peace and stability. Thus, he attempted to demonstrate that he had rightly interpreted all the rituals from ancient sources to persuade the Tokugawa shogunate to start performing the correct rituals. In this manner, Hakuseki's essay turned *kishin* discourse into a valuable means for Confucianists to delineate the political authority of the shogunate.

By contrast, Atsutane's purpose in taking up this topic was different. Even so, he made good use of the theoretical framework provided by Hakuseki's *Kishinron*, which thoroughly referenced all the important sources of Confucius, Zhu Xi, and other Song scholars of Neo-Confucianism to demonstrate the existence of the divine spirits. Atsutane's *Kishin shinron* begins:

As written in ancient books in China, people in China (*kano kuni*) have assumed rightly that the rulers in Heaven—*shangdi* (supreme ruler), *houdi* (celestial ruler), or *huangtian* (august heaven) and the like—, or what they simply call heaven (*tian*), or, whatever it is that sounds extremely awe-inspiring (*kashikoki*), are the deities of Heaven (*amatsukami*) [of Japan], and they are in charge of the affairs of the world (*yo no naka*). For example, one finds relevant passages in . . . [a page-long *katchū* starts here, listing quotations from *The Announcement to the Prince of Kang* (*Kanggao* in Chinese),

---

36. Arai, "Saishikō," 485.

Announcement of Tang (*Tanggao* in Chinese), and *Counsels of Gaoyao* (*Gaoy-aomo* in Chinese) in *The Classic of History* (*Shangshu* in Chinese), as well as *The Greater Odes of the Kingdom in the Book of Poetry* (*Maoshi Daya* in *Shijing*). Then, Atsutane concludes that "many references like these exist in China, and the Chinese ancient books correctly describe how miraculous the spirits of the creation deities (*musubi no taenaru mitama*) are, and how they created people and things."] However, do these words not sound like those of a quack (*kototsukekoto*)?[37]

Atsutane thus inserted the Japanese heavenly deities into the traditional Chinese concept of Heaven and the son of Heaven. His purpose was to use the references from China to validate the existence of the heavenly deities and explain how the creation deities of *musubi no mitama*, which Norinaga had identified in *Kojikiden*, had created people and things in the universe. Atsutane advanced Norinaga's discovery of the Japanese deities in antiquity, and by incorporating the sources from ancient China that discussed *kishin* at length, he replaced the claim made by Neo-Confucian metaphysics that all things in the universe were made of *yin* and *yang* with the miraculous power of the deities. According to Atsutane,

> It is not just that the later Confucian scholars (*zusa domo*) in China were wrong, but that these were the long-established customs (*narawashi*) of China. There is evidence for this. In foreign countries (*totsukuni*), they lost the real historical texts of the ancient (*inishie no tsutaegoto*), and even the extant documents were written ambiguously (*obo oboshii*) and incorrectly. Besides, China has presumptuous (*nama sakasiki*) manners and customs, so even if they had said it in the way the ancient written texts had done, it still would have sounded very much like a made-up thing.[38]

By referring to the historical texts that mention *kishin*, Atsutane positioned them as the sources of false information. In his understanding, because they had no access to the two chronicles, *Kojiki* and *Nihon shoki*, Chinese people were ignorant of real ancient history and did not know the true teachings of the gods. They remained ignorant of the gods'

37. Hirata, "Kishin shinron," 4.
38. Hirata, "Kishin shinron," 5.

extraordinary workings (*mishiwaza*) and wrongly believed that *kishin* were at work.

Atsutane closely followed Norinaga's scholarly footsteps by treating the chronicles as the real and only documents in learning. He continued to state the misguided nature of Chinese scholars as follows:

> These are all habits of scholars of Chinese learning (*kara no manabi*), who, without good reasons to support them, say that good things were founded by the sages. How narrow-minded and unwise of them to say this! Once born, everyone knows that we should revere *kishin* because this is the nature (*sei*) and "the way" (*michi*) shown by the deities of Heaven (*amatsu kami*). Even the Chinese (*karakuni hito*) should know this without being taught by the sages. How could one not know about respecting and worshiping *kishin* and one's own heart (*ono ga kokoro*)?[39]

By mixing the terms *kishin* and *kami* and using them interchangeably, Atsutane equated "the way" below Heaven with the way shown by *amatsu kami*. He also provided new readings for the characters *yin* and *yang*, respectively, "secretly" (*hisokani*) and "obviously" (*arawani*), replacing the metaphysical terms once used by the Zhu Xi scholars. The concepts of *hisokani* and *arawani* originated with Norinaga, who delineated the realm of the spirit (*kakuryo*) and the realm of the living (*arawanigoto*) in his discussions on *kami* (discussed shortly).[40] Throughout *Kishin shinron*, Atsutane imposed the language of Kokugaku onto the existing discourse of Neo-Confucian metaphysics and "translated" the Neo-Confucian metaphysical terms into Japanese Kokugaku terms. Quoting those Song scholars who said that *kishin* were the fine workings of two *ki* (*yin* and *yang*) and every creation in this world showed the signs of *kishin*, Atsutane went on to declare that "the truth is, two *ki* are fine workings of the deities" and reconstructed the cosmology of Confucianism by centering it on the deities of Heaven and Earth.[41]

Atsutane was able to produce a new view of cosmic order by confirming "the truth" shown in Norinaga's monumental work, *Kojikiden*. He

39. Hirata, "Kishin shinron," 6.
40. Hirata, "Kishin shinron," 6.
41. Hirata, "Kishin shinron," 13.

argued that the Japanese deities were the creators of not just the Japanese archipelago but the entire universe. On one hand, *Kojikiden* established the historical origin of Japan as *shinkoku* by identifying all the deities that created the Japanese archipelago. By highlighting the divine work of these deities, the *Kojikiden* made the term *kishin*, which was mostly used by the scholars of Chinese learning, irrelevant to those in the Motoori school. On the other hand, *Kojikiden* opened up the possibility for Atsutane to equate the deities of Heaven and Earth with *kishin* in the Confucian discourse and treat them all broadly as spirits. As we have seen in traditional understanding, *kishin* included the spirits of the deities in Heaven and Earth and the spirits of the dead. Atsutane recognized the value of *Kojikiden* as a device for authenticating the claim for *shinkoku* Japan and found a way to place Japanese antiquity within the broader context of East Asia. *Kojikiden* articulated the activities of *kamiyo* and the indigenous roots of the deities that had established Japan as the country of the divine deities, which allowed Atsutane to identify *kishin* as being original to Japan.

As a consequence, Atsutane declared that everything in this universe was caused as a result of the miraculous (*kushibi naru*) divine acts (*mishiwaza* or *miisao*) of the gods and completely rejected the theories of *yin* and *yang* and the metaphysics of Confucian scholars.[42] He marshaled the contradictions found in the definition of *yin* and *yang*—whether they were dead or alive, whether they had a spirit (*rei*) as the scholars said, or whether *yin* and *yang* were static or active, among other things. Quoting a dialogue between Confucius and one of his most faithful students, Zhong You (also known as Zilu, 542–480 BCE), Atsutane argued that later Confucian scholars held false concepts of the principles of the deities. Zhong You asked his teacher about death and how one might serve *kishin* in the afterlife, to which Confucius responded, "how could I possibly know about death when I have not mastered life?" Atsutane claimed that Confucius had indeed recognized the principles (*kotowari*) of the deities as being unknown to the ordinary people and that the invisible acts of *kishin* were the acts of the divine spirits. Based on Confucius's response, Atsutane concluded,

---

42.   Hirata, "Kishin shinron," 12.

to speculate about the birth of people or the principle after one's death is truly useless. Instead, cherish what we have learned from the past (*inishie no tsutaegoto*) and accept that the birth of people is caused by the wondrous and awesome (*kusushiku taenaru*) spirit of the creation deities (*musubi no mitama*) in Heaven that generates all things. The spirits made us to be born from our parents, and when we die, our spirits (*sono tama*) return to the world of the dead (*kakuryo*). Also, just accept that if people celebrate the dead, the spirit, too, will accept that gesture. Ask no more questions because the place above (*kono kami no tokoro*) is truly beyond human intelligence and cannot be measured or known.[43]

Following what Norinaga had said about the union of the deities and the birth of the Japanese islands, Atsutane identified that *musubi no mitama* prepared human lives to be born from their parents in the same way as many other things in the universe were created by the creation deity. Furthermore, he explained that when a person dies, the spirit goes to the world of the dead, which he called *kakuryo*. Norinaga identified the world after death as the land of the dead (*yomi*) and posited this world against the world of the living in his *Kojikiden*. In this regard, Atsutane, while accepting the world of *yomi*, invented *kakuryo* as a separate destination for the spirits of the dead and advanced his own theory about them. In *Kishin shinron*, Atsutane left readers with the advice that they should accept the divine workings of the deities and be thankful for their blessings. His work *Tama no mihashira* clarifies this world of *kakuryo* further by integrating Japanese and Chinese discourses with the spirits and with Western theology.

Atsutane's Theory of "Shinkoku" Japan

Tama no mihashira is based on Atsutane's *Kishin shinron*, where he argues that the spirits that Confucian scholars thought of as *yin*, *yang*, or *ki*, which generate all things in the universe, were actually the intricate workings of the spirits of the Japanese deities. When *Kishin shinron* was

43. Hirata, "Kishin shinron," 37.

written at the beginning of the nineteenth century, British and North American whalers were appearing frequently in Japanese waters, although there was not yet a Western military threat to Tokugawa Japan.[44] Atsutane's publication of *Tama no mihashira* was motivated by the desire to offer further explanations as to what the mysterious acts of the deities and the spirits meant to the students at Ibukinoya because he increasingly perceived Christianity as a threat corrupting the minds of the people. Composed of two parts, *Tama no mihashira* expounds what the divine spirits were, as well as identifying their relationship to Japan, to truly understand the teaching of antiquity. Atsutane clearly stated the purpose of writing this book in his preface:

> In order to master the ancient learning (*inishie manabi*), students shall obtain the way to calm down the Japanese heart (*yamato gokoro no shizumari*) . . . because the destination of the spirit could not be determined, the teaching of antiquity in our country got mixed up with theories from those countries that were made of bubbles and foam (*shionawa*) and those of a filthy country located below . . . it is unbearable to see this [confusion]. I have been thinking hard about how one can keep the thick pillar at heart and uphold it high [so it will help one stabilize his/her Japanese heart].[45]

By pushing forward Norinaga's theme of strengthening the Japanese heart, Atsutane asserted that maintaining a firm Japanese heart would allow students to obtain the true way (*makoto no michi*) that had been transmitted in Japan from ancient times. If we recall that Norinaga's focus on maintaining the Japanese heart required excluding the Chinese mode of understanding, it is clear that Atsutane's concern was different. Even though Atsutane wrote about how calming one's heart was invaluable for understanding the ancient way, his focus was on aiding those who had been confused by the "wrong" teachings of other countries. As he stated, the ancient way in Japan got mixed up with the teachings of polluted and unclean countries. He argued that these confusing theories clouded the minds of the Japanese people and brought about a weakening of the Japanese heart. Along with later scholars from the Bakumatsu era, Atsutane was intensely worried about the minds of the ordinary people, who,

---

44. Wakabayashi, *Anti-Foreignism and Western Learning*, 12.
45. Hirata, "Tama no mihashira," 4.

he argued, were overwhelmed by the "wrong" teachings of other countries, and it was feared that the masses would eventually lose faith in the perceived reality of their everyday lives.[46]

Reflecting this intellectual climate, Atsutane offered a vital message by clarifying the destination of spirits after death. *Tama no mihashira* presents a cosmology by advancing the discussion on Heaven, Earth, and the world of *yomi* Norinaga had elaborated in *Kojikiden*. By reiterating arguments supporting the creation of Heaven, Earth, and *yomi*, Atsutane sought to confirm the wondrous acts of the deities that were indeed unexplainable, while also identifying the end point of the journey of the spirits so that the followers were assured of their destination in the afterlife. In the first part of the text, Atsutane emphasized the significance of the formation (*narihajime*) of the three realms of Heaven, Earth, and *yomi*, including a description of their shapes and forms (*arikatachi*) and a narrative of the divine works (*isao*) of the gods in the making the realms. Largely referencing the theory of *On the Cosmic Triad* (*Sandaikō*, 1797), which was written by one of Norinaga's disciples, Hattori Nakatsune (1757–1824), Atsutane reenvisioned the creation of the Japanese archipelago by providing the reader with illustrations and a wealth of detail (figures 4.1–4.6).[47] The first illustration, for example, captures the emergence of Heaven in the vast sky, followed by the appearance of three deities. They came to constitute the three pillars of Japan: the Takami musubi no kami deity, the Ame no minaka nushi no kami deity, and the Kamumi musubi no kami deity.[48] Providing ten images to show the different stages

---

46. Koyasu, *Nihon nashonarizumu no kaidoku*, 73–79; Devine, "Hirata Atsutane and Christian Sources"; Wakabayashi, *Anti-Foreignism and Western Learning*; Harootunian, *Toward Restoration*; Katsurajima, "Kindai tennōsei ideorogī." For the official accounts and the strategy for controlling the confused minds of the people, see, for example, Yoshida and Satō, *Bakumatsu seijironshū*.

47. *Sandaikō* was written by Norinaga's disciple, but Norinaga included this theory as a supplement to volume seventeen of *Kojikiden*. Hattori N., "Kojikiden jūshichi fu no maki: sandaikō."

48. Nakatsune did not fully embrace the validity of *Kojiki* as Norinaga did. According to Mark McNally, Nakatsune tried to verify the descriptions in the *Kojiki* by using Western theories of the Earth, the globe, and other aspects of astronomy. He was familiar with those Western theories that articulated that the Earth was round, floated in the sky, and traveled around the sun and the moon, which convinced Nakatsune that the old legend of Japan perfectly matched the theories of Western people. McNally, "The Sandaikō Debate," 361.

第一圖

高皇産霊神
天之御中主神
神皇産霊神

此圖ノ内ハ大虚空ナリ・圖ハ假ニ圖ルノミゾ
実ニ此物アリトニハアラズ次々ニナルモ皆然リ
○三柱ノ神ノ座位ハ古傳ノ次弟ニ依テ假ニ如此
書ルノミナリ・必シモ據ルベカラズ

古傳曰古天地未生之時於天御虚
空所成坐神之御名者天之御中主
神次高皇産霊神次神皇産霊神此
三柱之神者並獨神成坐而隱御身

FIGURE 4.1. Atsutane's drawing: the first stage of the creation. This illustration shows the origins and creation of Heaven (*ame*), Earth (*tsuchi*), and the world of darkness (*yomi*). The circle signifies an empty sky, with three dots symbolizing the seats of the three pillars of the deities: Ame no minakanushi no kami (center), Takami musubi no kami (right), and Kamumi musubi no kami (left). However, they are hiding themselves to remain invisible. Hirata, *Tamano mihashira*, 1:16. Courtesy of the National Diet Library Digital Collections, http://dl.ndl.go.jp/info:ndljp/pid/2562762.

of the formation of the realms, Atsutane followed Norinaga's *Kojikiden* closely but restructured that account by identifying the ten developmental stages slightly differently.

Atsutane also drew on the ideas of Christianity, stating that it offered "better explanations about the vast sky and the feature of the land" (*daichi no arikata*), which had been discovered by the people of the distant West, who had investigated the globe by traveling the seas.[49] Atsutane argued

49.   Hirata, "Tama no mihashira," 6.

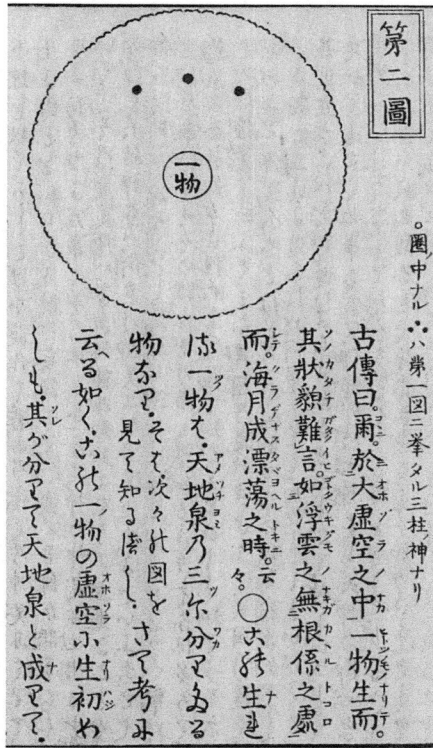

FIGURE 4.2. Atsutane's drawing: the second stage of the creation. This illustration shows the sudden emergence of an object (*hitotsu no mono*) in the center in the sky. This appears to be a rootless drifting cloud, which eventually separates the space into Heaven, Earth, and *yomi*. The three dots continue to represent the existence of the three pillars of the deities, who are all invisible. Hirata, *Tamano mihashira*, 1:17. Courtesy of the National Diet Library Digital Collections.

that Western theories pointed to more or less the same findings as outlined in his cosmology. For example, he argued that the story of the creation of Adam and Eve in Paradise was comparable to the union of the deities in Japan in the age of the gods.[50] Atsutane claimed that Japan (*sumera ōmikuni*) was the original country (*oya guni* or *moto guni*) for all other countries (*yorozu no kuni*), based on the fact that Japan appeared as a result of the union of the creation deities (*musubi no kami no musubi*).

50.　Hirata, "Tama no mihashira," 20.

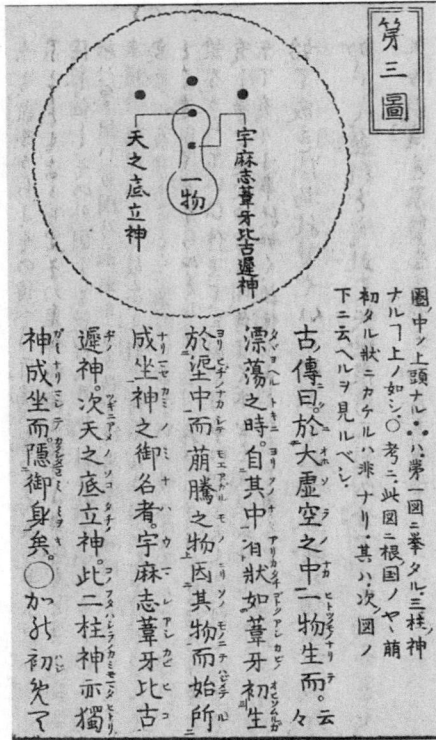

FIGURE 4.3. Atsutane's drawing: the third stage of the creation. This illustration shows the three pillars of the deities and the drifting cloud, which expands to house two new deities. They emerge from the drifting cloud like a flame; their names are Umare ashikabi hikoji no kami and Ame no sokotachi no kami. They, too, hide themselves and become invisible but are the rulers of Heaven, which is represented by the two black dots in the space of the object, the drifting cloud. Hirata, *Tamano mihashira*, 1:20. Courtesy of the National Diet Library Digital Collections.

He highlighted the union of the creation deities as supporting the case for supremacy and confirmed this special quality by referencing "some Western books," which described Japan as geographically privileged, protected from foreign invasions, and the unparalleled land of happiness.[51] He explained that the rich soil of the archipelago could be traced back to the blessings of the deities of Heaven and Earth, and he

51.   Hirata, "Tama no mihashira," 20–21.

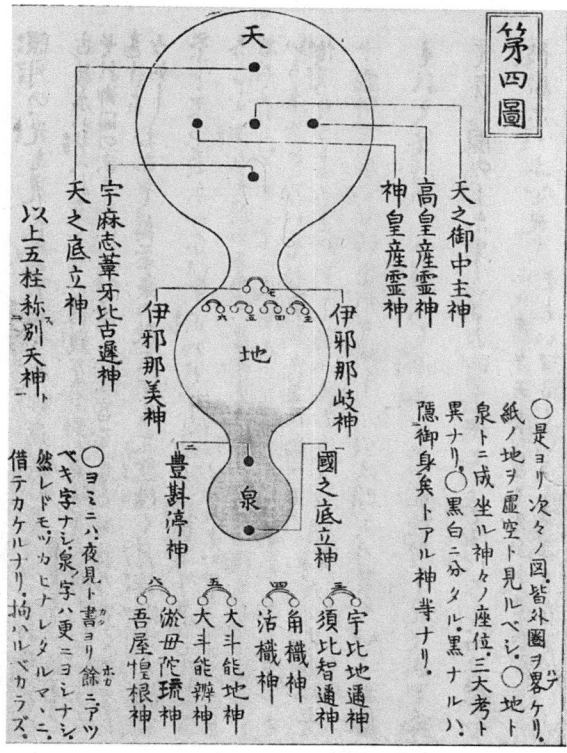

FIGURE 4.4. Atsutane's drawing: the fourth stage of the creation. This shows the creation of three spaces. It seeks to capture the separation of Heaven from Earth and *yomi*, although it is still connected in the image. At the bottom of *yomi*, the deity Kuni no sokotachi no kami is in charge, and another deity, Toyokumu nu no kami, acts as defense on the border between Earth and *yomi*. Both of them hide themselves to become invisible. In addition, four pairs of male and female deities are marked. They remain in Earth and *yomi* to rule with Izanami and Izanagi. They are represented by empty circles to show that they remain visible. They are Uhijini no kami and Suhichini no kami, Tsunugui no kami and Ikugui no kami, Ōtonoji no kami and Ōtonobe no kami, and Omodaru no kami and Aya kashikone no kami. Hirata, *Tamano mihashira*, 1:22. Courtesy of the National Diet Library Digital Collections.

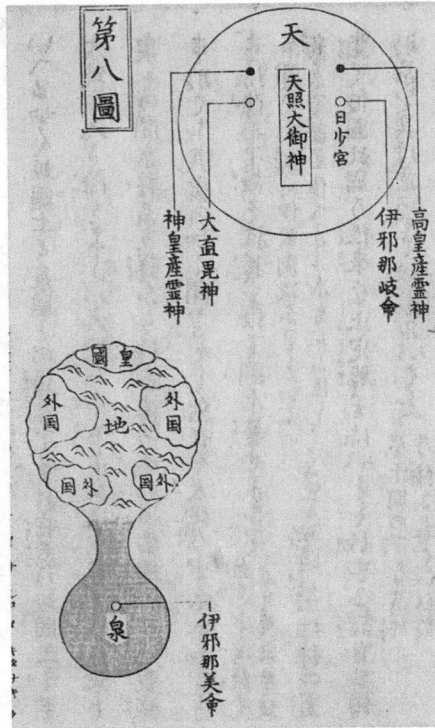

FIGURE 4.5. Atsutane's drawing: the eighth stage of the creation. The image shows the divine birth of Sun Goddess Amaterasu, who replaces the deity that was the central ruler of Heaven up to this point, Ame no minakanushi no kami. Takami musubi no kami and Kamumi musubi no kami were also present in Heaven, although they are marked by black dots to signify their invisibility. This illustration marks Izanagi and Ōnaobi no kami as visible gods, with Izanagi being present at the shrine of Hinowaka miya. In the lower image, Japan is located at the top of the space of Earth, beyond the four "foreign countries" that together inhabit the Earth. This image also shows that Earth is still connected to *yomi*, where Izanami is the ruler. Hirata, *Tamano mihashira*, 1:48. Courtesy of the National Diet Library Digital Collections.

used the character *ki*, which originally meant energy flow, by providing the readings of *ikioi* (force or energy) and *kokoro* (heart). Using information from Western theories to strengthen the existing narrative of *shinkoku* Japan, Atsutane added more validity to the claim of divinity.

Likewise, Atsutane identified various climatological effects, such as fog, haze, and mists in the mountainous areas, as the acts of the deities

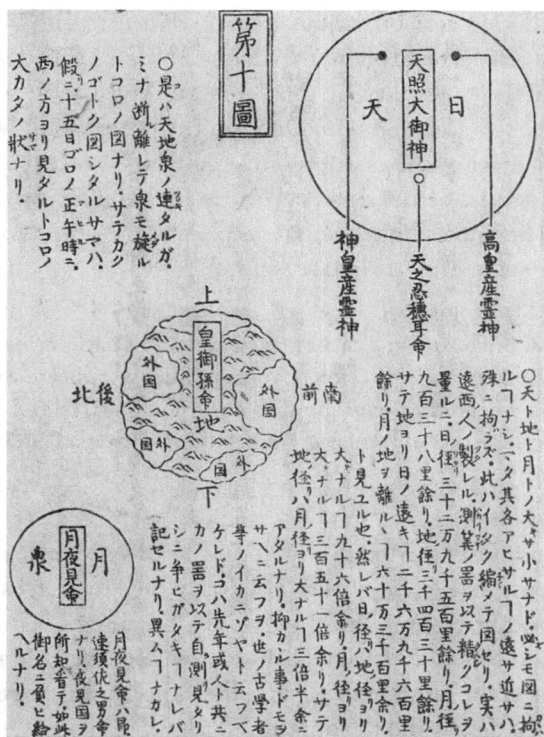

FIGURE 4.6. Atsutane's drawing: the tenth stage of the creation. The image shows the final separation of *yomi* from Earth and the emergence of three independent entities. *Yomi* is ruled by Tsuku yomi no mikoto, another name for Susanoo no mikoto, the brother of Amaterasu. In the space associated with Heaven, there is the presence of a deity, Ame no oshiho mimi no mikoto, just below Amaterasu. This is one of the sons of Amaterasu, also known as Masaka akatsu kachi hayabi, and he is the next ruler of Heaven after Amaterasu. Atsutane makes a note that this illustration is based on the map and astronomical calculations made by Western people from a distant land. Hirata, *Tamano mihashira*, 2:4. Courtesy of the National Diet Library Digital Collections, http://dl.ndl.go.jp/info:ndljp/pid/2562763.

of fire, earth, or wind in his elaboration on how the three realms came into being and the deities' role in the production.[52] In fact, Atsutane had already discussed these meteorological phenomena in *Kishin shinron*, attributing

52. Atsutane argues that Western people tried to explain climatic effects and mechanisms on Earth, but their theories were rootless. They did not know the principle

them to the divine acts of various deities (*miwaza*). In *Kishin shinron* reference was made to explain the divine role of each deity, such as claiming that the Sun deity lit up the world and the deities of water made rainfall.[53] In *Tama no mihashira*, on the other hand, he explained the cause and effect of the creation of the country to reveal more specifically the divine acts of the deities. For instance, following the creation stage of the different realms, Atsutane explained the origins of the deities of fire, wind, water, and the like as follows:

> Izanami gave birth to a god of fire (*hi no kami*) because *hi no kami* was necessary to make the land (*kuni*). And, in order to appease the ferocity (*arabi*) of the fire god, Izanami produced the god of earth and the god of water. All of these acts of Izanami originated in her deep affections for the land.[54]

Atsutane went on to describe the birth process of various deities as a way of explaining the love of the creation deities, which in turn explained the meteorological phenomena. In other words, because Izanami loved her land deeply and produced various deities, even seemingly "natural" phenomena, such as the wind blowing and the sun shining, were reflections of the love of the deities and the miraculous acts of the gods. Quite literally, the land, mountains, wind, and every other thing in the universe retained a god-like quality because the deities had made them. Therefore, all phenomena, whether climatic effects or the reproduction of life, were the results of the divine and miraculous acts (*mishiwaza*) of the gods in Atsutane's thought.

The second part of *Tama no mihashira* is focused on discussions about the land of the dead, *yomi*, and the spirits of the dead (*shinibito no tama*). Atsutane's theory centers on a god known as Ōkuninushi and his reign in the world of *yomi*. In Norinaga's interpretation, Ōkuninushi went to the land of permanent darkness (*tokoyo no kuni*) (another name for *yomi*) and hid himself in a place called Yasokumaji on his way to the Kizuki

---

of how the deities caused all these phenomena because they were not from the country of the deities (*shinkoku no hito naraneba*). Hirata, "Tama no mihashira," 31.

53.   Hirata, "Kishin shinron," 21–22.
54.   Hirata, "Tama no mihashira," 30.

Shrine (*kizuki no miya*). Atsutane took issue with this, arguing that Yaso-kumaji was not the same as *yomi* and its identity was unclear in historical documents. Claiming that Yasokumaji only meant "numerous" (*yaso* or *yae*) "paths in the deep recesses" (*kuma michi* or *kumaji*), Atsutane rejected the interpretation that Ōkuninushi had disappeared into *yomi*.[55] Instead, citing various references concerning Ōkuninushi's departure, he concluded that Ōkuninushi went to Kuzuki no miya to settle and rule (*shizumari mashisu*) there. He argued as follows:

> I have been thinking about the differences (*kejime*) between *arawanigoto* and *kamigoto*. When ordinary people (*tadabito*) live in this world (*utsusho*), this is a part of *arawanigoto* and they are the people of the emperor (*sum-eramikoto*). When they die, the god guides their spirits (*tama*), as we know through such notions as ghosts (*yūrei*) and the souls of the dead (*meikon*), so to speak, to the world of the dead (*yūmei*). In fact, the great god that rules the land of the dead (*kami no mikado*) is Ōkuninushi. Thus, the spirits of the dead go to his land to serve him and receive divine instruction (*miokite*) from Ōkuninushi.[56]

Using the terms developed by Norinaga, Atsutane created his terminology, such as the "affairs of the living" (*arawanigoto*) and the "affairs of the dead" (*kamigoto*), and presented a theory that the spirit of the dead went to a place called *yūmei*, which was part of the world of the dead including the *kami no mikado*. By identifying Ōkuninushi as ruler of the land of the dead, Atsutane presented a different view of the world of the dead than did Norinaga, who argued that the spirits went to the world of *yūmei* and entered the *kami no mikado*, the capital of the spirits. Awaiting the verdict of Ōkuninushi in the *kami no mikado* and serving him in *yūmei* are evocative of the idea of the final judgment in Christianity. Or, the role of Ōkuninushi reminds us of the god of Hell, Enma, in Buddhism, who judges whether the souls of people go to Heaven or Hell. Either way, Atsutane argued that after death, spirits did not disappear into the world of *yomi* but joined the world of Ōkuninushi and lived in *yūmei* by serving Ōkuninushi there.

55. Hirata, "Tama no mihashira," 53–55.
56. Hirata, "Tama no mihashira," 55–56.

According to Norinaga, *kamigoto* were the affairs of the deities, which were invisible to those who were alive, and it was unclear as to who was doing what in this realm of *kamigoto* because everything that happened in this world was caused by the will of the gods (*mikokoro*).[57] In contrast, Atsutane equated the world of Ōkuninushi with the events in *kamigoto* and explained that it was impossible for living people to see inside the world of *yūmei*—and that was why even Norinaga could not figure out where Ōkuninushi went. Atsutane's theory was that the destination of the spirit of the dead was not *yomi* but the place called *kami no mikado*, where Ōkuninushi was the ruler. By envisioning a meaningful life after death, Atsutane's theory offered a sense of relief to his followers and let them "calm their hearts." In fact, he moved further away from Norinaga's idea of *yomi* by rejecting the assertion that the spirits of the dead migrated to *yomi*. Instead, his explanation was rooted in the fact that the *yūmei* were invisible from the world of the living. Atsutane stated as follows:

> Where do the spirits go when the people of this country die? I say, the spirits stay in this country forever. Judging from our records from the past and the facts that we have today, we can clearly say this . . . because, *kami no mikado* is located in more than one place in this world of the living (*utsushi kuni*). However, *kami no mikado* is too faint (*honoka*) to see and one cannot distinguish the borders between the two worlds. Even the people in China spoke about the world of the dead as *yūmei* or *meifu*. From *kami no mikado*, they can see the acts of people [who are alive] (*hito no shiwaza*) (a *katchū* starts by stating: "about this, there are many records, so written that there is no need to give examples now."). However, from this side of the living (*utsusho*), it is impossible to see *yūmei*.[58]

Atsutane explained that the world of the dead was a place people could not see but was adjacent to the human realm. There, the dead lived the same kind of life they had lived so far. Thus, he reassured people that even if their bodies died, the spirits would reach *yūmei* and their souls (*reikon*) would join various deities and live in an unseen world much like our own. Just as the spirits stayed in the shrines, in the imperial tombs, or

---

57. Motoori, "Kojikiden ni no maki: kamiyo no tōmari futamaki to iu maki," 120.
58. Hirata, "Tama no mihashira," 82.

elsewhere, Atsutane stated, the spirits were rightly settled in their place (*shizumari mashinu*).[59]

Atsutane stated that his theory was nothing unique and foreign countries had similar explanations. He wrote:

> The destination of the spirits of the dead is not limited to the world of *yomi*. This can be proven from the facts of the divine age and the birth of people . . . the parents give birth to children, but the origin of their births is caused by the miraculous divine spirits (*mitama*) of the creation deities (*musubi no kami*). It results from the union of wind, fire, water, and earth, and the union of four kinds of thing (*yokusa no mono*), in addition to the spirit (*tamashii*) and happiness (*sachiwai*). (A *katchū* starts by saying, "although I cannot say how exactly this happens, I have seen it and am speaking truthfully, so please do not be suspicious.") When people die, it becomes water, earth, and corpse (*mukuro*), and the body is left in this world, while the divine soul goes with the wind and fire and leaves (*sakari saru*) [this world]. (Another *katchū* is inserted, stating, "when I said these things, someone said that my theory resembled the one in foreign countries [*adashi kuni no setsu*], but . . . I have verified my theory with the historical records of the past [*kamiyo no tsutae*] and facts . . . it is simply the case that their theories resemble my theory, not the other way around.")[60]

Even though Atsutane could not say for sure how the union of the deities or the divine spirits of the creation deities worked, he claimed that these were facts consistent with the accounts of the deities described in Norinaga's work. Building on his teacher's work, Atsutane conceived the theories of his own with the goal of "strengthening the Japanese heart." By explicating at length the nature of the world of the dead (something Norinaga refused to do), Atsutane made it familiar and knowable. Once they knew that the spirits of the dead stayed in the same space as the living after death, Atsutane's followers were not to be confused or misled by foreign teachings, but they should keep faith with the learning of the ancient. By making this theory a vital teaching of Kokugaku, Atsutane's theory of *kishin* was akin to spiritual guidance for the community.

59. Hirata, "Tama no mihashira," 84–85.
60. Hirata, "Tama no mihashira," 77–79.

In this way, Atsutane domesticated *kishin*, which had originally been the cause of popular anxiety in ancient China because of their invisibility and unknown potential. Atsutane visualized their ubiquitous existence and made them the sign of divine protection in Japan. He argued that it would not be odd to find records of extraordinary incidents because Japan was *shinkoku* and its space was historically populated by the spirits. Celebrating the supernatural phenomena, he actively excavated historical records about strange events as evidence of the gods and divine spirits. By reassuring his followers that they should feel consoled by the presence of numerous divine shields that existed in their community, Atsutane's strategy was to incorporate the supernatural dimension into popular spirituality. Building on the achievement of Norinaga, whose work had naturalized the idea that Japan was created by the deities, Atsutane led his followers to believe that traces of the deities were everywhere and that this was the defining quality of Japan.

Atsutane privileged historical records other than the chronicles, such as *fudoki*; the ancient prayers called *norito*; the five texts of *shintō*, which constituted the canonical texts for Ise Shinto (*shintō gobusho*); and the ninth-century imperial compilation of the *Newly Compiled Record of Clans* (*Shinsen shōjiroku* or *ujikabaneroku*), which showed the detailed history of powerful ancient families, including the ones that originally came to Japan from China and Korea.[61] Atsutane argued that the two chronicles of *Kojiki* and *Nihon shoki* did not record all the activities of the deities and differentiated himself from Norinaga. Instead, he strove to recover the "real" history of *kamiyo* through other sources, such as *norito*, the words of praise and worship for the gods that people offered during celebratory occasions, including festivals (*matsuri*) and rituals in the ancient past.[62] Many *norito* are found in volume eight of the *Engishiki*, and Atsutane valued old *norito* as evidence of the deities in

---

61.   Hirata, *Koshichō kaidaiki*, 245.

62.   In the past, words were perceived to have come to people through the divine will and acts of the gods. Thus, the ancient people attributed some spiritual notions to words. Typically, the first part of *norito* describes the origin of the festival, and the second part explains how the festival is conducted, and together it included a detailed list of information that identified who had ordered the performance of the festival. Takeda, "Norito: kaisetsu," 368–69.

the age of the gods.[63] In his essays "On *Norito* of Heaven and Earth" (*Amatsu norito kō*), "Correct Readings of *Norito*" (*Norito seikun*), and "Newly Transcribed: Procedures of *Norito*" (*Shinkoku norito shiki*), Atsutane interrogated the contexts and contents of the festivals the emperor ordered to be held in various regions to verify the actual words spoken by the gods.[64]

Atsutane prioritized these sources and integrated them into the major texts of his own teaching of Kokugaku, namely, the fifteen-volume *History of Ancient Japan* (*Koshi seibun*, 1811), the thirty-seven-volume *Commentaries on Koshi Seibun* (*Koshiden*, 1825), and the four-volume *On the Ancient History of Japan* (*Koshichō*, 1819), in addition to Norinaga's *Kojikiden*. Atsutane elaborated on his theory of *kishin* as the traces of *kami* in "On Great Japan" (*Daifusōkoku kō*, 1837) and "Additional Thoughts on the Three Divine Mountains" (*Sanshinzan yokō*), in which he explained that Japan was the location of the legendary three divine mountains and described how the deities caused marvelous phenomena to occur.[65] By claiming that the deities originated from the creation deities of Japan, Atsutane used the rich discussions on *kishin* in the Chinese sources on various festivals and rituals. In so doing, his new theory of *kishin* transformed *kishin* discourse that had originated in the teachings of the ancient Chinese sages into the basis of Kokugaku teaching and the foundational narrative of a social formation in nineteenth-century Japan.

As Harry Harootunian has written, Atsutane's success as a Kokugaku scholar derived from his talents in shifting the focus in the Kokugaku discourse of Norinaga from song, poetry, and aesthetics to the more popular concerns of the spirit. Atsutane demonstrated that spiritual "practice preceded the representations in language, song, and poetry that practical spirituality produced" based on textual authority.[66] Consequently, he changed the direction of Kokugaku discourse to provide his followers with spiritual guidance, and he made scholarly efforts to demonstrate that

63. *Engishiki* consists of fifty volumes total, with the first ten concerning the deities.

64. Hirata, "Amatsu norito kō," 1–13 and "Shinkoku norito shiki," 1–33.

65. Hirata, "Daifusōkoku kō" and "Sanshinzan yokō"; Miura K., *Chūgokujin no toposu*, 25–29.

66. Harootunian, *Things Seen and Unseen*, 26. See also McNally, *Proving the Way*.

the supernatural beings were really protective deities for the community. Atsutane's reworking of *kishin* merged the traditional discourse that had been circulating among Confucian scholars and the popular idea of the spirits of the dead, bringing them to the center of the narrative of Japan. By accentuating the activities of the divine spirits, Atsutane linked them with the evidence of *shinkoku* Japan and established a theory that everything in the universe was the result of the intricate workings of the divine deities. The transformation of the character *shin* or *kami* of the "spirits" shows the maturity of the discourse on Japan that had derived from the idea of *kishin* in ancient China.

We have now observed the naturalization and nativization of *kishin* discourse in early modern Japan. Scholars such as Ekiken, Razan, Hakuseki, Norinaga, and Atsutane employed *kishin* in the discursive production of Japan, and the formation of the *shinkoku* Japan narrative reveals the refinement of the discourse on community that came to overlap with the vision of a future Japan. In short, the production of Japan was a process of self-identification and self-representation vis-à-vis the dominant Other, China, accompanied by the tireless efforts of scholars who strove to produce the speaking subject of Japan. In this process, they negotiated and adopted foreign conceptual frameworks to represent Japan and ultimately naturalize the foreign cosmology and knowledge structure as they represented Japan as an independent country. Once Atsutane claimed *kishin* to actually be the divine *kami* of Japan, foreign traces in *kishin* discourse could be erased, and their presence became retrospectively inverted as if *kami* had existed from the very beginning in the discourse of Japan.

A series of reworkings of *kishin* in the narrativization of Japan testifies to the inevitable truth that defines the act of self-identification as only possible with the presence of the Other and, furthermore, a continuing act of erasing the trace of that Other. As Japan came to encounter more Others in the Bakumatsu era and beyond, Japanese scholars quickly abandoned China as their cultural reference point. Threatened by the invasive power of Western imperialism and capitalism, the new Meiji government devised ways to engage with the West. The next two chapters explore this process of identifying Japan vis-à-vis the Western powers in the changing order of East Asia and the world in the last decades of the nineteenth century. The shift from China to the West was accompanied by a series of political and social changes, including the overthrow of the Tokugawa shogunate, the establishment of the Meiji state, the invention of a modern nation-state under the symbolic unity of Emperor Meiji (1852–1912, r. 1868–1912), and the rapid industrialization of the center and periphery. In this process, the features of the narrative of Japan changed dramatically, and the discourse of *shinkoku* Japan was transformed into something completely different as Meiji intellectuals strove to produce a narrative of their country as sublime Japan.

CHAPTER 5

Philosophizing the Divine Country

Modern philosophy begins when the generally accepted basis
upon which the world is interpreted ceases to be a deity whose
pattern is assumed to have already been imprinted into the universe. The new philosophical task is therefore for human reason
to establish its own legitimacy as the ground of truth.

—Andrew Bowie, *Aesthetics and Subjectivity*

With an increasing number of foreign ships reaching Japanese
waters from the late eighteenth century onward, the growing vis-
ibility of the "barbarians" accelerated the fear of the foreign held by the
imperial court and populace. Rather than responding to these foreign
intruders as the "military general to subdue barbarians" (*seii taishōgun*),
which was the shogun's titular role, he allowed them to enter Japan's territory. Scholars perceiving the strength of the West in the teaching of
Christianity were fearful of its influence over the popular mind, and they
tried to produce ideological formulations to enhance the sense of community in Japan. As we observed in the previous chapter, for example,
Hirata Atsutane provided his followers with spiritual guidance to enable
them to live peacefully in the time of great anxiety by envisioning a society in which all beings were held tightly together in *shinkoku* Japan.

The Meiji Restoration of 1868 ended the 260 years of shogunate rule,
and the Meiji state identified the West as the new cultural authority,
replacing the Confucian metaphysics and cosmology from which the shogunate had drawn its legitimacy. Restoration activists quickly broke new
political ground via the teenage boy head of state, Emperor Meiji (1852–
1912, r. 1868–1912), launching a number of administrative reforms by vigorously incorporating radical Westernizing and nationalizing projects.
Hoping to transform Japan into a modern nation, Meiji statesmen introduced new worldviews and domains of knowledge from the West, which
gradually gave rise to a series of institutional frameworks that helped es-

tablish the modern nation-state by 1890.[1] However, building a modern nation in line with Western models, including the ideals of civil society and capitalism, proved a difficult path to tread. Although a heightened state of Westernization fever was outlandishly exemplified in the age of the "Deer-cry Hall" (*rokumeikan*) in the mid-1880s, local communities whose lifestyles were deeply rooted in the Tokugawa period model responded to the state's modernizing programs with dissent, indifference, and suspicion.[2] As Benedict Anderson has stated, nationalism, nationality, or nation-ness demands "such profound emotional legitimacy" from us because it completely replaces older ideas of legitimation and forms of loyalty and identification.[3] When citizens of a sovereign political state embrace these values, as well as nationality, patriotism, and a sense of loyalty to the state, a myth of the homogeneous space of nation begins to prevail.

The final two chapters of this book analyze how the narrative of *shinkoku* Japan changed in the transitional period from Tokugawa to Meiji with the emergent West as a new reference point and civilization model. One of the most prominent enlightenment leaders of the time, Fukuzawa Yukichi (1834–1901), insightfully remarked in his *Encouragement of Learning* (*Gakumon no susume*, 1872–76) that the difficulty with the modernizing process came from the fact that there was still no nation (*kokumin*) or any putative unity of the Japanese people after the decade-long struggle following the restoration.[4] He argued that for a sense of nation or nationalism to emerge, it was necessary for "the middle class" to form the majority of the population, with the members embracing a shared identity as a united people and the consciousness of the bourgeoisie.[5] This chapter demonstrates how "the middle-class consciousness" emerged in Japan in the closing decades of the nineteenth century as young intellectuals who contested the state's version of nationalism earnestly produced nationalist ideals.[6] Those who were educated and intelligent initiated

1. Karatani, "Japan as Art Museum," 43.

2. Fujitani, *Splendid Monarchy*; Platt, *Burning and Building*; Wigen, *Malleable Map*; Yasumaru, *Kamigami no Meiji ishin*.

3. Anderson, *Imagined Communities*, 4.

4. Fukuzawa, "Gakumon no susume," 52.

5. Fukuzawa, "Gakumon no susume," 52–54.

6. Karlin, *Gender and Nation*, 40–42. See also Furniss, *Edmund Burke's Aesthetic Ideology*, and Ashfield and de Bolla, eds., *The Sublime*, both of which analyze the discursive

the process of enlightening the masses and spreading the civic values and aspirations of the modern nation-state through the space created by journalism.

By focusing on one of the most politically active literary societies working against the Meiji state, Seikyōsha (Society for Political Education, 1888), this chapter analyzes how the members, most notably Miyake Setsurei (1860–1945, also known as Yūjirō), endeavored to reenvision an imaginary Japan by transforming the existing sets of values and worldview and allowing the Japanese to join the wider international community. He reinterpreted the significance of the historical experience of the East and through the prism of Western knowledge—most important, modern philosophy and the theories of evolution (*shinkaron*)—identified a new place for Japan in the modern world. In this new cosmological order, the distinct *fūdo* of Japan obtained a new identity as Setsurei reconfigured the philosophical basis of *fūdo* to claim for Japan the role of leading nation in East Asia.

The Rise of Intellectual Societies in the Late 1880s

Throughout his life, Miyake Setsurei published prolifically, including numerous works on philosophical and historical topics as well as world current affairs. From the time he graduated with a degree in philosophy from Tokyo University in 1883, he established himself as both a prominent philosopher and an outside (*zaiya*) scholar, one who stood in opposition to the Japanese state.[7] He taught philosophy at Tokyo Senmon Gakkō (Tokyo Specialized School, the present-day Waseda University) and Tetsugakkan (School of Philosophy, the present-day Tōyō University).

---

creations and transformations of the aesthetic ideology for the containment of revolution to secure the social formation in eighteenth-century Britain.

7.   After briefly working at the university and at the Ministry of Education, where he was engaged in researching the history of Buddhism in Japan with renowned philosopher Inoue Tetsujirō (1855–1944) and Ariga Nagao (1860–1921), Setsurei's research bureau moved from the university to the Ministry of Education. He did work for the Meiji state in the initial years of his career, leaving the ministry for good in 1887. Kano, *Nihon kindaika no shisō*, 74–81.

As one of the "new generation" in Meiji Japan, Setsurei was inspired by the teaching of Fukuzawa Yukichi, who encouraged learning while asserting the importance of "the independence of knowledge" (*gakumon no dokuritsu*) in his various works.[8]

Setsurei recalled the efforts and sacrifices of those who had first demanded a national assembly in 1874 as a historic achievement that subsequently evolved into the Freedom and Popular Rights movement (*jiyū minken undō*).[9] In 1874, the eight leaders of the movement, Itagaki Taisuke (1837–1919), Gotō Shōjirō (1838–1897), Soejima Taneomi (1828–1905), Etō Shinpei (1834–74), Yuri Kimimasa (1828–1909), Okamoto Kenzaburō (1842–85), Furusawa Shigeru (1847–1911), and Komuro Shinobu (1839–98), presented the "Petition for the Establishment of a Popularly Elected Assembly" (*minsen giin setsuritsu no mikotonori*) to the Meiji state, which at that time was largely controlled by those who came from the former Chōshū and Satsuma domains. This petition stirred up much attention and attracted others who shared a critical view of the authoritarian Meiji state. The demand for an elected legislature was the start of the Freedom and Popular Rights movement, which sought to distribute political power more evenly by expanding people's rights. In response to the petition, the imperial rescript of 1881 promised to establish a popularly elected assembly in 1890, and the 1881 rescript marked the first moment for people to be informed about the coming of parliamentary government. The promise of a democratic form of government inspired not only those who were involved in the Freedom and Popular Rights movement but also young students and scholars, who began to participate in discussions on the constitution and the nature of civil society.[10] The emergence of important intellectual groups in the late

---

8. Nagatsuma, *Kōkyōsei no ētosu* and *Miyake Setsurei no seiji shisō*, 70–83.

9. After withdrawing from the government over a disagreement about the invasion of Korea in 1873, which is known as the Meiji Six (1873) political crisis, the eight leaders submitted the petition, aiming to break the autocratic rule of the leaders from the Satsuma and Chōshū domains.

10. The 1881 (Meiji 14) political crisis ended with the expulsion of one of the most important Meiji government officials of the time, Ōkuma Shigenobu (1838–1922), who recommended that Japan should adopt a British-style parliamentary government for the national assembly. His elimination eradicated the possibility of either the British or French constitution becoming the model for Japan, and it strengthened the possibility

nineteenth century, such as the Min'yūsha (Friends of the People) in 1887 and the Seikyōsha in the following year, testified to the enthusiasm of the young intellectuals. In fact, one study estimates that more than 800 journals and magazines were published in 1888, and furthermore that 186 of these were new publications.[11] The literary activists wished to engage in the making of a democratic and civic nation with the timely arrival of the constitution and the National Diet.

Nevertheless, Setsurei concluded that the Freedom and Popular Rights movement was a failure because many of its leaders—either members of the Liberty Party (Jiyūtō), its supporters, or its sympathizers—were too concerned with obtaining rights and power for themselves. They did not think or believe that expanding the "popular rights" and freedom of "the people" could benefit the whole population.[12] The ongoing political antagonisms within the Meiji state and the factionalism in the leaderships of the state and opposition groups frustrated many young intellectuals. At the same time, Setsurei and others were frustrated by the destruction and violence caused by the Freedom and People's Rights movement, which proved that Japan was not ready to realize the Western ideals of a civil society, which for them was the symbol of a civilized nation.[13] The Meiji state failed to assume its responsibility for stabilizing the economy, and the popular protests proved to be damaging

---

that the constitution of Prussia would be the chosen model. The political struggles of 1881 made government circles more exclusive and dominant than ever before by removing the last opponent in the final stage of the nation-building project. See, for example, Gluck, *Japan's Modern Myths* and the more recent study by Kim, *Age of Visions and Arguments*.

11.   Nakanome Tōru cites a progress report titled "Meiji nijūichinen kōtei hōkoku," published by the Home Ministry (*Naimushō*) and explains that with the opening of the National Diet approaching fast, various local political parties were formed, and newspapers and magazines emerged to cover their opinions and activities. Nakanome, *Seikyōsha no kenkyū*, 143. See also Huffman, *Creating a Public*, 150–59.

12.   In particular, Miyake Setsurei's publication *Dōjidaishi* is an excellent source that reveals the skepticism of the young intellectuals toward the Meiji leaders and provides an analysis of current political conditions, including his views on the participants in the various popular protests. Miyake, *Dōjidaishi*.

13.   Setsurei expressed his disappointment in the essays he published in *Nipponjin*. These essays were long and appeared in a number of installments over several issues. See, for example, Miyake, "Ishin go seifu gai no seijika" and "Satchō no zento o uranau."

because they prevented Japan from establishing an enduring modern nation.

In this context, the founding of various intellectual groups and societies in the late 1880s suggests the changing dynamics of political participation and the replacement of popular protests with journalism. Precisely because of the direction and subsequent outcome of the Freedom and Popular Rights movement, the young student population realized that a prolonged campaign of popular protests would only exacerbate the sufferings of poor farmers in the countryside.[14] Those who organized the political societies shared a national vision of the political empowerment of the people, but they were far more inspired by the prospect of educating young readers and producing modern citizenry. Thus, university graduates like Setsurei no longer prioritized government positions as the ideal career path but were more inclined to enthusiastically pursue careers such as teachers, researchers, and journalists. A well-informed and sizable public was emerging, which anxiously awaited the promised promulgation of the institutional framework of a nation-state.

In spring 1891, popular excitement about the symbolic beginning of a new Japan peaked with the promulgation of the constitution and the opening of the first popularly elected assembly, the Diet. A scholar of modern Japanese literature and literary critic, Yanagida Izumi, described this culminating moment of hope and exhilaration as follows:

> Both pro and anti-Westernization camps placed their hopes in the promulgation of the Constitution and the emergence of the Diet and looked forward to the moment becoming real with an anticipation similar to the opening of New Year lucky bags (*fukubukuro*) from the God of Happiness (*fuku no kami*). However, once the first Diet had actually convened during the year 1890–91, those who had been eagerly waiting found nothing, not a single treasure came out of the lucky bag. The bag was supposed to

14.   Sohō was briefly a student at Tokyō Eigo Gakkō in 1876 and Dōshisha Eigo Gakkō in Kyoto until 1880, where he studied closely with Niijima Jō (1843–90). Sohō came to uphold industrialization, trade and commerce, and education as the top priorities of Japan after advancing his understanding with the People's Rights movement, directing his attention to the "gentlemen of the countryside" (*inaka shinshi*), who he believed would revitalize the local economy for the future leaders of Japan. See, for example, Kimura, *Seinen no tanjō*; Kano, *Nihon kindaika no shisō*, 75; Pierson, *Tokutomi Sohō*.

be filled with good fortune, but all they witnessed were huge disputes, bursting out in a chaotic manner as if pandemonium had broken out. This outcome drove many Japanese people to despair. Many people were deeply disappointed, feeling quite weary and deducing that there was no future for Japan.[15]

In spite of the culmination of their dreams, many were deeply disappointed and betrayed by the Meiji state. The political climate of 1891 proved that the state's interests were completely different and did not reflect the interests of the people.[16] As historian Kevin Doak has written, "the 1889 Constitution of the Great Empire of Japan not only defined the country as an empire (*teikoku*) rather than a nation-state (*kokumin-kokka*), but legally codified the previous announcement that the Japanese people were not a nation but merely subjects (*shinmin*) of their monarch."[17] Clearly, the constitution reflected the dominant view of the state leadership, namely, Itō Hirobumi (1841–1909), who was in charge of its drafting. Itō concluded that a series of popular protests in earlier decades proved the immature state of modern citizens in Japan and that they could not be trusted to correctly exercise their civil liberty to preserve civil society. By designating people as imperial subjects rather than the foundation stone of the regime, Itō legitimized the government as being independent of the will of a people who were not yet able to embrace and exercise their rights. As a result, a small but powerful political circle surrounding the emperor came to wield the actual power, rendering the political institutions of the modern Japanese nation undemocratic in future decades.

As Yanagida described it, the sense that a new beginning for Japan was dawning quickly turned to disappointment. Setsurei, too, was disenchanted, not just with the selfish politicians but also with the failure to create a united "people." Within and in opposition to this political situation, Setsurei wrote his book *Truth, Goodness, Beauty: The Japanese* (*Shin zen bi: Nipponjin*, 1891; hereafter cited as *Shin zen bi*) to inspire the weary

---

15.   Yanagida, "Kaidai," 424–25.

16.   Miyake, "Shakui rokuri no tomonawazaru chūkun," 566–72; Gotō B., *Taigu Miyake Setsurei*, 77–79; Nagatsuma, *Miyake Setsurei no seiji shisō*, 110. "Yohai dōshi wa ikanaru shugi o torite ka undō subeki," 5–7.

17.   Doak, *History of Nationalism*, 176.

people by reminding them that "the Japanese were a promising species (*yūi no shuzoku*) with important responsibilities to perform" in the modern world.[18] Intending to speak to the Japanese people and nation, even though it did not yet reflect national unity, he published the book to explain the role of modern citizens as members of the entire human race, not just the Meiji state. By carefully selecting the three philosophical notions of truth, goodness, and beauty from Western philosophy, Setsurei identified them as the foundation stones of the modern Japanese nation-building project. Before we examine this text, let us explore the prevalent intellectual climate of the 1880s, which was greatly affected by these manifestations of political turbulence.

The "Seikyōsha" and the Making of an Ideal Nation

Setsurei maintained a critical stance against the Meiji state's Westernization policies, cultivating a significantly different understanding of civilization than the intellectuals of earlier generations. In the first decade of the Meiji era, many leading scholars of Western studies (Yōgaku) who were related to the Meiji state had organized the Meiji Six Society (Meirokusha, 1873) with the aim of influencing people by providing images of national ideals and the state's future vision.[19] For many members, the idea of civilization (*bunmei*) meant Western civilization. By contrast, Setsurei repeatedly argued that there was something to be proud of in other cultures and civilizations and envisioned a world of various groups that would coexist with the civilizations of other countries. To spread the message and inform the public about Japan's potential to prosper in the modern world, Setsurei, along with Shiga Shigetaka (1863–1927), founded Seikyōsha in 1888 after graduating from Tokyo University.

18. Yanagida, "Kaisetsu," 425.

19. Hirota, "'Meirokusha' to 'Minyūsha'," 327–30. The members included Fukuzawa Yukichi, Katō Hiroyuki (1836–1916), Mitsukuri Rinshō (1846–97), Mitsukuri Shūhei (1826–86), Mori Arinori (1847–89), Nakamura Masanao (1832–91), Nishi Amane (1829–97), Nishimura Shigeki (1828–1902), Tsuda Mamichi (1829–1903), and Sugi Kōji (1828–1917).

The generational differences in relation to perceptions of civilization originated in the modern university education sector that had begun in the late 1870s. University students read widely in English and in translation, learning about Western views on civilizations of the world, particularly through the medium of world geography. In addition, the two national universities in Japan at this time, Tokyo University and Sapporo Agriculture College, employed many foreign nationals who were referred to as "hired foreigners" (*oyatoi gaikokujin* or *yatoi*). The Meiji state, prefectures, and companies (among others) hired foreign nationals to work in Japan temporarily, and they provided their students with textbooks and other learning materials from their own countries.[20] Japanese authors wrote numerous history and geography textbooks, in which, following the line of evolutionary theories, they designated the West as the center of enlightenment and civilization.[21] These textbooks unanimously positioned the rest of the world, particularly Asia and Africa, as being "barbaric" or "uncivilized." Fukuzawa Yukichi, in *Outline of the Theory of Civilization* (*Bunmeiron no gairyaku*, 1875), for instance, defined the three stages of civilization as "uncivilized" (*mikai*), "half-civilized" (*hankai*), and "civilized" (*bunmei*), placing Japan in the stage of half-civilized.[22] Drawing on various world history textbooks, including Henry Thomas Buckle's *History of Civilization in England* and François Guizot's *General History of Civilization in Europe*, Fukuzawa's hierarchy of civilization adhered to

20.   For the influence of Western literature, particularly British literature, on the formation of the Japanese Empire, see Saitō H., *Teikoku Nihon no eibungaku*.

21.   For example, Fukuzawa wrote geography books such as *Catalogue of the World's Countries in the Palm of One's Hand* (*Shōchū bankoku ichiran* 1869) and *Geography of Myriad Countries of the World* (*Sekai Kunizukushi*, 1869). *Sekai Kunizukushi* was a popular school textbook, along with *World Geography* (*Yochi shiryaku*, 1870–80) by Uchida Masao and *Introduction to Geography* (*Chigaku kotohajime*, 1870) by Matsuyama Tōan. Fukuzawa's *Gakumon no susume*, Nakamura Masanao's *Self-Help* (*Saigoku risshihen*, 1871), and Uchida's *Yochi shiryaku* were the three most popular books of the Meiji period (*Meiji no sansho*). Nakamura's *Saigoku risshihen* made numerous references to Alexander Mackay's *Manual of Modern Geography* (1861), J. Goldsmith's *Grammar of General Geography* (1834), and J. Kramers's *Geographical-Statistic-Historical Handbook* (*Geographisch-Statistisch-Historish Handboek*, 1850). These books tended to contain references to geographic determinism to highlight the privileged physical geography of Europe.

22.   Fukuzawa, "Bunmeiron no gairyaku," 16–37.

the developmental progress of human history and civilization, championing European civilization.[23] When Japanese students consumed these geography textbooks, where the European nations were presented as being supreme, they not only internalized the global hierarchies of social Darwinism but also set the Western nations and Western imperialism at the pinnacle of these hierarchies "as the goal and the model to follow."[24] By reading about Western explorers who had ventured to the Pacific, Africa, and Australia and exercised power in the name of enlightened leaders, Japanese students were encouraged to absorb Western ways of viewing parts of the world other than Japan and Europe. Consequently, they adopted a Eurocentric imperial gaze, observing the inferior "others" as those who lay beyond the borders of civilization and modernity.[25]

A predominant sense of crisis for the nation is reflected in the formation of Seikyōsha, but its journal reveals a rather optimistic response to the anxieties expressed by various leaders. The first issue of the Seikyōsha journal, *The Japanese* (*Nipponjin*, 1888), stated that Japan was re-created in 1868 and that its people were witnessing the epoch-making project of transforming it into a modern nation in East Asia. The task of nation-building was challenging; the biggest problem being how to decide what was right for Japan. In spite of the challenges and problems, the writer believed that the project would succeed as long as the Japanese people preserved their national essence (*kokusui hozon*).[26] Seikyōsha placed the highest value on Japan's indigenous culture by regarding it as the foundation of the nation (*kokuso*), and its members were the first group to mobilize culture as a way of forging the unity of the people. By "culture," the group meant a combination of religion (*shūkyō*), ethics (*tokkyō*), education (*kyōiku*), fine arts (*bijutsu*), politics (*seiji*), and the industrial and production system (*seisan no seido*), which together, they concluded,

---

23. The underlying objective of Buckle's *History of Civilization in England* is to reveal what separates the progress of civilization between European and non-European countries by separating the people by the "laws" that govern such progress. Buckle, *History of Civilization in England*, 4–26.

24. Ueda, *Concealment of Politics, Politics of Concealment*, 19.

25. Tierney, "Colonial Eyeglasses of Nakajima Atsushi," 152. See also Komori, *Posutokoroniaru*, 14–47.

26. The statement of determination appeared at the very beginning of the first and second issues of *Nipponjin*.

determined the tastes or sensibilities of the Japanese people (*Nippon jinmin no ishō*).[27] In fact, the group celebrated the establishment of the society on April 3, 1888, which was designated as the Emperor Jinmu Festival (Jinmu tennōsai), thereby enhancing the idea that Japan was a newly emergent power in East Asia and beyond.[28]

Although dealing with philosophical issues, the striking appeal of the journal is its mix of high-level intellectual discussions on politics, diplomacy, and various domestic problems, along with the encouraging tone of its writers, who were able to speak warmly to readers. Each issue was filled with a sense of excitement and enthusiasm for the nation-building project. For example, the third issue introduced an article starting with a series of poems on the cuckoo (*hototogisu*), one of the most referenced birds in Japanese traditional *waka* poetry because of its lovely voice. The section reads:

Lord Nobunaga said: *Hototogisu*! If you are not going to sing, I will just kill you.

Lord Hideyoshi said: *Hototogisu*! If you are not going to cry, I will make you cry.

Lord Ieyasu said: *Hototogisu*! If you are not going to cry, why not wait till you cry.

A Chinese said: *Hototogisu*! If you are not going to cry, I don't need you.

An American said: *Hototogisu*! If you are not going to cry, let us eat you.

A Frenchman said: *Hototogisu*! If you are not going to cry, that's just as entertaining.

A German said: *Hototogisu*! If you are not going to cry, you are not a bird.

A heartless man said: *Hototogisu*! If you are not going to cry, I will not care about you.

A compassionate man said: *Hototogisu*! If you are not going to cry, what a pitiable being you are.

27. *Nipponjin*, no. 1 and no. 2, back of the front cover; Shiga, "*Nipponjin* no jōto o hanamuke su."

28. Today, Emperor Jinmu is held as being Japan's first human emperor, but this belief emerged in the early Meiji era. In prior times, other emperors had also been identified as the "first" to have founded the imperial capital or to have done something else, but by the early 1870s, Jinmu was firmly established as having begun the imperial lineage, and April 3 was accordingly celebrated. See, for example, Takagi H., "Kindai ni okeru shinwateki kodai no sōzō" and *Kindai tennōsei no bunkashiteki kenkyū*.

A Seikyōsha member said: *Hototogisu*! If you are not going to cry, why should I not just teach you?[29]

This passage indicates that Seikyōsha men were playful and perhaps patient and hopeful, just like Ieyasu, who was presented as a man of tolerance, in contrast to the other characters. The difference between Ieyasu and the Seikyōsha men was the brotherly compassion manifested by the latter, who were not prepared to simply wait for the bird to sing but were willing to teach it how to perform. This article captures the spirit of the group, who were young and socially privileged, as well as eager to play the role of teacher in the space created by the journal.[30]

In this subtle and humorous manner, the Seikyōsha journal played a vital role in fostering nationalist ideals. The ten young men who made up the Seikyōsha membership, with the exception of Shimaji Mokurai (1838–1911), had university degrees, such as a bachelor's degree in agricultural studies (*nōgakushi*), a bachelor's degree in philosophy (*tetsugakushi*), and a bachelor of letters degree (*bungakushi*); their names, along with their degrees, are listed ahead of the table of the contents in the first two issues.[31] A specialist on Seikyōsha, Nakanome Tōru, identifies the Seikyōsha membership as "a group of scholars and critics (*gakushi ronkyaku*) who were contemporary with the Freedom and Popular Rights movement but did not directly participate in the movement."[32] Rather than fully taking part in the movement, they dedicated themselves to mastering modern Western knowledge in the educational institutions created by the Meiji

29. "Hototogisu no uta," 38. There is a note at the end of the article stating that this section was supposed to have appeared in the first issue of *Nipponjin*, but it had not been possible to accommodate it for unspecified reasons.

30. In this regard, Tsuda Sōkichi affectionately expressed his fondness for *Nipponjin* as not necessarily being for the debates or issues the journal raised but because of the writers' enthusiasm. Ienaga, *Tsuda Sōkichi no shisōshiteki kenkyū*, 16.

31. *Nipponjin*, no. 1 and no. 2, back of the front cover. Later the group expanded and included Miyazaki Michimasa (1852–1916), Naitō Konan (1866–1934), and Sugiura Jūgō (1855–1924). The original ten were Inoue Enryō (1858–1911), Kaga Shūichi (b. 1865), Kikuchi Kumatarō (1864–1904), Kon Sotosaburō (1865–92), Matsushita Jōkichi (1859–1931), Miyake Setsurei, Sugie Suketo (1862–1905), Tanahashi Ichirō (1863–1942), Tatsumi Kojirō (1859–1929), and Shiga Shigetaka (1863–1927).

32. Ariyama, "Kaidai: zasshi *Nipponjin Nippon oyobi Nipponjin* no hensen," 3–8; Nakanome, *Seikyōsha no kenkyū* and *Shosei to kan'in*, 10.

government. These students were called *shosei* (students), and Kenneth Pyle refers to this group by a different name, the "new generation" in Meiji Japan, who grew up in the time of political unrest and observed a series of crises during the transitional period from Tokugawa to Meiji.[33]

Pyle and Nakanome are correct in highlighting the liberal progressive intellectual current of the group, many of whom were well versed in Western literature, history, philosophy, and geography, plus the Confucian classics they had learned at home in their childhood. However, neither scholar has explored the implications of the "elite" status or the potential of the progressive intellectual orientation of the new generation. What does it mean that these young Japanese had mastered Western knowledge? What were they capable of doing with the specific knowledge they learned in the pursuit of Western knowledge? I argue that for them, "Western knowledge" meant the principles of natural selection, the survival of the fittest, social Darwinism, and Spencer's theory of social evolution, which became the central forces of imperialism and colonialism in the nineteenth century. In short, the new generation was trained to think and act in these terms by applying the principle of natural selection to their respective conditions. Adhering to the advice of Fukuzawa in *Encouragement of Learning*, many of them became teachers or engaged in literary activities to disseminate their ideals. As Fukuzawa outlined, the emergence of a modern nation was to rise from the middle, not from the government above or from a circle of people at the bottom. He also stated clearly that the role of scholars was to nurture "the middle class" that would form the mainstream of society.[34] Accepting Fukuzawa's idea that private individuals cultivated the nation's civilization while the government's role was to protect that civilization, the newly educated generation was poised to initiate a powerful influence over a large number of readers through their writing.

The young leaders were determined to be the national leaders for the young nation of Japan because many of them had direct experience with the invasive power of a superior race and had witnessed natural selection in operation during their college years. Indeed, the intellectual environment of young elites at university taught them the value of pragmatic

33.   Pyle, *New Generation in Meiji Japan*.
34.   Fukuzawa, "Gakumon no susume," 61.

thinking, in line with the idea of the survival of the fittest. Western scholars who took the opportunity to work in Japan made valuable contributions to seismology, geology, zoology, linguistics, and anthropology.[35] Many of them published the experimental theories and research results they developed in Japan in international journals and presented their work at international conferences. Foreign professors dominated the Japanese academy in the 1870s and 1880s, and they were in charge of the production of knowledge in Japan. It is well known that Ono Azusa (1852–86), the founder of Tokyo Senmon Gakkō (today's Waseda University), made a critical remark about this state of affairs in the university sector and broader academia in Japan, worrying about the independence of knowledge in Japan in the early 1880s. He argued that there was an indispensable need to teach in "our language" (*hōgo*) if Japan wanted to achieve the independence of "our knowledge" (*hōgaku*) when knowledge production was virtually all handled by foreigners in foreign languages.[36]

At the same time, Setsurei's publications also reveal the need for urgent domestic reforms for a new Japan to emerge in East Asia. A few months after his *Shin zen bi* appeared in 1891, he wrote about the ongoing political battles deriving from the old domain factionalism that hindered the Japanese nation's capacity to fully modernize in *Deceit, Evil, Ugliness: The Japanese* (*Gi aku shū: Nipponjin*, 1891; hereafter referred to as *Gi aku shū*).[37] Setsurei's explanatory notes (*kaidai*) to the *Gi aku shū* record that the political repression at that time did not allow for any discussion on political reform, and consequently there were no opportunities or

---

35. The academic activities that occurred during and after the appointment of these *yatoi* scholars are evidence of their determination to advance their careers. Many of them fully used the opportunities provided by the Meiji state. Bartholomew, *Formation of Science in Japan*; Beauchamp and Iriye, *Foreign Employees*; Burks, *Modernizers*; Gluck, "Review: *Live Machines*," 429; Notehelfer, *American Samurai* and *Japan through American Eyes*.

36. As Ueda notes, the independence of "our knowledge" did not mean teaching materials originally produced in Japan or by Japanese scholars. Rather, "our knowledge" referred to "a body of works that was endorsed as knowledge necessary in the path toward modernization," which had a "familiarity that granted them the status of 'our knowledge'." Ueda, "Colonial Ambivalence," 180–81.

37. Nagatsuma, *Kōkyōsei no ētosu*, 14–17. The sequel, *Nipponjin: Gi aku shū*, was published in May and July 1891 from Seikyōsha. Miyake, *Gi aku shū*, iii, and "Hanrei," *Shin zen bi*, iv.

means by which to reform the government. The government imposed heavy censorship on periodicals and other publications, and people were not permitted to openly discuss how to reform the current political system, its structure, participation, or other issues. He had firsthand experience of the restrictive space of journalism because his *Shin zen bi* was suppressed shortly after its appearance in March 1891.[38] The journal *Nipponjin* also experienced several occasions of suppression from 1891 through 1893, which forced him to launch *Asia* (*Ajia*) to continue their literary activities.[39] In spite of government pressure, Setsurei went on to publish *Gi aku shū* in May 1891 and courageously revealed to his readers why the governing of Japan continued to remain problematic.[40] Setsurei explained why Japan was not yet compatible with the civilized West, remarking as follows:

> Our state (*kokka*) has done much to remake the country [of Japan since the 1860s], but the evil customs (*inshū*) of the past thousand years are still present and remain unchanged. There are still many old ways that have to be destroyed completely. These old practices that need to be eliminated are

---

38. Nakanome, *Seikyōsha no kenkyū*, 190–92.

39. The first sign of censorship in relation to *Nipponjin* appeared in August 1888 when an article "On Meiji Clique Politics" (*Hanbatsu seiji*) was blacked out except for the title. The following edition included a letter from a reader who lived in Ushigome, Tokyo, titled "A Letter Concerning the editorial 'Hanbatsu seiji' ('Hanbatsu seiji' *no shasetsu ni kansuru shokan*). The sender asked Seikyōsha to print the article because he had been looking forward to reading it ever since he had seen an announcement in the prior edition. "Hanbatsu seiji"; Jichō, "'Hanbatsu seiji' no shasetsu ni kansuru shokan." There are a handful of articles that were censored in 1891, but censorship became really strict in 1892, forcing the Seikyōsha to start a new journal, *Ajia*, after the repeated suppression experienced by *Nipponjin*. *Ajia* remained their major journal until October 1893, when *Nipponjin* was resumed. *Nipponjin* suffered another bout of suppression, and the following anonymous articles preserve traces of state censorship, blocking any criticism leveled at the Meiji state and its foreign policies from the public viewpoint. "Genritsu seifu ni hantai suru mono"; "Itō Mutsu no gaikō seiryaku"; "Jōyaku reikō to sōsenkyo subekaraku zen daigishi o saisen subeshi"; "Satchō hankō hanbatsu igai no shohan ni gekisu"; "Taigai kōha no chijoku nari zenkokumin no fumenboku nari"; Tatsumi, "Seishin to goko zakkyo shikashite bōsu."

40. Setsurei explains that he did not intend to establish a symmetrical relationship between these publications, although one can see a certain level of correspondence in the notions he presents. Miyake, "Hanrei," *Gi aku shū*, iii.

preventing truth (*shin*) from being upheld. Deceit (*gi*) must be broken. Similarly, evil (*aku*) has to be defeated if goodness (*zen*) is to prevail. And, ugliness (*shū*) must be extinguished if beauty (*bi*) is to triumph.[41]

This passage criticized the evil forces of old customs, the abolition of which was called for by the Charter Oath of April 1868, the first guidelines for new state policies aimed at creating the modern nation of Japan. This preface echoes the responsibility of the state that Setsurei discussed in other texts, which needed to renew Japan's special characteristics (*tokushitsu*) and talents (*tokunō*). The failure to fulfill its responsibilities allowed the evil forces to remain powerful enough, even by 1890, to prevent the new political structure from taking hold. These forces, as Setsurei articulated, originated in the selfish desires of the current national leaders, who betrayed the spirit of the Meiji Restoration, as epitomized in the Charter Oath. Underlying this criticism lay his implicit condemnation of the ignorance of the people, who were incapable of ousting their irresponsible leaders.

In this regard, Marc Redfield's analysis of the emergence of aesthetic nationalism in Germany offers insights that were likely shared by Setsurei and other young intellectuals in 1890s Japan. Analyzing the *Addresses to the German Nation* that Johann Gottlieb Fichte (1762–1814) delivered at the Academy of Sciences in Berlin in the winter of 1807–8, Redfield has argued that it made German-ness "an imaginative act that imagines itself as the (national) repetition of itself," which could only be posited in their imagination.[42] Similar to how Fichte's address filled his audience with pain and uncertainty about the immediate future, Setsurei taught his readers about both the pain of abolishing the old ways and the excitement involved in building a modern nation at the turn of the century. In short, his philosophical texts were loaded with a range of issues that were heatedly debated at this historical and discursive moment in Japan, and it was not merely the philosophical pursuit of truth, goodness, and beauty but a philosophical intervention into the political conditions that led to reconceptualizing Japan in the 1890s. As I show in the second half of this chapter, Setsurei's attempt to produce a sense of national togetherness was

41. Miyake, *Gi aku shū*, 2.
42. Redfield, *Politics of Aesthetics*, 65.

achieved by mobilizing an earlier mode of representing Japan, the *fūdo*-based thinking rooted in the power of landscape. Placing it within the discourse of the philosophy of art, he presented Japan's national and imperial dreams within the mediation of the traditional discourse of Japanese *fūdo*.

As I will show, Setsurei's ideals of truth, goodness, and beauty reflected his adherence to a Western vision of civil society that was largely driven by the capitalism and imperialism of the time. His ideal vision of Japan, I argue, fully accepted these aspects of Western aggression, which in effect justified Japan's colonial expansion and exploitation, executed in the name of self-defense. On one hand, like the Protestant intellectuals who promoted Japan's expansionism by preaching their theology during the late nineteenth century, many texts of this era were strongly colored by nationalistic and patriotic tones.[43] On the other hand, although the politically charged nature of Setsurei's work is not extraordinary, I would note that his deployment of these philosophical notions does not simply translate into his cosmopolitanism. In light of the widely accepted view of Setsurei's cosmopolitanism or his highly celebrated belief in all civilizations and humanity in existing scholarship, my argument that his philosophy was profoundly charged with an imperial vision may be surprising to some readers.[44] However, my reading of his texts shows that he was fully aware of the Western ideas of progress and civilization, which were implicated in the colonizing strategies of the imperial West that were to subjugate weaker people, such as Africans, Chinese, and Indians, while occupying their lands and obliterating the native inhabitants from various parts of the world.[45] Accepting the fact that the superior moral leadership of Westerners was the flip side of their colonizing strategy of "educating" less civilized people, Setsurei also adopted this justification of violence in the name of bringing civilization and progress to the world. I now move to an examination of his philosophi-

43. Nirei, "Ethics of Empire."

44. Yanagida, "Kaidai," 425; Nagatsuma, *Kōkyōsei no ētosu* and *Miyake Setsurei no seiji shisō*. Morita's analysis is more nuanced in that it looks at the attention Setsurei paid to East Asian civilizations, but it does not emphasize the imperial visions that shaped Setsurei's view of Asia. Morita Y., *Hyōden*, 33, 118–32.

45. Gavin, *Shiga Shigetaka 1863–1927*; Kamei H., "Nihon kindai no fūkeiron," 31–37.

cal texts to analyze how he reconfigured the conception of Japan in the modern age.

Reconceptualizing the Cosmos through Philosophy

Setsurei first had to adopt a modern perception of the world and the universe and learn how to place Japan within it. To this end he selected philosophy as a means of envisioning the cosmos. His essay "A Few Drops of Philosophy" (*Tetsugaku kenteki*, 1889) is a survey of Western philosophy that had evolved up until the modern era, and in it he attempted to offer explanations for the evolution of human thought by highlighting the most genuine principles of the time from the major works of Western philosophy.[46] Under the section on empiricism in philosophy that had risen to prominence with the technological developments associated with Europe's early modern era, Setsurei tried to understand how the European philosophers had managed to challenge the supremacy of religion over science. He stated:

> Philosophy of this school is, in summary, a study (*gakumon*) that investigates all forms of knowledge (*chishiki*). First, it denies the absolute existence of innate ideas (*honzen no kannen*) through dialectic discussion. Second, it proves that all knowledge originates in experience (*keiken*) through deductive reasoning . . . in reality, principles that were thought to be universal or innate vary depending on time and place . . . [thus], it shall be the experience that constitutes the basis of knowledge.[47]

46. According to Yanagida, Setsurei read deeply and drew on the history of Western philosophy books to write *Tetsugaku kenteki*. He creatively interpreted these works and absorbed their philosophical notions, so this publication strongly represents his interpretation of the original work with regard to the evolution of Western philosophy through these schools of philosophers. Yanagida, "Kaidai," 424. Besides this piece, Setsurei wrote *Gakan shōkei* in 1892 about the nature of study of philosophy. It appears to me that he was trying to attain the cosmos within himself to be in philosophical union with the cosmos as suggested by the notion of Hegel's absolute spirit.

47. Miyake, *Tetsugaku kenteki*, 68–71.

By referencing René Descartes (1596–1650), Baruch Spinoza (1632–77), Gottfried W. Leibniz (1646–1716), and Nicolas de Malebranche (1638–1715), Setsurei went on to deny the existence of supernatural forces, such as *ki* in the traditional East Asian philosophy, or theological claims in Europe that were believed to have influenced the relationship between body (*shintai*) and spirit (*reikon*) as well as communication between spirit (*shin'i*) and things (*buttai*). Instead, he explained that human discoveries had revealed that changes and transformations of the natural world were caused by different factors, championing the method of observation and experience. He continued that these intellectual inquiries brought about the birth of new, specialized domains of knowledge, such as epistemology, ontology, logics, ethics, political sciences, physics, and psychology, among others, that were known as modern knowledge in his day.

Setsurei was interested in understanding the changing notion of universal truth that had first derived from a theological basis and then shifted to propositions, which were justifiable and knowable through observation. This suggested to him the nonuniversality of the truth of a single time or place, which prompted him to explore the ideas of truth in Eastern philosophy. Occasionally bringing aspects of Eastern philosophy into dialogue with Western philosophy in *Tetsugaku kenteki*, Setsurei highlighted Eastern philosophical notions that were akin to Western ones. He also challenged the idea of a superior Western civilization by pointing out the bygone days of advanced civilizations in the East, such as during the time of Marco Polo (1254–1324) or the age of the Qin (221–206 BCE) or Zhou (1046–256 BCE) dynasties of China, when Western travelers and scholars gathered in the prosperous Eastern cities. Furthermore, listing Confucian, Daoist, and Buddhist teachings as the three most important philosophical currents in the East and introducing them as compatible to Western philosophy in terms of their theories (*gakuri*), Setsurei argued that Eastern philosophy (*tōyō tetsugaku*) had a rich and noble rationale (*dōri*) and was as valuable as Western philosophy.[48] Although the term *philosophy* (*tetsugaku*) was largely unknown in popular circles before the department of philosophy was founded at Tokyo University in 1877, he tried to show the existence of "Eastern philosophy" before the formation of the discipline. With proper methods of explanation (*kaisetsu*

---

48. Miyake, *Tetsugaku kenteki*, 22–28.

no hōhō), he contended, Eastern philosophy would be a new subject of investigation for Western scholars. *Tetsugaku kenteki* was therefore his effort to demonstrate the compatibility of Eastern philosophy by introducing it into the Western conceptions, methodologies, and categories.

Tetsugaku kenteki projected an image of Japan as a highly sophisticated country that was willing to embrace various aspects of Eastern philosophy. By dividing the world into three philosophical traditions (Chinese, Indian, and European), he identified the impact of Chinese philosophy as enriching virtues and emotions (*jō*), whereas Buddhism sought to discipline human desires and helped people attain enlightenment (*i*), with Western philosophy helping refine human intellect and advance knowledge (*chi*).[49] Setsurei went on to state that, considering that Buddhism was no longer popular in India, Japan was a more appropriate heir to Buddhism because Buddhist traditions and practices had survived and were better preserved in Japan. Likewise, Japan had maintained strong Confucian traditions and remained as sagely as China. Having two of the three most important philosophical currents of the world, he remarked, Japan would be the ideal center of philosophy if the Japanese were to study European philosophy.[50] This declaration came from the fact that Setsurei himself was a philosopher of both the West and East, someone who recognized Japan's philosophical indebtedness to Buddhism and Confucianism. The knowledge of philosophy was clearly something Japanese people had yet to master, but Setsurei enthusiastically promoted the proliferation of Western philosophy in Japan because he saw an opportunity to establish this supposed advantageous position over Western philosophers.

Setsurei's identification of Chinese, Indian, and European philosophy with its respective focus on emotions/sensibilities, ideals/spirituality, and wisdom/knowledge roughly corresponds to Hegelian philosophy, which characterized the activities of the human spirit in the domains of art, religion, and philosophy. In Hegelian philosophy, these activities were expressions of the human mind, and Georg W. F. Hegel (1770–1831) placed philosophy as the highest activity of the mind, above both religion and

49. Miyake, *Tetsugaku kenteki*, 34.
50. Miyake, *Tetsugaku kenteki*, 36–37.

art.[51] Coincidentally, the culmination of Setsurei's history of Western philosophy in the text *Tetsugaku kenteki* is also the philosophy of the spirit, with him chiefly drawing on Hegel, Arthur Schopenhauer (1788–1860), and Karl R. E. von Hartmann (1842–1906). Setsurei was greatly inspired by Hegel and presented the goal of human thought as having a unity with the so-called Absolute Spirit (*dai-seishin*).[52] Arguing that humans were capable of obtaining and reproducing the universe within their own minds, Setsurei positioned self-consciousness as being absolute, which was truth in Hegel's terms. As Hegel had argued, Setsurei perceived that the production of thought (*shisō*) led to the production of reality (*jitsubutsu*) and privileged the mind as something capable of comprehending all things in the universe.[53] If the mind were capable of understanding how the universe operated, it could predict what the future might bring.

Setsurei interpreted that the privileged human mind was created rather naturally to be in sync with the environment. The beginning of the universe was in its primitive state, well before the emergence of humans. Every being had a soul (*reikon*), a name for the prior state of spirit (*seishin*), and soul became spirit through its exposure to the climate, weather, land, *fūdo*, and other environmental factors. Humans established such disciplines as art (*gigei* or *bijutsu*), religion (*shūkyō*), and philosophy (*tetsugaku*) as expressions of the spirit, and each respectively pursued beauty, goodness, and truth in their representation. Setsurei concluded:

> Indeed, all branches in philosophy that form the system of philosophy replicate the entirety of the cosmos (*uchū*) by reflecting the entirety of human thought (*shisō*). Because the totality of the cosmos is nothing but the wholeness of human thought, if one tries to imagine the wholeness of the cosmos by calmly investigating it, one might understand that there is no other vast universe [but the one in his/her mind]. Does this not prove the true state of independence of the spirit? . . . it seems almost impossible to articulate the ultimate truth of universal principles, but this merely shows the state of changing thought and its transformations (*shisō no hensen*).

51.　Hegel, "Selections," 383, 393.
52.　Hegel, "Selections," 427, 433–35.
53.　Miyake, *Tetsugaku kenteki*, 266–67.

Different systems of philosophy (*tetsugaku no taikei*) from various times, in fact, constitute all parts of my philosophy (*waga tetsugaku*).[54]

By adopting the philosophy of Hegel, which viewed reality as self-developing truth, Setsurei found a way to explain the changing reality of the modern world. If the mind or changing thought of humans were privileged in the name of intelligence or rationality, the path toward modernity would be justifiable, and so would the path toward imperialism. Setsurei's acceptance of Hegel's absolute spirit in essence gave him the means to justify Japan's imperial vision as a move toward becoming one with the cosmos. Setsurei called this process the genuine evolution of thought (*shisō shinka*).[55]

Clearly Setsurei's view of the absolute mind depended on the morality of individual thinkers, who were moral and capable of perceiving reality as a reflection of the ultimate principles and behaved righteously so as not to upset the ideal order. Of course, as is often the case with being correct or righteous, these conceptions are subjective and conceptual, not absolute. Only the mind has the capacity to confirm what is rendered as righteous. In fact, Setsurei's adaptation of Hegel may signal to some readers a certain mutation of *ri-ki* theory of Neo-Confucianism or the idea of training the heart (Shingaku), which is a valuable teaching point from Confucianism. Whether or not Setsurei's mastery of Western philosophy was mediated by the prior epistemology of Confucian traditions, with this understanding of the independence of the spirit, he discovered Wang Yangming (1472–1529), the leading figure of the Neo-Confucian school of thought that focused on the mind, as an embodiment of Hegel's absolute spirit. He prioritized the interpretation of Mencius during the Ming dynasty of China (1450–1750), and Setsurei emphasized the significance of Wang Yangming's belief that people were born with innate knowledge. Setsurei's publication *Wang Yangming* (*Ō Yōmei*, 1893), presented a great philosopher of the East, who denied the rationalist dualism of the Zhu Xi Neo-Confucianism but embodied thought that was identical to Kant, Hegel, Schopenhauer, and Friedrich W. J. Schelling (1775–1854).[56] Yanagida

54. Miyake, *Tetsugaku kenteki*, 284–85.
55. Miyake, *Tetsugaku kenteki*, 285.
56. Yanagida, "Kaidai," 427.

Izumi and others assessed that Setsurei's portrayal of Wang Yangming was indeed an image of himself, someone who exemplified the dignity of Eastern philosophy.[57]

Hegelian philosophy clearly inspired Setsurei to formulate Japan's potential in the modern world; in the process, it provided him with occasions to reinterpret Confucian virtues, the teachings of the sages and other thinkers, and to establish Japan's position in its role of systematizing Eastern philosophy. At the same time, Setsurei became convinced that to adopt Western ideas of progress and transform Japan into a member of the modern world, it was necessary to revolutionize the "popular intellect" (*chiryoku*) of the Japanese people. The strength of popular intellect was directly linked to the strength of the mind, and everything else, such as progress, civilization, enlightenment, rationalism, civil society, and people's rights, constituted the whole of modernity. Thus, he wrote vigorously on how one could strengthen one's critical mind, intelligence, and judgment at this time of transition from the old to a new era. Setsurei's acceptance of the supremacy of the mind became the basis of his legitimizing attempts to place Japan at the center of East Asia and halt the forces of Western imperialism.

Aesthetic Nationalism of Modern Japan

At the beginning of *Shin zen bi*, Setsurei upheld a principle, which also appeared in the first note of "Explanatory Notes" (*hanrei*), together with one more line that states, "the readers shall try their best to understand this principle (*kono ri*)" as they read the rest of the text.[58] The principle he wished to present reads as follows:

57. I note that Morita Yasuo has also pointed out the strong influence of *ki* philosophy and the Wang Yangming school of thought on Setsurei. Morita Y., *Hyōden*.

58. Miyake, *Shin zen bi*, iii. *Shin zen bi* was first published in March 1891, but Setsurei almost immediately revised and enlarged the text and published it again under the same title in May 1891. As he noted in the revised edition, Setsurei incorporated excerpts from other writers in order to borrow their expertise and help validate his claims. Consequently, the revised edition was considerably different from the original, al-

Doing one's best for one's country is the same as doing one's best for the world. The characteristics of a [group of] people (*minshu*) might complement the evolving growth (*kaiku*) of the entirety of mankind (*jinrui*). How could self-defense (*gokoku*) and love for mankind (*hakuai*) be contradictory?[59]

On one hand, one can interpret this principle as the direct connection between a country and the world, in which the good acts of a person in a particular nation might have a positive effect on the whole world. On the other hand, the opposite could also be true: if the world were connected in this way, then a vicious act committed by a person would affect the world and all of humanity negatively. Equally, one who is willing to defend a country for the sake of its security is also potentially someone who would kill others if they attacked it. Therefore, the health of all humankind is not well served if precious lives are lost. Similarly, "doing one's best for the country" may not be doing the best for the rest of the world if the country is ruled by a corrupt government that claims to be doing good, but whose actions might be harmful to people's lives.

This statement is perplexing, and the question Setsurei raised is rhetorical. How could the act of defending one's country be regarded as contradictory to the notion of expressing love for humanity? He answered in the negative, stating that it was not contradictory, that the two things were complementary. To be sure, the definition of self-defense is ambiguous in principle, but it is based on the assumption that by defending one's country one is standing up for the love for humanity by protecting people from the enemy. Thus, self-defense is worthy in the struggle to enhance world peace. Curiously, however, the principle never mentions the state, although Setsurei often wrote that the state was the basic unit in the international community and its role was to protect the people. Here, the matter of self-defense is left in the hands of the people, and the absence of the state makes it possible for the efforts of individuals to affect world peace directly, in turn making the thesis of the book a noble one. By upholding this principle on the front page of the text, from the very beginning

---

though he claimed that the experts' opinions regarding his original argument were complementary. Throughout this study, I use the first edition from March 1891.

59.   Miyake, *Shin zen bi*, front cover. This principle also appears at the beginning of *Gi aku shū*.

Setsurei was directing his readers to adopt this stance and encouraging them to defend their own country.

However, he was also speaking of all the existing states in the world by viewing them as champions in their respective regions. He explained that the region's survivors had exercised their special talents and special characters to remain strong, and the government's responsibility was to make every effort to maintain the special talents and characters of the people, while capitalizing on them to make the country economically competitive. Implicitly acknowledging the violence involved in the state's fight for survival in each region, Setsurei approved of the destruction and elimination of other tribes as being important and inevitable conditions for stabilizing a region. This idea is familiar in the natural selection process (*tōta*), which seeks to preserve the good and eliminate the weak. The destruction is presented as an important step toward the ideal state of a "world of harmony and happiness" (*enman kōfuku*), as part of the long process of achieving peace, which is the goal of humanity.[60] Setsurei highlighted the state of happiness and harmony without mentioning the lives lost in its pursuit. By consistently adhering to the principles of natural selection and the survival of the fittest, he never actually defined the exact meaning of "love for all mankind." Rather, his adherence to the idea of social Darwinism justifies the violence required to eliminate the less fit, seen as being a necessary condition for the triumph of the strong and the progress of the world.

Setsurei's principle was reflective of the reality of the times, with Japan acting as the region's survivor but facing overwhelming threats on various fronts from the Western powers. Defending Japan's position in the arena of regional competition, Setsurei noted that justice (*seigi*) was often threatened by the unequal balance of power in the world, and it was necessary to guarantee an equal balance between weak and strong countries.[61] Thus, he justified the possession of defense forces to counter the powerful Other and prevent the enemy from entering the country, and he further legitimized military preparations as a vital tool for preserving justice (*seigi o mamoru*). The sense of urgency that Setsurei felt in the late 1880s prompted him to adopt a kind of anti-imperialist position,

---

60. Miyake, *Shin zen bi*, 7–10.
61. Miyake, *Shin zen bi*, 43–44.

as seen in his ideals of world peace and love for all humanity. Yet his stance on self-defense as a means of challenging unequal power dynamics was clearly a contradiction of his earlier embrace of the right to rule for all peoples or the idea of the survival of the fittest. In other words, his support for a form of world peace that might work in favor of Japan was actually his version of a naturalized Western imperial discourse. In reality, he had become an imperialist by promoting the need for a strong self-defense force for Japan, regarding this as a necessary part of its right to establish its position in Asia. By placing the progress of the world as the highest priority, and thus adhering to social Darwinism, Setsurei's argument in *Shin zen bi* aimed to elevate the Japanese to the position of the strong, providing special permission to dominate the space of Asia, including the knowledge of Asia.

Setsurei's faith in the Japanese people was partly supported by his biological theory. For example, explaining why Japan managed to preserve its independence in Asia, in spite of the powerful waves of Western imperialism, he spoke about the "Mongolian racial component in Japanese blood," which was as advanced as the "Aryan race" (*Arian shu*). Reminding his readers that the Mongolians had cultivated their civilization near the Yellow River before the ancient Greeks had made their appearance in world history, he attempted to show the blood supremacy of the Japanese, who shared the Mongolian blood that had established its longstanding historical position in Asia.[62] To be sure, his use of race here is confusing, but when Japanese scholars and journalists actively used biological theories to establish the basis for blood, linguistic, or ethnic ties to define what the Japanese nation might mean in the late nineteenth century, they often used *race* as a term incorporating ethnicity.[63] Harking back to the past glory of the Mongol Empire and predicting another such glorious achievement of the Mongolian race as part of a cyclical pattern of history, Setsurei presented the Japanese as racially equal (if

62. Miyake, *Shin zen bi*, 20. However, this remark is misleading because the ancient Chinese civilization that prospered along the Yellow River was the Shang dynasty, not Mongolians, who were considered to be nomadic barbarians.

63. *Nipponjin* frequently included essays on Japan as being the only nation that had survived Western imperialism when India and China had come under the Western domination. See, for example, Kon, "Nippon no jitsuryoku"; Miyazaki, "Jitsuryoku yōseiron"; "Waga Nippon o shii seru hōkoku wa mina horobitari."

not superior) to the Euro-American nations. The Japanese shared not only a bloodline with the supreme Asian ethnic group but also the linguistic family (*gengo no keitō*) associated with another strong ethnic group, the Manchurian Tatars (*Manshū Dattan*).[64] Differentiating the Manchurian Tatar language from the language spoken in China (*Shina*), he attempted to list the distinct abilities of the Japanese, who were related to the most ethnically powerful Asian people in history.

In this fashion, Setsurei enthusiastically demonstrated the adept nature of the Japanese people by underscoring the ties with the Manchurian Tatars and Mongolians. He was able to broaden the historical stage of non-Western players by introducing the philosophy and history of non-Western people who had thus far been excluded from Western-centered history. By slightly shifting the center and inserting the experiences of the East into the Euro-centric understanding of history, Setsurei sought to include Eastern experiences that led to the modern age as being vital aspects of the history of the world. Furthermore, to reposition Japan as the historical leader of Asia, he strove to secure Asia as a place for Japan and stop Western imperialism from taking further root. These attempts are indications that Setsurei did not fully uphold the idea that every nation was entitled to emerge. Instead, he accepted the subjugation of the less fit as a necessary step in establishing the security of the region and was happy to espouse the conquest and colonization of the less civilized.

Likewise, in *Shin zen bi*, he spoke about the formation of a comprehensive knowledge of Asia as one of Japan's responsibilities in the stabilization of the region. Arguing that Japan could take charge in the advancement of comparative studies in Asia by establishing museums and research centers as the Western countries had done in their colonized regions, Setsurei championed Japanese skills in the fields of research, excavation, and historical investigation that had been nurtured in recent decades as a result of the modern educational curricula. He stated that the Japanese could establish the discipline of comparative Asia studies as the

64. Miyake, *Shin zen bi*, 17–19. Setsurei notes that in the recent past a new linguistic discovery had been made about the Japanese language and its relationship to Manchurian Tatar, but he discloses nothing about the discovery. He was, however, well informed about the wider discourse of the theories of contemporary anthropologists and linguists who had studied the origins of the Japanese or the Japanese language and comparatively drew a distinction between Japan and China.

center of the new knowledge. The center could incorporate the Western archeological and historical methods to classify and periodize the vast number of art and archeology artifacts that emanated from Asiatic civilizations. Suggesting that the Meiji state expand its current Imperial Museum (*teikoku hakubutsukan*) to house an Eastern Museum (*tōyō hakubutsukan*), as well as the establishment of more libraries to store the records, historical materials, and objects from China and all of East Asia, he stated:

> We should focus on the historical achievements of the East (*tōyō no jiseki*). The Asiatic continent is located very closely to us (*ichii taisui o hedatete aisetsu suru*). We obtained our knowledge from their (Chinese) historical and cultural developments, so it is easy for us to research (*kenkyū suru*) their history and culture. The Chinese will not feel left out or feel restrained or limited (*seichū seraruru tokoro naku*). On the contrary, they can fully count on our fair judgment. We can keep seeking and inquiring (*tankyū shi kyūmei suru*) about the matters and conditions of India, China, and the surrounding countries. Additionally, if we employ the newly imported Western theories (*taisei no riron*) and utilize the historical achievements of the Orient as materials for comparative research and make fair analyses (*kōmyō no dantei*), Japan might naturally become the Orient of Alexandria in the domain of inquiry into reason and justice (*rigi kyūmei*).[65]

Similar to Okakura Tenshin's (1863–1913) statements about Japan being the storehouse of Asia in his 1903 *Ideals of the East*, Setsurei assumed Japan's supremacy over China and any other country in the East with regard to absorbing Western knowledge.[66] Completely ignoring the sovereignty of Asian countries that had their own artistic and material culture, he positioned Japanese scholars as being the best qualified and most capable to manage the production and preservation of knowledge, culture, and tradition. Setsurei had internalized the Western gaze and adopted this superior position of ordering things in the rest of Asia.

Without a doubt, the suggestion of establishing research centers for Asia in Japan emerged as part of the competition with Western Orientalists.

65. Miyake, *Shin zen bi*, 34–35.
66. Okakura, *Ideals of the East.*

They enthusiastically founded various intellectual and academic societies, such as the Asiatic Society of Japan in Yokohama in 1872 and the
Royal Asiatic Society of London, established to promote the knowledge
of Japan, referred to as Nihonology or Japanology for Westerners.[67] The
Society in Yokohama was to "produce and record hitherto unpublished
information about all manner of aspects of Japan and the Far East" to
"place Japanese studies in the pattern of Western academic disciplines,"
and the society actively disseminated its research findings in the journal
Transactions of the Asiatic Society of Japan.[68] Resisting the forces that
threatened independence of knowledge, Setsurei advocated that Japanese
historians, archeologists, and classicists should be in charge of the production of Eastern knowledge.

Notably, the newly established domain of art was particularly at risk
because of the activities of Ernest F. Fenollosa (1853–1908). He came to
"teach Spencer's theory of social evolution and Hegel's philosophy" in 1878
but had extensive influence beyond his teaching role at the university.[69]
Offering financial assistance to Japanese artists and his perspectives on
Japanese art, Fenollosa shaped the course of Japanese painting (*Nihonga*)
by directing and defining what *Nihonga* should be in relation to oil painting in the West (*Yōga*).[70] Together with his student Okakura Tenshin,
he founded the Tokyo School of Fine Arts (Tokyo Bijutsu Gakkō) in
1889 and instructed government officials on how to preserve and classify
Buddhist arts and treasures from the past that were housed in temples
and shrines and ultimately how to create the art history of Japan. Fenollosa's enthusiasm earned Meiji government support because he placed
Japanese art at a higher level than Western art and proposed the poten-

67.   For example, the British Empire vigorously shaped the knowledge of the region as it expanded its sphere of influence. The development of Egyptology, Indology,
and Sinology progressed closely in line with the activities of intellectual and academic
groups. See Kenrick, *Century of Western Studies of Japan*, 58.

68.   Kenrick, *Century of Western Studies of Japan*, 13–14.

69.   Karatani, "Japan as Art Museum," 43.

70.   Foxwell notes that a dichotomy of Western/Japanese painting (*Yōga*/*Nihonga*)
emerged in a complicated, competing manner, and that there was not a single general
shift toward *Nihonga* or an entity that was opposed to Western painting. Foxwell, *Making Modern Japanese-Style Painting*, 1–10. See also Murakata, *Ānesuto F. Fenorosa shiryō*;
Kitazawa, *Me no shinden*; Satō, *Meiji kokka to kindai bijutsu* and *'Nihon bijutsu' tanjō*.

tial for "intellectual exports [of Japanese art] to the industrialized West."[71] Some of the "new generation" were in Fenollosa's class at Tokyo University and learned aesthetic theories and philosophy from him. In fact, challenging Fenollosa's theory of art, they voiced their interpretations of the beautiful. For instance, Tsubouchi Shōyō argued in *The Essence of the Novel* (*Shōsetsu shinzui*, 1885) that art (*bijutsu*) needed to have no practical use other than to "[delight] the minds of the viewers and make[s] their refineness (*kikaku*) noble (*kōshō*)."[72]

Setsurei also debated about the nature of Japanese art by identifying its major quality as "lightness" and "exquisiteness" (*tegaruku sara sara toshite keimyō*) in his 1891 *Shin zen bi*, "not sublime (*sōgon*), although there are some works of art that contain sublime elements."[73] Considering that the exotic appeal of Japanese art was the object of a feverish interest among the Westerners at this time, Setsurei's comment on light and delicate gracefulness (*keimyō*) as the main characteristics of Japanese art is insightful. As he continued to argue, this quality allowed the viewer to insert their own subjective viewpoint and judgment, dominate the artwork, and interpret the art in any way they liked. He concluded that the popularity of Japanese art among Westerners lay in the fact that it allowed them to dictate the aesthetic experience by ignoring the expressions of Japanese artists.

We can see that Setsurei recognized the need to transform the nature of Japanese art, if art was the expression of truth and the expression of the Japanese mind, to the level of lofty spiritual delight and ultimately to advance the stature of Japanese art by incorporating the sublime quality. Setsurei confronted his readers by asking how it was that Japanese works of art had been attracting large foreign audiences and challenged

71. Fenollosa, "Bijutsu shinsetsu," 57. Thomas Rimer states that "Fenollosa's relative success derives from his ability to gauge the level of knowledge" of his audience who "knew nothing of Plato and Aristotle, nor of Descartes and Kant" at this point in history. Rimer, "Hegel in Tokyo," 105.

72. Shōyō referenced Fenollosa as "someone knowledgeable from the United States, who recently lectured on the principle of art (*bijutsu no ri*) and became quite famous," but in the section "Shōsetsu sōron" of his *Shōsetsu shinzui*, Shōyō disagreed with Fenollosa by proposing a different definition of art that was more focused on the realism approach. Tsubouchi, *Shōsetsu shinzui*, 2–3.

73. Miyake, *Shin zen bi*, 70–71.

them to consider if there were different ways of experiencing art. Critically assessing how and why Western collectors were infatuated with Japanese art, he concluded that the contemporary frenzy originated in the problems created by the overt Westernization of the Meiji state. He argued,

> If we, the Japanese, are thinking about adopting their culture and using it for our own purposes, shouldn't we first undertake thorough research and weigh what are the advantages and disadvantages of doing that? It used to be that the Japanese envied the state of progress (*kaika*) in the West and wished to become like them. The Meiji state declared that we would borrow their strength and supplement our weakness. What hypocritical words (*biji*) they are! It was more like adopting the shortcomings of the West to enhance our own weakness. . . . . If we carefully study and consider (*shinshi jukuryo*) the loss and gain [of adopting another culture], we would only take what works well for us (*ware ni ōzuru mono*). Then, we could cultivate it and encourage everyone to use it. Then, one day, this foreign thing would surely emerge as our own (*wagakuni no tokushoku*).[74]

The main point of this passage comes down to the ability to think, something Setsurei repeatedly emphasized throughout his career. He was critical of the lack of this ability among the Japanese, especially the leadership, who blindly absorbed things from foreign cultures that were not necessarily appropriate to "our culture." In Setsurei's view, it was a mistake to heedlessly absorb someone else's customs and culture, but he recognized this happened because people lacked the ability to think for themselves. According to him, the adaptation of the knowledge or culture of another society required critical thinking in relation to what was in accordance with the manners and customs of one's native land.

We have thus far explored the complex thought of Setsurei, who at times critically diagnosed the premature state of popular intellect, while holding double standards in relation to his theorization of Japan's self-defense strategies. His philosophical intervention with regard to conditions in Japan during the 1880s and 1890s was aimed at elevating the country's status to that of a modern nation, but intriguingly, his belief in the

74. Miyake, *Shin zen bi*, 77–78.

special qualities exhibited by the Japanese people did not always originate from scientific or empirical evidence. For instance, Setsurei also stated in *Shin zen bi* that

> There is absolutely no doubt that Japanese people could significantly augment the flaws (*kekkan*) of white people by maximizing our special ability (*tokunō*). By pursuing truth, goodness, and beauty, Japan could play an important role in moving the world toward peace and happiness. This is possible because Japan is located in a place where pure (*suizen taru*) and exceptionally spiritual *ki* (*reishū no ki*) gathers. The lofty summit of Mt. Fuji that Yamabe no Akahito [700–736] wrote about in his poem shines so clearly and brilliantly while the blue sea that invigorated the genius of Lady Murasaki [973–1014] at the Ishiyamadera distinctly reflects the shadows of pine trees that are more delicate than flowers . . . . It is widely known, both inside and outside Japan, that the Japanese who were born and raised in this [place of luminous natural beauty] have made historic accomplishments as a result of the characteristics of their ideals (*risō no tokushoku*), their refined taste for rituals and exchange (*reibun fūshō*), and their artistic talent for writing (*jishō bigei*).[75]

This passage is reminiscent of earlier chapters, where Japan's location in the East was prioritized as the place of *yang ki*. In a way that was quite identical to that rhetoric, Setsurei privileged the distinct beauty of the Japanese landscape, referring to it as a place of amazingly spiritual *ki* that had historically nurtured the *fūdo* of Japan. His extensive list of scenic spots, examples of this special *ki*, was evidence in support of his belief in the "exceptionally spiritual *ki*" that demonstrated the potential of the Japanese people. Together with the law of evolution and biological theories, the *ki*-inspired philosophy from the earlier period quietly but assuredly formed the basis for his justifications.

As we may recall, Setsurei explained that philosophy was a domain of knowledge that studied various forms of knowledge so as to articulate the entirety of knowledge through experience, and he denied the mythical power of *ki* and other Eastern metaphysical notions that could not be experienced. He admitted that the universe (*uchū*) had originally consisted

75. Miyake, *Shin zen bi*, 11–12.

of a vast collection of gas (*kitai*) and it was impossible to explain what existed inside it. However, the advancement of knowledge made it possible, through observation, to uncover the mythical constituents of the universe.[76] Even though Setsurei's philosophical essays show that he fully endorsed the empirical facts about the nature of the universe, the realm of Japanese art as an expression of the Japanese spirit remained quite equivocal. Considering the Western frenzy for Japanese art, which fueled the trend for Japonism in Europe, reaching its peak in the 1860s and 1870s, the Western acceptance of Japanese art might have implied that Japanese art required no explanation of its beauty or its popularity. Without explaining what nurtured Japanese aesthetic sensitivity, Setsurei uncritically promoted the dissemination of Japanese art, which would also support the spread of the peace-loving sentiments of the Japanese people throughout the world. He remarked:

> To maximize beauty, one must harmonize and cultivate the various ideas that come from the notion of beauty (*bi no kannen*) and select, nourish, and extract the real essence of the ideas. I think our people can make a vital contribution to the world in this field. Our people are convinced of their potential, but I believe that foreigners would likely agree with us on this issue.
>
> Our Japan has a mild climate and its scenery (*fūbutsu*) is pure and beautiful. Besides the Three Scenic spots of Japan (*sankei*), there are numerous absolutely amazing views, such as Mt. Mikasa, known for the rising moon [as read in the poem of Abe no Nakamaro (698–770)] and Awaji Island for the sad songs of plovers [which Minamoto no Kanemasa (d. 1120) read about] . . . To summarize, the beautiful views of mountains and rivers are everywhere in Japan. All things that have grown in the beautiful nature of this country have a blissful feel (*iitaru no fū*) to them as if they have emerged from the divine *ki* (*shinki*), and all these things offer, not just the function of utility, but, more importantly, comfort and relaxation to those who look at them.[77]

76. Miyake, "Uchū," 40.
77. Miyake, *Shin zen bi*, 63–64.

The rationale Setsurei used in this section is once again conceptual and not based on scientific evidence. By referencing the power of scenic places with the mystical power of *ki*, he emphasized the exceptional qualities and beauty of the Japanese landscape.[78] Without articulating concrete evidence for the extraordinary geographic beauty of the landscape, he endorsed the privileged nature of Japan's location and its *fūdo*, echoing the *ki*-saturated space of the archipelago. The special power of *ki* is again mobilized to defend the special quality in Japanese aesthetic sensibility, and the knowledge of Japanese art produced in this space should be spread throughout the world.

By reminding readers that their country was surrounded by special *ki* that made the scenic beauty, Setsurei invoked the distinct history of Japan that had shaped its identity, which contrasted with his emphasis on the importance of Japan's self-defense as a condition for the triumph of strength. Although the presence of the *ki*-inspired landscape and rhetoric justifying the violence required to eliminate the less fit makes this text inconsistent in focus, the incompatibility still captures the essence of the land as the symbolic representation of unity and independence. Presenting the contradictory claim for self-defense as a truthful pursuit along with the survival of the fittest, he projected Japan's rule of East Asia as a valuable step toward the realization of world peace. In an attempt to make a philosophical intervention in response to the political conditions that existed after the Meiji state had stripped power from the people by designating them as imperial subjects, Setsurei articulated the transcendental values of humanity and its need to join the community of humankind, which could not be realized if Japan was prevented from defending itself. This one-sided interpretation of modern conceptions was the only way for Japan to rise, and his call began to shape the "middle-class"

78. Seikyōsha members unanimously accepted Japanese art as one of Japan's strong points. Sugiura Jūgō (1855–1924), for instance, stated that art in Japan required no help from the West, although all other disciplines needed to incorporate Western knowledge. Shiga Shigetaka argued that the art of Japan could emerge triumphantly by harmonizing with the notion of art in the Western civilization because the enlightenment of Japan originated in a state of harmony (*chōwa*) as an amalgam of a variety of ideas and methods. Shiga, "Yamato minzoku no senseiryoku," 2; Sugiura, "Nippon gakumon no hōshin."

consciousness as a concerted, if not coordinated, result of the emergence
of the modern Japanese nation.

Nevertheless, Setsurei's attempt to decenter the historical experience
of the West by introducing the historical experience of the East to the
world stage bore little fruit and was doomed to fail precisely because it
was simply a one-sided application of Western imperialism. His model
did not move away from West–East binarism and did not provide Japan
with any new spaces to rule. His privileging of Japan as the home of the
leading people behind the historic rise of Asia stood on the shaky ground
that was the special quality of *ki*. Modern geography was needed to re-
align *ki* philosophy and map out the colonial spaces into which Japan could
expand. I now turn to the final chapter, where I discuss the work of geographer Shiga Shigetaka, who introduced a new spatialization of Japan
as a means of relinquishing the *shinkoku* idea.

CHAPTER 6

Geography of the Divine Nation

The sublime is not confined to sentiment alone. It belongs to description also; and whether in description or in sentiment, imports such ideas presented to the mind, as raise it to an uncommon degree of elevation, and fill it with admiration and astonishment. This is the highest effect either of eloquence or poetry: and to produce effect, requires a genius glowing with the strongest and warmest conception of some object awful, great, or magnificent.

—Hugh Blair, "A Critical Dissertation of the Poems of Ossian (1763)"

In response to the ever-increasing presence of Western imperial endeavors in the waters surrounding Japan, Shiga Shigetaka (1863–1927), who emerged as one of the major writers for Seikyōsha, published a book called *The Conditions in the South Seas* (*Nan'yō jiji*) in 1887. By specifically mentioning which nations were expanding their spheres of influence, Shiga forewarned his readers about the urgent nature of current conditions in the South Seas.[1] He informed his readers that Japan had the potential to enter into imperial competition with Western nations, dominate a share of the waters, and ultimately become the ruler of the Eastern Seas. This was dependent on Japan taking immediate action—before China could do so. Then, he continued, Japan would be able to establish itself as the "Britain of the Eastern Seas" (*Tōyō no Eikoku*) by emulating New Zealand,

---

1. Shiga initially planned to publish his personal travel account (*kikō*) of the South Seas but revised his account into *Nan'yō jiji* to convey the urgency of the matter to Japanese readers. Later, "Diary of the South Seas Tour" (*Nan'yō junkō nikki*) was serialized in Fukuzawa Yukichi's newspaper, *Jiji Shinpō*, from May 25 to June 11, 1888. As Kamei Hideo notes, Shiga made considerable revisions in the new edition, so one needs to be careful about the changes in the contents depending on the edition. Kamei H., "*Nan'yō jiji* kenkyū," 75.

which he called England of the South Seas (*Nan'yō no Eikoku*), a successful case of nation founding. By following the glorious example of New
Zealand, Japan would emerge as the Britain of the Eastern Seas, which
would be followed by the establishment of Britain as the "Japan of the
Western Seas" (*Seiyō no Nippon*).[2] As optimistic as this remark might
seem, Shiga informed his readers about real examples of the developing
imperial competition in the nearby waters, hoping to portray Japan as the
next imperial power, one that was capable of protecting Asia from the
threat of Western imperialism.

Distinguishing themselves from state leaders, whom they referred to
as the old men of the Tenpō Era (1830–44), the "new generation" in Meiji
Japan consisted of progressive intellectuals with a sophisticated understanding of modern knowledge.[3] They mastered the language of the
principles of social evolution and published their ideas in newspapers and
journals by using such terms as the race for survival in the world of living
beings (*seibutsu shakai no seizon kyōsō*) and the principle of the survival
of the fittest (*yūshō reppai no taihō*). Having naturalized social evolution
theories and the rhetoric of Western imperialism in their understanding of
the modern world, however, they were anxious to secure Japan's survival
in the coming decades. With firsthand opportunities to observe how foreign advisers (*yatoi*) and foreign scholars dominated the production of
knowledge in Japan, the writers for the Seikyōsha magazine *Nipponjin*
made many suggestions for how Japan should modernize in accordance
with the universal laws of evolutionism. Their slogan was the preservation
of the Japanese national essence by incorporating Western knowledge so
as to strengthen its culture as the basis of the nation (*kokuso*).

This final chapter examines Shiga's thought and his initiatives for encouraging Japan's nation-building project by analyzing his narrative of
Japan, which embodied nationalist aestheticism. Drawing from a domain
of geography called physical geography (*chimongaku*) and grounded in the

2. Shiga regrettably admitted that at the time of the production of his text Japan
was not yet capable of achieving the vision of becoming the Britain of the East. Shiga,
"Nan'yō jiji," 53–54.

3. For example, *Nipponjin* made a number of references to "Tenpō," such as "old
men of the Tenpō era" (*Tenpō no rōjin*) and "the ignorant and deceiving merchants of
the Tenpō era" (*Tenpō nenkan no mushiki hiretsu kanshō yakara*), signaling their unre-
fined manners and outdated mode of thought.

distinct geographic beauty of Japan, Shiga's geographic aestheticism sought to inspire young men's "adventurous spirits to explore the world."[4] His first publication, *Nan'yō jiji*, expressed the importance of the landscape and people's affinity with the land, among other things, by drawing on the example of the British colonization of the Australian continent. In his second publication, *On the Landscape of Japan* (*Nippon fūkeiron*, 1894), he presented the image of a sublime Japan by explaining the geological, geographical, climatological, and meteorological processes that substantiated the beauty of its landscape. This text was the culmination of his nationalist ideals, and it became an instant best-seller, appearing in October 1894, shortly after the outbreak of the Sino-Japanese War.[5]

Founded on the idea that the survival of the Japanese nation would critically depend on a stable economy derived from the strengths of the local *fūdo*, which would then enhance the beauty of the local landscapes, Shiga's theory centered on the strength and beauty of the landscape.[6] Thus *Nippon fūkeiron* transformed the traditional *fūdo*-based discourse of Japan by moving away from the divine land of the deities to the scientific explication of the national land or homeland (*kokudo*), which would unite people through a sense of belonging.[7] By paying attention to how Shiga strategically propelled the geographic affinity between land and people, I begin the final analysis of the symbolic emergence of the Japanese landscape.

Growing Up with Colonizing Forces

Shiga Shigetaka was born into the household of a Confucian lecturer at the domain school of Okazaki in Mikawa province (present-day Aichi prefecture) in 1863. From 1874 to 1878, he attended a private school, the

4. Shiga, "Chirigaku," 270.
5. Kamei H., "Nihon kindai no fūkeiron," 19.
6. Shiga, "Nippon zento no nidai tōha," 26. This article initially emerged in June 1888 in *Nipponjin*.
7. Wigen, "Discovering the Japanese Alps," 6. See also Kamei H., *Meiji bungakushi*, 81–101; Ōmuro, '*Nihon fūkeiron' seidoku*; Thomas, *Reconfiguring Modernity*, 173–74; Yamamoto and Ueda, *Fūkei no seiritsu*.

Kōgyoku-juku, in Tokyo, which was founded in 1863 by Kondō Makoto (1831–86). Kondō was one of the six most influential educators of the Meiji period and promoted Western learning (Yōgaku), in particular navigation and naval operations. Shiga's connection with navy personnel proved valuable later because it allowed him to join navy tours and other expeditions as an observer. After graduating from Kōgyoku-juku, Shiga studied at a preparatory school for Tokyo University (Tokyo Daigaku Yobimon), but instead of Tokyo University, he became a student at the Sapporo Nōgakkō (Sapporo Agricultural College) in July 1880.

Unlike Tokyo University, the government paid "all their expenses while in college," which encouraged many students to choose the Agricultural College over Tokyo University.[8] The college was founded in the newly added prefecture of Hokkaidō, with the aim of nurturing the future leaders and educators there. These leaders would assume the central role in developing the land formerly known as Ezo and enlightening the people of Hokkaidō about their role as part of the Japanese Empire. After entering the college, students from "all parts of the Empire" were expected to "become its employès [employees] after graduation, and to remain in its service for a term of five years," and convert the island of Ezo into a prefecture analogous to the rest of Japan in accordance with the policy of the assimilation of imperial subjects (*kōka*).[9] The college was also established to offer the "most thorough instruction in the theory and practice of Agriculture and Horticulture [to] prompt the colonization of Hokkaido." According to the "Object and Plan of Organization" in the first annual report of the college, the emphasis was placed on the following subjects:

the Japanese and English Languages; Elocution, Debate, Composition and Drawing; Book-keeping and the Forms of Business; Algebra, Geometry, Trigonometry, Surveying, Civil Engineering, so far as it was required in

8. The college attracted students by upholding the promise of future employment and tuition waiver but canceled these promises when the Colonization Department (Kaitakushi) was abolished in 1882. The abolition of the department was a serious blow to the college and threatened its existence by temporarily terminating student admissions in 1882. Takakura, "Kaisetsu," 9.

9. Hokkaidō Daigaku Tosho Kankōkai, *First Annual Report*, 41; Kamei and Matsuki, *Chōten niji o haku*, 51.

the construction of ordinary roads and railroads, and in works for drainage and irrigation; Physics, with particular attention to Mechanics; Astronomy; Chemistry, with especial regard to Agriculture and Metallurgy; Structural, Physiological and Systematic Botany; Zoology; Human and Comparative Anatomy and Physiology; Geology; Political Economy; Mental and Moral Science; Physical Culture; Military Science and Tactics.[10]

There was a heavy focus on acquiring technology to build cities and living spaces for the new prefecture. In accordance with this line of thinking, Director Kuroda Kiyotaka (1840–1900) of the Colonization Department (Kaitakushi) in Hokkaidō enthusiastically promoted the education of the children of local people, "previously those who inhabited the land (*kyū dojin*), who are known as the Ainu today, while paying particular attention to the education of Japanese female students." Kuroda's aim was to populate Hokkaidō with educated families, and he argued that educated mothers could teach their children the value of home and their place of origin, in effect nurturing a sense of belonging to the land. The need to cultivate such an attachment rooted in the land was the basis of Kuroda's view, and he believed that the success of immigration and colonization in Hokkaidō depended on creating a special sentiment to be shared by the people living there.[11] Although the Kaitakushi and other government institutions in Hokkaidō lasted fewer than five years, from the very beginning, the Kaitakushi had a clear goal of educating female and the native Ainu students along with the male students.[12]

The Kaitakushi recruited William Smith Clark (1826–86), who was the founder, designer, and manager of the Massachusetts Agricultural College at Amherst, as the first president of the Sapporo Agricultural College.[13] Clark's stay in Sapporo was short, but he profoundly influenced

10. Hokkaidō Daigaku Tosho Kankōkai, *First Annual Report*, 41.

11. Kuroda and Higashikuze, "Joshi ryūgakusei haken no giseiin e ukagai (1871)," 57. See also Hokkaidō Daigaku, "Kaitakushi no setchi to kari gakkō," for further information concerning education in Hokkaidō.

12. The Kaitakushi consistently faced problems and criticism, but their difficulties were intensified by the financial crisis triggered by the Matsukata deflation, which led to the agency's abolition in 1882.

13. Clark's appointment was for only nine months, but during this short stay, he established a distinct academic culture by combining his religious beliefs and pioneering

the college by steadily building the groundwork for the Japanese Empire in Japan's first colony of Hokkaidō. Like Kuroda, Clark believed the stability of local life must be rooted in the people's ties to the land, and he argued that the people's devotion and special emotional attachment to the land were critical forces for transforming natural resources into national wealth.[14] Clark was thus a firm believer in agriculture, which he thought could significantly improve social welfare. He proposed, among other things, a manual labor class for the purpose of teaching young Japanese students the value, joy, and reward of work. This lesson was very new to many students, including Shiga. However, they quickly became used to the idea of the rewards of work and held "five *sen*" snack parties (*gosen kashikai*) regularly with the money they received for their manual work.[15]

When he graduated from the Sapporo Agricultural College in 1884 with a degree in agricultural studies, Shiga proceeded to work as a geography teacher for about a year at a normal school in Nagano prefecture.[16] He switched jobs for the Maruzen bookstore and worked there for about three months, helping publish J. C. Hepburn's English–Japanese dictionary. Around this time he wrote a textbook in English, to

---

spirit. He inspired numerous students with his Christian morals and high values, leaving with his famous farewell speech, "Boys, be ambitious." Maki, *William Smith Clark*; Ōsaka, *Kurāku sensei shōden*; Ōshima, *Kurāku sensei to sono deshi tachi*; Yamamoto H., *Hokumon kaitaku to amerika bunka*.

14. Hokkaidō Daigaku Tosho Kankōkai, *First Annual Report*, 1–2; Takakura, "Kaisetsu," 2–3.

15. In a diary he kept in college, now available under the title of the *Morning Sky Spews Out a Rainbow* (*Chōten niji o haku*), Shiga recorded numerous events that happened throughout his college years by employing classical Chinese poetry, *kanshi*, and poetic expressions. The diary is a valuable window that gives witness to life in Sapporo in the 1880s when colonization had yet to penetrate the inner parts of Hokkaidō. Kamei and Matsuki, *Chōten niji o haku*, 71.

16. Shiga specialists suggest that he was fired after an argument with the principal of the school, but Shiga seems to fondly remember his students, who excitedly debated with him about Darwin's survival of the fittest and other aspects of geography. Takabayashi cites one of the Australian newspapers, the *Echo Saturday*, dated April 10, 1888, which records Shiga's writing as follows: "There you may observe tiny urchins with rosy cheeks and raven black hair resisting your Darwin's 'Survival of the fittest' and telling how coral isles are constructed, how a delta is formed, etc." Takabayashi, "Atarashii shiryō ga kataru," 204. About his work at the Maruzen, see, for instance, Kamei S., *Nashonarizumu no bungaku*, 100; Yamamoto and Ueda, *Fūkei no seiritsu*, 29.

be published as *History of Nations* (1888).[17] He wrote this textbook under the supervision of W. D. Cox, one of his English language instructors at the Sapporo Agricultural College, and the textbook was intended to be used in a world history class. Shiga eventually established himself as a leading scholar of geography; he delivered a lecture for the Tokyo Geographic Society (Tokyo Chigaku Kyōkai, 1879) in 1887 and began teaching geography at Tokyo Senmon Gakkō (present-day Waseda University) in 1889. He was awarded honorary membership of the Tokyo Geographic Society and, from 1917, held the title of Honorary Corresponding Member of the UK Royal Geographical Society.

Shortly after Shiga left his job at Maruzen, he traveled to the border between Tsushima and Korea in December 1885 on the naval battleship *Tsukuba*, the aim being to inquire into a territorial dispute between Britain and Russia over Komundo Island (Port Hamilton).[18] He went as an educated observer, someone knowledgeable in the fields of agricultural studies and natural science, although he was not employed by the government. Shiga traveled widely in his lifetime, but this trip left a lasting impact on him because he was in his early twenties when he witnessed the conflict between two Western nations over an Asian island.[19] After this trip, Shiga seized the opportunity to journey on the *Tsukuba* for ten months. This time, he petitioned Navy Minister Saigō Tsugumichi (1843–1902) and joined the tour to the South Seas, including the Caroline Islands, Australia, New Zealand, Fiji, Samoa, and Hawaii in 1886. By this time, Shiga had read expedition books by British captains and was very fond of Charles Darwin's *The Voyage of the Beagle* (1839). He carried these books throughout the journey and made travel reports modeled on those he read.[20] Whenever he had a chance to meet people during the trip, Shiga identified himself as "the Darwin from Japan."

17. Shiga, *History of Nations*.

18. Kamei Hideo writes that what enabled Shiga to take part in the tour with the navy at this time, and later in the longer one in 1886, was his connection with the naval academy, Kōgyoku-juku, before starting college. Kamei H., "*Nan'yō jiji* kenkyū," 55–56.

19. Gavin, *Shiga Shigetaka 1863–1927*, 10; Mita, *Yama no shisōshi*, 59–60.

20. According to Kamei, Shiga sent reports from the South Seas, which were serialized in Fukuzawa Yukichi's *Jiji shinpō*. Shiga's reporting style, which began with descriptions of the terrain (*chisei*), climate (*kikō*), vegetation (*shokubutsu*), animals (*dōbutsu*), trade (*bōeki*), race, and language (*jinshu gengo*), established an archetype of a

During his ten-month journey, he learned of Australia and New Zealand's independence histories, which had been achieved from Great Britain at the cost of eliminating the native tribes from the map of Australia.[21] Shiga encountered a number of stories of indigenous peoples in the Southern Hemisphere who had been wiped out in accordance with the principle of the survival of the fittest. Shiga saw the realities of how "Anglo-Saxons" had colonized indigenous peoples and extinguished them by killing them and spreading the diseases they brought to the islands. He learned about the visible and invisible superiority of the Westerners, as inscribed on the land of the Australian continent, and became truly convinced of Darwin's theory of evolution and the applicability of the idea of natural selection and survival of the fittest in social contexts.[22] In the early part of *Nan'yō jiji* he stated that the superiority of Westerners lay with the white race (*hakuseki jinshu*) and that they were defined as superior people (*yūtō jinmin*).[23] Shiga remarked that, as history had proven, the Indo-European race excelled around the globe and overwhelmed everyone else, including the yellow, black, copper, and Malay races. He offered a detailed account of how the Anglo-Saxon people (*minzoku*) had expelled the natives from their lands and became the new masters of the South Seas, including a discussion on how Hawaii had been turned into a "lifeless shell" (*semi no nukegara*) because the merciless killing of native people by Westerners.[24] He argued that similar threats to existence were rapidly approaching Japan, with the Western powers continuing to advance their spheres of influence in the South Seas. This realization inspired him to write the *Nan'yō jiji*, which was aimed at informing the Japanese people about the actual approaching threat posed by the Westerners.

---

reporting style when writing about the South Seas, which inspired Yano Ryūkei to write *Ukishiro monogatari* (The Tale of Ukishiro, 1890). Kamei H., "*Nan'yō jiji* kenkyū," 57–58.

21. Kamei H., "*Nan'yō jiji* kenkyū," 81–84.

22. Specifically, British economist Herbert Spencer (1820–1903) used the phrase "survival of the fittest" in relation to Darwin's idea of natural selection when he compared Darwin's theory to an economic principle.

23. Shiga, "Nan'yō jiji," 3–5.

24. Shiga, "Nan'yō jiji," 105–7.

Moreover, by including an account of a dream he had had in Australia where he spoke with the ghost of a promising indigenous warrior (*yūi no shi*) who was probably a tribal chief, Shiga's narrative suggested that Japan was the welcome successor to the ill-fated natives.[25] He claimed that the chief, who represented a group of savages according to the civilization hierarchy scale, had entrusted this knowledge to Shiga, who was a member of a half-civilized community of peoples according to the hierarchy. His "Dream Story in Australia" (*Ōshū yume monogatari*) sadly but powerfully made a case for the superiority and adaptability of the white race, which had destroyed the native tribes on Kusaie (also known as Strong) Island in the South Seas. Interestingly, the story does not end there but continues to reveal the causes of the unity of the Anglo-Saxons in Australia. The tribal chief spoke to Shiga about a battle between the Anglo-Saxons and Franco-Latin people, who were also interested in dominating the South Seas. According to the chief, the Anglo-Saxon movement against the French threat culminated in the establishment of Australia when the Anglo-Saxon people who had migrated there wished to preserve the everyday landscape of the mountains, rivers, and lakes that had become the intimate images of home for them.[26] Their love of Australia and the Australian *fūdo* was the source of their enthusiasm and unity, and in this dream the tribal chief taught Shiga that national essence was rooted in the *fūdo* of the area where people actually lived, not their original, faraway motherland.

The fact that Shiga included this dialogue with an "uncivilized savage" leader suggests that he was critical of the fate they suffered in the name of civilization. However, he never privileged the "inferior" native tribes, whom he referred to elsewhere as "an incomparably brutal cannibal race" (*kyōaku muhi no shokujinshu*).[27] This account confirms that Shiga was convinced of the law of natural selection, that is, that weaker races are destined to die out. More important, even the stronger races, in this case the Anglo-Saxons, needed to constantly improve and adapt to remain strong. The original British Anglo-Saxon did not immediately prosper in the Southern Hemisphere, but the later migrants and their descendants were capable

25. Shiga, "Nan'yō jiji," 38–41.
26. Shiga, "Nan'yō jiji," 41.
27. Shiga, "Nan'yō jiji," 60.

of adjusting to the new Australian environment, and they became the ultimate winners, assuming an Australian identity. The major lesson here was the necessity of adapting to new circumstances, which the old Anglo-Saxons had failed to do. They were unable to develop any affinity with their new living environment and did not succeed or prevail in the new continent. Shiga ended *Nan'yō jiji* by hypothesizing on the possible situation in the South Seas in the seventieth year of Meiji (1937), when the region might be flourishing with the Teutonic, Latin, and Slav *minzoku* who had successfully migrated there. He wrote of the possibility that the future readers of his revised *Nan'yō jiji* might include Teutonic, Latin, and Slav peoples, indicating a possibility that Japan might be occupied by these foreign ethnic groups in the near future. In April 1887, only five months after Shiga's return from the tour, the book was published, describing the South Seas as a "region to which the general public (*sejin*) has yet to pay serious attention."[28]

    Nan'yō jiji was a warning to Japanese readers, but Shiga playfully began the book with a two-page poem he had composed in English, "Arise! Ye Sons of Yamato's Land!" He told his readers to awake from their long, dreamy slumbers and urged the "sons of Yamato's land" to engage in the grand task of obtaining the "holy independence" of Japan.[29] As stated earlier, he incited his readers to make Japan the ruling power of the Eastern Seas so as to maintain its autonomy. I do not provide the details of Shiga's production guidelines and economic plans here; suffice it to say that he encouraged his readers to build more robust trade relations with Australia as a way of ensuring Japan's survival as leader in the East Asian

28.   When writing this chapter, I consulted the 1887 March version of *Nan'yō jiji*, which appears in volume three of *Shiga Shigetaka zenshū*. The *zenshū* version includes a separate supplementary section called "*Nan'yō jiji* furoku" (Supplement to *Nan'yō jiji*), which was published in June 1889. In the supplement, Shiga includes his theories on how to use the land of Ezo, Tsushima, and Taiwan to increase Japan's productivity, as well as policies regarding trade and immigration, with the same purpose of increasing productivity. Shiga, "Nan'yō jiji," 105.

29.   Shiga, "Nan'yō jiji," i–ii. To wake up his readers, Shiga employs such phrases as "hope," "sweet smile," "three treasures of spirit, science and gold," and "divine Self-help" in reference to the profoundly influential book by Samuel Smiles (1812–1904). Smiles's *Self-Help* was translated by Nakamura Masanao (1832–91) under the title "Saigoku risshi hen" in 1870–71. It soon became a best-selling book, introducing such concepts as success and personal ambition. Kinmonth, *Self-Made Man in Meiji Japanese Thought*.

region. *Nan'yō jiji* highlights the importance of *nan'yō* to Japan, thus allowing the text to revise the existing East–West relationship narrative, one in which Japan is destined to be inferior. In other words, by creating the conceptual space of *nan'yō* and breaking the dichotomy of East (*tōyō*) and West (*seiyō*), Shiga sought to position Japan as the direct benefactor of South Seas trade. The invention of a third space elevated the status of Japan in the civilization hierarchy, even though it remained in the half-civilized position, that is, in between the savages and the civilized. The designation of *nan'yō* provides Japan with a place to rule, which decenters the West and complicates the binary East–West relationship. As a scholar of Japanese literature, Robert Tierney has argued that Shiga created "room for a non-Western colonial power" in the globalizing world because he realized that Japan could not become the West within the existing Euro-centric hierarchy of colonialism, where only the "colonizing West" and the "subjugated East" existed.[30] By creating the South Seas as a middle ground, Japan could establish itself as the center of the East and subjugate other Asian neighbors to confront the colonizing West.

What is noteworthy about the *Nan'yō jiji* is, as observed in Shiga's dream account with the tribal chief, that he identified the limitations of the old Anglo-Saxons (namely, the British) and distinguished them from the newly emerging colonizing powers that were the Anglo-Saxon descendants in Australia and New Zealand. In Shiga's conceptualization, the multiple groups or generations of Anglo-Saxons highlighted how the Australian Anglo-Saxon groups survived. *Nan'yō jiji* includes a chapter on the deserted villages that Shiga discovered during his explorations in Australia, which are presented as the dark side of the glory that was the British colonization of the continent. He connected the abandoned and empty villages with the limitations of the British settlers, who were initially adventurous, courageous, and daring but no longer able to adjust to the new environment or establish new roots there once colonization had been achieved. Shiga described the decline of the valuable qualities that had brought them to the Southern Hemisphere in comparison with the failure of policies in the old civilized nations (*kyū kaikoku*): they could not adequately deal with the diverging levels of wealth and equality that existed in their homeland, and there was the problem of overpopulation in the

30. Tierney, *Tropics of Savagery*, 22.

capital city and motherland, as well as low wages and the shortage of jobs, to name just a few challenges. The narrative of the *Nan'yō jiji* is consistent with social Darwinian theories of natural selection, but it crucially stresses the constant improvements needed by the superior race as being an important aspect of the law of evolution and progress (*shinka no hōsoku*).

In short, the historic rise of Australia marked the rise of the "new civilized nations" (*shin kaikoku*). By promoting Japan as the ideal partner of Australia and New Zealand, Shiga elevated the promising species of *Yamato minzoku* to the status of "new civilized nation." Furthermore, to prove the validity of Japan as being one of the nations of *shin kaikoku*, Shiga actively publicized the civilized aspects of the modern Japanese nation. In April 1886, a series of articles he wrote for the Australian newspaper *The Sydney Echo* appeared in English, titled "The Japan of Today: The Land of the Mikado." Divided into three parts and reported on three different days (April 10, 17, and 24), Shiga introduced himself as a "naturalist on board," posing again as the Darwin of Japan. These articles created a positive impact in *The New Zealand Mail*, which praised these essays as being written by a "fine English scholar and a gentleman of keen observation."[31] Shiga introduced Japan to the Australian public, including his proposal regarding Japan's potential for partnership in the South Seas trade in the near future. He assumed the role of publicist, expressing his view of the Australian public as follows:

> The Australian public possesses less pure information or entertains more numerous erroneous opinions concerning Japan, than even Japanese do concerning Australia. . . . Perhaps you imagine that we have no such comforts of civilization as railroads, telegraph, newspapers, system of postage, etc., whilst we believe that your country is still a barren waste, where awful bands of brutal cannibals ramble in search of prey . . . . But now that commerce and intercourse of these two countries are slowly [but] steadily progressing, we ought to shake off the prejudices and want of knowledge, associated with ignorant and rude ages, when we only looked beyond the boundary of our own with distrust and hostility.[32]

31. This is a newspaper article titled "New Zealand and Japan: A Japanese Naturalist" in the *New Zealand Mail* dated on May 21, 1886.

32. Shiga, "The Japan of Today: The Land of the Mikado."

Clearly assuming the status of enlightened scholar, Shiga showed his surprise at how little the Australian public, originally Anglo-Saxon people
who migrated to the Southern Hemisphere, actually knew about Japan.
Shiga accepted the fact that the Australian public shared widespread prej-
udicial images of Japan, but without hesitation, he bluntly wrote that
Australia was a "barren wasteland" where the native tribes still practiced
cannibalism, demonstrating their "uncivilized" aspects. Having observed
the actual state of affairs in the South Seas, Shiga was ever more convinced of the validity of social Darwinism and Spencer's theories of
evolution. These principles indicated the possibility of either success or
decline, without assuming the rule of a single imperial power. This allowed
him to reconceptualize the modern world by adding the categories of old
and new to his analysis of civilized nations. The most important message
was the need to constantly maintain efforts to improve the potential of
the people.

Vision, Physical Geography, and the Space of Japan

Shiga's eloquent writing, especially his excellence in composing *kanshi*, is
well known, and he is remembered as one of the three most prolific writers
of his day, along with Tōkai Sanshi (1852–1922) and Tokutomi Sohō (1863–
1957).[33] Sohō was the lead writer for a popular journal, *Nation's Friend*
(*Kokumin no tomo*, 1887), and he expressed his fondness for Shiga's writing as follows: "Even though the preservation of national essence (*kokusui
hozon shugi*) is not something that I pay considerable attention to, I always

33.   Kojima Usui (1873–1948), who was inspired by Shiga's *Nippon fūkeiron* and became an amateur climber, provided "Kaisetsu" (explanatory notes) to Shiga's text published by Iwanami Shoten. He claimed that Shiga's *Nippon fūkeiron* was listed in Fukuzawa's *Jiji shinpō* magazine as the book next to the Fukuzawa's publications in the "100
Favorite Books of All Ages" (*kokon no aidokusho hyakushu*). Kojima, "Kaisetsu" (1937),
3–4; Kojima "(Iwanami bunko shohan) Kaisetsu," 368–69. On the other hand, Nakanome Tōru lists Miyake Setsurei, Shiga, and Tokutomi as the three most influential
writers (*bundan san meishi*) by referencing a journal, *Shōnen sekai* 1, no. 20 (1895). Nakanome, *Seikyōsha no kenkyū*, ii. See, also, Anzai, "Shiga Shigetaka *Nihon fūkeiron* ni
okeru kagaku," 2; Hamashita, "Shiga Shigetaka *Nihon fūkeiron* ni miru Nihonteki
suikō," 5.

enjoy reading his essays. I do not like all the essays [in the journal *Nip-ponjin*], but only the ones written by the lead writer, Shiga Shigetaka."[34] Similarly, Uchimura Kanzō (1861–1930), who also graduated from the Sapporo Agricultural College, was impressed by Shiga's writing.[35] Uchimura also wrote about geography and was the author of *On Geography* (*Chirigakukō*), completed in 1894, which was later revised and published as *Man and Earth* (*Chijinron*, 1897). Uchimura and Shiga were important writers who introduced the ideas of geographers at a time when "formal courses in the subject were not [yet] offered in Japanese universities."[36] In the review he wrote for Shiga's *Nippon fūkeiron*, Uchimura named Shiga as the "Ruskin of Japan" and noted the similarities that existed in their depictions of beauty to be found in nature, with Shiga locating all the beauty of the world in the Japanese archipelago, whereas Ruskin discovered beauty in nature.[37] The impact of John Ruskin (1819–1900) on the formation of naturalism (*shasei shugi*) in Japanese literature is profound, and Shiga's generation enthusiastically read his works. Quoting lines from Shiga describing pine trees in Japan, Uchimura compared them with the lines in which Ruskin described lichens and mosses in his *Modern Painters* (1843).

Did Uchimura mean to say that Shiga's keen observation captured what caused nature to create such beauty in the landscape? Or did he mean to say that Shiga's special talent for writing made it possible for readers to vividly imagine the world he depicted? In fact, Uchimura's remarks in the review of Shiga's *Nippon fūkeiron* witness a change in tone, revealing criticism of Shiga's excessively nationalistic language, which coexisted with the patriotic fever that accompanied the Sino-Japanese War of 1894.[38] Uchimura criticized Shiga's "patriotic bias" for claiming that Japan housed all the beauty in the natural world, which was, of course, hard to prove.

34. Nakanome quotes a section from the *Kokumin no tomo* 32, which was printed in 1888. Nakanome, *Meiji no seinen*, 14–15.

35. Uchimura belonged to the second-year class and entered the college in 1877, whereas Shiga was in the fourth-year class. In his diary, Shiga wrote about Uchimura and how exceptionally bright he was, especially in biology. Kamei and Matsuki, *Chōten niji o haku*, 436.

36. R. Okada, "'Landscape' and the Nation-State," 93.

37. Uchimura, "Shiga Shigetaka-shi cho *Nippon fūkeiron*," 363.

38. Uchimura, "Shiga Shigetaka-shi cho *Nippon fūkeiron*," 365–67.

In spite of his criticism, it is noteworthy that Uchimura identified Shiga's text so closely with the rise of patriotic sentiment in Japan at this time and remained critical of the abstract connection between patriotism and the landscape.

How did Shiga manage to locate "all the beauty in the world" in the Japanese archipelago, and how did he describe it to his readers? How was his depiction of the Japanese landscape different from the scenic beauty of earlier periods that had aestheticized poetic places and other sites? These questions direct our attention to the importance of vision in the discovery of beauty in the "natural" world. Geographer Denis Cosgrove explains the significance of a Western conception of the universe as "a divine geometrical exercise," which was developed by a psalmist in the Old Testament, cosmographers of the Renaissance, and the theoretical geometries of astronomical geography in Europe.[39] This particular focus on nature's beauty remained profoundly influential in relation to the human imagination and intellect of the eighteenth century, furthering the belief during Ruskin's time that the image of God's handiwork was manifest in the real natural world. As is well known, Ruskin had an acute awareness of the importance of vision and carefully maximized the power of vision to express the beauty existing in nature because he sought to promote the idea that the external world reflected the ideal aesthetics of the Creator's work and went further by committing himself to validating this claim. For instance, when he taught at Oxford University in the newly founded School of Geography, Ruskin argued that artists were able to draw more accurately and imaginatively if they understood the mechanisms behind different natural phenomena. Therefore, he required that artists must be able to see nature perfectly, which was "as much a spiritual act as a physical one," and they needed to "possess imaginative insight into the mysterious infinity of things."[40] He was so preoccupied with the need for the artist to articulate details, such as geological formations, climatic principles, and meteorological mechanisms, that in his drawing class he taught his students the climatic and geological processes that generate fog, mist, showers, or the rough scars of water erosion that

39. This idea originates in *Timaeus*, a cosmological text written by Plato. Cosgrove, *Geography and Vision*, 16–17.
40. Colley, *Victorians in the Mountains*, 165.

were left on the surface of a rock. In this manner, Ruskin insisted that artists, especially landscape painters, had to know the "specifics of the natural world: 'every class of rock, earth, and cloud, must be known by the
painter with geologic and meteorological accuracy.'"[41]

Ruskin's obsessive concern with depicting nature resembles that of
Shiga, who described the landscape of Japan by placing a similar emphasis on the climatic and geological process that generate various kinds of
effect. The following long excerpt reveals how Shiga visualized a number
of views of beautiful rivers and mountains and finally highlights the effects that produced the beautiful landscape. The passage appears at the
beginning of *Nippon fūkeiron*, introducing Japan's unparalleled beauty.

> Ōtsuki Bankei [1801–78] once expressed, "Truly beautiful (*junbi*) rivers and
> mountains (*kōzan*)! And, that is my home." Are there people who would
> not wax on about their own home (*waga kyō*)? . . . There was an exhibition
> of a village of the indigenous Eskimo people [now referred to as "Inuit
> people"] at the Chicago World's Fair, and there were many indigenous
> people there. However, they did not want to be in Chicago and attempted
> to return to their homeland in the icy rocks and snowy mountains. How
> frail human emotions (*hito no jō*) are! Who would not wax on about one's
> own home? [We all do so because] this is a kind of notion (*isshu no kan-
> nen*). In the case of Japan, however, there is only one reason for the Japa-
> nese to talk about the true beauty of the "rivers and mountains" in their
> homeland. The reason is that beautiful rivers and mountains actually exist
> in Japan in an absolute sense (*jitsu ni zettaijō*). Foreign travelers find Japan
> the land of happiness (*gokurakudo*) in this world and think very hard about
> why this is the case. They agree with Rai San'yō [1781–1832] who composed
> the following:
>
>> Observing the gradual dawn of spring that is
>> Coming out of cherry blossoms that surround entire Yoshino
>> Chinese (*morokoshi bito*) and Koreans (*koma bito*) altogether
>> Obtain the heart of Yamato (*yamato gokoro*).
>
> I think, looking around the changing phenomena of the natural world
> (*zōka*) that boundlessly spread across Japan, the masterwork of craftsman-
> ship (*daiku no kyoku*) is gathered in Japan. This makes the landscape of

41. Andrews, *Landscape and Western Art*, 182.

Japan an unparalleled beauty on earth. The reasons for the Japanese to speak about the true beauty of mountains and rivers are as follows:

1. There are varieties and various changes in climate (*kikō*) and ocean currents (*kairyū*) in Japan.
2. There is an overabundant amount of vapor (*suijōki*) in Japan.
3. There are numerous volcanic rocks (*kazangan*) in Japan.
4. Water erodes very violently in Japan.

Before explaining each of these elements, one must first realize the [climatic and geographic] differences observed in the Japan Sea side and the Pacific Ocean side of the Japanese archipelago.[42]

Shiga first declared that the longing for home was universal, but he quickly distinguished Japanese longing from universal sentiments. Japanese people spoke about the beautiful homeland and felt sentimental about where they belonged because the beautiful landscapes existed within the borders of the nation. Then Shiga listed the factors necessary for creating the absolute beauty in the space of Japan as being the following climatic conditions: (1) vapor, (2) ocean currents, (3) volcanic rocks, and (4) water erosion. He listed them as the factors that produced the absolutely extraordinary beauty of the landscape and implied that this beauty could be further investigated to prove the actual mechanisms through reference to science.

By introducing to his readers the mechanisms lying behind the different natural phenomena, Shiga's *Nippon fūkeiron* resembles Ruskin's insistence on knowing the meteorological processes to depict the beauty of showers and different formations of cloud. Shiga discussed at great length the process of how *suijōki* was formed and how the vapor affected the climate and various animals and creatures in the archipelago. His attention is focused on something invisible, vapor and air, or volcanic rocks and ocean currents that are formed in the interior of the Earth. Clearly, Shiga drew considerably from the domain of knowledge known as physical geography (*chimongaku*), which was introduced to Japan in the early 1880s as part of geography and brought about a new understanding of the Earth, invisible air, and the constituent materials of the Earth.

42. Shiga, *Nippon fūkeiron* (1st ed.), 1–3.

According to the section on *Chimongaku* in *Encyclopedia* (*Hyakka zensho*, 1882), this knowledge is explained as follows:

> The origin of the study of the Earth (*chigaku*) is geography, which comes from a Greek word that means the descriptions of the Earth. The main idea of *chigaku* is to study things (*jibutsu*) and the formation (*keisei*) of the Earth, and there are two divisions in this study. One is called physical geography (*chimongaku*), which studies the surface (*hyōmen*) of the Earth, including the location of water and land (*kairiku no ichi*), the size of water and land areas (*daishō*), the height of water and land (*kōtei*), the depth of water and land (*shinsen*), flow (*ryūdō*), and all other aspects of the Earth (*issai no seishitsu*). Indeed, this study articulates the distribution of water and land (*suiriku no bunpu*), the inconsistency of the ground (*jimen no sansa*), unevenness (*ōtotsu*), the heat and cold of the climate (*kandan kikō*), the distribution of animals and plants (*dōshokubutsu no bunpu*), and the like. The second is called administrative geography (*hōsei chigaku*), which is all about the man-made making of the country, such as the division of provinces and counties.[43]

This excerpt shows the newness of this domain of knowledge, *chimongaku*, which is implicit in the coarseness of the translation. Yet the excerpt tries to convey the objective of the knowledge, namely, to systematically investigate the Earth's surface and surrounding environment, such as the oceans, air, and atmospheric environments. It is a new area of study that deals with the parts of the globe not visible to the naked human eye, although they might be quite familiar in everyday weather phenomena.

An English physical geography text, *Elementary Lessons in Physical Geography*, which was originally published in 1877, emphasizes the important place of atmospheric phenomena in the field of physical geography. The author, Archibald Geikie (1835–1924), explains the reasons for focusing on the atmospheric phenomena: they are "among the most familiar and universal features of the globe," and these examples can "be used with singular advantage to illustrate how the facts of science are ob-

43. Sekifuji (trans.), *Chimongaku*, 1. *Hyakka zensho* was translated from the edited volume of William Chambers's *Encyclopedia*. The Ministry of Education initiated the translation for use in school textbooks.

served and its laws are deduced."[44] Kamei Hideo also identified Shiga's *Nippon fūkeiron* as an example of *chimongaku*, and he argues that Shiga particularly tried to explain the mystery of atmospheric occurrences because the translated texts available in Japan, including Fujitani Takao's *Physical Geography of Archibald Geikie* (*Geishi chimongaku*, 1887) and Yazu Masanaga's *Physical Geography of Japan* (*Nippon chimongaku*, 1889) did not fully explore such mechanisms.[45] At that time the audience was greatly interested in learning how the invisible air becomes transformed into varying forms, such as snow, clouds, and mists, and therefore Shiga's *Nippon fūkeiron* captured their attention.

Shiga was familiar with the original English text of physical geography, which describes physical geography as an instrument to inspire the learner's imagination and promote critical observation of the living environment.[46] Geikie's text, for example, states:

> [*Physical Geography*] tries to gather together what is known regarding the Earth as a heavenly body, its constitution, and probable history. In describing the parts of the Earth—air, land, and sea—it ever seeks so to place them before our minds as to make us realize, not only what they are in themselves, but how they affect each other, and what part each plays in the general system of our globe. Thus, *Physical Geography* endeavors to present a vivid picture of the mechanism of that wonderfully complex and harmonious world in which we live.[47]

As this introductory remark indicates, Geikie strove to show his readers how the Earth was a heavenly body. By drawing their attention to familiar climatic phenomena, the author encouraged readers to use the knowledge

44. Geikie, *Elementary Lessons in Physical Geography*, xi.

45. Kamei H., "Nihon kindai no fūkeiron," 24–28. Yazu makes a note in the small preface, "*Nippon chimongaku shōin*," that this text was produced as a textbook for college students (*chūtō gakkō kyōkasho*), but the editors of the book hoped to incite the entrepreneurs (*jigyōka*) to venture something new. Yazu, *Nippon chimongaku*, 1.

46. In 1884, Shimada Yutaka (dates unknown) translated Geikie's *Physical Geography* into Japanese, *Chimongaku* and published it with Kyōeki Shōsha. Shiga proofread the manuscript and offered his expertise by verifying some of the phenomena discussed in the text. Shimada Y. (trans.), *Chimongaku*.

47. Geikie, *Elementary Lessons in Physical Geography*, 1.

they learned in the book in their everyday lives and "compare and contrast what they see take place from day to day."[48] Geikie also introduced the importance of atmosphere:

> No matter how dry the air may appear to be, more or less of this invisible water-vapor is always diffused through it. Every mist or cloud which gathers in the sky—every shower of rain, snow, or hail which falls to the ground—every little drop of dew . . . the importance of this ingredient of the atmosphere in the general plan of our world can hardly be overestimated. It is to the vapor of the atmosphere that we owe all the water-circulation of the land—rain, springs, brooks, rivers, lakes—on which the very life of plants and animals depends, and without which, as far as we know, the land would become as barren, silent, and lifeless as the surface of the moon.[49]

Shiga's *Nippon fūkeiron* greatly reflects some of the words that were introduced in Geikie's *Physical Geography*. As seen already, Shiga identified vapor, climate, and ocean currents as the elements that helped make Japan's beautiful landscapes. In other words, in *Nippon fūkeiron* Shiga demonstrated how the invisible factors that made the Japanese landscape reflected the knowledge of *chimongaku*. He followed up by providing a list of examples of the various *suijōki* effects, such as light from the sun (*kōsen*) reflecting the moisture on leaves or water (*tsuyu*), misty showers in early summer (*samidare*), and fogs (*kiri*) and haze in spring (*kasumi*). Shiga described the secret workings of the invisible elements and persuaded his readers that vapor, ocean currents, volcanic rocks, and water erosion did indeed contribute to creating such unique geographic beauty.

To demonstrate that these secret workings of the Earth were familiar to the Japanese people, Shiga offered a long list of poems by ancient poets to prove that the ancient people also had aesthetic responses to these phenomena. As we know, the Japanese *waka* poems thematize the topic of vapor effects that evoke emotions in response to aesthetically pleasing views. Thus, Shiga tried to claim that these phenomena had been historically recurring in Japan since classical times and that the Japanese people

---

48. Geikie, *Elementary Lessons in Physical Geography*, 5.
49. Geikie, *Elementary Lessons in Physical Geography*, 49.

had always found them fascinating, recording such effects in poetry. He highlighted the example of a mirage of Nagonoura Bay in Yokkaichi, Ise province (today's Mie prefecture), but insisted that the beauty of the mirage should not be mistaken for the deities traveling somewhere (*shinrei no yūkō*), as suggested in the *Illustrated View of the Famous Places on the Tōkaidō Road* (*Tōkaidō meisho zue*, 1797). Instead, Shiga explained to his readers that the *suijōki*, not the power of the deity, had generated this marvelous view.[50] By incorporating geological, geographical, and meteorological processes and explaining them, he offered a scientific explanation for the natural beauty witnessed in Japan throughout history.

Shiga's explanations of the geographical processes that create various beautiful landscapes suggest that like Ruskin and also Kuroda and Clark in Hokkaidō, he believed that love for nature among the country's citizens was central to the maintenance of communal life and the further expansion of the spatial borders of the nation. He understood that the everyday lived-in landscape was "a fundamental concept central to a people's sense of community, heritage, and nationhood" and shared the understanding of the importance of everyday space in relation to beauty in nature.[51] Geography was perceived as integral to the process of enlightening people in an age of imperialism because it was a tool that empowered people to defend their living spaces against foreign threats. Along with his insistence on the preservation of a national essence, Shiga's interest in the potential of geography timely reflected the historical moment.

In addition, Shiga paid particular attention to remembering the important explorers, natural scientists, and others who contributed to the enrichment of national geography in various ways. For instance, he visited the home of Mamiya Rinzō (1780–1844) in 1907 and encouraged local communities to publicize and honor Mamiya's achievements.[52] According to Shiga, Mamiya had learned about methods used for surveying the coastline from Inō Tadataka (1745–1818) and was sent to the northernmost area (*kyūhoku no chi*) by the shogunate and traveled alone to Manchuria. There, he investigated the areas from Sakhalin to mainland Asia,

---

50. During the Tokugawa period, there existed a belief that some giant deep-water seashells produced the mirage. Geikie, *Elementary Lessons in Physical Geography*, 42–43.

51. Osborne, "Interpreting a Nation's Identity," 230.

52. Nakanome, *Shosei to kan'in*, 166–69.

discovering that Sakhalin was an island, separating Asia from the Russian territory.[53] When Shiga began lecturing on his geography course at the school that would become Waseda University, he encouraged his students by remarking that the "true study of geography is not only aimed at enlightening the minds of young men, but also at enriching their knowledge about the world and, furthermore, inspiring adventurous spirits to explore the world."[54]

Observed in this light, one dimension of geography, *chimongaku*, provided Shiga with an overarching explanation for describing the geographic constituents of the Japanese archipelago. *Chimongaku* was, however, more than an explanation of the composition of Japan's Earth surface. *Physical Geography* spoke about the constant changes that occur on the surface of the Earth, stating that "the faunas and floras of the earth's surface today would not remain the same" forever, as witnessed in the modern horse and cattle breeds that had been "preceded by other kinds which are no longer living."[55] In short, specifically for the purpose of explaining the beautiful landscape, Shiga employed the mighty law of natural selection that runs throughout the knowledge of physical geography. The law of natural selection underscores Shiga's vision of the survival of the modern Japanese nation, which is also visible in the map of "Nipponkoku" (Country of Japan) (figure 6.1) that Shiga created and inserted in *Nippon fūkeiron*.[56] I now turn to the text of *Nippon fūkeiron* and explore how it defines the essential elements that make the landscape distinctly Japanese, with a special emphasis on the map of Nipponkoku that visualizes what constituted the geographic distinctiveness of the Japanese landscape.

53. This discovery by Mamiya led to the naming of Mamiya Strait (Mamiya kaikyō) in the Pacific Ocean that connects the Sea of Okhotsk with the Sea of Japan. Shiga, "Mamiya Rinzō tōtatsu yuki hyakunen kinen." This essay first appeared in *Ōsaka mainichi shinbun* (Osaka Daily Newspaper) on July 11, 1909.

54. Shiga, "Chirigaku," 270.

55. Geikie, *Elementary Lessons in Physical Geography*, 363.

56. Toby, "Mind Maps and Land Maps," 1; Wood, *Power of Maps*, 111.

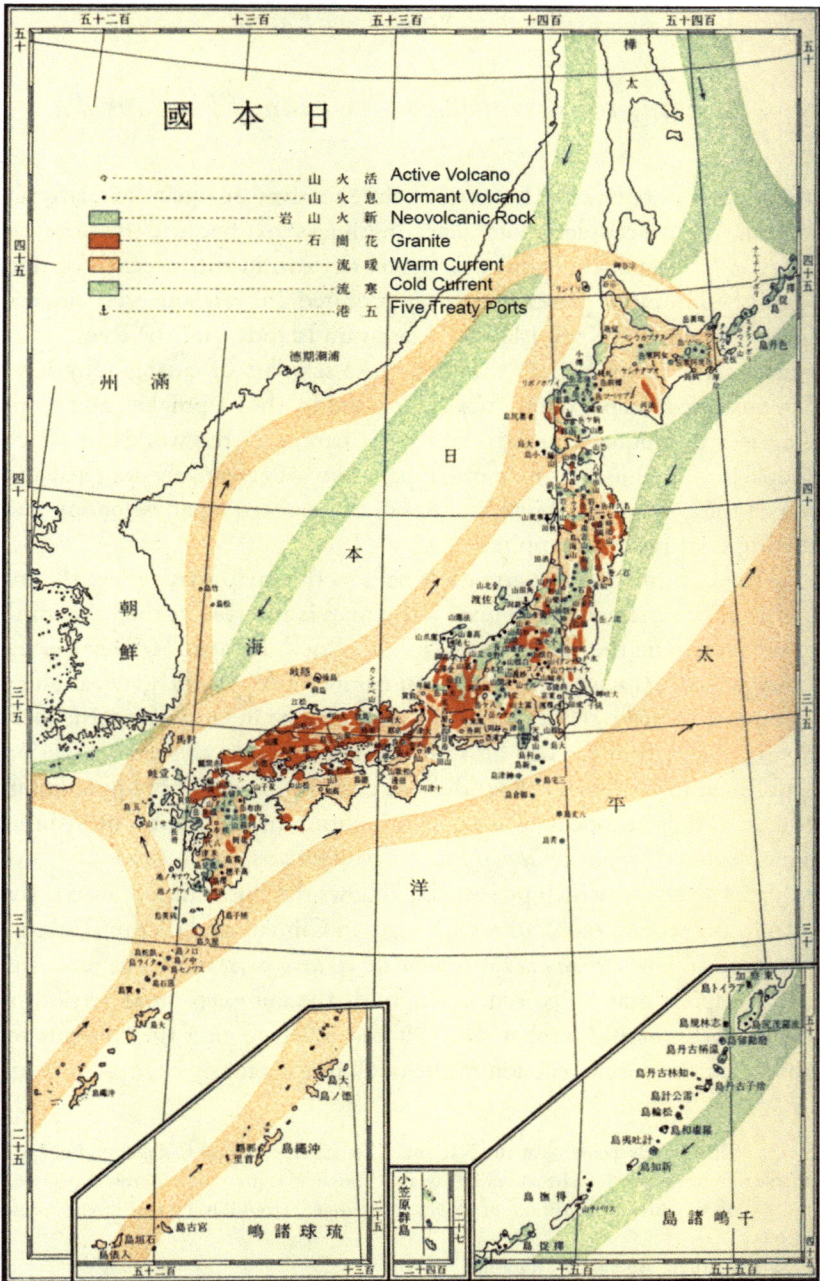

FIGURE 6.1. Map of Japan, "Nipponkoku." To view and analyze its contents, I used this reproduced map from the *Meiji bungaku zenshū*, vol. 37. Courtesy of Chikuma Shobō.

Valorizing the Archipelago: The Map of Nipponkoku

The map of Nipponkoku has never before received adequate scholarly attention, but it occupies a vital place in Shiga's text because the map appears as "the Japanese Empire" (*Nippon teikoku*) in the fifteenth edition (published in 1903), presenting newly acquired Taiwan squeezed into the space between the Kuril Islands, Ogasawara Islands, and the Ryūkyū Islands in the lower half of the map.[57] As scholars of cartography have demonstrated, maps contain objects selected by the mapmaker, and mapping is a technique "to engender the re-shaping of the worlds in which people live."[58] Thus, this map of Nipponkoku also creatively designed and staged the conditions of new realities of the modern Japanese nation and the imperial Japanese empire.

The lack of scholarly attention paid to this map may reflect the inconsistency inherent in the text.[59] The map is inserted at the beginning of the section on the "Numerous Volcanic Rocks in Japan" (*Nippon ni wa kazangan no tata naru koto*) in the first edition of *Nippon fūkeiron*; as Shiga continued to make slight changes to the contents in later issues, the location of the map in the text also shifted. For example, the second edition (published in December 1894) did not contain the map of Nipponkoku, while the map reappeared in the third edition in the section on "Abundant Vapor in Japan" (*Nippon niwa suijōki no taryō naru koto*). The later Kōdansha version, which presumably follows the third edition, inserts the map in the section on "Various Changes in Climate and Ocean Currents in Japan" (*Nippon niwa kikō kairyū no tahen tayō naru koto*). The inconsistency implies that Shiga did not publish the complete final version of *Nippon fūkeiron* in October 1894 but continued to alter the contents by observing the public reaction to the book in the rapidly changing politi-

---

57. This map is available at the National Diet Library Digital Collection, but I am unable to reproduce it here because of its quality. The map is inserted in between pages 64 and 65 of the fifteenth edition of *Nippon fūkeiron*. http://dl.ndl.go.jp/info:ndljp/pid /1150843.

58. Corner, "Agency of Mapping," 213.

59. For more details about the differences in editions, see Kamei H., "Nihon kindai no fūkeiron," 19; Kojima, "Kaisetsu" (1937), 5–6; Ōmuro, *Shiga Shigetaka 'Nihon fūkeiron' seidoku*, 231.

cal context of the last decade of the nineteenth century. Indeed, originally, *Nippon fūkeiron* appeared in 1893 in Seikyōsha's journal, *Ajia*, the replacement journal when *Nipponjin* was suppressed. Even though the first appearance in *Ajia* garnered almost no attention, its reappearance in 1894, following the outbreak of the Sino-Japanese War, attracted wide support, and many copies were rapidly sold.[60] The numerous reviews of *Nippon fūkeiron* published at the beginning of new editions of the text testify to its popularity.

Let us start with the legend featured in the map of Nipponkoku (see figure 6.1). It shows two kinds of volcano, active (*kakkazan*) and dormant (*sokukazan*); neovolcanic rocks (*shin kazangan*); granites (*kakōseki*); two kinds of ocean current, warm (*danryū*) and cold (*kanryū*); and five treaty ports (*gokō*), all of which configure the Japanese archipelago. These items roughly correspond with the textual detail provided in *Nippon fūkeiron*, which stipulated the four defining elements that mark the unparalleled beauty of Japan's landscape. The items included in the legend immediately raise a number of questions. Why are volcanoes seen as so important?[61] More curiously, why is the set of five treaty ports designated as one of the defining elements? How could the treaty ports, which had been "forced" to open up for the importation of foreign goods in the 1850s, contribute to making the beautiful landscapes in the same way volcanoes and granites might have done?

The major attribute of these ports is their significance in the symbolic "opening" of Japan to the West in the last decade of the Tokugawa shogunate. After the arrival of Commodore Matthew Perry (1794–1858) in 1853, the Tokugawa shogunate negotiated and concluded a series of treaties with the Western Powers. The conclusion of the Harris Treaty in 1858

---

60.   The text published in *Nipponjin* in October 1894 was similar but not identical to the version published in *Ajia* in December 1893.

61.   The importance of volcanoes in the Japanese archipelago was not limited to Shiga. Shimada Yutaka, who translated Geikie's *Physical Geography*, also stressed the importance of the abundant volcanoes. Shimada recommends that prospective learners of physical geography should study earthquake theories (*jishin no setsu*) to understand the physical geography of Japan. Shimada makes a note that chapter 23, "Rikuchi no undō" (movement of the land), draws largely on John Milen's work, although the actual chapter is titled "Daichi no shindō" (shaking of the Earth) not "Rikuchi no undō." Shimada Y. (trans.), *Chimongaku*, 2:79–86.

marked the beginning of a new phase in foreign relations for the Japanese and designated the five ports, Hakodate, Nagasaki, Yokohama, Kōbe, and Niigata, as open for trade with the Western nations.[62] These ports were the entrance through which Western technologies and civilization flowed into Japan, changing social and economic structures. The Westernization and modernization program led by the Meiji state after 1868 cannot be seen separately from the story of these ports, and the symbolic meaning of the treaty ports on this map is to confirm the role played by the Westernization of Japan as a whole and the integration of Japan into the realm of Western capitalism. However, how could the West—or the Westernization of Japan for that matter—make the Japanese landscape beautiful?

Nowhere in the textual section does Shiga mention the five treaty ports, and the ports appear only in the legend and the map of Nippon-koku. In spite of this silence, including these ports in the legend endorses them as essential features, and they are a defining element in making the Japanese landscape beautiful. Given Seikyōsha's logic of the *kokusui hozon*, their repetitive explanation about how to adopt someone else's culture into one's own, and the claim that supplementing the abilities of Japan with the stronger Western culture would strengthen them, including these ports must have something to do with how Japan would be able to strengthen its *kokusui*. It suggests that Japan would need to accept, adopt, and appropriate Western knowledge and imperialism to strengthen its culture and combat the power of Western imperialism. A closer look at the map reveals the seven different keys in the legend, which are minutely applied to the map of the Japanese archipelago, with the other three islands shown in the enlarged sections. The four items in the legend are related to the geological surface features of Japan's national land, such as volcanoes, neovolcanic rocks, and granite, which confirms that the archipelago is a heavily volcanic land. In particular, neovolcanic rocks are specifically designated to "zones of recent volcanic activity," referring to younger extrusive rocks.[63] Hokkaidō and the Kuril Islands are colored in green, as if to explain how the abundant neovolcanic rocks there helped

62. Auslin, *Negotiating with Imperialism*, 11.

63. *McGraw-Hill Dictionary of Scientific & Technical Terms, 6E*. S.v. "neovolcanic." Retrieved August 17, 2017 from http://encyclopedia2.thefreedictionary.com/neovolcanic.

the expansion of Japanese territory in the recent past. The main island is also intensely annotated to show the distributions of granite and the location of neovolcanic rocks and other volcanoes, which makes it almost impossible to clearly distinguish which volcanoes are dormant and which are active. Simply put, Shiga's map shows the ubiquity of volcanoes on the surface of the archipelago.

One notices that Shiga's conceptualization of Japan within the space of Nipponkoku includes the Kuril Islands (Chishima shotō), the Ogasawara Islands (Ogasawara guntō, also known as the Bonin Islands), the Ryūkyū Islands (Ryūkyū shotō), and Hokkaidō as part of the space of Japan, but none of these belonged to the domains ruled by the former Tokugawa shogunate (figure 6.1).[64] By enlarging these smaller groups of islands with labels showing their names, the map of Nipponkoku shows the reader the details of these island groups (*guntō* or *shotō*), as if to introduce them as newly added territories of Japan. These islands were forcibly annexed into the Meiji state in the 1860s and 1870s. Nonetheless, the newness of these added islands is not particularly jarring because the map includes actual foreign lands of the day, such as Manchuria (Manshū), the Korean peninsula (Chōsen), and Sakhalin (Karafuto). The Nipponkoku leaves the really foreign countries unmarked, and the contrasting presentation of blank foreign spaces and the densely annotated space of the territories suppresses memories of the recent violent history of the colonization of Hokkaidō and the Ryūkyū Islands. They are presented as being naturally connected parts of Japanese territory, whose geological surfaces share the same volcanic rocks.

The natural presence of the added territories of Hokkaidō and Ryūkyū is generated by the unity of the Japanese archipelago that is presented at the center of Nipponkoku. As one can see in figure 6.1, the archipelago is not just placed in the middle but also circled in orange and green,

64. Shiga wrote about various islands in Japan and the surrounding seas throughout his life, but he had a considerable interest in the Ogasawara Islands because of their rich resources, such as sugar, vegetables, and citrus fruits. More important, he focused on the strategic importance of the Ogasawara. For example, in his analysis, the Ogasawara Islands offered a good port for transporting goods and a good location for distant fisheries, and they would make a great hub within the trading empire by connecting the Japanese ports and the ports in the Pacific Ocean and South Seas. Shiga, "Ogasawara gentō."

indicating the movement of the ocean currents. Nipponkoku precisely portrays Japan within a grid of latitude and longitude lines and positions the archipelago at the center, surrounded by Sakhalin, Korea, and Manchuria. The neighboring areas remain blank, while the Sea of Japan, the Pacific Ocean, the Japanese archipelago with enlarged sections of the Ryūkyū shotō, Chishima shotō, and Ogasawara shotō are labeled with symbols colored in different zones, with arrows marking the direction of the winds.[65] Within the archipelago, there are numerous volcanic rocks that are both dormant and active. By focusing on the great natural power of volcanoes (*shizen no dai katsuryoku*), Shiga identified volcanoes as the ultimate expression of grandiosity in the universe.[66] The intensity and density of these annotations indicate the potential for volcanic explosions on the archipelago, which would have the capacity to blow up existing landscapes and transform the surface of Japan. The colors and symbols make it possible to visualize the movement of the winds and the routes of the ocean currents. In particular, the orange and green zones of ocean currents, with the arrows indicating the direction of water currents, represent energy dispelling beneath the ocean. Portraying these currents moving perfectly over the Ryūkyū and the Kuril Islands, respectively, the topographic display of ocean currents suggests that these islands are part of Japanese territory because they lie within the travel routes of the same ocean currents and circulating winds that travel across the space where the archipelago is located.[67]

65. The map of Nipponkoku in the version of *Meiji bungaku zenshū* is colored, but the other editions present this map in black and white, with shading and dotted highlighting, among other features, which still succeeds in clearly articulating the various symbols and annotations.

66. Shiga, *Nippon fūkeiron* (1st ed.), 59.

67. Although Shiga does not specifically comment that the arrows on the map indicate the direction of water or air currents, he appears to have understood that tidal and air movements act together as a set and in synchronization. For example, his strategic economic plans for Japan, laid out in *Nan'yō jiji* or elsewhere, emphasized the use of trade winds (*bōekifū*) because the combination of currents and winds would shorten the duration of a journey by allowing the ship to move faster. However, I am not aware of any evidence that shows the existence of any concurrent relationships between the pattern of winds and ocean currents. See, for example, Shiga, "Nippon seisanryaku," 65–66. This essay originally appeared in July 1888 in *Nipponjin* in four installments.

As natural phenomena, the currents and winds are able to slightly shift their routes and influence the climatic conditions of the neighboring areas. In other words, the map reveals Japan's interest in expanding its sphere of influence by portraying these winds and currents as running closely to the shores of Vladivostok, the Korean peninsula, northern China, Sakhalin, and the chain of islands between Japan and Russia. Moreover, the topographic display of ocean currents and winds on Nipponkoku traces not only the direction of the movement but also the presence of the nearby islands. More precisely, the warm ocean current emerges around Tsushima Island in the southwestern section of the map, and continues up to Dōzen and Dōgo in the Oki Islands, and to the Ōshima and Kojima Islands set next to the Matsumae peninsula of Hokkaidō. It continues as far as the Okushiri and the Rishiri Islands on the northwestern tip of Hokkaidō. The ocean current connects these islands almost like the shipping route proposed by Shiga in "Nippon seisanryaku."[68] Similarly, another warm ocean current branches out from Tsushima Island to reach the Matsushima and Takeshima Islands near the Korean peninsula, moving upward to meet at Rishiri Island. These ocean currents on the map for Nipponkoku are identical to the potential travel routes and locations of future trading ports, as Shiga suggests in his essays on Japan's production methods and future trade. The map therefore envisions the possible economic expansion of Japan, which might be achieved by maximizing the natural resources in accordance with the strengths of the nation's natural features and resources that were available in the archipelago.

In this fashion, the map of Nipponkoku communicates a sense of the life, energy, and various movements that exist within the space of the archipelago. Reflecting the knowledge of *chimongaku*, Shiga's descriptions recast various movements within the Earth's surface of the Japanese archipelago and convey the power within the archipelago to the reader. Dynamic leaps caused by the currents might jump-start the island chain toward Russia or Korea, and numerous volcanoes (marked all over the archipelago) could potentially explode and change mountain formations. Such volcanic eruptions might melt the existing mountain ranges or invent new islands to merge with the natural borders. The projection of

68. Shiga, "Nippon seisanryaku," 66.

these movements and the potential destruction and renewal cycle in the landscape produces a sense of life that is innately contained within the Japanese archipelago. In addition, by including the routes of wind and ocean currents on the map so skillfully—almost touching the borders of neighboring nations—the map of Nipponkoku begins to overlap with Japan's imperial desires for territorial and economic expansion.

The Nipponkoku map displays the scientific evidence that generates the grandiose beauty of the landscape in the form of a map by maintaining close parallels with the written textual part of *Nippon fūkeiron*, which expounded on the meteorological, climatological, and geographic mechanisms of the Japanese archipelago. The map explains what constituted modern Japan's nationhood by articulating the geographic constituents, thereby defining concretely the "geo-body" of Japan, to borrow Thongchai Winichakul's term.[69] By providing a more concrete sense to the notions of nation and national essence through the technology of mapping and modern geography, *Nippon fūkeiron* visualizes a section of Earth, the heavenly body of the Japanese archipelago.

Dynamic Japan, Sublime Language

The sense of dynamic movement that emerges from the map of Nipponkoku is further enhanced by Shiga's poetic, lyrical descriptions of the climatic processes. He combines geographic knowledge to explain the mechanisms of mist, haze, and vapor with a poem depicting the fresh morning mist on grass. As a result, his writing generates vivid imagery, a rolling rhythm and movement within the narrative. Together with illustrations that carefully follow the evocative narrative, the reader could visualize and imagine a world where the various winds, ocean currents, and climates produce a beautiful landscape.

The descriptive explanations become much more effective in the second and subsequent editions of *Nippon fūkeiron*, in which the text structures the argument slightly differently than in the first edition by developing it on the basis of the three major aesthetic qualities of beauty (*bi*), elegance

69. Thongchai, *Siam Mapped*.

(*shōsha*), and sublimity (*tettō*).[70] In these versions, Shiga described the quality of "elegance" by referencing the splendor of colored maple trees when describing the Japanese fall. The quality of "beauty," on the other hand, is symbolized by Japan's spring, when plums, cherry blossoms, and other flowers are in full bloom and bush birds (*uguisu*) are in flight. Illustrations of such captivating views of the fall and spring follow, providing readers with an image of these beautiful times. Equally, the third aesthetic quality, *tettō* (the state of the infinitely grand and dynamic, in short, sublimity), is presented as being the central element in making the landscape so beautiful. The expression of *tettō* is focused on the destructive power of corrosive water and lava. These violent processes are presented as making strangely beautiful views (*kikan*), sturdy and heroic sights (*gōken no shō*), and absolutely stunning scenery (*zesshō*) from the explosive energy of volcanoes and water.

In the discussion on the quality of *tettō*, Shiga presented volcanoes as the embodiment of the vitality of nature and declared that volcanoes and volcanic rocks were defining features of the Japanese landscape. As observed earlier, the map of Nipponkoku depicts numerous volcanoes. In the textual descriptions, too, Shiga defined Japan as a nation of volcanic mountains (*kazan*), due to the sheer number of volcanoes.[71] According to him, *kazan* was another name for beautiful mountains (*meizan*); as if to validate this fact, he provided a diagram that lists the existing volcanoes on the mainland of Japan, starting with Iwaki Mountain in Aomori and ending with Mt. Aso in Kumamoto prefecture (figure 6.2). Each mountain is identified by its location and an ancient Japanese *waka* poem, evidence that poets had been appreciating them since ancient times. In fact, the poems recorded in classical anthologies never actually described the beauty of the volcanic mountain, nor did they mention the volcanic quality of the mountain. Rather, their authors were more intrigued by the autumn view or the clear air of summer, without actually realizing that the mountain was a volcano. Shiga even admitted that the ancient

---

70. In the first edition, these terms are used throughout the text to describe the processes or phenomena by calling them beautiful or sublime-like. The term *tettō*, for instance, is used throughout the text, most often to discuss volcanoes and the water erosion process. Shiga, *Nippon fūkeiron* (2nd ed.), 3–7.

71. Shiga, *Nippon fūkeiron* (1st ed.), 56–59.

poets did not call these mountains volcanic mountains but simply mountains and that none of the poems in the chart mentions the power of volcanic mountains.[72] Forced to create historical continuity in these poems and volcanic mountains, Shiga forged a connection between them and sublime aesthetics, presenting these *waka* poems as proof that the ancient poets had recognized the beauty of the mountains. His desire to claim the historical development of Japanese aesthetics that centers on volcanoes is clear, even though no ancient poet gave it much thought.

This sort of twisted logic is not rare in this treatise on the Japanese landscape. For example, Shiga provided an explanation for the long history of nature worship in Japan under the section "Worshipping Nature by Japanese" (*Nipponjin no shizen haisū*), highlighting that famous mountains have always had a place dedicated to the worship of the deities (*kami*) or Buddha (*hotoke*), typically a shrine (*jinja*).[73] These mountains historically attracted pilgrims (*junreisha*) and others, who came to revere the deities believed to live there. Nevertheless, Shiga insisted that these sacred mountains attracted spiritual people because the beautiful mountains and volcanoes were identical.[74] By claiming that the beautiful or sacred mountains were always volcanoes, Shiga argued that the Japanese people had historically worshiped the geographic beauty of the mountains, not the superficial divinity attributed to the mountains.

The designation of volcanoes as another name for beautiful mountains leads to another list of the numerous volcanic mountains found throughout the Japanese archipelago, starting with the Kuril Islands, Hokkaidō, the mainland, and the southern part of Japan, including the Ryūkyū and Ogasawara Islands.[75] The ownership of the Kuril Islands, even today, is disputed between Japan and Russia, and in 1875 they became a Japanese possession with the conclusion of the Treaty of St. Petersburg. Describing the Kuril Islands, Shiga wrote,

72. The reason for the absence of volcanic mountains in the poem is apparently that classical aesthetic sensibilities did not focus on the violent nature of volcanoes as a theme.

73. Shiga, *Nippon fūkeiron* (1st ed.), 157–58.

74. Shiga, *Nippon fūkeiron* (1st ed.), 157.

75. Shiga, *Nippon fūkeiron* (1st ed.), 63–98.

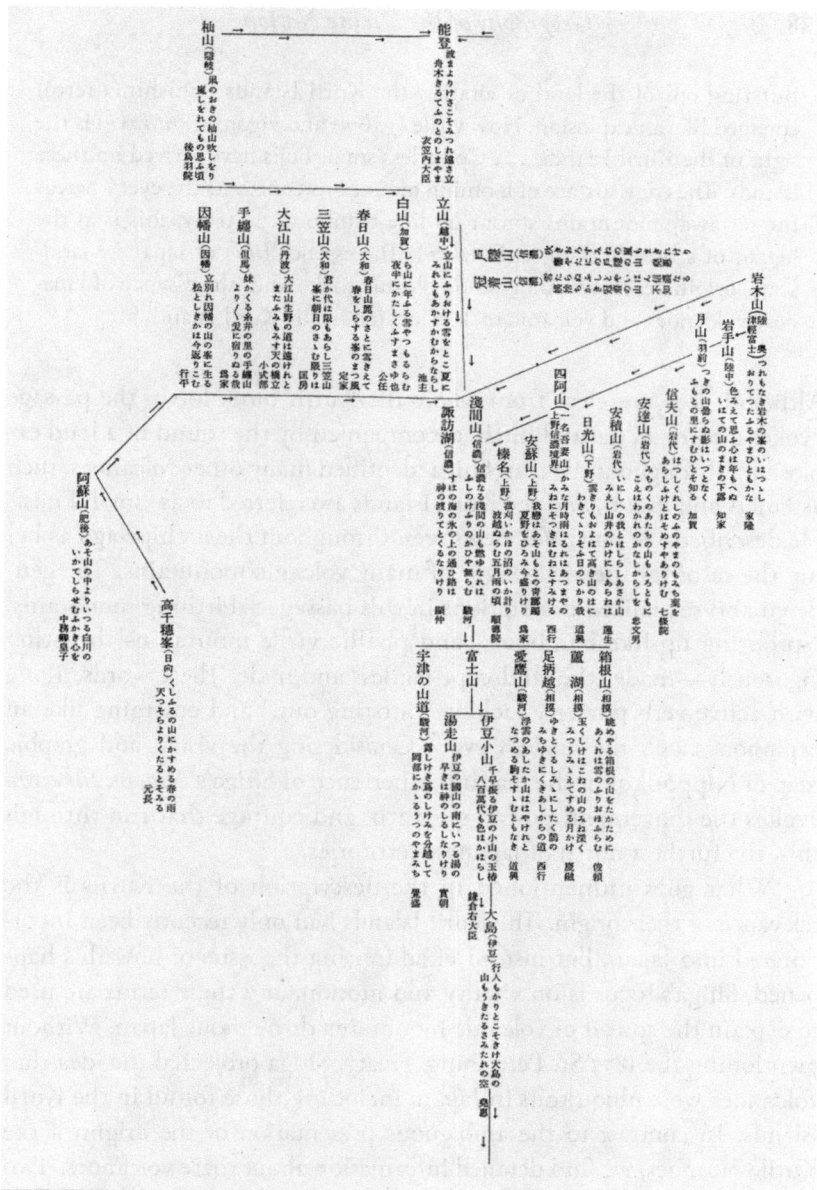

FIGURE 6.2. A diagram of mountains with their best-known *waka* poems. The diagram starts with Mt. Iwaki in Aomori and ends with Mt. Aso in Kumamoto prefecture. Each mountain is identified by the provincial name of the Tokugawa era and an ancient *waka* poem. *Meiji bungaku zenshū: Seikyōsha bungakushū*, vol. 37. Courtesy of Chikuma Shobō.

Bursting out of the land of vitality, the Kuril Islands (Chishima rettō) emerged like an explosion. How virile (*gōken*) and vigorous (*rairaku*) is the sight of the Kuril Islands! . . . Countless small Fujis have arrived on these islands. The edgy surface of looming mountains confronts the eye, whereas the far away mountains sprout up like bamboos . . . truly, this is at the height of a breathtaking sight (*ikan*). The essence (*iki*) of Japanese landscape originates in volcanoes and volcanic rock. And, the essence of Japanese volcanoes and volcanic rock is located in the Kuril Island.[76]

Although it is not clear from where the Kurils burst forth, the passage evokes a scene of natural birth, accompanied by the sound of a loud explosion. Throughout the text, Shiga identified many other volcanoes, such as Fuji A and Fuji B, and the Kuril Islands are referred to as "small Fujis." He described the powerful views seen throughout the archipelago as being the result of the virile vigor of many volcanic mountains. The gendered and sexualized descriptions in this passage—birthing mountains, "sprouting up like bamboos," and phallic virile mountains thrusting vigorously—render the landscape fearless and male. These words, along with active verb phrases, such as "bursting out," and emerging like an explosion, catch the reader's eye.[77] Considering the visual and graphic map of Nipponkoku, the reading experience of Shiga's *Nippon fūkeiron* evokes the movement, power, strength, and courage that run through this, the furthest north of Japanese territories.

What goes unmentioned in the description of the Kurils is the relevance of their origin. The Kuril Islands had only recently been incorporated into Japan, but instead of addressing the issue of how this happened, Shiga's focus is on vitality and motion, and these terms are used to explain the spread of volcanic mountains throughout Japan. Without mentioning the 1875 St. Petersburg Treaty, Shiga projected the idea that volcanoes were ubiquitous in Japan, including those found in the Kuril Islands. In contrast to the ambiguous presentation of the origin of the Kuril volcanoes, we find detailed information about these volcanoes. Two

76.   Shiga, *Nippon fūkeiron* (1st ed.), 62–63.
77.   In her analysis of Alexander von Humboldt (1769–1859), who revolutionized popular imaginations of America, Pratt similarly highlights his use of charts, graphs, drawings, and maps, interweaving with visual and emotive language. Pratt, *Imperial Eyes*, 111–37.

more diagrams follow to illustrate the volcanoes of the Kuril Islands (figure 6.3) and those of Japan (figure 6.4). Together with information on volcanoes in the Chishima Island, Shiga demonstrates his mastery of the geography of the Kuril Islands and these mountains by depicting the shape, height, and location of different volcanoes, as well as their relationship with each other.

While reiterating that "beautiful mountains" (*meizan*) are always volcanoes, Shiga offered additional evidence by introducing representative volcanoes found throughout Japan. Starting with those found in northeastern Japan, the diagram flows from right to left, top to bottom, and ends with the volcanoes in southwestern Japan. The flow of the diagram continues from the Atlasova Island (Araito tō) in the Kuril, located at the "northeastern tip of the Japanese Empire" to Mt. Aso in southwestern Kumamoto prefecture, passing a series of islands of Izu shotō and ending with Miharayama Mountain, the biggest mountain in the Izu Islands. By laying out images of volcanic mountains, one by one, followed by a brief description of the mountain, the diagram invites the reader's eye to follow these images and words, thus creating an outline of the Japanese archipelago. In other words, Shiga creates a mental map of Japan through the representative volcanic mountains, and reading the diagram becomes an experience of spatializing the empire through these volcanic mountains. This diagram blurs the fact that some of these islands had been added to the territory of Japan in the previous twenty years. In fact, the caption instructs the reader to refer to the section of the text that lists, in detail, the location, volcanic activity, shape, and rock formations, and outlines how these volcanoes might be connected to and part of the larger mountain ranges and mountain chains.

By explicating the deeper connections between and relatedness of these volcanoes one with another, Shiga reminded the reader of the violent cycle of destructive eruptions and renewal process of volcanoes, hinting at the continuous productive cycle of energies in the Japanese landscape. The detailed description of the larger network of mountain ranges implies that it is natural to suppose that some of the volcanoes were once part of larger mountain ranges. In the same way, the Japanese archipelago can be expanded as a result of the movements of Mother Nature. In the remainder of the text, Shiga describes the powerfully energetic aspect of Japan's nature, including the water erosion processes that make sharp

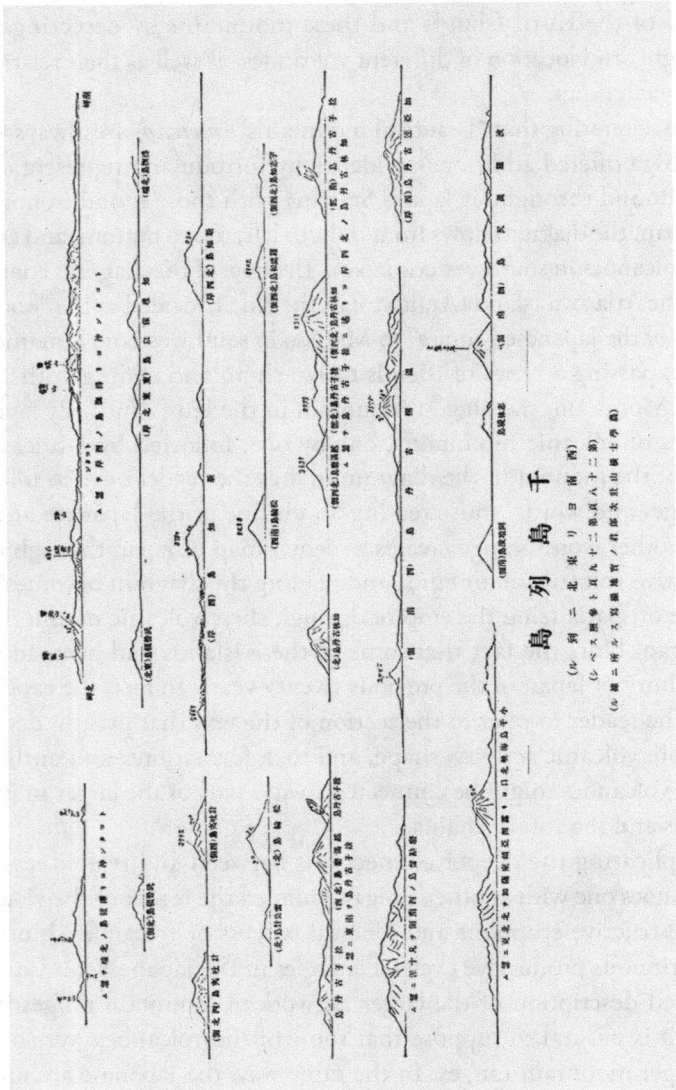

FIGURE 6.3. A diagram of volcanoes in the Kuril Islands. Shiga makes a note that the line of volcanoes begins in the southwest and heads northeast toward the Kuril Islands. *Meiji bungaku zenshū*, vol. 37. Courtesy of Chikuma Shobō.

FIGURE 6.4. A diagram of volcanoes in Japan. Shiga notes that he has listed the volcanoes from northeast to southwestern Japan and adds a line below the caption that all beautiful mountains are volcanic mountains. *Meiji bungaku zenshū*, vol. 37. Courtesy of Chikuma Shobō.

and edgy coastlines, cliff lines, and mountain lines. The visual and textual components of *Nippon fūkeiron* make the point that the *kokusui* evolves around such ideas as energy, birth, dynamic motion, absorption, and the destructive power of nature. Nature's energy displays uncontrollable power and force in volcanic eruptions and the fierce eroding forces of rain and wind that oxidize and corrode the surfaces of shores and rocks. Shiga attributes these powerful, often wild and aggressive aspects of nature to the representative character of the Japanese landscape and Japan's cultural identity. The essence of Japan's identity revolves around these vigorous movements of energy. By rendering these forces into natural phenomena, Shiga's treatise on the beautiful Japanese landscape offers language justifying territorial expansion, or an expansion of the sphere of influence, as natural.

The analysis so far has suggested that mountains, oceans, trees, and other things are not depicted as something static or something to be looked at but as active forces, whether they are the volcanic veins penetrating the deep Earth, ocean currents diving deeply to the bottom of the sea, or mountain ranges running through the elongated archipelago. The use of active verbs such as *run, jump, penetrate*, and *surge* generates an effect that excites the reader with a sense of motion while revealing the energy captured within the Japanese landscape. The mental effect caused by these exciting events is signified in the aesthetic category of the sublime, which is the most powerful aesthetic experience according to Hugh Blair (1718–1800). Blair wrote that while the effect of sublimity could be either visual or mental, the sublime experience fills the mind of the viewer/reader with aesthetic sensibilities, even if they have never seen the object or view. The reasons are as follows:

> It produces a sort of internal elevation and expansion; it raises the mind much above its ordinary state; and fills it with a degree of wonder and astonishment, which it cannot well express. The emotion is certainly delightful; but it is altogether of the serious kind: a degree of awfulness and solemnity, even approaching severity; commonly attends it when at its height; very distinguishable from the more gay and brisk emotion raised by beautiful objects.[78]

78.   Blair also explains, "the simplest form of external Grandeur appears in the vast and boundless prospects presented to us by nature." As for those objects that appear

In this theory, the experience of sublimity involves an internal elevation of the mind, generating some intensely noble yet fervent feelings that do not allow the person to simply feel delighted. Blair continued to write about sublimity, comparing it with a sense of beauty, saying that beauty was "always conceived by us, as something residing in the object which raises a pleasant sensation," and beautiful objects remained to be appreciated as objects.[79] On the other hand, sublimity raises a feeling that is too violent to be sustainable.[80] In short, a capable writer could invent an experience to overwhelm the reader by using the rhetoric of the sublime, and a reader who is the subject of the experience undergoes an internal elevation and expansion that raises the mind high above its ordinary state.

Shiga read a good deal of Western literature when he was a student at the Sapporo Agricultural College, and he studied the nineteenth-century notions of the sublime and beautiful through the rhetoric course and by reading *Rhetoric and Belles-Lettres* (*Shūji oyobi kabun*, 1879) by Kikuchi Dairoku (1855–1917). Viewed in the light of Blair's lecture, Shiga's *Nippon fūkeiron* produces the sublime effect that fills the reader with a degree of wonder, exhilaration, and astonishment about their living space. At the same time, the text implicitly conveys the message that such ideas of a beautiful home could easily disappear if Japan lost the war with China. The timing of this text's publication reflected such a sense of vulnerability. Japan had been, after all, at war with China since August 1894, and Shiga's text appeared in October 1894 as if to challenge the reader on their willingness to defend the nation. Given the fact that the first and second editions of the text sold rapidly, and the third edition of *Nippon fūkeiron* appeared in March 1895, it clearly had the potential to ignite a reader's passion regarding the beauty of the national homeland.

With a supplementary section called "Encouragement of the Creation of a New Spirit of Mountaineering" (*Tozan no kifū o kōsaku subeshi*), Shiga's text incited readers to climb the beautiful mountains throughout the national homeland. The text promoted the culture of mountaineering,

---

sublime but have no relation to space, such as "great loudness of sound," they always give rise to sublime ideas. He also writes, "nothing is more sublime than mighty power and strength." Blair, *Lectures on Rhetoric and Belles Letters*, 26.

79.   Blair, *Lectures on Rhetoric and Belles Letters*, 48.

80.   Blair, *Lectures on Rhetoric and Belles Letters*, 45.

which was just being introduced in Japan through the Western Orientalists, who actively hiked across the Japanese countryside. Climbing and hiking were not yet familiar sports in the 1890s, but Walter Weston (1861–1940) introduced the Western culture of mountaineering around this time, and this quickly gave rise to the establishment of the Japanese Alpine Club (*Nihon Sangakukai*, 1905).[81] As Kären Wigen has noted, it was Kojima Usui (1874–1948) who actively promoted Shiga and his work, reinvented the Japanese Alps, and promoted Alpine culture in Japan.[82] Kojima expressed his fascination and the awe-like sentiments he felt on reading Shiga's *Nihon fūkeiron* for the first time; even as late as 1935, Kogure Ritarō (1874–1944) recalled the excitement he experienced when reading Shiga's masterpiece. Shiga's text prompted Kogure to venture forth and climb in the Kiso region mountain range in the summer in 1896, and he wrote about the volcanic mountains of Kisokoma and Kaikoma.[83] The influence of *Nippon fūkeiron* was therefore profound. As Blair's account of the sublime explains, Shiga's text produced a sort of internal elevation and expansion, and this triggered delightful emotions in the mind of the reader. His theory on the landscape of Japan successfully inspired young men to unleash their adventurous spirits because his nationalist aestheticism was grounded in the "true study of geography."

At the same time, my analysis indicates that the degree of maturity of modern geography in his text *Nippon fūkeiron* is highly debatable. As scholars have already pointed out, the fusions of East and West, modern and nonmodern, scientific and nonscientific coexist in this text. I would

81.   The Japanese Alpine Club started as an informal social gathering named Nihon hakubutsu dōshikai (Japanese Natural History Club) among those who were interested in mountaineering. Based on the advice given by Walter Weston, they organized the club, which centered its activities on hiking in the mountains and publishing their reports. In 1921, one of the members, Aritsune Maki, successfully climbed the east ridge of the Eiger in the Swiss Alps, and members began to adopt the Western Alps style of climbing and climbed mountains with similar conditions to those of the Alps in winter. Shiga was the second recipient of an honorary membership from the Japanese Alpine Club after Weston. Shidei, "Nihon sangakukai e no teigen," 3. See Andrews, *The Search for the Picturesque*, for the rise of landscape aesthetics since eighteenth-century Britain.

82.   Kojima, "Kaisetsu" (1937) 7–11; Wigen, "Discovering the Japanese Alps," 15–18.

83.   Kogure, "Kisokoma," 489–90. Kogure makes a note that the essay on Kisokoma first appeared in the November 1935 issue of the journal *Tozan to haikingu* and the essay on Kaikoma appeared in the January 1936 issue of *Yamato keikoku*.

agree that Shiga's aestheticism was a product of the rapid importation of Western knowledge that reorganized the domains of knowledge into the new Western academic disciplines that were also being formed. Thus, it embodied the intellectual climate of the 1880s and 1890s. However, when we consider the temporary attractiveness of the discipline of physical geography, and the fact that it gained popularity only in the 1880s without taking root as an independent subject of modern knowledge, it suggests that the subject itself was in a state of development. Shiga and others were easily able to own this knowledge and explain the formation of the Earth's surface on which Japan was located because they could imagine the various movements in the space of Japan. The ocean currents, winds, and mountain ranges made these energies and were the vehicles for moving the modern Japanese nation forward. The focus on the movement of the oceans and mountains overlaps with the earlier epistemology that perceived the universe as consisting of the incessant movement of *ki*.

Shiga rarely mentions *ki* in his writings, and he denied that spiritual beings played a role in making Japanese landscapes beautiful. However, his worldview clearly demonstrates a line of continuity with earlier cosmology theories, in which *ki* energies were dynamically moving and constituted the actual universe. Indeed, his uncritical acceptance of the Japanese landscape reminds us of the vision of Miyake Setsurei, and even Kaibara Ekiken, who identified the direction of the East as the privileged reservoir of *ki*. Later historians, including myself, have made artificial links between historical figures. In this sense, it is notable that Shiga's *Nippon fūkeiron* maintained a crucial link to Ekiken's understanding of landscape. Shiga actively created an intellectual and historical relationship to Ekiken's scholarship by including a page-long excerpt, titled "Infinite bliss" (*Kagirinaki tanoshimi*), with an indication that the author is Ekiken.[84] By highlighting the internal happiness one gains through travel, Shiga implicitly valorized travel as a special experience for explorers who are ambitious and have daring visions. His gesture toward Ekiken is

---

84. Although Shiga makes no clear acknowledgment of Ekiken, nor registers his intellectual indebtedness to him, *Nihon fūkeiron*, from the second edition onward, always included "Kagirinaki tanoshimi." The excerpt is not a direct quotation from Ekiken's particular text; rather, Shiga seems to have drawn mainly from Ekiken's *The Precept for Happiness* (*Rakukun*, 1711), in which he discusses how one might enrich one's internal happiness through travel.

subtle, and especially when the country was getting charged for territorial expansion, Shiga seemed to be aware of a deep continuity between the scholars, given that they found the essence of cultural identity in the local topography and the notion of *fūdo*.

We have observed the transformation of the idea of *fūdo* since the early modern era, but as we saw in Shiga's landscape treatise, Japan continued to be presented as a privileged land that was designed specifically for the Yamato *minzoku*. As he stated in *Nippon fūkeiron*, "even Westerners admire the land of Japan by calling it a paradise in the world (*sekai no gokuraku*)" and accepted this "land of paradise in the world" as another name for the superior natural environment of Japan.[85] The concept of the privileged space was never questioned but was equated with the essential elements that created the distinct geographic beauty. The superior geographic location and conditions of the Japanese archipelago had become naturalized by the end of the nineteenth century, and the Japanese *fūdo* remained so for centuries to come.

85.   Shiga, *Nippon fūkeiron* (1st ed.), 5.

CONCLUSION

Landscape and National History

In this study, I sought to understand Japan's experience of modernity from a subjective point of view by exploring how the idea of Japan as a unifying narrative came into being, how such an idea circulated throughout the country, and how it changed its form throughout history. Beginning with an analysis of the divine traces found in the local topography of the seventeenth century, I argued that local scholars played an instrumental role in validating the claim that Japan was *shinkoku*. The initial discovery of divine vestiges in local places inspired scholarly interest in the divine age narrative of Japan, which then contributed to the founding of the Kokugaku school in the late eighteenth century. These divine indications predictably stimulated the intellectual desire to excavate the experience of the divine age in the first half of the Tokugawa era but became far more important when that desire overlapped with a thirst for finding solutions to contemporary problems. With an increase in popular anxieties and moral decline in the eighteenth century, Kokugaku scholars such as Motoori Norinaga and Hirata Atsutane reinvented the *shinkoku* narrative as a salvation force for their community. Their sincere wish was to help followers maintain the essence of the Japanese heart. This idea of community was emotionally charged, and the sense of belonging provided members with spiritual guidance that would suffice and save them, even if the end of the world came about. Changing the nature of *shinkoku* Japan from Kaibara Ekiken's time onward, the community of faith produced by Kokugaku scholars inspired the development of social cohesiveness.

The social formation of Japan further escalated as a result of the changing geopolitics in East Asia in the 1850s and 1860s. The overwhelming presence of the Western powers in Asia in the late nineteenth century prompted the import of Western knowledge into the existing political, social, economic, and cultural structures in Japan by replacing the hitherto cultural authority of China. Meiji statesmen were enthusiastic about absorbing and borrowing Western ways of doing things since this was seen as a way of transforming Japan into a modern nation like the West. When we comparatively examine these experiences of imagining Japan in the early modern and modern eras, we learn that Japanese scholars had historically been engaged in this type of translation, seeking a cultural authority to use as a reference point for representing themselves. Thus, there was hardly anything new about "translating the West" or adopting Western chronology and other practices in the Meiji era.[1] The act of "translation" in the Meiji was made modern because Japan's counterpart at that particular moment was the modern West. The current periodization of Japanese history follows Western models of modernity and emphasizes the emergence of the nation-state as a sign of modernity. I have demonstrated that the imaginative mapping of Japan in both eras was essentially part of the same attempt to imagine a culturally defined community. Through these processes of translating the foreign, Japan's system of knowledge became more advanced. This study highlights the process of maturing the structure of knowledge as representing Japan's subjective progress toward modernity.

This book suggests that the discursive progress of the idea of Japan corresponds with the process whereby the collective identity of people as Japanese grew stronger and more solidified in any given historical time. My aim has been to demonstrate how certain aspects of culture were identified as distinctly Japanese and how these features and characteristics formed the basis of the discourse of Japan as a community. To posit these defining Japanese qualities, one must assume the presence of the foreign Other as the fundamental condition. In response to the Other, it became

---

1. Howland, *Translating the West*; S. Tanaka, *Japan's Orient* and *New Times in Modern Japan*.

possible for an awareness of Japan to emerge, to be sought, and to be represented; the imagining of Japan was motivated by a desire to establish an intellectual relationship with the Other. Thus, even the irreducible qualities that define the subjective position of the Self were discovered in the light of the Other, and these tireless subjective engagements with the Other testify to the awareness of Japan in the early modern and modern eras. The significance of the Tokugawa era is not the temporal order that places it before the Meiji but the cultivation of this communal identity that facilitated the imagination of Japan.

In standard narratives of Japanese history, the Meiji Restoration of 1868 is positioned as the start of the modern era, a time when the country, headed by nationalist leaders, strove to create Japan's place in the modern world. By vigorously adopting Western ways of doing things, their policies contributed to the transformation of the political framework into a modern nation-state by 1890. The promulgation of the Meiji Constitution, the establishment of the national assembly of the Diet, and the Imperial Rescript on Education that pronounced the duties of the imperial subject established the appearance of a modern Japanese nation. As this study has shown, however, the exterior transfiguration of the country alone did not turn Japan into a modern nation, and Miyake Setsurei's 1891 *Shin zen bi* was written precisely as a means of empowering the people. Similarly, Shiga Shigetaka wrote *Nippon fūkeiron* shortly after the outbreak of the Sino-Japanese War in 1894 to mobilize his readers to support Japan's territorial expansion and preserve the distinct *fūdo* of their country. Aesthetic nationalism expressed through the landscape became a profound engine that was capable of moving the nation forward over the decades. To advance the project of imperial Japan, they produced idealistic images of the nation, focusing on the feelings readers might hold dear to their hearts: special sentiments for native places. Their support for Japan's imperial vision in the last decade of the nineteenth century became the unifying force that eventually gave rise to the bourgeois "middle class," an objective that Fukuzawa Yukichi had expounded on in the 1870s.

My analysis has only focused on the successful attempts of Setsurei and Shiga, who spoke directly to their readers and educated them about the changing political situation in the world. The popularity of their texts alone may not conclusively prove that these readers actually embraced the imperial agenda that Seikyōsha intellectuals were promoting. However, without offering empirical evidence in support of the effectiveness of their nationalist narratives, I have directed the reader's attention to the actualization of the Japanese empire in the subsequent decades and, furthermore, the realization of the discourse of Japan that Shiga and Setsurei explicated in the late nineteenth century. As they argued, by the turn of the century, Japan's distinct geographic beauty and its moral and aesthetic supremacy had become manifest in perceived reality. The state and private sectors sponsored and established a number of Japan-centered research institutions and museums throughout the empire. Similarly, nationalist claims that advocated the preservation of local traditions and the Japanese way of life produced various groups that idealized native places and culture. As Narita Ryūichi (among others) has demonstrated, social groups consisting of members who came from the same region or hometown (*kyōrikai* or *dōkyōkai*) flooded the cities after the 1880s, holding meetings to stop the disappearance of native places (*kyōri* or *furusato*) and their culture from Japanese life.[2] These trends coincided with the slogan delivered by the Seikyōsha, the preservation of Japan's national essence. They shared the anxiety over the vanishing culture of Japan and strove to retain the country's indigenous identity in the modern world.

Likewise, my analysis of Kaibara Ekiken's *kishin*-inspired narrative of *shinkoku* Japan may face criticism in that I did not reveal the faces of the readers who responded to this narrative. My focus was to highlight how Ekiken's narrative was guided by the pacification of the spirits, *kishin*, which were historically believed to cause misfortune and tragedy and how he promoted celebration of the deities as a necessary principle for ensuring enduring peace. The metaphysical relationships guided the initial articulation of the experience associated with the early history of Japan, being inscribed in the local landscape. In turn, the inscribed landscape explicated the history of Japan. By showing how the discursive productions of *shinkoku* Japan came to overlap with the geographic borders of Japan and became the central identity of Japan in the early modern and modern eras, I have tried to illustrate the dialectic relationship between discourse and reality.

2.   Narita, *Kindai toshi kūkan no bunka keiken*, 14, 73–76. See also Narita, *Kokyō to iu monogatari*; Narita et al., *Kokyō no sōshitsu to saisei*.

The landscape as the epitome of the unique national spirit conceals, of course, the historical development of the discourse of Japan that has obliterated the remnant of the Other. As this study has repeatedly argued, the special sentiments expressed in relation to Japan's divine landscape, the community protected by divine spirits, and the irreducible qualities of the Japanese nation derived from its remarkable *fūdo* were never inherently Japanese but developed in response to the cultural authority of the dominant Other. Moreover, such feelings were represented by mediation of foreign conceptualizations. However unique and distinct the presentation of Japanese identity was, there was obviously nothing purely Japanese about it; more accurately, Japanese-ness was historically made possible by erasing the traces of the foreign Other. As we have seen through the case of the *kishin* that initially formed the discourse of Japan for Ekiken, we are blinded to the presence of the foreign by forgetting its very origins. In this sense, the analyses presented in this book differ considerably from those of later philosophers, such as cultural theorist Kuki Shūzō (1888–1941), whose work Leslie Pincus carefully explores in *Authenticating Culture in Imperial Japan: Kuki Shūzō and the Rise of National Aesthetics*, or the literary group of the Japan Romantic School (*Nihon rōmanha*) that Kevin Doak has extensively analyzed.[3] Twentieth-century intellectuals were disillusioned with the ubiquity of the West in Japanese life and sought to return to the "eternal forms of community," which existed only in their idealized vision. As these studies have confirmed, the discovery of an original space to return to is a modern phenomenon, and it only becomes possible when subjects identify themselves with the dominant cultural reference point for the other inferior Others.

In this regard, it is intriguing to recall Naitō Konan (1866–1934), Sinologist at Kyoto Imperial University, who perceived the modernizing attempts of Japan following the Meiji Restoration as merely passing moments in a longer process that had originated in the early modern era. He presented a different conceptualization of modernity in the twentieth century. For example, in 1921 Konan identified the post–Ōnin War (1467–77) period through to the Sino-Japanese War of 1894 as an era of

---

3. Pincus, *Authenticating Culture in Imperial Japan*; Doak, *Dreams of Difference*.

Japan's social and "cultural renaissance."[4] He remarked that a distinct culture of Japan (*Nihon bunka*) grew and prospered in the period after the Ōnin War, which removed the privileged groups of court aristocrats (*kizoku kaikyū no hito*) and brought about the rise of common people (*heimin no kōki*) in Japanese history.[5] Furthermore, when speaking about the warriors who fought and ousted the aristocrats from the imperial capital and then rebuilt the capital and periphery in the aftermath of the Sengoku turmoil, Konan defined the Tokugawa period as a time of cultural restoration. He refuted the claims of those who criticized Japan as a country with no original culture of its own (*jibun no bunka*), one that only absorbed other cultures from China and the continent. Instead, Konan emphasized how the courtiers, emperors, warriors, and others together invented the national culture (*kokumin bunka*) by recovering and reproducing many of the lost imperial anthologies and Buddhist scriptures.[6] For today's readers, Konan's periodization may sound perplexing and unsettling, but it offers a valuable viewpoint on how some Meiji intellectuals perceived the formation of the Japanese empire originating in the late sixteenth century. They understood that the modernizing efforts of the Meiji state were the final phase of the modernizing process of the Japanese nation as it prepared itself for transformation into an imperial power.

When Konan envisioned this periodization, Japan was finally becoming a great power within the international community. As we know very well, after World War I (1914–18), Japan was not only an empire with overseas colonies in Asia and the Pacific but, in 1919, had also gained a perma-

---

4.   Naitō, "Ōnin no ran ni tsuite," 130–48. Before becoming a professor, Konan was an active journalist who wrote for Seikyōsha's *Nipponjin*, *Ōsaka Asahi Shinbun* (Osaka Asahi News), and *Taiwan Nippō* (Taiwan Daily News). He worked under Miyake Setsurei and often wrote Setsurei's essays on his behalf when they both worked for the Seikyōsha. Konan became influential in the twentieth century by proposing a new periodization of Chinese history, one in which the Song dynasty marked the beginning of the early modern period. Although his thesis is no longer popular or influential, his argument that republicanism in China originated during the beginning of the Song, reemerging as modern China in 1914, attracted a degree of attention in the mid-twentieth century among Japanese scholars of China. Tackett, *Destruction of the Medieval Chinese Aristocracy*, 4. See also Fogel, *Politics and Sinology*, xx–xxi; S. Tanaka, *Japan's Orient.*
5.   Naitō, "Nihon kokumin no bunkateki soshitsu," 226–40.
6.   Naitō, "Nihon kokumin no bunkateki soshitsu," 226–40.

nent seat on the council of the League of Nations. Nonetheless, Japan's experience at the Paris Peace Conference was by no means glorious or victorious. Even though Japan belonged to the victorious side, the proposed racial equality clause was rejected by the European leaders and did not become part of the Treaty of Versailles. By being denied full membership of the other great powers, many national leaders were awakened to the idea that Westernization alone was insufficient, or, more accurately, the Westernizing programs the country had followed thus far might have been completely wrong. Finally recognizing that Japan would never become the West, the intellectual leaders began eliminating the signs of the West from Japanese culture and identity. They began searching for ways to return to the past and retrieve the lost culture of indigenous Japan, which prompted the country's isolation in the international community in the 1920s, 1930s, and 1940s.

The naturalized West as part of Japan's identity became the element that had to be removed in the twentieth century; on the other hand, we can see this discursive shift signaling the stabilization of Japan as a signifier and the discursive saturation of Japanese-ness. Around this time Japanese historians outright denied the validity of Norinaga's *Kojikiden* and Atsutane's "*Kishin shinron*." For example, intellectual historian Tsuda Sōkichi (1873–1961) openly declared in his *New Research on the Early History of Japan (Jidaishi no atarashii kenkyū*, 1913) that the accounts of the Divine Age in the two chronicles were fabricated myths (*shinwa*).[7] Tsuda was not alone in denouncing the invented nature of the divine age in the twentieth century, and this rejection shows that by this point the *shinkoku* idea had reached a saturation point, with Japanese scholars perceiving it in a more matter-of-fact manner. Whether or not the gods had inhabited the Japanese archipelago or whether the emperors were descended from the deities, it was clear that Japan was a fully fledged empire in the modern world, with or without the spiritual power of the deities. In 1942, Yasuda

---

7.   Kaizuka, Ienaga, and Ueda, "Tōron," 19–23. The debate concerning the "myths" of Japan's Divine Age began in 1891 with an essay written by Kume Kunitake (1839–1931) that questioned the nature of State Shinto as religion (*shūkyō*). At that time, responses from Shinto enthusiasts led to Kume's forced resignation from academic positions, subsequent attacks on those who defended him, and the abolition of the Historiography Section (*shishi hensan gakari*) at the Tokyo Imperial University. This became known as the Kume Incident. Matsuzawa, *Shigeno Yasutsugu to Kume Kunitake*, 66–75.

Yojūrō (1910–81) of the Japan Romantic School went on to express the belief that the landscape meant the "native place of Japan" (*kokyō toshite no fūkei*) and that the landscape had itself become Japan's history (*rekishi sonomono*).[8]

The Japanese government had widely employed the *shinkoku* idea ever since the Meiji Restoration to substantiate a number of state efforts, such as the reorganization of *shintō* shrines, the establishment of the imperial household with an accompanying narrative of divine age origins, and the creation of the emperor system. In such an environment, most Japanese scholars felt it unnecessary to pinpoint the exact historical texts in which the *shinkoku* idea originated. The divine power that was once believed to reside in the landscape became less important when claiming the remarkable quality of the Japanese nation, and the Japanese landscape as the peerless symbol of Japan's national spirit continued to hold sway throughout the twentieth century. However, given that the ultranationalists in the 1930s and 1940s forced ordinary people to worship the emperor and show reverence toward the divinities in the Japanese landscape, this scholarly "indifference" to the historical origin of the *shinkoku* ideology and their apathy toward the historical relevance and validity of the divine age narrative are deeply problematic. What did Yasuda mean when he claimed that the landscape was the "native place of Japan"? Was he suggesting that if we come to the landscape, we will locate the indigenous past and experiences there?

Although questions remain, Yasuda romanticized and made the landscape into the embodiment of the nation's historical accomplishments—its history itself—and the landscape emerged as a witness to the long history of Japan. Whether we deny or celebrate its historical accomplishments, the landscape as Japanese history is a powerful, emotional source of impact as we look at it. The historical idea of *shinkoku* Japan is embedded in the landscape, and it reverberates subtly even today by being fused into the sense of place of the spiritual, habitual, and recreational.[9] Having come to understand the naturalizing power of the landscape in this study, how might we confront a landscape that invites us to engage in a dialogue by charming us with its seductive beauty? I hope that it is pre-

8.   Yasuda Y., *Fūkei to rekishi*, 425.
9.   Nelson, *Enduring Identities*, 243.

cisely the valorization of landscape as history that allows us to maintain a critical distance from both history and landscape and also allows us to be aware of ideological power. By reminding ourselves of its recurring collaboration with ideology, landscape serves as a keepsake of the value of the spirit of criticism, which navigates the dangers associated with a naive acceptance of the claim that history repeats itself.

Bibliography

Abe Akio. "Juka shintō to kokugaku." In *Nihon shisō taikei*, vol. 39, *Kinsei shintōron zenki kokugaku*, ed. Bitō Masahide, Ienaga Saburō, Inoue Mitsusada, Ishimoda Shō, Maruyama Masao, Nakamura Yukihiko, Sagara Tōru, and Yoshikawa Kōjirō, 497–506. Tokyo: Iwanami Shoten, 1972.

———. "Shushi no kyūri no nisokumen."*Geppō* 34, no. 7, 2–3. Tokyo: Iwanami Shoten, 1970.

Abe Shinzō. *Utsukushii kuni e.* Tokyo: Bungei Shunjū, 2006.

Abe Yoshio. *Nihon shushigaku to Chōsen.* Tokyo: Tokyo Daigaku Shuppankai, 1965.

Akimoto Kichirō. *Fudoki no kenkyū.* Osaka: Osaka Keizai Daigaku, 1963.

Anderson, Benedict. *Imagined Communities: Reflections on the Origin and Spread of Nationalism.* New York: Verso, 1991.

Andrews, Malcolm. *Landscape and Western Art.* New York: Oxford University Press, 1999.

———. *The Search for the Picturesque: Landscape Aesthetics and Tourism in Britain, 1760–1800.* Stanford, CA: Stanford University Press, 1989.

Anzai Shin'ichi. "Shiga Shigetaka *Nihon fūkeiron* ni okeru kagaku to geijutsu: mubaikaisei to kokusui shugi." *Tōhoku geijutsu bunka gakkai* 11 (2006): 1–15.

Aoki, Michiko Y. *Izumo Fudoki.* Tokyo: Sophia University, 1971.

Aoyama Sadao. *Tō Sō jidai no kōtsū to chishi chizu no kenkyū.* Tokyo: Yoshikawa Kōbunkan, 1963.

Aoyama Tadamasa. "Joshō: kinsei ni 'han' wa atta ka." In *Meiji ishin no gengo to shiryō*, 1–12. Osaka: Seibundō Shuppan, 2006.

Arai Hakuseki. "Kishinron." In *Arai Hakuseki zenshū*, vol. 6, ed. Ichishima Shunjō, 1–23. Tokyo: Yoshikawa Hanshichi, 1907.

———. "Saishikō." In *Arai Hakuseki zenshū*, vol. 6, ed. Ichishima Shunjō, 482–88. Tokyo: Yoshikawa Hanshichi, 1907.

Araki Kengo. "Kaibara Ekiken no shisō." In *Nihon shisō taikei*, vol. 34, *Kaibara Ekiken Muro Kyūsō*, ed. Bitō Masahide, Ienaga Saburō, Inoue Mitsusada, Ishimoda Shō,

Maruyama Masao, Nakamura Yukihiko, Sagara Tōru, and Yoshikawa Kōjirō, 467–91. Tokyo: Iwanami Shoten, 1970.

Arano Yasunori, Ishii Masatoshi, and Murai Shōsuke, eds. *Kinseiteki sekai no seijuku*, vol. 6, *Nihon no taigai kankei*. Tokyo: Yoshikawa Kōbunkan, 2010.

Ariyama Teruo. "Kaidai: zasshi *Nipponjin Nippon oyobi Nipponjin* no hensen: sono genron to dōjin." In *Zasshi 'Nipponjin' 'Nippon oyobi Nipponjin' mokuji sōran*, vol. 1, ed. Nihon Kindai Shiryō Kenkyūkai, 1–54. Tokyo: Hayakawa Tosho, 1977.

Asano Sanpei. "Kaisetsu: Arai Hakuseki to *Kishinron*." In *Genbun gendaigo yaku Kishinron Kishin shinron*, 271–86. Tokyo: Kasama Shoin, 2012.

———. "Kaisetsu: Hirata Atsutane to *Kishin shinron*." In *Genbun gendaigo yaku Kishinron Kishin shinron*, 287–302. Tokyo: Kasama Shoin, 2012.

Asao Naohiro. *Shōgun kenryoku no sōshutsu*. Tokyo: Iwanami Shoten, 1994.

———. "Tenkabito to Kyoto." In *Tenkabito no jidai: jūroku jūnana seiki no Kyoto*, ed. Asao Naohiro and Tabata Yasuko, 19–62. Tokyo: Heibonsha, 2003.

Ashfield, Andrew, and Peter de Bolla, eds. *The Sublime: A Reader in British Eighteenth-Century Aesthetic Theory*. Cambridge: Cambridge University Press, 1996.

Asukai Masamichi. *Nihon kindai seishinshi no kenkyū*. Kyoto: Kyoto Daigaku Gakujutsu Shuppankai, 2002.

Auslin, Michael R. *Negotiating with Imperialism: The Unequal Treaties and the Culture of Japanese Diplomacy*. Cambridge, MA: Harvard University Press, 2004.

Bartholomew, James R. *The Formation of Science in Japan: Building a Research Tradition*. New Haven, CT: Yale University Press, 1989.

Batten, Bruce L. *Kokkyō no tanjō: Dazaifu kara mita Nihon no genkei*. Tokyo: Nihon Hōsō Kyōkai, 2001.

———. *To the Ends of Japan: Premodern Frontiers, Boundaries, and Interactions*. Honolulu: University of Hawaii Press, 2003.

Beauchamp, Edward, and Akira Iriye, eds. *Foreign Employees in Nineteenth-Century Japan*. Boulder, CO: Westview Press, 1990.

Berque, Augustin. *Japan: Cities and Social Bonds*. Northamptonshire: Pilkington Press, 1997.

Berry, Mary Elizabeth. *Hideyoshi*. Cambridge, MA: Harvard University Press, 1982.

———. *Japan in Print: Information and Nation in the Early Modern Period*. Berkeley: University of California Press, 2006.

Blair, Hugh. *Lectures on Rhetoric and Belles Letters*. Carbondale: Southern Illinois University Press, 2005.

Bol, Peter K. "The Rise of Local History: History, Geography, and Culture in Southern Song and Yuan Wuzhou." *Harvard Journal of Asiatic Studies* 61, no. 1 (June 2001): 37–76.

Bowie, Andrew. *Aesthetics and Subjectivity from Kant to Nietzsche*. Manchester: Manchester University Press, 2003.

Breen, John, and Mark Teeuwen. *A New History of Shinto*. Malden, MA: Wiley-Blackwell, 2010.

Brown, Philip C. *Central Authority and Local Autonomy in the Formation of Early Modern Japan: The Case of Kaga Domain*. Stanford, CA: Stanford University Press, 1993.

Buckle, Henry Thomas. *History of Civilization in England*. New York: Appleton, 1884.
Burks, Ardath. *The Modernizers: Overseas Students, Foreign Employees, and Meiji Japan*. Boulder, CO: Westview Press, 1985.
Burns, Susan L. *Before the Nation: Kokugaku and the Imagining of Community in Early Modern Japan*. Durham, NC: Duke University, 2003.

Carter, Steven D. "Sōgi in the East Country: Shirakawa Kikō." *Monumenta Nipponica* 42, no. 2 (Summer 1987): 167–209.
Clements, Rebekah. "Rewriting Murasaki: Vernacular Translation and the Reception of *Genji Monogatari* during the Tokugawa Period." *Monumenta Nipponica* 68, no. 1 (2013): 1–36.
Colley, Ann C. *Victorians in the Mountains: Sinking the Sublime*. Farnham, UK: Ashgate, 2010.
Corner, James. "The Agency of Mapping: Speculation, Critique and Invention." In *Mapping*, ed. Denis Cosgrove, 213–52. London: Reaktion Books, 1999.
Cosgrove, Denis E. *Geography and Vision: Seeing, Imagining, and Representing the World*. London: I.B. Tauris, 2008.
———. *Social Formation and Symbolic Landscape*. Madison: University of Wisconsin Press, 1998.

Devine, Richard. "Hirata Atsutane and Christian Sources." *Monumenta Nipponica* 36, no. 1 (1981): 37–54.
Doak, Kevin M. *Dreams of Difference: The Japan Romantic School and the Crisis of Modernity*. Berkeley: University of California Press, 1994.
———. *A History of Nationalism in Modern Japan: Placing the People*. Leiden: Brill, 2007.

Ekikenkai, ed. "Ekiken sensei nenpu." In *Ekiken zenshū*, vol. 1, ed. Ekikenkai, 1–42. Tokyo: Ekiken Zenshū Kankōbu, 1910.
Endō Jun. *Hirata kokugaku to kinsei shakai*. Tokyo: Perikansha, 2008.
———. "Hirata Kokugaku to yūmei shisō: kinsei shintō ni okeru shi no shudaika." In *Shirīzu Nihonjin to shūkyō: kinsei kara kindai e*, vol. 3, *Sei to shi*, ed. Hayashi Makoto, Shimazono Susumu, Takano Toshihiko, and Wakao Masaki, 143–68. Tokyo: Shunjūsha, 2015.
Endō Katsumi. *Kinsei on'yōdōshi no kenkyū, Shintei zōho ban*. Tokyo: Shinjinbutsu Ōraisha, 1996.

Fenollosa, Ernest F. "Bijutsu shinsetsu." In *Nihon kindai shisō taikei*, vol. 17, *Bijutsu*, ed. Aoki Shigeru and Sakai Tadayasu, 35–65. Tokyo: Iwanami Shoten, 1989.
Fogel, Joshua. *Politics and Sinology: The Case of Naitō Konan (1866–1934)*. Cambridge, MA: Harvard Council on East Asian Studies, 1984.
Foucault, Michel. "Questions on Geography." In *Power/Knowledge: Selected Interviews and Other Writings, 1972–1977*, ed. Colin Gordon, 63–77. New York: Vintage Books, 1980.
Foxwell, Chelsea. *Making Modern Japanese-Style Painting: Kano Hōgai and the Search for Images*. Chicago: University of Chicago Press, 2015.
Fujii Jōji. *Edo jidai no kanryōsei*. Tokyo: Aoki Shoten, 1999.

———. "Kinsei zenki no daimyō to jikō." In *Kaibara Ekiken: tenchi waraku no bunmeigaku*, ed. Yokoyama Toshio, 117–43. Tokyo: Heibonsha, 1995.

———. *Tokugawa shōgunke ryōchi ategaisei no kenkyū*. Kyoto: Shibunkaku Shuppan, 2006.

Fujita Satoru. *Kinsei no sandai kaikaku*. Tokyo: Yoshikawa Kōbunkan, 1989.

Fujitani, Takashi. *Splendid Monarchy: Power and Pageantry in Modern Japan*. Berkeley: University of California Press, 1988.

Fujizane Kumiko. "Santo no hon'ya nakama." In *Shirīzu hon no bunkashi*, vol. 4, *Shuppan to ryūtsū*, ed. Yokota Fuyuhiko, 29–68. Tokyo: Heibonsha, 2016.

Fukuoka, Maki. *The Premise of Fidelity: Science, Visuality and Representing the Real in Nineteenth-Century Japan*. Stanford, CA: Stanford University Press, 2012.

Fukuzawa Yukichi. "Bunmeiron no gairyaku." In *Fukuzawa Yukichi zenshū*, vol. 4, ed. Jiji Shinpōsha, 1–212. Tokyo: Iwanami Shoten, 1959.

———. "Gakumon no susume." In *Fukuzawa Yukichi zenshū*, vol. 3, Jiji Shinpōsha, 21–144. Tokyo: Iwanami Shoten, 1959.

———. "Shōchū bankoku ichiran." In *Fukuzawa zenshū*, vol. 2 ed. Jiji Shinpōsha, 523–64. Tokyo: Kokumin Tosho, 1925–26.

Funke, Mark C. "Hitachi no kuni fudoki." *Monumenta Nipponica* 49, no. 1 (1994): 1–29.

Furniss, Tom. *Edmund Burke's Aesthetic Ideology: Language, Gender and Political Economy in Revolution*. New York: Cambridge University Press, 2008.

Furth, Charlotte. *A Flourishing Yin: Gender in China's Medical History: 960–1665*. Berkeley: University of California Press, 1999.

Gavin, Masako. *Shiga Shigetaka 1863–1927: The Forgotten Enlightener*. Richmond, UK: Curzon, 2001.

Geikie, Archibald. *Elementary Lessons in Physical Geography*. London: Macmillan, 1884.

"Genritsu seifu ni hantai suru mono." *Nipponjin* 9 (February 1894): 7–12.

Gluck, Carol. *Japan's Modern Myths: Ideology in the Late Meiji Period*. Princeton, NJ: Princeton University Press, 1985.

———. "Review: *Live Machines: Hired Foreigners and Meiji Japan*." *Journal of Japanese Studies* 7, no. 2 (1981): 428–32.

Goldsmith, J. *Grammar of General Geography*. London: Longman, 1834.

Goree, Robert D. "Fantasies of the Real: Illustrated Gazetteers in Early Modern Japan." Ph.D. diss., Yale University, 2010.

Gotō Bee. *Taigu Miyake Setsurei*. Tokyo: Bugeisha, 1916.

Gotō Yasushi and Yamao Yukihisa. *Rakusei tanbō: Kyoto bunka no saihakken*. Kyoto: Tankōsha, 1990.

Haga Noboru. *Kokugaku no hitobito: sono kōdō to shisō*. Tokyo: Hyōronsha, 1977.

Haga Shōji. *Shisekiron: jūkyū seiki Nihon no chiiki shakai to rekishi ishiki*. Nagoya: Nagoya Daigaku Shuppankai, 1998.

Hamashita Masahiro. "Shiga Shigetaka *Nihon fūkeiron* ni miru Nihonteki suikō no kanōsei: tettō sangaku shinkō to kokusui." *Bungeigaku kenkyū* 8 (2004): 1–25.

"Hanbatsu seiji." *Nipponjin* 10 (August 1888): 1–5.

Hardacre, Helen. *Shintō and the State, 1868–1988*. Princeton, NJ: Princeton University Press, 1991.

Harootunian, Harry D. *Things Seen and Unseen: Discourse and Ideology in Tokugawa Nativism*. Chicago: University of Chicago Press, 1988.

———. *Toward Restoration: The Growth of Political Consciousness in Tokugawa Japan*. Berkeley: University of California Press, 1970.

Haruno Shirube. *Kyoto rakusai sanjūsan ka sho gaido*. Osaka: Toki Shobō, 2009.

Hashimoto Manpei. "Kaisetsu: 'Ōzassho' no keitō to tokushoku." In *Kan'ei kyūnenban Ōzassho* ed. Hashimoto Manpei and Koike Jun'ichi, 146–214. Tokyo: Iwata Shoin, 2002.

Hashimoto Masayuki. *Kofudoki no kenkyū*. Osaka: Izumi Shoin, 2007.

Hattori Nakatsune. "Kojikiden jūshichi fu no maki: sandaikō." In *Motoori Norinaga zenshū*, vol. 10, ed. Ōno Susumu, 297–316. Tokyo: Chikuma Shobō, 1968.

Hattori Yukio. *Ōinaru koya: kinsei toshi no shukusai kūkan*. Tokyo: Heibonsha, 1986.

Hayashi Razan. "Honchō jinjakō." In *Shintō taikei*, vol. 20, *Ronsetsu hen: Fujiwara Seika Hayashi Razan*, ed. Shintō Taikei Hensankai, 31–272. Tokyo: Shintō Taikei Hensankai, 1988.

Hegel, Georg Wilhelm Friedrich. "Selections from *The Philosophy of Fine Art*." Trans. F. P. B. Osmaston. In *Philosophies of Art and Beauty: Selected Readings in Aesthetics from Plato to Heidegger*, ed. Albert Hofstadter and Richard Kuhns, 382–445. Chicago: University of Chicago Press, 1976.

Hellyer, Robert I. *Defining Engagement: Japan and Global Contexts, 1640–1868*. Cambridge, MA: Harvard University Asia Center, 2010.

Higo Kazuo. "Kiki seiritsu no rekishi shinri teki kiban." In *Koten Nihon bungaku zenshū*, vol. 1, *Kojiki, Nihon ryōiki, fudoki, kodai kayō*, ed. Fukunaga Takehiko, Ishikawa Jun, and Kurano Kenji, 368–80. Tokyo: Chikuma Shobō, 1960.

Hirano, Katsuya. *The Politics of Dialogic Imagination: Power and Popular Culture in Early Modern Japan*. Chicago: University of Chicago Press, 2013.

Hirata Atsutane. "Amatsu norito kō." In *Hirata Atsutane zenshū*, vol. 2, ed. Muromatsu Iwao, 1–13. Tokyo: Itchidō Shoten, 1911.

———. "Daifusōkoku kō." In *Hirata Atsutane zenshū*, vol. 14, ed. Hirata Atsutane Zenshū Kiseikai, 1–68. Tokyo: Hōbunkan Shoten, 1917.

———. "Kishin shinron." In *Hirata Atsutane zenshū*, vol. 3, ed. Muromatsu Iwao, 1–50. Tokyo: Hirata Gakkai, 1911.

———. *Koshichō kaidaiki*. Tokyo: Iwanami Shoten, 1936.

———. "Sanshinzan yokō." In *Hirata Atsutane zenshū*, vol. 15, ed. Hirata Gakkai, 1–50. Tokyo: Hōbunkan Shoten, 1918.

———. "Shinkoku norito shiki." In *Hirata Atsutane zenshū*, vol. 2, ed. Muromatsu Iwao, 1–33. Tokyo: Itchidō Shoten, 1911.

———. *Tamano mihashira*, vols. 1–2. Unpublished paper, engraved by Kikuchi Mohee. Tokyo, 1813. Naitonal Diet Library Digital Collection, http://dl.ndl.go.jp/info:ndljp/pid/2562762; http://dl.ndl.go.jp/info:ndljp/pid/2562763.

———. "Tama no mihashira." In *Hirata Atsutane zenshū*, vol. 2, ed. Muromatsu Iwao, 1–102. Tokyo: Itchidō Shoten, 1911.

Hirota Masaki. "'Meirokusha' to 'Minyūsha'." In *Min'yūsha to sono jidai*, ed. Kitano Akihiko, Nishida Takashi, Wada Mamoru, and Yamada Hiromitsu, 325–40. Kyoto: Mineruva Shobō, 2003.

Hokkaidō Daigaku, ed. "Kaitakushi no setchi to kari gakkō." In *Hokudai hyakunenshi*, vol. 1, *Tsūsetsu*, 3–28. Sapporo: Gyōsei, 1982.

Hokkaidō Daigaku Tosho Kankōkai, ed. *First Annual Report of Sapporo Agricultural College, 1877 Fukkokuban*. Sapporo: Kaitakushi, 1877.

"Hototogisu no uta." *Nipponjin* 3 (May 1888): 38.

Howell, David L. *Geographies of Identity in Nineteenth Century Japan*. Berkeley: University of California Press, 2005.

Howland, Doughlas R. *Translating the West: Language and Political Reason in Nineteenth-Century Japan*. Honolulu: University of Hawaii Press, 2002.

Huffman, James L. *Creating a Public: People and Press in Meiji Japan*. Honolulu: University of Hawaii Press, 1997.

Idemitsu Sachiko. "Ike Taiga hitsu Manpukuji tōhōjō fusumae saikozu o meguru mondai: keikan ni hyōgen sareta imi ni tsuite." In *Nihon bijutsu no kūkan to keishiki: Kawai Masatomo kyōju kanreki kinen ronbunshū*, ed. Kawai Masatomo Kyōju Kanreki Kinen Ronbunshū Kankōkai, 251–77. Tokyo: Kawai Masatomo Kyōju Kanreki Kinen Ronbunshū Kankōkai, 2003.

Ienaga Saburō. *Tsuda Sōkichi no shisōshiteki kenkyū*. Tokyo: Iwanami Shoten, 1972.

Ihara Saikaku. *Nihon eitaigura*. Osaka: Kaneya, Morita Shōtarō, 1688.

Ikegami, Eiko. *Bonds of Civility: Aethetic Networks and the Political Origins of Japanese Culture*. Cambridge: Cambridge University Press, 2005.

Inoue Atsushi. "Kindai Nihon ni okeru Li Taikei kenkyū no keifugaku: Abe Yoshio Takahashi Susumu no gakusetsu no kentō o chūshin ni." *Sōgō seisaku ronsō* 18 (2010): 61–83.

Inoue Tadashi. *Kaibara Ekiken*. Tokyo: Yoshikawa Kōbunkan, 1963.

Ishida Ichirō. "Zenki bakuhan taisei no ideorigī to shushigakuha no shisō." In *Nihon shisō taikei*, vol. 28, *Fujiwara Seika Hayashi Razan*, ed. Bitō Masahide, Ienaga Saburō, Inoue Mitsusada, Ishimoda Shō, Maruyama Masao, Nakamura Yukihiko, Sagara Tōru, and Yoshikawa Kōjirō, 411–48. Tokyo: Iwanami Shoten, 1975.

Ishida Ichirō and Takahashi Miyuki. "Kaidai." In *Shintō taikei*, vol. 20, *Ronsetsu hen: Fujiwara Seika Hayashi Razan*, ed. Shintō Taikei Hensankai, 19–63. Tokyo: Shintō Taikei Hensankai, 1988.

Isomae, Jun'ichi. *Japanese Mythology: Hermeneutics on Scripture*. Sheffield, UK: Equinox Publishing, 2010.

———. "Myth in Metamorphosis: Ancient and Medieval Versions of the Yamatotakeru Legend." *Monumenta Nipponica* 54, no. 3 (1999): 361–85.

Isomae, Jun'ichi, and Sarah E. Thal. "Reappropriating the Japanese Myths: Motoori Norinaga and the Creation Myths of the Kojiki and Nihon shoki." *Japanese Journal of Religious Studies* 27, no. 1/2 (2000): 15–39.

Itasaka Yōko. "Chihō no bungaku." In *Iwanami kōza Nihon bungakushi*, vol. 10, *Jūkyūseiki no bungaku*, ed. Fujii Sadakazu, Hino Tatsuo, Kubota Jun, Kuritsubo Yoshiki, and Noyama Kashō, 269–91. Tokyo: Iwanami Shoten, 1996.

————. "Kaibara Ekiken *Azumaji no ki Kishi kikō* to Edo zenki no kikō bungaku." In *Shin Nihon koten bungaku taikei*, vol. 98, *Azumaji no ki Kishi kikō Seiyūki*, ed. Kubota Jun, Nakano Mitsutoshi, Ōsone Shōsuke, and Satake Akihiro, 417–60. Tokyo: Iwanami Shoten, 1991.

————. "Kaibara Ekiken no *kikōbun*: sono seisaku jōkyō to koko no sakuhin ni tsuite." *Gobun kenkyū* 12 (1972): 32–41.

————. "Kaibara Ekiken to kikōbun." *Aichi kenritsu daigaku bungakubu ronshū* 28 (1978): 21–34.

————. "Kaibara kazō 'Azumaji no ki' no hen'yō." *Edo jidai bungakushi* 3 (1983): 177–89.

————. "Kaisetsu." In *Kinsei kikōbun shūsei*, vol. 1, 3–17. Fukuoka: Ashi Shobō, 2002.

————. "Meisho zue rui no fūkei byōsha." *Gobun kenkyū* 38 (1975): 16–26.

"Itō Mutsu no gaikō seiryaku." *Nipponjin* 11 (March 1894): 1–10.

Itō Tasaburō. *Kinseishi no kenkyū*, vol. 4, *Bakufu to shohan*. Tokyo: Yoshikawa Kōbunkan, 1984.

Izumi Seiji. *Kinsei zenki gōsondaka to ryōshu no kisoteki kenkyū: Shōhō no gōchō kuniezu no bunseki o chuūshin ni*. Tokyo: Iwata Shoin, 2008.

Jichō Sei. "'Hanbatsu seiji' no shasetsu ni kansuru shokan." *Nipponjin* 11 (September 1888): 29–30.

Jingūshichō Kojiruien Shuppan Jimusho, ed. *Kojiruien*, vol. 37, *Jingibu 1*. Tokyo: Jingūshichō, 1896–1914.

"Jōyaku reikō to sōsenkyo subekaraku zen daigishi o saisen subeshi." *Nipponjin* 7 (January 1894): 6–9.

Kageki Hideo. *Shōken Kō zenchū*. Osaka: Seibundō Shuppan, 1998.

Kaibara Ekiken. "Chikuzen no kuni zoku fudoki." In *Ekiken zenshū*, vol. 4, ed. Ekikenkai, 1–713. Tokyo: Ekiken Zenshū Kankōbu, 1911.

————. "Fusō kishō." In *Ekiken zenshū*, vol. 7, ed. Ekikenkai, 310–542. Tokyo: Ekiken Zenshū Kankōbu, 1911.

————. "Hōkoku kikō." In *Nihon shomin seikatsu shiryō shūsei*, vol. 2, *Tanken, kikō, chishi: saigoku hen*, ed. Haraguchi Torao, Miyamoto Tsuneichi, and Tanigawa Ken'ichi, 477–99. Tokyo: San'ichi Shobō, 1969.

————. "Isei shūyō." In *Ekiken zenshū*, vol. 7, ed. Ekikenkai, 815–16. Tokyo: Tosho Kankōkai, 1973.

————. "Jingikun." In *Ekiken zenshū*, vol. 3, ed. Ekikenkai, 641–85. Tokyo: Ekiken Zenshū Kankōbu, 1911.

————. "Jinshin kikō." In *Kinsei kikō shūsei*, vol. 17, *Sōsho edo bunko*, ed. Takada Mamoru and Hara Michio, 5–48. Tokyo: Kokusho Kankōkai, 1991.

————. "Keijō shōran." In *Ekiken zenshū*, vol. 7, ed. Ekikenkai, 1–44. Tokyo: Ekiken Zenshū Kankōbu, 1911.

————. "Nihon shakumyō." In *Ekiken zenshū*, vol. 1, ed. Ekikenkai, 1–83. Tokyo: Ekiken Zenshū Kankōbu, 1910.

————. "Taigiroku." In *Ekiken zenshū*, vol. 2, ed. Ekikenkai, 148–75. Tokyo: Ekiken Zenshū Kankōbu, 1910.

———. "Wajiga." In *Ekiken zenshū*, vol. 7, ed. Ekikenkai, 543–752. Tokyo: Ekiken Zenshū Kankōbu, 1911.

———. "Wakan meisū." In *Ekiken zenshū*, vol. 2, ed. Ekikenkai, 821–61. Tokyo: Tosho Kankōkai, 1973.

———. "Washū junranki." In *Ekiken zenshū*, vol. 7, ed. Ekikenkai, 45–81. Tokyo: Ekiken Zenshū Kankōbu, 1910.

———. "Zoku wakan meisū." In *Ekiken zenshū*, vol. 2, ed. Ekikenkai, 862–924. Tokyo: Tosho Kankōkai, 1973.

Kaibara Toshiko. "Honkoku Ekiken shiryō: *Kōtō kikō/Kumano ji no ki*." *Kashiigata: kokubungaku kenkyūshi* 13 (August 1967): 78–87.

Kaiho Mineo. "Tōitsu seiken, Matsumae han, Ezochi." In *Hokkaidō no kenkyū*, vol. 3, *Kinseihen I*, ed. Kaiho Mineo, 39–76. Osaka: Seibundō Shuppan, 1983.

———. "Wajin seiken no seiritsu." In *Hokkaidō no kenkyū*, vol. 3, *Kinseihen I*, ed. Kaiho Mineo, 1–37. Osaka: Seibundō Shuppan, 1983.

Kaizuka Shigeki, Ienaga Saburō, and Ueda Masaki. "Tōron: Tsuda Sōkichi no gakumon to shisō." In *Hito to shisō: Tsuda Sōkichi* ed. Ueda Masaaki, 7–58. Tokyo: San'ichi Shobō, 1974.

Kamei Hideo. *Meiji bungakushi*. Tokyo: Iwanami Shoten, 2003.

———. "Nan'yō jiji kenkyū." In *Hokudai hyaku nijūgo-nen shi: ronbun shiryō hen*, 54–110. Sapporo: Hokkaidō Daigaku Tosho Kankōkai, 2003.

———. "Nihon kindai no fūkeiron: Shiga Shigetaka Nihon fūkeiron no baai." In *Iwanami kōza bungaku*, vol. 7, *Tsukurareta shizen*, ed. Komori Yōichi, 17–41. Tokyo: Iwanami Shoten, 2003.

Kamei Hideo and Matsuki Hiroshi, eds. *Chōten niji o haku: Shiga Shigetaka 'zai Sapporo nōgakkō dai-ni nenki chū nikki'*. Sapporo: Hokkaidō Daigaku Tosho Kankōkai, 1998.

Kamei Shunsuke. *Nashonarizumu no bungaku: Meiji seishin no tankyū*. Tokyo: Kōdansha, 1988.

Kamens, Edward. *Utamakura, Allusion, and Intertextuality in Traditional Japanese Poetry*. New Haven, CT: Yale University Press, 1997.

Kamio Tokiko. *Kodai ritsuryō bungaku kō: shiseki to chishi*. Tokyo: Ōfū, 1996.

Kamo no Toshiharu. "Kamosha nenjū gyōji." In *Nihon sairei gyōji shūsei*, vol. 1, ed. Nihon Sairei Gyōji Shūsei Kankōkai, 141–50. Tokyo: Heibonsha, 1970.

Kanai Madoka. *Hansei*. Tokyo: Shibundō, 1962.

Kanaya Osamu. *Rōsōteki sekai: Enanji no shisō: sāra sōsho 11*. Kyoto: Heirakuji Shoten, 1959.

Kanda Chisato. "'Tendō' shisō to 'shinkoku' kan." In *Shirīzu Nihonjin to shūkyō: kinsei kara kindai e*, vol. 2, *Shin, ju, futsu no jidai*, ed. Shimazono Susumu et al., 19–47. Tokyo: Shunjūsha, 2014.

Kano Masanao. *Nihon kindaika no shisō*. Tokyo: Kenkyūsha Shuppan, 1972.

Karatani, Kōjin. "Japan as Art Museum: Okakura Tenshin and Fenollosa." In *A History of Modern Japanese Aesthetics*, ed. Michael F. Marra, 43–52. Honolulu: University of Hawaii Press, 2001.

Karlin, Jason G. *Gender and Nation in Meiji Japan: Modernity, Loss, and the Doing of History*. Honolulu: University of Hawaii Press, 2014.

Kasaya Kazuhiko. "Joron: Tokugawa jidai tsūshi yōkō." In *Tokugawa shakai to Nihon no kindaika*, ed. Kasaya Kazuhiko, 3–87. Kyoto: Shibunkaku, 2015.

————. *Sekigahara kassen: Ieyasu no senryaku to bakuhan taisei*. Tokyo: Kōdansha, 1994.

————. *Sekigahara kassen to Ōsaka no jin*. Tokyo: Yoshikawa Kōbunkan, 2007.

Katō Akira. "Nanbuhan ni okeru chihō chigyōsei no seisakuteki igi: chihō chigyōsei no sonzoku no riyū ni tsuite." In *Kinsei hōken shihai to minshū shakai: Wakamori Tarō sensei kanreki kinen*, ed. Wakamori Tarō sensei kanreki kinen ronbunshū henshū iinkai, 49–80. Tokyo: Kōbundō, 1975.

Katsu Kokichi. *Musui's Story: The Autobiography of a Tokugawa Samurai*. Trans. Teruko Craig. Tucson: University of Arizona Press, 1991.

Katsurajima Nobuhiro. *Bakumatsu minshū shisō no kenkyū: bakumatsu kokugaku to minshū shūkyō*. Kyoto: Bunrikaku, 1992.

————. "Kindai tennōsei ideologī no shisō katei: Tokugawa shisō oyobi Hirata Atsutanezō no tenkai o chūshin ni." In *Tennō to ōken o kangaeru*, vol. 4, *Shūkyō to ken'i*, ed. Amino Yoshihiko, Kabayama Kōichi, Miyata Noboru, Yamamoto Kōji, and Yasumaru Yoshio, 217–46. Tokyo: Iwanami Shoten, 2002.

Kawahira Toshifumi and Katsumata Motoi. *Fusō meishōzu-kō: Kyūdai-bon o chūshin ni*. Kyushu University Institutional Repository Kyushu University Library, https://catalog .lib.kyushu-u.ac.jp/opac_download_md/10358/po16.pdf.

Kawamura Hirotada. *Edo bakufu no Nihon chizu: kuniezu, shiroezu, Nihonzu*. Tokyo: Yoshikawa Kōbunkan, 2010.

————. *Edo bakufusen kuniezu no kenkyū*. Tokyo: Kokon Shoin, 1984.

Kawasaki Rie. "Kinsei shakai ni okeru rekisen no jittai: Hirose Kyokusō to Furutani Dōan o sozai ni." *Kyoto joshi daigaku daigakuin bungaku kenkyūka kenkyū kiyō shigakuhen* 9 (2010): 27–47.

Kawase Kazuma. *Shoshigaku nyūmon*. Tokyo: Yūshōdō Shuppan, 2001.

————. *Zōho Kokatsujiban no kenkyū*. Nihon Koshoseki Shōkyōkai, 1967.

Keene, Donald. *Travelers of a Hundred Ages: The Japanese as Revealed through 1,000 Years of Diaries*. New York: Columbia University Press, 1999.

Kenrick, Douglas Moore. *A Century of Western Studies of Japan: The First Hundred Years of the Asiatic Society of Japan*. Tokyo: Asiatic Society, 1978.

Kim, Kyu Hyun. *The Age of Visions and Arguments: Parliamentarianism and the National Public Sphere in Early Meiji Japan*. Cambridge, MA: Harvard University Asia Center, 2007.

Kimura Naoe. *Seinen no tanjō: Meiji Nihon ni okeru seijiteki jissen no tenkai*. Tokyo: Shin'yōsha, 1998.

Kinmonth, Earl H. *Self-Made Man in Meiji Japanese Thought: From Samurai to Salary Man*. Berkeley: University of California Press, 1981.

Kitajima Masamoto. *Edo bakufu no kenryoku kōzō*. Tokyo: Iwanami Shoten, 1964.

Kitazawa Noriaki. *Me no shinden: 'bijutsu' juyōshi nōto*. Tokyo: Bijutsu Shuppansha, 1989.

Kobayashi Junji. "Kinsei ni okeru chi no haibun kōzō: Genroku Kyōhō-ki ni okeru shoshi to jusha." *Nihonshi kenkyū* 439 (1999): 72–102.

Kogure Ritarō. "Kisokoma." In *Yama no omoide*, vol. 1, 489–532. Tokyo: Heibonsha, 1999.

Kojima Usui. "Kaisetsu." In Shiga Shigetaka, *Nippon fūkeiron*, 3–17. Tokyo: Iwanami Shoten, 1937.

———. "(Iwanami bunko shohan) Kaisetsu." In Shiga Shigetaka, *Nippon fūkeiron*, 368–82. Tokyo: Iwanami Shoten, 1995.

Komori Yōichi. *Buntai toshite no monogatari: zōhoban*. Tokyo: Seikyūsha, 2012.

———. "Kaisetsu: shisō toshite no buntai, buntai toshite no shisō." In *Nihon bungaku kenkyū shiryō shinshū*, vol. 11, *Kindai bungaku no seiritsu: shisō to buntai no mosaku*, 249–63. Tokyo: Yūseidō, 1986.

———. *Posutokoroniaru*. Tokyo: Iwanami Shoten, 2001.

Kon Sotosaburō. "Nippon no jitsuryoku." *Nipponjin* 4 (May 1888): 14–18.

Konta Hirofumi. *Edo no hon'ya san: kinsei bunkashi no sokumen*. Tokyo: Heibonsha, 2009.

Koyasu Nobukuni. *Edo shisōshi kōgi*. Tokyo: Iwanami Shoten, 2010.

———. *Hōhō toshite no Edo: Nihon shisōshi to hihanteki shiza*. Tokyo: Perikansha, 2000.

———. *Jiken toshite no Soraigaku*. Tokyo: Seidosha, 1990.

———. *Kishinron: kami to saishi no disukūru*. Tokyo: Fukutake Shoten, 1992.

———. *Kokka to saishi: kokka shintō no genzai*. Tokyo: Seidosha, 2004.

———. "'Kōsetsuka' Atsutane no tōjō to kyūzai no gensetsu." *Edo no shisō: kyūzai no shinkō* 1 (1995): 53–72.

———. *Nihon nashonarizumu no kaidoku*. Tokyo: Hakutakusha, 2007.

———. *Norinagagaku kōgi*. Tokyo: Iwanami Shoten, 2006.

———. *'Norinaga mondai' towa nanika*. Tokyo: Chikuma Shobō, 2000.

———. *Norinaga to Atsutane no sekai*. Tokyo: Chūōkōronsha, 1977.

———. *Shisōshika ga yomu rongo: 'manabi' no fukken*. Tokyo: Iwanami Shoten, 2010.

———. "Shushigaku to Kindai Nihon no keisei: tōa shushigaku no dōchō to ishu." *Taiwan tōa bunmei kenkyū gakkan* 3, no. 1 (June 2006): 81–96.

———. *Soraigaku kōgi: "Benmei" o yomu*. Tokyo: Iwanami Shoten, 2008.

Kozakai Daigo. *Kinsei Nihon no dogō to chiiki shakai*. Osaka: Seibundō Shuppan, 2018.

Kramers, Jacob Janszoon. *Geographisch-Statistisch-Historisch Handboek*. Gouda: van Goor, 1850.

Kurano Kenji. "Kaisetsu." In *Koten Nihon bungaku zenshū*, vol. 1, *Kojiki, Nihon ryōiki, fudoki, kodai kayō*, ed. Fukunaga Takehiko, Ishikawa Jun, and Kurano Kenji, 287–305. Tokyo: Chikuma Shobō, 1960.

Kuroda Kiyotaka and Higashikuze Michitomi. "Joshi ryūgakusei haken no giseiin e ukagai (1871)." In *Hokudai hyakunenshi*, vol. 3, *Sapporo nōgakkō shiryō 1*, ed. Hokkaidō Daigaku, 6. Sapporo: Gyōsei, 1981.

Kurokawa Dōyū. *Yōshū fushi: kinsei Kyoto annai*. Tokyo: Iwanami Shoten, 2002.

Kyoto Shinbunsha, ed. *Rakusai no Kannon san: reijō meguri*. Kyoto: Kyoto Shinbunsha, 1979.

Kyoto Shiseki Kengakukai, ed. *Kyoto rakusai rakuhoku sanpo nijū-ni kōsu*. Tokyo: Yamakawa Shuppansha, 2004.

Kyūshū Shiryō Kankōkai, ed. "Ganko mokuroku" and "Kazōsho mokuroku." In *Ekiken shiryō: Hoi*, vol. 4. Kyūshū: Kyūshū Shiryō Kankōkai, 1955.

———. *Ekiken shiryō: shokanshū*, vol. 5. Kyūshū: Kyūshū Shiryō Kankōkai, 1955.

Lewis, Mark Edward. *The Construction of Space in Early China*. Albany: State University of New York Press, 2006.

Mackay, Alexander. *Manual of Modern Geography: Mathematical, Physical, and Political*. London: Blackwood, 1861.

Maeda Kōji. *Aizuhan ni okeru Yamazaki Ansai*. Tokyo: Nishizawa Shoten, 1935.

Maeda Tsutomu. "Shin, ju, butsu no sankyō to Nihon ishiki." In *Shirīzu Nihonjin to shūkyō: kinsei kara kindai e*, vol. 2, *Shin, ju, butsu no jidai*, ed. Shimazono Susumu et al., 111–43. Tokyo: Shunjūsha, 2014.

Maki, John M. *William Smith Clark: A Yankee in Hokkaido*. Sapporo: Hokkaidō University Press, 1996.

Marcon, Federico. *The Knowledge of Nature and the Nature of Knowledge in Early Modern Japan*. Chicago: University of Chicago Press, 2015.

Marra, Michael F., trans and ed. *The Poetics of Motoori Norinaga: A Hermeneutical Journey*. Honolulu: University of Hawaii Press, 2007.

Matsumoto Shigeru. *Motoori Norinaga no shisō to shinri: aidentitī tankyū no kiseki*. Tokyo: Tokyo Daigaku Shuppankai, 1981.

Matsumura Kōji. "Kunshi no chi: Ekiken no 'hakugaku' o megutte." In *Kaibara Ekiken: tenchi waraku no bunmeigaku*, ed. Yokoyama Toshio, 179–98. Tokyo: Heibonsha, 1995.

Matsuno Genkei. "Fusō keikashi." In *Shinshū Kyoto sōsho*, vol. 22, *Fusō keikashi, Yamashiro meiseki junkōshi, Yamashiro meisho jisha monogatari*, ed. Shinshū Kyoto Sōsho Kankōkai, 1–220. Kyoto: Rinsen Shoten, 2004.

Matsuyama Tōan. *Chigaku kotohajime*, vols. 1–3. Tokyo: Keiō Gijuku Shuppankyoku, 1870.

Matsuzawa Yūsaku. *Shigeno Yasutsugu to Kume Kunitake: "seishi" o yumemita rekishika*. Tokyo: Yamakawa Shuppansha, 2012.

McNally, Mark. *Proving the Way: Conflict and Practice in the History of Japanese Nativism*. Cambridge, MA: Harvard University Asia Center, 2005.

———. "The Sandaikō Debate: The Issue of Orthodoxy in Late Tokugawa Nativism." *Japanese Journal of Religious Studies* 29 (2002): 359–78.

Mita Hiroo. *Yama no shisōshi*. Tokyo: Iwanami Shoten, 1973.

Mitani, Hiroshi. *Escape from Impasse: The Decision to Open Japan*. Trans. by David Noble. Tokyo: International House of Japan, 2006.

Mitchell, W. J. T., ed. *Landscape and Power*. Chicago: University of Chicago Press, 2002.

Miura Kunio. *Chūgokujin no toposu: dōkutsu, fūsui, kochūten*. Tokyo: Heibonsha, 1988.

———. "Shushi kishinron no rinkaku." In *Kami kannen no hikaku bunkaron teki kenkyū*, ed. Seki Hiroshi and Minamoto Ryōen, 741–84. Tokyo: Kōdansha, 1981.

———. *Shushi to ki to shintai*. Tokyo: Heibonsha, 1997.

Miura Shūichi. "Taigiroku ni itaru michi." In *Kaibara Ekiken: tenchi waraku no bunmeigaku*, editied by Yokoyama Toshio, 199–233. Tokyo: Heibonsha, 1995.

Miyake Setsurei. *Dōjidaishi*, vols. 1–2. Tokyo: Iwanami Shoten, 1949.

———. "Gakan shōkei." In *Kindai Nihon shisō taikei*, vol. 5, ed. Motoyama Yukihiko, 3–54. Tokyo: Chikuma Shobō, 1975.

———. *Gi aku shū: Nipponjin*. Tokyo: Seikyōsha, 1891.

———. "Ishin go seifu gai no seijika." *Nipponjin* 8 (July 1888): 8–11.

———. "Satchō no zento o uranau." *Nipponjin* 2 (April 1888): 9–14; *Nipponjin* 3 (May 1888): 9–12; *Nipponjin* 5 (June 1888): 15–19.

———. "Shakui rokuri no tomonawazaru chūkun aikoku." In *Sōkon: Kaitei shukusatsu*, 563–75. Tokyo: Shiseidō Shoten, 1916.

———. *Shin zen bi: Nipponjin*. Tokyo: Seikyōsha, 1891.

———. *Tetsugaku kenteki*. Tokyo: Bunkaidō, 1889.

———. "Uchū." In *Meiji bungakuzenshū*, vol. 33, *Miyake Setsureishū*, ed. Yanagida Izumi, 3–144. Tokyo: Chikuma Shobō, 1967.

Miyamoto Tsuneichi. "Tanken, kikō, chishi: saigoku hen: jo." In *Nihon shomin seikatsu shiryō shūseii*, vol. 2, *Tanken, kikō, chishi: saigoku hen*, ed. Haraguchi Torao, Miyamoto Tsuneichi, and Tanigawa Ken'ichi, 1–4. Tokyo: San'ichi Shobō, 1969.

Miyazaki Michimasa. "Jitsuryoku yōseiron." *Nipponjin* 11 (September 1888): 18–21.

Mizuno Aki. *Eki, fūsui, reki, yōjō, shosei: higashi ajia no kosumorojī*. Tokyo: Kōdansha, 2016.

Mizutani Futō. *Shinsen retsudentai shōsetsushi*. Tokyo: Shun'yōdō, 1929.

Morita Toyoko. "Daizassho kenkyū josetsu: *Eitai ōzassho manreki takisei* no naiyō bunseki kara." *Nihon kenkyū* 29 (2004): 247–76.

Morita Yasuo. *Hyōden: Miyake Setsurei no shisōzō*. Osaka: Izumi Shoin, 2015.

Morohashi Tetsuji. *Dai kanwa jiten*, vol. 3. Tokyo: Taishūkan Shoten, 1968.

Motoori Norinaga. *Ashiwake obune Isonokami sasame goto: Norinaga 'mono no aware' karon*. Annot. Koyasu Nobukuni. Tokyo: Iwanami Shoten, 2003.

———. "Kojikiden ichi no maki." In *Motoori Norinaga zenshū*, vol. 9, ed. Ōno Susumu. Tokyo: Chikuma Shobō, 1968.

———. "Kojikiden ni no maki." In *Motoori Norinaga zenshū*, vol. 10, ed. Ōno Susumu. Tokyo: Chikuma Shobō, 1968.

———. "Kojikiden san no maki." In *Motoori Norinaga zenshū*, vol. 11, ed. Ōno Susumu. Tokyo: Chikuma Shobō, 1969.

———. "Uiyama bumi." In *Motoori Norinaga zenshū*, vol. 1, ed. Ōno Susumu, 1–30. Tokyo: Chikuma Shobō, 1968.

Motoyama Yukihiko. *Kinsei jusha no shisō chōsen*. Kyoto: Shibunkaku Shuppan, 2006.

Murai Shōsuke, Satō Makoto, and Yoshida Nobuyuki. *Kyōkai no Nihonshi*. Tokyo: Yamakawa Shuppansha, 1997.

Murakami Tadashi, ed. *Edo bakufu Hachiōji sennin dōshin*. Tokyo: Yūzankaku Shuppan, 1988.

Murakata Akiko, ed. *Ānesuto F. Fenorosa shiryō: Hāvādo daigaku Hōton raiburarī zō*. Tokyo: Myūjiamu Shuppan, 1982.

Muraoka Tsunetsugu. "Hirata Atsutane ga suzunoya nyūmon no shijitsu to sono kaishaku." In *Shinpen Nihon shisōshi kenkyū*, ed. Maeda Tsutomu, 165–90. Tokyo: Heibonsha, 2004.

Nagashima Fukutarō. *Nara bunka no denryū: Unebi shigaku sōsho*. Tokyo: Chūōkōronsha, 1929.

Nagatsuma Misao. *Kōkyōsei no ētosu: Miyake Setsurei to zaiya seishin no kindai*. Kyoto: Sekai Shisōsha, 2002.

———. *Miyake Setsurei no seiji shisō*. Kyoto: Mineruva Shobō, 2012.

Naikaku bunko shozō shiseki sōkan, vols. 55–56, *Tenpō gōchō*. Tokyo: Kyūko Shoin, 1984.

Naitō Konan. "Nihon kokumin no bunkateki soshitsu." In *Naitō Konan zenshū*, vol. 9, 226–40. Tokyo: Chikuma Shobō, 1969.

———. "Ōnin no ran ni tsuite." In *Naitō Konan zenshū*, vol. 9, 130–48. Tokyo: Chikuma Shobō, 1969.

Najita, Tetsuo. *Visions of Virtue in Tokugawa Japan: The Kaitokudō Merchant Academy of Osaka*. Honolulu: University of Hawaii Press, 1987.

Nakagawa Kiun. *Kyō warabe*, vol. 1. Kyoto: Yamamori Rokubei, 1658.

Nakai, Kate Wildman. *Arai Hakuseki no seiji senryaku: jugaku to shiron*. Tokyo: Tokyo Daigaku Shuppankai, 2001.

———. "The Naturalization of Confucianism in Tokugawa Japan: The Problem of Sinocentrism." *Harvard Journal of Asiatic Studies* 40, no. 1 (June 1980): 157–99.

Nakamura Masanao. *Saigoku risshihen*. Tokyo: Kihira Aiji, 1871.

Nakanome Tōru. *Meiji no seinen to nashonarizumu*. Tokyo: Yoshikawa Kōbunkan, 2014.

———. *Seikyōsha no kenkyū*. Kyoto: Shibunkaku Shuppan, 1993.

———. *Shosei to kan'in: meiji shisōshi tenkei*. Tokyo: Kyūko Shoin, 2002.

Naoki Kōjirō, ed. *Shoku Nihongi*, vol. 1. Tokyo: Heibonsha, 1986.

Narita Ryūichi. *Kindai toshi kūkan no bunka keiken*. Tokyo: Iwanami Shoten, 2004.

———. *Kokyō to iu monogatari: toshi kūkan no rekishigaku*. Tokyo: Yoshikawa Kōbunkan, 1998.

Narita Ryūichi, Fujii Hidetada, Iwata Shigenori, Uchida Ryūzō, and Yasui Manami. *Kokyō no sōshitsu to saisei*. Tokyo: Seikyūsha, 2000.

Narumi Kunitada. "Kinsei ezu ni miru sokuryō no kiroku to sono hyōgen." *Rekishigaku kenkyū* 842 (2008): 13–24.

Nelson, John K. *Enduring Identities: The Guise of Shinto in Contemporary Japan*. Honolulu: University of Hawaii Press, 2000.

Nenzi, Laura. *Excursions in Identity: Travel and the Intersection of Place, Gender, and Status in Edo Japan*. Honolulu: University of Hawaii Press, 2008.

Ng, On-cho. *Mirroring the Past: The Writing and Use of History in Imperial China*. Honolulu: University of Hawaii Press, 2005.

Nirei, Yōsuke. "The Ethics of Empire: Protestant Thought, Moral Culture, and Imperialism in Meiji Japan." Ph.D. diss, University of California, Berkeley, 2004.

Notehelfer, Fred. *American Samurai: Captain L. L. Janes and Japan*. Princeton, NJ: Princeton University Press, 1985.

———. *Japan through American Eyes: The Journal of Francis Hall 1859–1866*. Boulder, CO: Westview Press, 2001.

Numata Satoshi. "Kishin, kaii, yūmei: Hirata Atsutane shōron." In *Nihon kinseishi ronsō*, vol. 2, ed. Bitō Masahide sensei kanreki kinenkai, 295–324. Tokyo: Yoshikawa Kōbunkan, 1984.

Ogawa Takeo and Yoshioka Masayuki, eds. *Kinri-bon to kotengaku*. Tokyo: Hanawa Shobō, 2009.

Ōishi Kyūkei. *Jikata hanreiroku*. Tokyo: Kondō Shuppansha, 1969.

Okada, Richard. "'Landscape' and the Nation-State: A Reading of *Nihon fūkei ron*." In *New Directions in the Study of Meiji Japan*, ed. Helen Hardacre with Adam L. Kern, 90–107. Leiden: Brill, 1997.

Okada Takehiko. *Edoki no jugaku*. Tokyo: Meitoku Shuppansha, 2010.

———. "Kaibara Ekiken." In *Edo no shisōkatachi*, vol. 1, ed. Sagara Tōru, Matsumoto Sannosuke, and Minamoto Ryōan, 289–322. Tokyo: Kenkyūsha, 1979.

———. *Yamazaki Ansai to Ri Taikei*. Tokyo: Meitoku Shuppansha, 2011.

Okakura, Kakuzō. *The Ideals of the East with Special Reference to the Art of Japan*. London: John Murray, 1903.

Ōmuro Mikio. *Shiga Shigetaka 'Nihon fūkeiron' seidoku*. Tokyo: Iwanami Shoten, 2003.

Ōno Izuru. *Ganzan Daishi mikuji-bon no kenkyū: omikuji o yomitoku*. Kyoto: Shibunkaku Shuppan, 2009.

Ōno Mizuo. "'Ryōchi hanmotsu/ shuinjō' sairon." *Tōyō daigaku bungakubu kiyō* 53, no. 25 (1999): 1–28.

Ōno Susumu, ed. "Kaidai." In *Motoori Norinaga zenshū*, vol. 1, 5–27. Tokyo: Chikuma Shobō, 1968.

Ooms, Herman. *Charismatic Bureaucrat: A Political Biography of Matsudaira Sadanobu 1758–1829*. Chicago: University of Chicago Press, 1975.

———. *Tokugawa Ideology: Early Constructs, 1570–1680*. Ann Arbor: University of Michigan Press, 1998.

———. *Tokugawa Village Practice: Class, Status, Power, Law*. Berkeley: University of California Press, 1996.

Ōsaka Shingo. *Kurāku sensei shōden*. Sapporo: Kurāku Sensei Shōden Kankōkai, 1956.

Osborne, Brian S. "Interpreting a Nation's Identity: Artists as Creators of National Consciousness." In *Ideology and Landscape in Historical Perspective*, ed. Alan R. H. Baker and Gideon Biger, 230–54. Cambridge: Cambridge University Press, 1992.

Ōshima Masatake. *Kurāku sensei to sono deshi tachi*. Tokyo: Kyōbunkan, 1993.

Paramore, Kiri. *Japanese Confucianism: A Cultural History*. Cambridge: Cambridge University Press, 2016.

Pierson, John D. *Tokutomi Sohō, 1863–1957: A Journalist for Modern Japan*. Princeton, NJ: Princeton University Press, 1980.

Piggott, Joan R. *The Emergence of Japanese Kingship*. Stanford, CA: Stanford University Press, 1997.

Pincus, Leslie. *Authenticating Culture in Imperial Japan: Kuki Shūzō and the Rise of National Aesthetics*. Berkeley: University of California Press, 1996.

Platt, Brian. *Burning and Building: Schooling and State Formation in Japan, 1750–1890*. Cambridge, MA: Harvard University Asia Center, 2004.

Plutschow, Herbert E. *A Reader in Edo Period Travel*. Leiden: Brill, 2006.

Pratt, Mary Louise. *Imperial Eyes: Travel Writing and Transculturation*. New York: Routledge, 1992.

Pyle, Kenneth B. *The New Generation in Meiji Japan: Problems of Cultural Identity, 1885–1895*. Stanford, CA: Stanford University Press, 1969.

Redfield, Marc. *The Politics of Aesthetics: Nationalism, Gender, Romanticism*. Stanford, CA: Stanford University Press, 2008.

Rimer, Thomas J. "Hegel in Tokyo: Ernest Fenollosa and His 1882 Lecture on the Truth of Art." In *Japanese Hermeneutics: Current Debates in Aesthetics and Interpretation*, ed. Michael F. Marra, 97–108. Honolulu: University of Hawaii Press, 2002.

Roberts, Luke S. *Mercantilism in a Japanese Domain: The Merchant Origins of Economic Nationalism in 18th-Century Tosa*. Cambridge: Cambridge University Press, 1998.

———. *Performing the Great Peace: Political Space and Open Secrets in Tokugawa Japan*. Honolulu: University of Hawaii Press, 2012.

Saitō Hajime. *Teikoku Nihon no eibungaku*. Kyoto: Jinbun Shoin, 2006.

Saitō Mareshi. *Kanbunmyaku no kindai: Shinmatsu Meiji no bungakuken*. Nagoya: Nagoya Daigaku Shuppankai, 2005.

———. *Kanbunmyaku to kindai Nihon: mōhitotsu no kotoba no sekai*. Tokyo: Nihon Hōsō Shuppan Kyōkai, 2007.

———. *Kanji sekai no chihei: watashitachi ni totte moji towa nanika*. Tokyo: Shinchōsha, 2014.

Sakai, Naoki. *Translation and Subjectivity: On "Japan" and Cultural Nationalism*. Minneapolis: University of Minnesota Press, 1997.

Sakai Shigeyuki. *Kinri-bon kasho no zōshoshiteki kenkyū*. Kyoto: Shibunkaku Shuppan, 2009.

Sakamoto, Tarō. *The Six National Histories of Japan*. Vancouver: University of British Columbia Press, 1991.

"Satchō hankō hanbatsu igai no shohan ni gekisu." *Nipponjin* 10 (March 1894): 6–10.

Satō Dōshin. *Meiji kokka to kindai bijutsu: bi no seijigaku*. Tokyo: Yoshikawa Kōbunkan, 1998.

———. *'Nihon bijutsu' tanjō: kindai Nihon no 'kotoba' to senryaku*. Tokyo: Kōdansha, 1996.

Screech, Timon. *The Shogun's Painted Culture: Fear and Creativity in the Japanese States, 1760–1829*. London: Reaktion Books, 2000.

Seikyōsha, ed. *Nipponjin*. Tokyo: Seikyōsha, 1888–1895.

Sekifuji Shigeo, trans. *Chimongaku: Hyakka zensho*. Osaka: Umehara Kamehichi, 1882.

Shidei Yasuhiko. "Nihon sangakukai e no teigen: kindai arupinizumu o koeru hōkō wa nanika." *Yama* 746 (July 2007): 1–3.

Shiga Shigetaka. "Chirigaku." In *Shiga Shigetaka zenshū*, vol. 4, ed. Shiga Fujio, 269–418. Tokyo: Shiga Shigetaka Zenshū Kankōkai, 1928.

———. *History of Nations: Especially Adapted for Japanese Students*. Tokyo: Maruya, 1888.

———. "The Japan of Today: The Land of the Mikado." *Sydney Echo* (April 10, 1886). Reprinted in Masako Gavin, *Shiga Shigetaka 1863–1927: The Forgotten Enlightener*, 145–51. London: Routledge, 2013.

———. "Mamiya Rinzō tōtatsu yuki hyakunen kinen." In *Shiga Shigetaka zenshū*, vol. 2, ed. Shiga Fujio, 18–33. Tokyo: Shiga Shigetaka Zenshū Kankōkai, 1928.

———. "Nan'yō jiji." In *Shiga Shigetaka zenshū*, vol. 3, ed. Shiga Fujio. Tokyo: Shiga Shigetaka Zenshū Kankōkai, 1927.

———. "New Zealand and Japan: A Japanese Naturalist." *New Zealand Mail* (May 21, 1886). Reprinted in Masako Gavin, *Shiga Shigetaka 1863–1927: The Forgotten Enlightener*, 163–64. London: Routledge, 2013.

———. *Nippon fūkeiron*. 1st ed. Tokyo: Seikyōsha, 1894.

———. *Nippon fūkeiron*. 2nd ed. Tokyo: Seikyōsha, 1894.

———. "*Nipponjin* no jōto o hanamuke su." *Nipponjin* 1 (April 1888): 1.

———. "Nippon seisanryaku." In *Shiga Shigetaka zenshū*, vol. 1, ed. Shiga Fujio, 62–85. Tokyo: Shiga Shigetaka Zenshū Kankōkai, 1928.

———. "Nippon zento no nidai tōha." In *Shiga Shigetaka zenshū*, vol. 1, ed. Shiga Fujio, 26–34. Tokyo: Shiga Shigetaka Zenshū Kankōkai, 1928.

———. "Ogasawara gentō." In *Shiga Shigetaka zenshū*, vol. 2, ed. Shiga Fujio, 168–75. Tokyo: Shiga Shigetaka Zenshū Kankōkai, 1928.

———. "Yamato minzoku no senseiryoku." *Nipponjin* 7 (July 1888): 1–4.

Shimada Kenji. "Kaisetsu." In *Shintei Chūgoku kotensen*, vol. 4, *Daigaku Chūyō*, 1–16. Tokyo: Asahi Shinbunsha, 1967.

Shimada Yutaka, trans. *Chimongaku*, vols. 1–2. Tokyo: Kyōeki Shōsha, 1884.

Shirai Tetsuya. *Nihon kinsei chishi hensanshi kenkyū*. Kyoto: Shibunkaku, 2004.

Shirane, Haruo. *Traditional Japanese Literature: An Anthology, Beginnings to 1600*. New York: Columbia University Press, 2012.

Shōji Kichinosuke, ed. *Aizu fudoki fūzokuchō: Kanbun fudoki*, vol. 1, 33–493. Tokyo: Yoshikawa Kōbunkan, 1979.

———. "Hanrei." In *Aizu fudoki fūzokuchō: Kanbun fudoki*, vol. 1, 18–20. Tokyo: Yoshikawa Kōbunkan, 1979.

———. "Josetsu." In *Aizu fudoki fūzokuchō: Kanbun fudoki*, vol. 1, 1–17. Tokyo: Yoshikawa Kōbunkan, 1979.

———. "Kaidai." In *Aizu fudoki fūzokuchō: Kanbun fudoki*, vol. 1, 25–31. Tokyo: Yoshikawa Kōbunkan, 1979.

Sugimoto Fumiko. *Ryōiki shihai no tenkai to kinsei*. Tokyo: Yamakawa Shuppansha, 1999.

Sugimoto Fumiko, Hirai Shōgo, Isonaga Kazuki, Nakano Hitoshi, Onodera Atsushi, and Ronald P. Toby. *Ezugaku nyūmon*. Tokyo: Tokyo Daigaku Shuppankai, 2011.

Sugiura Jūgō. "Nippon gakumon no hōshin." *Nipponjin* 1 (April 1888): 4–6.

Suzuki Ikkei. *On'yōdō: jujutsu to kishin no sekai*. Tokyo: Kōdansha, 2002.

Suzuki Shōsei. *Edo no meisho to toshi bunka*. Tokyo: Yoshikawa Kōbunkan, 2001.

Suzuki Tōzō. *Kinsei kikō bungei nōto*. Tokyo: Tōyōdō Shuppan, 1968.

Tachikawa Yoshihiko. *Kyōtogaku no koten Yōshū fushi*. Tokyo: Heibonsha, 1996.

Tackett, Nicolas. *The Destruction of the Medieval Chinese Aristocracy*. Cambridge, MA: Harvard University Asia Center, 2014.

Tahara Tsuguo. "Kaisetsu: Tamano mihashira igo ni okeru Hirata Atsutane no shisō ni tsuite." In *Nihon shisō taikei*, vol. 50, *Hirata Atsutane, Ban Nobutomo, Ōkuni Takamasa*, ed. Bitō Masahide, Ienaga Saburō, Inoue Mitsusada, Ishimoda Shō, Maruyama Masao, Nakamura Yukihiko, Sagara Tōru, and Yoshikawa Kōjirō, 565–94. Tokyo: Iwanami Shoten, 1973.

"Taigai kōha no chijoku nari zenkokumin no fumenboku nari." *Nipponjin* 15 (July 1894): 5–8.

Taira Shigemichi. "Kaisetsu: kinsei no shintō shisō." In *Nihon shisō taikei*, vol. 39, *Kinsei shintōron*, ed. Bitō Masahide, Ienaga Saburō, Inoue Mitsusada, Ishimoda Shō, Maruyama Masao, Nakamura Yukihiko, Sagara Tōru, and Yoshikawa Kōjirō, 507–58. Tokyo: Iwanami Shoten, 1972.

———. *Kinsei Nihon shisōshi kenkyū*. Tokyo: Yoshikawa Kōbunkan, 1969.

Tajiri Yūichirō. "Kinsei Nihon no 'shinkoku'ron." In *Seitō to itan: tennō, ten, kami*, ed. Katano Tatsurō, 109–25. Tokyo: Kadokawa Shoten, 1991.

Takabayashi Kōki. "Atarashii shiryō ga kataru Shiga Shigetaka no shōgai." In *Shiga Shigetaka: kaisō to shiryō seitan hyaku sanjū nen kinenshi* ed. Toda Hiroko, 194–204. Tokyo: Toda Hiroko, 1994.

Takagi Gen. "Shoshi, kashihon'ya no yakuwari." In *Iwanami kōza*, vol. 10, *Nihon bungakushi*, ed. Kubota Jun, 245–65. Tokyo: Iwanami Shoten, 1996.

Takagi Hiroshi. "Kindai ni okeru shinwateki kodai no sōzō: Unebiyama, Jinmuryō, Kashihara Jingū, sanmi ittai no Jinmu 'seiseki'." *Jinbun gakuhō* 83 (2000): 19–38.

———. *Kindai tennōsei no bunkashiteki kenkyū: tennō shūnin girei, nenjū gyōji, bunkazai*. Tokyo: Azekura Shobō, 1997.

———. "'Kyōdo ai' to 'aikokushin' o tsunagu mono: kindai ni okeru 'kyūhan' no kenshō." *Rekishi hyōron* 659 (2005): 2–18.

Takagi Shōsaku. "Edo bakufu no seiritsu." In *Iwanami kōza*, vol. 9, *Nihon rekishi kinsei 1*, ed. Asao Naohiro et al., 117–53. Tokyo: Iwanami Shoten, 1975.

Takahashi Akinori. "Kinsei kōki no rekishigaku to Hayashi Jussai." *Tōhoku daigaku Nihon shisōshi kenkyū* 21 (1989): 1–18.

Takahashi Miyuki. "Kinsei juka shintō no itanron." In *Seitō to itan: tennō, ten, kami*, ed. Katano Tatsurō, 93–108. Tokyo: Kadokawa Shoten, 1991.

Takahashi Satoshi. *Edo no heiwaryoku: sensō o shinakatta Edo no nihyakugojūnen*. Tokyo: Keibunsha, 2015.

Takakura Shin'ichirō. "Kaisetsu." In *Sapporo nōgaku nenpō: kaisetsu mokuji hen*, 2–11. Sapporo: Hokkaidō Daigaku Tosho Kankōkai, 1976.

Takano Nobuharu. *Daimyō no sōbō: jidaisei to imējika*. Osaka: Seibundō Shuppan, 2014.

———. *Hankoku to hanpo no kōzu*. Tokyo: Meisho Shuppan, 2002.

———. *Kinsei daimyōke kashindan to ryōshusei*. Tokyo: Yoshikawa Kōbunkan, 1997.

———. *Kinsei seiji shakai eno shiza: 'hihyō' de amu chitsujo, bushi, chiiki, shyūkyōron*. Osaka: Seibundō Shuppan, 2017.

Takeda Yūkichi. "Norito: kaisetsu." In *Nihon koten bungaku taikei*, vol. 1, *Kojiki norito*, ed. Kurano Kenji and Takeda Yūkichi, 367–82. Tokyo: Iwanami Shoten, 1958.

Takei Jirō and Mark P. Keane, eds. *Sakuteiki: Visions of the Japanese Garden*. Boston: Tuttle, 2001.

Takemura Toshinori. *Shinsen Kyoto meisho zue*, vol. 5. Shirakawa Shoin, 1963.

Tanaka, Stefan. *Japan's Orient: Rendering Pasts into History*. Berkeley: University of California Press, 1993.

———. *New Times in Modern Japan*. Princeton, NJ: Princeton University Press, 2009.

Tanaka Takashi. "Kaidai." In *Shintō taikei koten hen*, vol. 7, *Fudoki*, 7–26. Tokyo: Shintō Taikei Hensankai, 1994.

Taniguchi Shinko. "Junshi, adauchi, shinjū." In *Shirīzu Nihonjin to shūkyō: kinsei kara kindai e*, vol. 3, *Sei to shi*, ed. Shimazono Susumu et al., 79–108. Tokyo: Shunjūsha, 2015.

Tatsumi Kojirō. "Seishin to goko zakkyo shikashite bōsu." *Nipponjin* 1 (October 1893): 24–26.

Teeuwen, Mark. "From Jindō to Shinto: A Concept Takes Shape." *Japanese Journal of Religious Studies* 29, no. 3/4 (Fall 2002): 233–63.

Thomas, Julia A. *Reconfiguring Modernity: Concepts of Nature in Japanese Political Ideology*. Berkeley: University of California Press, 2001.

Thongchai, Winichakul. *Siam Mapped: A History of the Geo-Body of a Nation*. Honolulu: University of Hawaii Press, 1994.

Tian, Xiaofei. *Tao Yuanming and Manuscript Culture: The Record of a Dusty Table*. Seattle: University of Washington Press, 2005.

Tierney, Robert T. "The Colonial Eyeglasses of Nakajima Atsushi." *Japan Review* 17 (2005): 149–96.

———. *Tropics of Savagery: The Culture of Japanese Empire in Comparative Frame*. Berkeley: University of California Press, 2010.

Toby, Ronald P. "Foreign Texts/Native Readings: Matsushita Kenrin (1637–1703) and the Challenge of Chinese/Korean Histories." In *Japan and Its Worlds: Marius B. Jansen and the Internationalization of Japanese Studies*, ed. Martin Collcutt, Kato Mikio, and Ronald P. Toby, 143–74. Tokyo: I-House Press, 2007.

———. "Mind Maps and Land Maps: The Cognitive Geography of 'the Village' in Tokugawa Japan." Unpublished paper.

———. *'Sakoku' to iu gaikō*, vol. 9, *Nihon no rekishi*. Tokyo: Shōgakkan, 2008.

———. *State and Diplomacy in Early Modern Japan: Asia in the Development of the Tokugawa Bakufu*. Stanford, CA: Stanford University Press, 1984.

———. "Why Leave Nara? Kanmu and the Transfer of the Capital." *Monumenta Nipponica* 40, no. 3 (Autumn 1985): 331–47.

Tokuda Kazuo, ed. *Chūsei bungaku to rinsetsu shogaku*, vol. 8, *Chūsei no jisha engi to sankei*. Tokyo: Chikurinsha, 2013.

Tokugawa Yoshinori. *Shinshū Tokugawa Ieyasu monjo no kenkyū*. Tokyo: Tokugawa Reimeikai, 1983.

Traganou, Jilly. *The Tōkaidō Road: Traveling and Representation in Edo and Meiji Japan*. New York: RoutledgeCurzon, 2004.

Tsubouchi Shōyō. *Shōsetsu shinzui*. Tokyo: Shōgetsudō, 1885.

Tsuda Sōkichi. *Banzan Ekiken: dai kyōikuka bunko*, vol. 4. Tokyo: Iwanami Shoten, 1984.

Tsujimoto Masashi. "'Gakujutsu' no seiritsu: Ekiken no dōtokuron to gakumonron." In *Kaibara Ekiken: tenchi waraku no bunmeigaku*, ed. Yokoyama Toshio, 147–78. Tokyo: Heibonsha, 1995.

———. *Kinsei kyōiku shisōshi no kenkyū*. Kyoto: Shibunkaku Shuppan, 1990.

———. "Kinsei ni okeru 'ki' no shisōshi oboegaki: Kaibara Ekiken o chūshin ni." In *Kindai Nihon no imi o tou: seiji shisōshi no saihakken*, ed. Mizobe Hideaki, 39–76. Tokyo: Bokutakusha, 1992.

———. *Manabi no fukken: mohō to seijuku*. Tokyo: Kadokawa Shoten, 1999.

———. "Moji shakai no seiritsu to shuppan media." In *Shin taikei Nihonshi*, vol. 16, *Kyōiku shakaishi*, ed. Tsujimoto Masashi and Okita Yukuji, 121–46. Tokyo: Yamakawa Shuppansha, 2002.

———. *Shisō to kyōiku no mediashi: kinsei Nihon no chi no dentatsu*. Tokyo: Perikansha, 2011.

Tsutsumi Kunihiko. *Kinsei bukkyō setsuwa no kenkyū: shōdō to bungei*. Tokyo: Kanrin Shobō, 1996.

Tsutsumi Kunihiko and Tokuda Kazuo, eds. *Jisha engi no bunkagaku*. Tokyo: Shinwasha, 2005.

Tucker, Mary Evelyn. *Moral and Spiritual Cultivation in Japanese Neo-Confucianism: The Life and Thought of Kaibara Ekken (1630–1714)*. Albany: State University of New York, 1989.

Uchida Masao. *Yochi shiryaku*. Osaka: Meizendō, 1882.

Uchimura Kanzō. "Shiga Shigetaka-shi cho *Nippon fūkeiron*." In *Nippon fūkeiron*, Shiga Shigetaka, 363–67. Tokyo: Iwanami Shoten, 1995.

Ueda, Atsuko. "Colonial Ambivalence and the Modern *Shōsetsu*: *Shōsetsu shinzui* and De-Asianization." *Traces* 3 (2004): 179–206.

——. *Concealment of Politics, Politics of Concealment: The Production of "Literature" in Meiji Japan*. Stanford, CA: Stanford University Press, 2007.

Umeda Chihiro. "Rekisensho no shuppan to ryūtsū." In *Shuppan to ryūtsū*, ed. Yokota Fuyuhiko, 109–39. Tokyo: Heibonsha, 2016.

Umemura Kayo. "Kinsei ni okeru minshū no tenarai to dokusho: kodomo no kiryō keisei o chūshin toshite." In *Shoseki bunka to sono kitei*, ed. Wakao Masaki, 123–55. Tokyo: Heibonsha, 2015.

Unno, Kazutaka. "Cartography in Japan." In *Cartography in the Traditional East and Southeast Asian Societies*, ed. J. B. Harley and David Woodward, 346–477. Chicago: University of Chicago Press, 1995.

Unoda Shōya. "Kinsei juka no keiseiron: sōkoku suru 'Tokugawa Nihon' no shohyōshō." *Edo no shisō: jukyō towa nanika* 3 (1996): 25–47.

Uranishi Tsutomu. "Edo jidai chūki no ichi shintō-ka no katsudō ni kansuru oboegaki: Tada Yoshitoshi no katsudō." In *Nihon kinsei bungaku kenkyū no shin ryōiki*, ed. Munemasa Isoo, 77–119. Kyoto: Shibunkaku Shuppan, 1998.

Vaporis, Constantine N. *Tour of Duty: Samurai, Military Service in Edo, and the Culture of Early Modern Japan*. Honolulu: University of Hawaii Press, 2008.

"Waga Nippon o shii seru hōkoku wa mina horobitari." *Nipponjin* 2 (April 1888): 37–39.

Wakabayashi, Bob Tadashi. *Anti-Foreignism and Western Learning in Early-Modern Japan: The New Theses of 1825*. Cambridge, MA: Harvard University Council on East Asian Studies, 1986.

Wakao Masaki. "Kinsei ni okeru 'Nihon' no ishiki no keisei." In *Kakusei suru chiiki ishiki*, vol. 5, *Edo no hito to mibun*, ed. Wakao Masaki and Kikuchi Isao, 14–45. Tokyo: Yoshikawa Kōbunkan, 2010.

——. "Shin, ju, butsu no kōsaku." In *Shirīzu Nihonjin to shūkyō: kinsei kara kindai e*, vol. 2, *Shin, ju, butsu no jidai*, ed. Shimazono Susumu et al., 49–86. Tokyo: Shunjūsha, 2014.

——. "Shin, ju, butsu no jidai." In *Shirīzu Nihonjin to shūkyō: kinsei kara kindai e*, vol. 2, *Shin, ju, butsu no jidai*, ed. Shimazono Susumu et al., 3–17. Tokyo: Shunjūsha, 2014.

———. "Sōron: shoseki bunka to sono kitei." In *Shoseki bunka to sono kitei*, ed. Wakao Masaki, 7–41. Tokyo: Heibonsha, 2015.

———. '*Taiheiki yomi' no jidai: kinsei seiji shisōshi no kōsō*. Tokyo: Heibonsha, 2012.

Wakimura Yoshitarō. *Tōzai shoshigai kō*. Tokyo: Iwanami Shoten, 1979.

Watanabe Hiroshi. *Sōgaku to kinsei Nihon shakai*. Tokyo: Tokyo Daigaku Shuppankai, 1985.

Watanabe Kinzō. *Hirata Atsutane kenkyū*. Tokyo: Rokkō Shobō, 1942.

Watanabe Takashi. *Kinsei hyakushō no sokojikara: mura kara mita Edo jidai*. Tokyo: Keibunsha, 2013.

White, Hayden. *The Content of the Form: Narrative Discourse and Historical Representation*. Baltimore, MD: Johns Hopkins University Press, 1990.

Wigen, Kären. "Discovering the Japanese Alps: Meiji Mountaineering and the Quest for Geographical Enlightenment." *Journal of Japanese Studies* 31, no. 1 (2005): 1–26.

———. *A Malleable Map: Geographies of Restoration in Central Japan, 1600–1912*. Berkeley: University of California Press, 2012.

Wood, Dennis. *The Power of Maps*. New York: Guilford Press, 1992.

Yakuwa, Tomohiro. "Kinsei minshū no ningen keisei to bunka." In *Shin taikei Nihonshi*, vol. 16, *Kyōiku shakaishi*, ed. Tsujimoto Masashi and Okita Yukuji, 171–244. Tokyo: Yamakawa Shuppansha, 2002.

Yamada Yasuhiko, ed. *Hōi yomitoki jiten*. Tokyo: Kashiwa Shobō, 2001.

Yamaguchi Keiji. *Bakuhansei seiritsushi no kenkyū*. Tokyo: Azekura Shobō, 1974.

———. "Han taisei no seiritsu." In *Yamaguchi Keiji chosakushū*, vol. 2, *Bakuhansei shakai no seiritsu*, 157–229. Tokyo: Azekura Shobō, 2008.

Yamamoto Hiroteru. *Hokumon kaitaku to Amerika bunka: Kepuron to Kurāku no kōseki*. Sapporo: Bunka Shoin, 1946.

Yamamoto Norihiko and Ueda Toshimi. *Fūkei no seiritsu: Shiga Shigetaka to 'Nihon fūkeiron'*. Osaka: Kaifūsha, 1997.

Yamazaki Ansai. "Aizu fudoki jo." In *Aizu fudoki fūzokuchō: Kanbun fudoki*, vol. 1, ed. Shōji Kichinosuke, 36–37. Tokyo: Yoshikawa Kōbunkan, 1979.

Yanagida Izumi. "Kaidai." In *Meiji bungaku zenshū*, vol. 33, *Miyake Setsurei shū*, ed. Yanagida Izumi, 424–30. Tokyo: Chikuma Shobō, 1966.

———. "Kaisetsu: Nihon no *bi* toiu mono: Miyake Setsurei no *bi* no shisō." In *Meiji bungaku zenshū*, vol. 33, *Miyake Setsurei shū*, ed. Yanagida Izumi, 387–423. Tokyo: Chikuma Shobō, 1966.

Yasuda Airō. "Yamato meguri nikki." In *Nihon shomin seikatsu shiryō shūsei*, vol. 2, *Tanken, kikō, chishi: saigoku hen*, ed. Haraguchi Torao, Miyamoto Tsuneichi, and Tanigawa Ken'ichi, 452–60. Tokyo: San'ichi Shobō, 1969.

Yasuda Yojūrō. *Fūkei to rekishi*. Tanbashi, Nara: Tenri Jihōsha, 1942.

Yasumaru Yoshio. *Kamigami no Meiji ishin: shinbutsu bunri to haibutsu kishaku*. Tokyo: Iwanami Shoten, 1979.

Yazu Shōei. *Nippon chimongaku*. Tokyo: Maruzen Shōsha, 1889.

"Yohai dōshi wa ikanaru shugi o torite ka undō subeki." *Nipponjin* 11 (September 1888): 5–7.

Yokota Fuyuhiko. "Edo jidai minshū no dokusho." *Rekishi chiri kyōiku* 718 (2007): 76–81.

———. "Ekiken-bon no dokusha." In *Kaibara Ekiken: tenchi waku no bunmeigaku*, ed. Yokoyama Toshio, 315–53. Tokyo: Heibonsha, 1995.

———. "Kinsei minshū shakai ni okeru chiteki dokusha no seiritsu: Ekiken-bon o yomu jidai." *Edo no shisō: dokusho no shakaishi* 5 (1996): 48–68.

———. "Kinsei no shuppan bunka to 'Nihon'." In *Rekishi no egakikata*, vol. 1, *Nashonaru hisutorī o manabi suteru*, ed. Sakai Naoki, 93–133. Tokyo: Tokyo Daigaku Shuppankai, 2006.

———. *Nihon kinsei shomotsu bunkashi no kenkyū*. Tokyo: Iwanami Shoten, 2018.

———. *Nihon no rekishi*, vol. 16, *Tenka taihei*. Tokyo: Kōdansha, 2002.

———. "'Rōnin hyakushō' Yoda Chōan no dokusho." *Hitotsubashi ronsō* 134, no. 4 (2005): 612–35.

———. "Shomotsu o meguru hitobito." In *Chishiki to gakumon o ninau hitobito*, vol. 5, *Mibun teki shūhen to kinsei shakai*, ed. Yokota Fuyuhiko, 1–16. Tokyo: Yoshikawa Kōbunkan 2007.

Yokoyama Toshio. "Jo: antei shakai o ikiru: Ekiken'ō no uwasa ni koto yosete." In *Kaibara Ekiken: tenchi waraku no bunmeigaku*, ed. Yokoyama Toshio, 9–22. Tokyo: Heibonsha, 1995.

———. "Ōzassho kō: tashin sekai no baikai." *Jinbun gakuhō* 86 (2002): 25–79.

———. "Tatsujin e no michi: *rakukun* o yomu." In *Kaibara Ekiken: tenchi waraku no bunmeigaku*, ed. Yokoyama Toshio, 25–68. Tokyo: Heibonsha, 1995.

Yonemoto, Marcia. *Mapping Early Modern Japan: Space, Place, and Culture in the Tokugawa Period, 1603–1868*. Berkeley: University of California Press, 2003.

Yoshida Asako. *Kōkyō suru shisha, seisha, kamigami*. Tokyo: Heibonsha, 2016.

Yoshida Masaki. *Hirata Atsutane: reikon no yukue*. Tokyo: Kōdansha, 2017.

Yoshida Tsunekichi and Satō Seizaburō, eds. *Nihon shisō taikei*, vol. 56, *Bakumatsu seijironshū*, ed. Bitō Masahide, Ienaga Saburō, Inoue Mitsusada, Ishimoda Shō, Maruyama Masao, Nakamura Yukihiko, Sagara Tōru, and Yoshikawa Kōjirō. Tokyo: Iwanami Shoten, 1976.

Yoshikawa Kōjirō. "Kaisetsu." In *Chūgoku bunmeisen*, vol. 3, *Shushishū*, ed. Yoshikawa Kōjirō and Miura Kunio, 1–7. Tokyo: Asahi Shinbunsha, 1976.

Yoshikawa Kōjirō and Miura Kunio, eds. *Chūgoku bunmeisen*, vol. 3, *Shushishū*. Tokyo: Asahi Shinbunsha, 1976.

Yoshino Yutaka. *Fudoki*. Tokyo: Heibonsha, 1969.

Zachmann, Urs Matthias. *China and Japan in the Late Meiji Period: China Policy and the Japanese Discourse on National Identity, 1895–1904*. London: Routledge, 2009.

Online Sources

Japan Knowledge, https://japanknowledge.com/library/en/.

McGraw-Hill Dictionary of Scientific & Technical Terms, 5th ed., S.v. "neovolcanic," http://encyclopedia2.thefreedictionary.com/neovolcanic.

Museum of Motoori Norinaga, http://www.norinagakinenkan.com.

Nagoya City Museum website, http://www.museum.cicty.natoya.jp.
National Archives of Japan Digital Archive, https://www.digital.archives.go.jp/DAS
/pickup/view/category/categoryArchives/0300000000/default/00.
National Diet Library Digital Collections, http://dl.ndl.go.jp/.
National Institute of Japanese Literature, *Union Catalogue of Early Japanese Books*, http://
base1.nijl.ac.jp/infolib/meta_pub/KTGSearch.cgi.

Index

Page numbers for tables and figures are in italics.

Harvard East Asian Monographs

(most recent titles)